life be full of wonderful adventures.

Through the Looking Gl[ass]

For Decla[n]

May you[r]

Hong Kong University Press thanks Xu Bing for writing the Press's n[ew]
Word Calligraphy for the covers of its books. For further information,

Through the Looking Glass
China's Foreign Journalists from Opium Wars to Mao

Paul French

香港大學出版社
HONG KONG UNIVERSITY PRESS

Hong Kong University Press
14/F Hing Wai Centre
7 Tin Wan Praya Road
Aberdeen
Hong Kong

© Paul French 2009

ISBN 978-962-209-982-1

All rights reserved. No portion of this publication may be reproduced or transmitted in any form or by any means, electronic or mechanical, including photocopy, recording, or any information storage or retrieval system, without prior permission in writing from the publisher.

British Library Cataloguing-in-Publication Data
A catalogue record for this book is available from the British Library.

Secure On-line Ordering
http://www.hkupress.org

Printed and bound by Kings Time Printing Press Ltd., Hong Kong, China.

Hong Kong University Press is honoured that Xu Bing, whose art explores the complex themes of language across cultures, has written the Press's name in his Square Word Calligraphy. This signals our commitment to cross-cultural thinking and the distinctive nature of our English-language books published in China.

"At first glance, Square Word Calligraphy appears to be nothing more unusual than Chinese characters, but in fact it is a new way of rendering English words in the format of a square so they resemble Chinese characters. Chinese viewers expect to be able to read Square Word Calligraphy but cannot. Western viewers, however are surprised to find they can read it. Delight erupts when meaning is unexpectedly revealed."
— Britta Erickson, *The Art of Xu Bing*

Contents

Acknowledgments vii

Names and Spelling ix

Introduction — Through the Looking Glass 1

1 God, Mammon and Flag 15

2 Civil and Other Wars — Rebels, Mercenaries and More Dope 39

3 Boxers and Treaty Porters — Headlines Change History 63

4 The Vultures Descend 87

5 Writing in a Republic — Printing What They Damn Well Liked 99

6 The Roaring Twenties — Substituting Action for Talk 119

7 The Decadent Thirties — Celebrities, Gangsters and the Ladies
   of the Press 143

8 The Dirty Thirties — Left Wing, Right Wing, Imperialists
   and Spies 165

9 Too Hot — China Fights for Its Life 195

10 In Air Raid Shelters and Caves — Covering the War 227

11 Interregnum — End of a War, Start of a Revolution 249

Notes 269

Bibliography 277

Appendix 283

Index 285

Acknowledgments

To attempt a complete directory of every member of the foreign press corps in China from the 1820s to the 1950s would be both probably impossible and very likely dreary. Therefore, the characters included in this book represent a selection of the major figures and those who piqued my interest for one reason or another. Hopefully dreariness has been avoided. Along the way, plenty of people weighed in with their own personal favourite members of the old China press corps and often lobbied hard for their inclusion. Needless to say, any errors of fact, omission or interpretation in this book are the author's own shortcomings.

Perhaps unsurprisingly, the most helpful contributors to this project were those journalists who have been part of the foreign press corps of China for the last 30 years and have found themselves naturally interested in their predecessors while producing not a few books of analysis and memoir between them. Those that offered suggestions for inclusion and encouragement included Jasper Becker, Gary Bowerman, Sam Chambers, Thomas Crampton, Steven Crane, Laura Daverio, Geoff Dyer, Graham Earnshaw, Robert Elegant, Simon Elegant, Jonathan Fenby, Rob Gifford, John Gittings, Peter Goff, Duncan Hewitt, Isabel Hilton, Gary Jones, Arthur Kroeber, James Kynge, Ed Lanfranco, Louisa Lim, Melinda Liu, Simon Long, Richard McGregor, Calum McLeod, Tom Miller, Mark O'Neill, Hugo Restall, Rosemary Righter, Catherine Sampson, Bill Savadove, Richard Spencer, Joe Studwell, Graham Thompson, Jonathan Watts, Adam Williams and Rupert Wingfield-Hayes.

Many people with an interest in the period also offered their thoughts and suggestions including Julia Boyd, Kerry Brown, Matthew Crabbe, Patrick Cranley, Dennis Crow, Nenad Djordjevic, Peter Hibbard, Jim Hoare, Tess Johnston, Bobo Lo, JFK Miller and Lynn Pan.

Thanks also to the staff of various libraries that were always helpful, including the Shanghai Municipal Archives, the University of Hong Kong Library and the British Library newspaper archive in London. Once again, thanks to Hong Kong University Press, including Colin Day, Dennis Cheung and Winnie Chau for taking up this project so enthusiastically.

Lisa stoically grinned and bore another book. I always forget to tell her how much her support means to me, so now it's officially "on the record". She agreed to live with one troublesome foreigner in China and unwittingly found herself surrounded by books written by hundreds of them. It can't have been pleasant but she was never less than totally supportive.

Illustration Credits

The numbers below refer to the numbers in the plates section after p. 118.

1, 6, 8, 11, 12, 13, 17, 18, 19, 20, 21, 23, 28. Author's collection

2. Courtesy of the State Library of New South Wales

3, 4, 5. Courtesy of the collection of Peter Hibbard

7. Courtesy of the John Emett Woodall (Tienstin Grammar School) Collection and the School of Oriental and African Studies, University of London

9. Courtesy of the John Benjamin Powell Papers, 1910–1952, Western Historical Manuscript Collection – Columbia, MO.

10. Courtesy of the Western Historical Manuscript Collection — Columbia, Missouri

14. Courtesy of Indiana University and the Lilly Library

15. With the kind permission of the Estate of Peter Fleming and special thanks to Kate Grimond

16, 22, 26, 27. Courtesy of the Malcom Rosholt Collection and Mei-fei Elrick

24, 29, 31, 32. With permission from Corbis

25. Courtesy of the John F. Kennedy Presidential Library and Museum, Boston

30. Courtesy of The Lois Snow and the Edgar Parks Snow (1905–1972) Papers, University of Missouri-Kansas City

Names and Spelling

The problem of uniform spelling of Chinese names and words is quite simply insurmountable. Therefore, all Chinese names and words in the text have been rendered into modern pinyin (e.g. Chongqing rather than Chungking), except where they are included in the original titles of books or within contemporary quotes (e.g. the city of Hankou was home in the 1930s to the "Hankow Last Ditchers"). Given the many spelling variations in numerous sources over a period of 200 years, a list of China's provinces and major cities and their various pre-1949 and post-1949 names is included at the end of this book as an appendix.

Chinese names are used with the family name indicated first followed by their patronymic, as is standard in China. While most are in modern pinyin, some exceptions include those that are spelled in various ways but are well known to readers in a particular form, such as Sun Yat-sen (rather than Sun Zhongshan). Where they were commonly used, the English names adopted by Chinese people are included.

INTRODUCTION
Through the Looking Glass

"He (the foreign correspondent in China) deals with a difficult subject, there are no established sources of news, hardly two persons view the same incident in the same light, there are critics on all sides ready to condemn a reporter as having turned a propagandist, and so on, and difficulties by the score could be enumerated."

> The problems faced by foreign correspondents in China as expounded by "One of Them", *China Weekly Review,* 1928

"Trained newspapermen are supposed to be able to dive into a new environment and, no matter how murky the medium, come up briskly and triumphantly with the pearl of truth. If that is the safe general rule, then I was a shocking exception when I first went to the Far East early in 1926, for I was wrong from the beginning, and my errors of appraisal were continuous ..."

> Hallett Abend, *New York Times* China correspondent, 1927–41

It's a cliché, but journalists and foreign correspondents are in many ways mirrors of the society they exist in and write about. They try to reflect often-complex events in faraway lands in a way their readers can hopefully understand. This was especially true of the old China press corps that started in the Canton Factories of the opium-dealers in the 1820s and reached its high point, both in terms of word count and number of reporters, in the 1930s and during the Second World War. Whether they wrote for an audience back in Europe or America, Japan or elsewhere, or worked on the foreign language press in China attempting to interpret events to the foreign community through their own newspapers, magazines and journals, the China press corps was the major interpreter of China to the outside world then as it is now.

The foreign press corps of China, from its very small beginnings to its heyday, experienced China's history and development; its convulsions and upheavals; revolutions, reforms and wars. The members of the press corps were uniquely privileged in that they, as a group, and collectively *Zelig*-like, had front row seats for nearly every major twist and turn in China's fortunes. They witnessed the Opium Wars; stood on the sidelines as the Taiping Rebellion rose and fell; saw the Summer Palace burn; endured the Siege of the Legations and the onslaught of the Boxers; witnessed the collapse of the Qing dynasty, the birth of a Nationalist China; its struggle for survival against rampant warlordism; the Japanese encroachment; the rise of the Communists; total war and then revolution. When the Treaty of Tientsin was signed in 1858, opening China forcibly to foreign trade, the foreign press corps was there; when the Allied Relief Force occupied Beijing at the end of the Siege of the Legations in 1900 they were present too; and they saw the Republic born in 1911 and a young, increasingly politically strident China assert itself on May Fourth 1919. The old China press corps stood in the street witnessing the blood-letting of the First Shanghai War in 1932 as the Nationalists slaughtered the Communists and they were blown off their feet by the convulsions of the Second Shanghai War on Black Saturday in 1937. They tracked Japan's incursions into China from the invasion and annexation of Manchuria in 1931, the bombing of Shanghai and the Rape of Nanjing through to the assault on the Nationalist wartime capital of Chongqing as they sheltered in the same bomb shelters as everybody else until the conflict ended. They took tea with the Generalissimo and Madame Chiang and visited Mao and his comrades in the caves of Yenan. They witnessed the civil war, the flight of Chiang Kai-shek to Taiwan and the early days of the People's Republic. The members of the old China press corps were the witnesses and the primary interpreters of the history of modern China to millions around the world.

Like journalists everywhere, they took sides and brought their own assumptions and prejudices to China but a fair number also brought their personal hopes, dreams and fears with them too. They certainly weren't infallible; they got the story completely wrong as often as they got it partially right. Most did their jobs ably and professionally, some even passionately and a select few with rare flair and touches of genius. They were human beings with all the flaws inherent in the species. A fair few were drunks, philanderers and frauds and more than one was a spy; they changed sides, they lost their impartiality, they displayed bias and a few were downright scoundrels and liars of the first order.

What united virtually all of the old China press corps from the first journalists cranking out small papers on hand-presses in the Canton Factories to the foreign correspondents telegraphing back articles to the great newspapers of the world in London or New York was a desire to try to understand China and somehow share that knowledge with their readers. This was what essentially made China such a fascinating and challenging "beat" for so many men and women from the 1820s to the 1949 revolution. The problem they collectively found was that there were no easy interpretations of China. They were like Lewis Carroll's Alice who, after passing through her looking glass, found herself in The Garden of Live Flowers where she realised that no path ever leads where she expects, and the twists and turns on the journey result in unexpected places and chance encounters:

> "I should see the garden far better," said Alice to herself, "if I could get to the top of that hill: and here's a path that leads straight to it — at least, no, it doesn't do *that* ..." (after going along the path and turning several sharp corners), "but I suppose it will at last. But how curiously it twists! It's more like a corkscrew than a path! Well, *this* turn goes to the hill, I suppose — no it doesn't! This goes straight back to the house! Well then, I'll try it the other way".

Characters Like No Others

The story of the old China press corps starts with a duel between two editors over the smuggling of opium into China in the 1820s and ends with an affable Belgian reporter sharing his booze with his beleaguered colleagues as the "bamboo curtain" fell after the revolution. It would be possible to write a history of accountants, lawyers or engineers in China but you wouldn't uncover anything like as interesting a group of people. The old China press corps was top heavy with mavericks, individuals and compelling characters. Unlike any other profession they roamed free, mostly, though at times they encountered resistance and outright hostility from the officials of the Qing dynasty, the Nationalist government or, finally, the Communists. They could be out of contact for weeks, even months without postal services or telegraph stations for hundreds of miles. They wrote when they could and wired their despatches when possible; and they frustrated their editors who tore their hair out until a cable or finally a letter arrived. Even those tied to their desks on local publications such as the *North-China Daily News* in Shanghai or the *Peking and Tientsin Times* regularly wrote features, travelled and pursued their own personal interests for their readers' amusement.

Why were so many journalists attracted by China? Some were posted for obvious reasons such as their knowledge of the Chinese language and their experience of the East; and many were the children of missionaries, born and raised in China as "mishkids". Others were sent, or hired, frequently pulled away from very different beats, though they often ultimately became experts and Old China Hands. For example, Tom Millard, who became a legend in the Shanghai press corps in the early part of the twentieth century, had been a drama critic in New York before being sent to cover the Boxer Rebellion; Carl Crow left the crime beat on the *Fort-Worth Star Telegram* to join Millard in Shanghai on the eve of the Nationalist revolution; and J. B. Powell followed both men from their roots in Missouri to China. Times of war called for a redistribution of labour on the world's major newspapers. Willard Dickerman Straight was poached from the China Imperial Maritime Customs Service to cover the 1905 Russo-Japanese War for Reuters while "accidental Orientalist" Brooks Atkinson was the *New York Times* chief drama critic before he was plucked off Broadway where he was championing the plays of Eugene O'Neill and sent to China's besieged wartime capital of Chongqing in 1941. It was a contrast to say the least, and one they all came to fully appreciate and revel in.

Some were natural-born adventurers looking for a better life. William Wood left the opium business to start a newspaper in 1831; and Shanghai's leading auctioneer founded the *North China Herald* in 1850. Also, James Ricalton resigned as a school teacher in New Jersey to report on China in the 1890s, while Gareth Jones resigned as British prime minister David Lloyd George's foreign affairs adviser to become a freelance reporter until his untimely death at the hands of Mongolian bandits, or perhaps Soviet spies, or possibly Japanese mercenaries (his murderers have never been positively identified) in the mid-1930s. In addition, Ralph Shaw bought himself out of the Durham Light Infantry after being posted to Shanghai on the eve of the Second World War and became a reporter with the *North-China Daily News*, a job which was much more to his liking.

Not a few desperately needed a touch of glamour and danger to spice up their reputations. War junkies a plenty headed to China over the decades. They ranged from Jack London, who became a leader of the self proclaimed "Vultures" — the band of foreign correspondents that covered the Russo-Japanese War in Manchuria — to many of the members of the so-called "Hankow Last Ditchers" who clustered in the besieged and heavily bombed Nationalist retreat of Hankou in 1938, chasing another war after having covered Abyssinia, Spain and a dozen other conflicts. As the Nationalist government retreated further inland to make its last stand at Chongqing, yet more war junkies arrived looking for action, including Ernest Hemingway and Martha Gellhorn. For others, China was to be an important stop on an international trail to a sparkling career. Vincent Sheean was only 27 when he arrived in China but he already knew that China would be a stepping stone to greater things and had already cultivated the air of the "roving reporter deluxe".[1] Teddy White, who was to become the doyen of the China press corps, was only 23 when he arrived. Between the wars, a stint in China was almost essential for any truly serious would-be top flight international correspondent.

There were a large number of correspondents with a background in sinology who mixed a passion for China with a love of journalism. China-born Arthur de Carle Sowerby combined being the foremost authority on China's flora and fauna with being the founder, editor and proprietor of the highly regarded *China Journal of Science and Arts* from 1912 till the Japanese shut it down after Pearl Harbour. Also, H. G. W. Woodhead, the long-serving editor of the *Peking and Tientsin Times*, had a strong background in China and Chinese affairs and eventually entered partial retirement in the 1930s as the editor of the respected quarterly journal *Oriental Affairs*. There were also a few missionaries who liked the journalistic life. They had little else to do in the evenings in their remote inland missions and provided valuable services as stringers, sending news of China's mysterious interior to their editors in Shanghai or Hong Kong.

The 1930s saw an influx of refugees from the Great Depression. Edgar Snow originally shipped out to China after finding himself disillusioned, unemployed and broke in America; and Jack Belden jumped ship in Tianjin by bribing a customs officer with $200 and his gold watch to be let ashore. Indeed a surprising number of jobless hacks in Europe, America or Australia worked their passage to China to find employment on the China coast press. They were determined young men and women, anxious to see the world and write about it. Others were refugees from revolutionary upheavals. For example, Sapajou, the prolific cartoonist of the *North-China Daily News* was a graduate of the Aleksandrovskoe Military School in Moscow and a lieutenant in the Russian Imperial Army, and had been aide-de-camp to a czarist general before the Bolsheviks swept his Russia away. Also, a young Israel Epstein arrived in Tianjin with his Polish Marxist parents, who were unable to get along with the Bolsheviks and were forced into exile. When Epstein was barely 15 years old, he was hired as a cub reporter by H. G. W. Woodhead and he went on to stay in China after 1949 and eventually took Chinese citizenship in 1957.

From the start, the foreign press corps in China took political stands. The Philadelphian William Wood launched the *Canton Courier* in 1831 after becoming disillusioned with the opium trade; the chief opium-dealer William Jardine had already launched the *Canton Register* to spread his free-trade views; and the missionaries who wished to bring God to China followed shortly afterwards. Arguably the first full-time China correspondent, G. E. Morrison ("Morrison of Peking") was hired by the London *Times* which felt sure he would remain a trenchant voice of the British Empire even when far from home — and they were not to be disappointed. Also, Woodhead in Tianjin stoutly and unwaveringly supported extraterritoriality in the 1920s and 1930s while J. B. Powell in Shanghai equally as stoutly and unwaveringly opposed the system whereby foreigners were not subject to Chinese law, and he was criticised for his efforts by the Shanghai Municipal Council and thrown out of the American Chamber of Commerce for his apparently radical views.

Journalists reflected the politics of their contemporary world. Some correspondents were committed Trotskyists while working as journalists — such as Frank Glass, a South African who worked on most of the English-language dailies in Shanghai in the 1930s, Rayna Prohme of the *Peking People's Tribune* and prolific freelancer Harold Isaacs, the son of a New York real estate magnate. Others were Stalinists, while Arthur de Carle Sowerby was admired for his thoughtful writing on China but despised by many as the head of Shanghai's *Fascisti*.

Long-time China Hands and journalists such as Carl Crow, J. B. Powell and Hallett Abend sounded an early alarm about Japanese meddling in Chinese affairs and its inevitable escalation, but others like George Bronson Rea, who ran the right-wing *Far Eastern Review*, actively supported Tokyo and Japanese expansion into China. Also, of course, we should not forget those who found themselves becoming sympathetic to the communist cause, ranging from dedicated revolutionaries such as Agnes Smedley, who covered China for years for the *Frankfurter Zeitung* and the *Manchester Guardian*, to open sympathisers such as Edgar Snow, to the numerous "softliners" who found themselves gravitating away from the Nationalists towards the Communists during the late 1930s and the Second World War.

And then, inevitably, some were just plain weird. Englishman Edwin Dingle was a Shanghai-based journalist who walked to Tibet in 1909, wrote, edited and founded a number of publications in China and then packed it all in to establish a strange religious cult in California.

Sojourners to Differing Degrees

The foreign press corps, more than any other group of foreigners in China in the last 200 years, represented the three strands of the foreign experience. Some immersed themselves in China's culture, language and mores, and others remained resolutely foreign sojourners to their dying days, or the day their ships departed from a Chinese dock. A third group became archetypal China coast foreigners who adopted what Arthur Ransome — himself a journalist who spent time in China after covering the 1917 Bolshevik Revolution — called the "Shanghai mind", the mindset of the "hermetically sealed glass case" that was the privileged foreign-controlled treaty port life of China.

Among those who immersed themselves deeply in China and revelled in the contrasts was Emily Hahn. In the late 1930s Hahn straddled the lush life of high-living foreign Shanghai but also edited *avant garde* Chinese magazines with her poet lover and man-about-town Zau Sinmay. She famously became a concubine, got hooked on opium, got off it and then wrote it all up for the *New Yorker*. Others didn't cross the lines in the way Hahn did but their sympathies lay with sections of Chinese society. Millard, Crow and Powell actively supported the Guomindang after the founding of the Nationalist republic. As founder and managing editor of the *China Press* in 1911, Millard was the first foreign editor to declare the events of 1911 a "revolution"; Crow started work on Sun Yat-sen's authorised biography, which was never completed; and Powell's *China Weekly Review* was considered the best foreign propaganda possible for the Nationalists by Chiang Kai-shek (a rather backhanded compliment Powell felt). However, a later generation such as Snow and others rejected the Nationalists to support the Communists. Interestingly a large number of these reporters started their China careers on the publications founded, edited and managed by Millard, Crow and, especially, Powell. Though its numbers grew, the old China press corps was always in many respects a village where everyone knew everyone else and allegiances, relationships and assignments overlapped constantly.

For many of the foreign press corps, their experiences as reporters in China led them to ultimately become more directly engaged in the country and its development, rather than simply reporting events, however partisan their interpretations one way or the other. A surprising number of foreign journalists moved from being commentators to being activists and direct agents in China's development. For instance, Morrison of Peking left the *Times* to become an adviser to China's erratic "strongman" leader Yuan Shih-kai; prolific journalist B. L. Putnam Weale became an adviser to any number of warlords before becoming involved in one intrigue too many and ending up being assassinated on a Tianjin street; Tom Millard left Shanghai to become a lobbyist for the Nationalist government in Washington; and Bill Donald became well-known as "Donald of China", advising first a warlord and then most famously Chiang Kai-shek and Madame Chiang. Also, Hallett Abend was offered the job of publicity manager for the Old Marshal Zhang Zuolin, a warlord known as the Tiger of Mukden, but, though thanking him profusely, Abend turned down the job. This tradition of moving from reporting to advising and actively lobbying on behalf of various Chinese political interests was to be a major theme of the old China press corps, particularly its American members and it's worth noting at the start that rarely, if ever, was this move from impartiality to advocacy undertaken for money. Whether supporting the status quo or revolutionary change, the decision to engage actively rather than simply observe was invariably heartfelt and committed.

Some, of course, only came for weeks or months, though often their vivid impressions have lived on. The handsome and dashing Peter Fleming of the *Times* visited only a handful of times, yet his two China books — *One's Company* and *News From Tartary* — remain classics and he became a pin-up for many an English schoolgirl. Also, the English writers Auden and Isherwood came for only a matter of months in 1938, but their recollections gathered together in *Journey to a War* remain one of the most atmospheric descriptions of China on the brink of total conflict. The same cannot be said of others. For instance, Hemingway and Gellhorn wrote nothing of substance while in Chongqing during the war. China knowledge was not a pre-requisite for the sojourner: most came with little or no knowledge of the country, though some were less willing to admit their ignorance than others. Typically Peter Fleming positively boasted of his inadequacies:

> The recorded history of Chinese civilisation covers a period of four thousand years. The population of China is estimated at 450 millions. China is larger than Europe. The author of this book is twenty-six years old. He has spent, altogether, about seven months in China. He does not speak Chinese.[2]

Others devoted their entire working and productive lives to China. Millard, Crow, Powell, Epstein, Woodhead and many others stayed for 20, 30, 40 or more years. Some knew nowhere else. For example, Epstein had arrived as a child and the knowledge-fixer and journalist Roy Anderson had been born in China, the son of the founder of Suzhou University. And some died practising their craft. For example, the popular London *Times* correspondent Thomas Bowlby was the sole reporter on the ill-fated Elgin Mission in 1860 to affirm British and French treaty rights, the so-called "Unequal Treaties", and he was kidnapped, tortured and died in incarceration. When Elgin torched the Summer Palace and unleashed a massive looting spree, he declared as his justification: "What would the *Times* say of me if I did not avenge its correspondent?"

Bowlby was the first, but not the last, foreign correspondent to die in China. Among others, Pembroke Stephens of the *Daily Telegraph* was shot dead by a Japanese sniper in Shanghai's old Chinese city; the intrepid Italian journalist Sandro Sandri was mortally wounded when Japanese fighter planes strafed and bombed the American gunboat *Panay* as the ship was evacuating Americans and other neutrals from Nanjing in December 1937; and the veteran J. B. Powell tragically died as a result of Japanese torture in the 1940s.

The China Obsession in Perspective

By looking back at the men and women who have reported and written on China since the late 1820s, it might just be possible to gain some perspective on the media's current obsession with the China story. For a start, such a glance at those who wrote, edited and launched newspapers in China, as well as those correspondents who visited briefly to report back, might constructively give us pause for thought about the accepted wisdom that today the West is obsessed with China as never before. Arguably, more column inches were devoted to China in the second half of the nineteenth century and the first half of the twentieth century than since. In an article entitled "Work of the Foreign Newspaper Correspondent in China" written anonymously for *The China Weekly Review* in 1928 and simply signed "By One of Them", the author opened by writing: "During the past two years more space in the world's press has probably been given to China than during the previous decade".[3] The anonymous author was referring to the start of Chiang Kai-shek's Northern Expedition from Guangzhou to unite the country under Nationalist rule and rid it of warlords in 1926. This did indeed seem to be the case. In 1928 the Sunday edition of the *New York Times* was "… running seven and sometimes eight columns of material on China"[4] from their correspondent Hallett Abend and sending urgent telegrams instructing him to send yet more China news.

Even then, this heavy volume was not necessarily anything new. Starting around the time of the Boxers and the Siege of the Legations in 1900, the world's public began to want significantly more information about China, and so the world's great newspapers started sending and hiring full-time correspondents backed up by an army of stringers. Their numbers grew and then spurted in the 1920s, as "One of Them" notes. China was among the biggest and most prestigious foreign postings since the First World War as the fragile country appeared besieged on all sides, internally as well as externally.

It is certainly true that the foreign press corps from 1900 until 1937 was significantly larger than it has been at any time since. There were more magazines and non-academic journals devoted to understanding China then than now. From long- running publications such as J. B. Powell's *China Weekly Review* to short-lived upstarts such as Edgar Snow's *Democracy*, their number fluctuated but compared to today's handful of serious publications they were legion. And, of course, foreigners established, edited and filled numerous newspapers published in China from Guangzhou to Shanghai and on to Tianjin and Beijing. Those are now all gone and there are no equivalents of the *North-China Daily News* or the *Peking and Tientsin Times* today, except in Hong Kong. It was also arguably true that, despite the large number of books now appearing on China and fighting desperately for shelf space, the period between 1930 and 1945 produced more and better-selling books on China, many by former members of the old China press corps, than the period between 1990 and the present day. There had already been several libraries full offered to the reading public. As the highly regarded J. O. P. Bland of the *Times* had noted at the start of the twentieth century, "Remembering all the tomes [on China] which burdened our shelves ... one wonders, as the stream of books rolls on, what and where are the people who buy them?" The flood of China books didn't recede. When, in 1937, the long-time Shanghai-based journalist Earl Leaf was set the task of compiling a list of ten recently published books that "... will provide a sound knowledge of China", he wrote:

> As I write I have here before me a list of 400 books dealing with China and the Far East, including such atrocities as "Ways That Are Dark" by Ralph Townsend who suffers from cirrhosis of the literary liver, "The Road to Shanghai", all about the white slave traffic in Shanghai by M Henry Champli, who doubtless never saw Shanghai, and "China in the Making" by HD Capper, which is guaranteed to put the reader to sleep quicker than counting sheep. Between these extremes are many excellent books well worth reading but which cannot be included because my "required reading list" is limited to only ten inexpensive books.[5]

Interestingly, his top ten list included books by several members of the old China press corps, including Edgar Snow, Gunther Stein, Agnes Smedley, H. G. W. Woodhead and occasional freelancer Pearl S. Buck, all of whom feature in this history. Despite only supposedly listing ten, Leaf goes on to note a host of other members of the China press corps who had turned to book writing to leverage their China experiences, such as Vincent Sheean, Victor Yakhontoff, Rodney Gilbert, Hallett Abend and J. O. P. Bland. Arguably too, those China books of the 1920s and 1930s heyday sold larger numbers to wider audiences than any by foreign reporters or China Hands do today. For instance, Peter Fleming became an overnight star and publishing sensation in England with his 1935 book *One's Company* and Carl Crow's 1937 *400 Million Customers* went into multiple reprints and multiple languages and sold strongly for the next 12 years. Also, novels such as Alice Tisdale Hobart's *Oil for the Lamps of China* and Pearl Buck's *The Good Earth* were best-sellers in the 1930s, staying on the book charts for months on end and becoming movies and stage plays; and Edgar Snow's *Red Star over China* had an enormous impact upon publication in 1937, going through five reprints within a month. In addition, superstar correspondents Teddy White and Annalee Jacoby's book of their experiences in wartime Chongqing — *Thunder out of China* — sold over half a million copies at its first printing and became one of the best-selling books of the Second World War through the 1950s.

By the late 1930s foreign correspondents in China were complaining that publishers were refusing their manuscripts sight unseen as they thought the China books market flooded and overdone. By the 1940s, even at the height of the war, publishers such as Harper and Brothers, which had been at the forefront of publishing books on China by former journalists, were turning down manuscripts that weren't either by star correspondents with household names or personally recommended by powerful newspaper editors who could guarantee vast publicity and correspondingly stellar sales numbers.

It's also worth considering whether there are now editors and newspaper proprietors with the personal commitment to and stake in China that many of the employers of the old China press corps had. This includes not just those who lived and worked in China for most of their lives such as Millard, Woodhead, Powell, Sowerby and others but also the likes of Henry Luce whose *Time-Life* empire constantly covered China, partly because it was a major story but also partly because Luce was himself a "mishkid". He had been born and raised in China, with the country in his blood and its fortunes, so he felt, deeply intertwined with his own.

In order to appreciate why China was such a big story between the 1820s and 1949 it is necessary to push aside the media immediacy of the current times, dominated as it is by the instantaneousness of constantly rolling news and the Internet. The first English-language newspapers in China were established to make vocal to a wider public the arguments of the China trade lobby, the opium smugglers and the businessmen looking to open China and force trade upon her. Spats over quotas, intellectual property and dumping may cause some media ripples as the European Union and Washington argue with Beijing, but these hardly compare to the trade spats that ended in the two so-called "Opium Wars" and the Unequal Treaties, the Elgin Mission that ended in the burning and looting of the Summer Palace and the Treaty of Tientsin that enforced the treaty port system.

Similarly, events in recent times such as the 1999 American bombing of the Chinese embassy in Belgrade or the 2001 American spy plane incident, awful as they were and where some hostility to foreigners in China was seen, can hardly compare to the Boxer Rebellion of 1900, the subsequent Siege of the Legations or the outpourings of anger and rebellion in May 1919 as China was deserted by the Great Powers at Versailles. The international media may show concern for poverty in China but can this compare to the poverty that engulfed China during the convulsion of the Taiping Rebellion or the Japanese invasion? The media may uncover corrupt and almost feudal-like local officials in obscure parts of China today but can this compare to the warlord period when men known as the Dogmeat General and the Tiger of Mukden ruled territories the size of European countries? Today correspondents debate who really makes decisions in China and the relative strength of the central government but after 1912 the debate was whether there was any effective government in China at all, central or otherwise. People opposed to government rule are uncovered by the media occasionally but can these compare to the ferocity of the civil war between the Nationalists and the Communists in the 1920s, 1930s and through to 1949? The media may cover the rise of organised groups, "cults" as Beijing would have it, such as Falun Gong and speculate on how large and influential they really are, but can these movements really compare to the Taiping Heavenly Kingdom in the mid-nineteenth century that left tracts of China laid waste and perhaps as many as 20 million people dead, or the Boxers severing heads at the turn of the century? Fortunately there is also nothing to compare with the global news events of the bombing of Shanghai in 1937 (arguably the point at which the Second World War became inevitable), the horrific Rape of Nanking and the numerous atrocities of the Japanese invasion.

Throughout the nineteenth century China appeared as "the sick man of Asia", a dangerously unstable, badly governed, poverty-stricken country. Bad leadership, a succession of seemingly never-ending natural disasters from floods to earthquakes, and the constant threat of coup and revolution united everyone from William Jardine to Karl Marx in the belief that China was constantly on the verge of complete disintegration, most probably in a horrible and deadly conflagration of some sort. These nineteenth-century opinions were, if anything, strengthened after 1911 when the young Republic sunk into chaotic warlordism before enduring 14 years of invasion by Japan from the 1931 "annexation" of Manchuria to Japan's final defeat in 1945. Peace was momentary and civil war and revolution soon followed. From the 1820s the China story was one of a country on the brink of collapse.

Of course, there is a story in China now — a massive and significant one. But in historical terms it is tamer, far more stable and, given the number of foreign journalists who came to China alive and left dead for one reason or another, an altogether safer beat than it was during the span of this book from 1827 to the 1950s or thereabouts. Having said all that, there is little use in looking back at the past as if those were purely glory days. The foreign press in China itself was a product of the Unequal Treaties and foreign intervention in China's affairs, and so much of the media's interest in China came down to how its people, products and resources could further enrich the Great Powers. The stories that made the careers of so many of the old China press corps and thrilled and intrigued readers at home were nightmarish horrors for those Chinese forced to live through them, as behind the adventure and excitement of the old China press corps lies a mass of death, destruction and chaos.

Still, if there were more larger-than-life characters in the foreign press corps in China then than today, it was because the times were in many ways larger, the world certainly less known and the story more compelling. The old China press corps, flawed as its members so often were, is a crucial part of China's story and, perhaps most importantly, of our collective memory of a China now passed into history. As Mark Twain famously said, history may not repeat itself but it often rhymes.

The Old China Press Corps

Trying to compress approximately 150 years of history into one book is not necessarily a straightforward task. Historical events and significant periods overlap and decades do not always start neatly, while the members of the press corps themselves vary from short-time sojourners to "China lifers" who remained for decades. There is no neat solution to this problem. This book begins with the first stirrings of a foreign press and interest in China before the Opium Wars and continues through the flourishing that occurred after the foreign powers gun-boated their way into the country around the middle of the nineteenth century. This led to the treaty port system and the expansion of a foreign press in those enclaves, notably Shanghai.

It seems more logical to follow the old China press corps through the decades. The Boxer Rebellion in 1900 was really when the full-time foreign correspondent in China emerged, most obviously in the figure of Morrison of Peking, and the period immediately following saw a combination of growth in both full-time correspondents for the international press and an increasing number of foreigners working on titles in English and other European languages in China.

The Nationalist Revolution of 1911 saw the world once again sit up and take notice of China and led to more China coast newspapers being launched and more foreign correspondents disembarking. From 1919 and the May Fourth Movement, a more noticeable trend of foreign journalists starting to identify themselves more with China's causes and grievances emerges. Simultaneously, and in particular in the 1930s, many journalists not only began to take sides — Nationalist vs Communist and pro- or anti-extraterritorial rights — but also reflected the worldwide political divisions of left and right that became so stark in that chaotic and fascinating decade.

The situation changed sharply once again in 1937 with the onslaught of the might of Japanese militarism upon China. Foreign journalists, more than at any time before, became partisan for their chosen side and ideology as well as overt targets for retribution by the Japanese. The left-right divisions of the early to mid-1930s became yet starker. The war against Japan itself saw political divisions among the journalists accentuate as well as the forming of clear cliques in the wartime centres of Hankou and Chongqing; and the war was also a high point for foreign correspondents resident in the country as China became a major front in the global Second World War. When that war finished in most parts of the world, conflict continued in China as the civil war between Nationalists and Communists resumed and culminated in the 1949 Communist "liberation", a period that posed significant new challenges for the immediate post-war correspondents. After the revolution, foreign journalists were left fighting a losing battle and eventually their numbers dwindled to zero and the old China press corps passed into history.

This then is the story of the men and women who were the old China press corps.

1
God, Mammon and Flag

"That which we require now is, not to lose the enjoyment of what we have got."

> Arthur Wellesley, the Duke of Wellington, speaking to the China debate in Parliament shortly before the First Opium War

"We have no eternal allies and we have no perpetual enemies. Our interests are eternal and perpetual, and those interests it is our duty to follow."

> Lord Palmerston in the House of Commons, 1848

Rivals for the Mud Press — The Trenchant Voice of the Opium Merchants

The birth of foreign newspapers and a foreign press corps in China really begins in the small enclave of Canton, the city now known as Guangzhou, in what were called the Factories, the somewhat fortified and mostly self-sufficient warehouses where a select group of foreigners was begrudgingly permitted to trade by the Qing dynasty. The twin European imperatives in China were to trade and proselytise to advance their various national agendas, empires and treasuries. This meant that the very earliest newspapers and journals to be produced reflected a tripartite of interests: God, Mammon and flag. From the start the first newspapers were intended as much to influence the decision makers back home, which initially meant London, as to provide a forum for debate and news among the foreign community of merchants and missionaries in China. Though it was to be the merchants rather than the missionaries who were to be the first to enter into the newspaper business, the men of God were never to be far behind the men of Mammon.

The roots of the foreign press are, like so many other aspects of early European involvement in China, revealed in opium. The nineteenth century British-dominated "mud trade", based on opium as a narcotic smoked for pleasure or relaxation rather than medicinal purposes, was already over 50 years old by the time the first English-language newspapers appeared in China, coincidentally sponsored by the largest suppliers. Warren Hastings, the governor-general of British India, had started shipping "Indian treacle" or, as the self-declared opium-eater and essayist Thomas De Quincey termed it, "the celestial drug", from India to China in 1772 in exchange for Chinese-made goods and tea. Starting out as a luxury item for the rich, opium had inevitably trickled down the social scale and first raised alarm among China's rulers when it became increasingly popular with the common folk. This coincided with a dramatic fall in price due to large-scale British importation.

On 8 November 1827 the first English-language newspaper to be written, printed and distributed in China appeared — the *Canton Register*. Soon to follow were the *Canton Courier* and the *Canton Press* in July 1831 and September 1835 respectively. All of them were printed on small-scale hand-presses in the cramped Canton Factories. The *Canton Register and Price Current*, to give the paper its full name, was published twice monthly on the first and 15th of each month, though it was often late when nobody showed up to crank the press. At first it was an extremely local read: the first edition reported on the decision to enclose the small open square in the Factories, and featured a description of Chinese coins and a report of a double drowning of two sailors at Whampoa. The *Price Current* in the title referred to the fact that, like all the earliest papers, it contained as its major selling point a list of the current prices of goods received at Canton. The *Register*'s opening editorial declared:

> The want of a printed register of the commercial and other information of China, has long been felt, and its utility and convenience, full appreciated. With a view to remedy this deficiency, we have been induced to commence our present undertaking, the origin of which may be principally attributed to the kindness, and, public spirit, of a gentleman, who has obliged us with the use of his press.[1]

The *Register* owed its origins and patronage to Jardine Matheson, the trading company founded in 1828 by the Scottish merchants William Jardine and James Matheson (Alexander Matheson, James's nephew was the "gentleman" who provided the hand-press). It was no surprise, therefore, that its slogan was "the organ of free merchants in China" as they were looking to break the long-standing monopoly of the East India Company on the British-China trade. The

Register combined the latest departures and arrivals of ships with price information and notes on Chinese life from opera performances to snake charmers. Naturally, given its backers, the paper approved of the opening up of trade, was supportive of the opium business and did not look favourably upon the East India Company which was at the time the main competition to the independent traders like Jardine and Matheson. The opening issue declared that "... the free trade and the trade of the Company now move in different spheres".[2] The *Register* was to be a major shot in the war fought by the free traders to end the monopoly of the so-called "Honourable Company".

The monthly *Canton Courier*, launched in 1831 and referred to by the British as "that American publication", was founded and edited by a Philadelphian called William Whiteman Wood who had sailed to China in the 1820s in the hope of getting rich and worked as a clerk for the American opium-dealers Russell and Company. The problem was that Wood, the son of a famous American actor, was a romantic, a poet and an incessant talker with a quick temper but he had absolutely no business acumen. He was well-read and witty but also completely unsuited to the opium business. He was a skilled draughtsman and caricaturist who gave art classes to other like-minded foreigners in Macau, where he fell in love with Harriet Low, a vibrant young American woman from Massachusetts who was living in the Portuguese enclave as companion to her aunt and was generally considered the most attractive and vivacious available white woman in town. Wood courted her and attempted to marry her, proposing in secret. She accepted his proposal and they were engaged, but the nuptials were thwarted by her uncle, a senior partner in Wood's former employer Russells, who refused to give her away to a "penniless adventurer". Wood and the *Courier* were not overly fond of the opium business. He had come to have contempt for the mud trade while at Russells, and he particularly disliked the East India Company and regularly inveighed against it in his editorials. Indeed, he managed to annoy the Honourable Company to such an extent that Charles Marjoribanks, the President of the East India Company's powerful Select Committee, cancelled the company's regular order of 24 copies, which were divided among its stations at Guangzhou, Bengal, Madras, Macau and, the rather remote, St Helena. Wood appealed to the company to renew the subscription as 24 copies was a major component of his total sales. However, his assaults against the business of the Honourable Company were deemed so severe that the head of the company's even more powerful Court of Directors, Charles Ravenshaw himself, wrote to Wood confirming the cancellation and noting that the decision was "irrevocable".

The competition increased again when the *Canton Press* started in 1835 as the first weekly, published every Saturday at the "No. 3 British Hong", and was strongly under the influence of Dent's which was Jardine and Matheson's major rival in the opium trade. The paper differed slightly from the *Register* and the *Courier* by containing a lot more news from England, in particular the ongoing China debate in Parliament, the opium trade and the imminent revocation of the Honourable Company's monopoly on the China trade. Despite both Dent's and Jardine Matheson standing to benefit from the repeal of the Honourable Company's privileges, Dent's English founder, Lancelot Dent, had an intense dislike of Matheson and the former surgeon Jardine, which the two Scots reciprocated with equal ferocity.

The first three English-language newspapers in China also led to the first newspaper wars — quite literally. When Wood had launched the *Courier*, his sweetheart in Macau, Harriet Low, declared: "I am afraid he will make enemies".[3] He did indeed. They included the missionary Robert Morrison and Arthur Saunders Keating, the *Register*'s hot-blooded Irish-born editor who was a staunch and rather zealous supporter of the opium trade and took strong exception to Wood's anti-opium editorials. Keating became so incensed that he demanded Wood apologise, but Wood refused and a challenge was immediately issued for a duel, which Wood accepted. As was his privilege, Wood got to choose the time and place of the fight and chose the Factories. Naturally, the duel was a major event for the foreign community because, first, many foreign residents were still employed by the Honourable Company and so many were a bit miffed by Wood's strident editorialising and, second, a good duel certainly livened up life. Wood prepared to defend his honour and all the foreign community took sides. However, not only did his challenger fail to show up for the fight but Keating actually fled the Factories for the opium supply station of Lin Tin Island in the Pearl River estuary, never to return. Wood considered himself "honourably exonerated". An afternoon's entertainment was cancelled and Wood returned to his editorial desk unscathed. However, his anti-opium stance meant he was shunned by many in the miniscule Guangzhou and Macau foreign community and he left for Manila in 1833 where he worked on a coffee plantation, played around with a *camera obscura* and, after having been thwarted in his passion for Harriet Low by her opium-dealing uncle, never married.

Aside from duels to the death, more familiar forms of rivalry were also immediately in evidence. After it was launched at a charge of 50 cents, the *Register* had been annoyed to find Wood coming on the scene and charging just 25 cents for the *Courier*. Price wars had begun as soon as there were two papers and the potential customers arriving at the "Europe Bazar" operated in the Factories by Messers Markwick and Lane at the No. 3 Imperial Hong could not only choose which paper's politics they preferred but also which price suited them better. However, duelling editors aside, life in the Factories offered few distractions and so most bought any and all papers available. They also bought the *Canton Miscellany*, a non-political and anonymous journal which was written and edited by the community and was launched in May 1831. It offered some expression for the creative and intellectual juices of those in the Factories, on Lin Tin Island and Macau, featuring essays on subjects as diverse as Lord Amherst's Mission to China in 1816, the vagaries of the Chinese language, the military secrets of the Marmelukes and Lord Byron's genius.

All the papers and the *Miscellany* were written largely by the members of the self-named "Funny Club", a group of foreigners stationed in the Factories who took boat trips on the Pearl River at night to escape the claustrophobia and oppressive heat. The local Chinese thought it most odd to see a group of strangely dressed foreigners bobbing around on the river at midnight in heated debate and gossip. Members of the Funny Club regularly wrote sarcastic and pointed letters to the papers signing themselves by various *nom de plumes* such as Anglosinesis, Citizen of the World, Common Sense and Amicus.

But by day commercial rivalry resumed. In the 1830s both Jardine's and Dent's were engaged in the so-called "country trade" in commodities between China and India — opium as well as other goods to China, and other stops en-route — in defiance of the East India Company's monopoly. It was not an insignificant business. By 1830 the mud trade constituted 19,000 chests of opium a year, rising to 30,000 in 1835 and 40,000 by 1838, the first full year of Queen Victoria's reign, which also translated into something between four and 12 million opium addicts created in China.

The emergence of the *Register*, *Courier* and the *Press* saw the end of the China trade as the monopoly of the Honourable Company which had established its first base in China in 1715. The company, along with what Joseph Conrad called "the dark interlopers of the eastern trade"[4], had dominated the trade for over a century from its headquarters on London's Leadenhall Street. It took a much-debated Act of Parliament but the company finally closed its China station to hand over to the, now more respectable, "country men" such as Jardine, Matheson and Dent. They were to emerge as the first China coast versions of the Indian *nabobs*, the British who had made their fortunes in India and returned home extremely wealthy while also becoming stock characters in English newspapers, novels and plays, combining their crass *nouveau riche* lifestyle with an image of decadence and debauchery many back home associated with life in the Orient. In the December 1833 issue of the *Chinese Repository,* a missionary paper that appeared soon after the merchant papers, an article appeared, similar to what would now be called an op-ed, signed by a "British Merchant' which declared that the trade was now finally wide open. With the ending of the Honourable Company's monopoly, the entrepreneurs were massing their forces to maximise the business opportunities which were becoming increasingly apparent. If Jardine — "Old Rat with Iron Head" as the Chinese called him after he emerged unscathed from a ruckus in which he received and survived a rather fulsome blow to the skull at Guangzhou's Petition Gate — did not write the piece himself then it was someone with very similar views.

The editorial bemoaned the fact that during the Honourable Company's monopoly little had changed to open the market to foreign merchants and argued that the company had been too conciliatory and subservient in its dealings with China to truly serve the interests of *laissez-faire* capitalism. The piece was extremely strong for the time. It even accused the Honourable Company of not being very honourable at all in its actions and so compliant with the Chinese authorities as to have actually handed over a Royal Navy gunner to be put to death in 1784 for "inadvertently" killing a Chinese man. A ship, the *Lady Hughes*, had fired a salute near Hong Kong and a Chinese man was accidentally killed by a cannon-ball rather carelessly left in one of the guns. For their part, the Chinese had threatened to stop the trade and the company had caved in. This still clearly annoyed the merchants 50 years later: "Has not the immolation up to this day remained unavenged? There is the smell of blood still" raged the author in fine tabloid style. Jardine himself or not, it reflected the changing mood of the freebooting merchant community. They were not actually very bothered about the luckless navy gunner but, in order to compel the British to hand over the man, the Chinese had kidnapped an English merchant, George Smith. This was a possible trend the merchants did not want to be continued. If the worst came to the worst, navy gunners could be sacrificed but surely not merchants! And such was the case as the luckless gunner was tried, found guilty and strangled.

This sort of tirade was something new in print and was clearly the voice of a surging British capitalism positioning itself for a new era of trade relations that could either be agreed to by China (on England's terms) or forced upon them (on England's terms). The merchants by and large didn't care how the aim was achieved as long as it didn't cost them too dearly financially. A combination of assumed racial superiority, British nationalism, trade before all else and English blood needing to be avenged were to be familiar themes to readers as the *Press* and *Register* became the major English-language organs of the China coast merchants. Along with the more independently minded *Courier*, both the *Press* and the *Register* also soon became somewhat more independent and intense rivals. Still, all of them ran shipping announcements, an essential service for the business community in the Factories, Lin Tin Island and Macau, who were waiting anxiously for news of their cargoes having arrived safely. All also ran adverts for newly arrived shipments of products that those Britons far away from home would want to buy — primarily ale, bitter and other varieties of booze, it seems. And, of course, they all listed the current prices for opium.

The single most important function of the papers was that they published prices on opium and goods for all to read. Such information had previously been the sole knowledge of the Honourable Company and was a crucial part of their trading advantage. Suddenly everybody knew what everyone else was up to. The nascent China coast English-language press did much to level the commercial playing field. In addition, with everyone knowing everything about trading conditions and sharing information about what was happening in China, back in Europe and in related places such as India, the merchants were able to unify their position in relation to the Honourable Company, co-ordinate their ongoing campaigns in Parliament to open up the China trade and appear as one (to a point) in their individual dealings with the Chinese.

The Jardine's-backed *Register* was the most successful of the papers. It constituted one part of the overall campaign Jardine Matheson waged to promote the China trade. It also came to be supported by the power of the English manufacturers back home and that sizeable section of Parliament which was feeling rather bullish given British victories in Europe (Trafalgar and Waterloo, though some years before, still loomed foremost in the national consciousness). Despite the skeleton of opium in the cupboard, Jardine and Matheson worked extremely hard to win over political and commercial opinion in Britain to their way of thinking on free trade. In reality, the influence the *Register* and *Press* were able to wield in the debate in Britain was out of proportion to their local readership. In 1832 the British staff of the Honourable Company in the Factories and Macau totalled about 25 with another assorted 32 Britons resident in the area, and by 1839 this number had reached perhaps 200 at most. Among these were private merchants, four shopkeepers, a watchmaker and the notorious and invariably indebted painter George Chinnery — not exactly a mass readership. However, this was to be a trend repeated along the China coast. Twenty years later the *North China Herald* in Shanghai was to be highly influential in shaping the debate in Britain on treaty port policy despite there being only 175 full-time foreign residents in the Shanghai Settlement at the time.

The decade of the 1830s just prior to the First Opium War, or the Anglo-Chinese War, was to see the start of a serious and detailed foreign English-language press in China that was read and contributed to by the two major foreign communities in China — missionaries and merchants — both on the China coast and in Europe and America. What was interesting was that a broad accommodation appears to have been reached between these two groups that would hold for some time: the High Victorian ideal of ruling the world whilst also redeeming it. This was perhaps not that surprising given shifts in British economic and philosophical thinking. In the eighteenth century influential thinkers such as Adam Smith had been largely hostile to imperialism but the rising Victorian thinkers were to take a different line and see British culture, trade and imperialism as bringing the benefits of what they considered England's advanced culture to the world: spiritual rejuvenation was linked to economic advancement promoted by trade. Evangelical Protestant Christianity meshed theoretically with capitalism.

Eventually many in the missionary community would come to openly condemn and campaign against the opium trade, but not immediately by any means, in what can be seen as a re-run of the English church's acceptance of and then repudiation of slavery slightly earlier. The presence of Protestant missionaries as translators for Jardine Matheson and the Honourable Company in the 1830s showed that the line between God and Mammon could be blurred, as these missionaries had gone ashore along the China coast engaged in opium smuggling but had also surreptitiously handed out religious tracts. In part, it appears to have been a case of taking the devil's money to do God's work and it was also partly a communality of interest in forcing both Western things and thinking upon the Chinese. This theory was supported by Maurice Collis, the Irish-born former British diplomat who was demoted down the ranks of the Indian Civil Service for being too pro-Burmese. In *Foreign Mud*, a study of the opium trade and wars that was widely read later, he wrote:

> In this way their (*the missionaries*) point of view is seen not to have differed very profoundly from Jardines. He wanted to force everything western upon China, including opium, which he considered indispensable. They wanted to force everything western upon China, except opium, for, being without commercial experience they were not convinced of its indispensability.[5]

Throughout the 1830s the two sides were to coexist until the Opium Wars forced divisions. While the merchants continued to publish the *Register* and *Press*, the missionaries formed their own journal, which voiced their concerns but rarely openly attacked the merchants and often ran parallel to them in its aims. This was not surprising given the fact that those involved with the endeavour included missionaries who had worked as translators for the opium-dealers, including Robert Morrison, Karl Gützlaff and E. C. Bridgman. Indeed Bridgman, an American missionary, had had his fare to China paid by an American trading company with opium connections. As Collis noted of the period, "… trade and the Bible were allies, and after them came the flag".[6]

The Circumspect Voice of the Missionaries

Robert Morrison and William Milne of the London Missionary Society (LMS) had started publishing the *China Monthly Magazine* in 1815. Though largely about China, it was actually produced in Malacca rather than in China itself. So it was to be the *Chinese Repository* that was the first journal of Chinese studies actually produced in China. It was published quarterly out of Macau and Guangzhou from 1832 until 1851 and was clearly the product of the missionaries who, in this case, were Protestants. The *Repository* ran to 12 volumes before ceasing publication. Remarkably each volume ran to a lengthy 650 pages with an average of 1,800 words per page, suggesting that many readers were either patient or had good eyesight (or both), while certainly indicating that the missionaries and their invited contributors had plenty to say about China and not much else to read on the long lonely nights.

The *Repository* lived up to its name in many ways and provides a fascinating snapshot of China just prior to the Opium Wars. It was a collection of essays on Chinese history, literature and geography as well as current events and reviews of all books published in Europe and America concerned with China and the Far East. The *Repository* set the standard for its many later followers in the English-language press by combining a detailed record of events and concerns of the day with an attempt to understand this strange land in which the missionaries had settled. The *Repository*'s political tone was reasonably impartial and often without bias by contemporary standards on subjects other than the spread of the Christian religion which was unsurprisingly consistently seen as a good thing. For the times, it could be judged to be not only the first serious publication in English to emerge from China but also one of the first decidedly liberal offerings. In fact, this was not a problem for the bulk of the readership — the Guangzhou and Macau merchant and missionary community — who in the 1830s and 1840s made less of a distinction between free trade and the desirability of religious conversion than later generations of businessmen did when the prevailing view became one of seeing the missionaries as annoying irritants. However, it was also most definitely a product of its time and declared in its inaugural issue in May 1832 that it would seek to uncover the culture and society of China but also declared: "We have no very strong expectation of finding much that will rival the arts and sciences, and various institutions of the Western nations".[7] Though interested in China, the *Repository* was quite clear that European and Christian superiority were real and indisputable.

The *Repository* was essentially the brainchild of two missionaries, Elijah Coleman "E. C." Bridgman and Robert Morrison. E. C. Bridgman continued to edit it until he left Guangzhou for Shanghai in 1847, whereupon his nephew the Reverend James Granger "J. G." Bridgman succeeded him as editor till September 1848 when Samuel Wells Williams took charge of the publication. Still, E. C. remained a constant contributor until the journal finally ceased publication in 1851 and the *Repository* was to be his life's major labour of love. E. C. believed that it was essential for missionaries to keep abreast of the wider developments in China and valued the political as highly as the commercial, the social and the historical, as well as random China coast scuttlebutt. As the *Repository* grew, he widened its content to include details of events and missionary activities in Singapore, Malacca, Penang, Batavia and Indo-China.

Bridgman had been one of the first American Protestant missionaries to arrive in China prior to the Opium Wars. He had graduated from Andover Theological Seminary in Massachusetts where he had started corresponding with Robert Morrison who had reached Guangzhou as early as 1807. Bridgman had been ordained and appointed for service in China by the American Board of Commissioners for Foreign Missions in 1829 and arrived in Guangzhou in 1830, where he finally got to meet his hero Morrison. With the links between commerce and missionaries still strong at the time, an American firm engaged in the opium trade had paid for his passage as a philanthropic donation. He immediately started studying the Chinese language, which became a lifelong passion.

In 1834 he became the first joint secretary of the wonderful-sounding Society for the Diffusion of Useful Knowledge that had been founded in London in 1828 with the objective of publishing information to people who had been unable to obtain a formal education. The Society produced the *East-West Monthly Examiner*, a journal that sought to introduce Chinese readers to information regarding the world outside. It was a popular society, with William Jardine himself attending its first meeting in Guangzhou in October 1835. Bridgman was also a founder of the Morrison Education Society in 1836 and remained its president for many years while also being active in organizing the Medical Missionary Society in China in the late 1830s. This society had been established following a pamphlet issued by Dr. Peter Parker, another American-born Guangzhou resident who later became a diplomat in China alongside Caleb Cushing, President Tyler's envoy extraordinary and minister plenipotentiary to China; and it was to be responsible for many good works in Guangzhou, including the founding of the city's Ophthalmic Hospital. All of these good works needed recording too.

Bridgman decided he liked the publishing business and in 1832 started the Canton Mission Press just before launching the *Chinese Repository*. At the same time, during the negotiations to secure American access to China in the early 1840s, Bridgman was working as a translator and adviser to the US government.

(As Americans had come later than the Brits to the China trade, they were known as "Second Chop Englishmen" by the Chinese.) He remained the editor for many years, eventually handing over to his nephew J. G. Bridgman in 1847. E. C. had chosen to change direction after baptizing his first Chinese convert, an experience that moved him deeply (and had taken him fully 17 years to achieve). This reactivated his missionary zeal and led him to decide to go Shanghai where he prepared a Chinese translation of the Bible, which appeared shortly after his death.

J. G. had also graduated in theology before heading to Guangzhou to study Chinese with his uncle. However, he was to die in China at a young age just a few years after taking over the editor's post. His successor was to be yet another missionary, Samuel Wells Williams, originally from New York and a graduate of the Rensselaer Polytechnic Institute in Troy, Ohio who had arrived in China in 1833 as a printer with Bridgman's Canton Mission Press. He was certainly prolific: while editing the *Repository*, Williams contributed over 180 lengthy articles. Though a noted sinologist, he remained a missionary first and foremost, high-handedly declaring the role of the *Repository* to be bolstering "the introduction of China into the family of Christian nations, her elevation from her present state of moral, intellectual, and civil debasement, to that standing which she should take, and the free intercourse of her people and rulers with their fellow men of other climes and tongues, is a great work, and a glorious one".[8] Men like Williams appeared to be deeply interested in what China could become, while also having an interest in what it actually was. The problem was that they had clearly already decided that whatever they discovered about China it could never be a cultural or intellectual equivalent of the West.

The *Repository*'s other founder was the Englishman Robert Morrison, the first English Protestant missionary to China. As a boy in Morpeth and Newcastle, he had dreamed of being a missionary in Africa while apprenticed to his father as a boot-tree maker. He joined the Presbyterian Church, was ordained, and after an interview with the LMS, it was decided he would go to China rather than Africa. Arriving in 1807, he spent several years hiding from the Chinese authorities who had outlawed missionaries. When he did leave his house, he adopted traditional Chinese garb to try to avoid attention, but this strategy didn't fool anyone. To get permission to stay in Guangzhou, Morrison became a translator at the Honourable Company's factory by day while translating the Bible into Chinese at night and also producing a *Commercial Guide* to China that formed the first modern practical "how-to-do-business" book on China. All this meant that he didn't actually get many converts but did get a job as a translator on Lord Amherst's abortive diplomatic mission in 1816 to the Qing emperor. Though not a great converter of souls, he did spread the Word in China through the *Repository* as well as Malacca's Anglo-Chinese College that trained missionaries, baptised the first Protestant Chinese Christian and ordained the first native Chinese pastor.

The *Repository* also had a wide variety of writers who weren't missionaries, and were mostly occasional rather than full-time staff members: the whole publication was rather *ad hoc* in its organisation. In the mid-1830s the *Repository* ran a series of pieces by a certain Dr. Twogood Downing, a British surgeon who visited China with the English fleet. Downing's articles gave a marvellous flavour of Guangzhou and Macau at the time.[9] Downing spiced up the pages of the *Repository* with tales of the Flower Boat floating brothels on the Pearl River, something we can hopefully assume the missionaries weren't too familiar with. He also recalled, among other sites, Hog Lane, a small alley close to the British Factory where visiting sailors, who at the time were allowed two visits to the city while their ships were moored up, could get drunk on a rather lethal mixture of alcohol, tobacco, juice, sugar and arsenic called "Canton Gunpowder".[10] In the time-honoured traditions of the Royal Navy, the sailors quickly became completely paralytic whereupon their pockets were picked and fights broke out. The officers would then have to bundle the booze-sodden Tars, drunk on the local *Samshoo*, back to the boats before they were lynched by angry locals they had offended and Chinese tavern-owners they had neglected to pay. Downing believed that the establishments of Hog Lane killed more British in Guangzhou than disease did in the 1830s. The pious Protestant owners of the *Repository*, though often deeply involved in the opium trade, were happy to run pieces like this showing the evils of drink and sin which left readers with vivid and (unintentionally we can assume) not a little titillating impressions of life on the China coast. They were often accompanied by illustrations by the well-known London artist, Thomas Rowlandson, who had died in 1827, but not before capturing Jack Tar in all his drunken and roistering glory.[11] To be fair, the wealthy foreign traders of Guangzhou were not any more averse to a tipple than the Royal Navy's Matlows; long boring evenings in the Factories were enhanced somewhat by the liberal imbibing of Canton Gunpowder too.

The *Repository* also contained more serious items for those who needed to get to grips with the workings and thinking of the Chinese government at the time. Just how to deal with the Chinese in terms of diplomatic niceties and customs had been a tricky issue since Lord McCartney's refusal to kow-tow to the emperor in the 1790s and then Lord Amherst's similar frustrations a quarter of a century later. By the 1830s the British were still trying to decipher the mysterious etiquette of the Flowery Court. The *Repository* was able to provide some of the earliest guides to Confucian business etiquette in China, thanks to Morrison who translated official court edicts and documents originally published in the Qing court's daily internal newspaper and summary of court records, the *Imperial Gazette: The Emperor's Epitome of Past Events* (later to be more commonly called the *Peking Gazette*), for the benefit of the *Repository*'s readership. The *Gazette*, which later sourced much of its news directly from the *Tsungli Yamen*, the imperial Chinese foreign office which was established in 1861, was a fascinating record of the minutiae of court life, recording everything from the emperor's schedule to cataloguing gifts received as tribute. It was also not always just a slavish publication of the court, as occasionally an editorial would take issue with a court document carried in the paper on the same day. The *Repository* also produced regular translations of classical Chinese legends and poems to further elucidate the Middle Kingdom to its readers. Morrison was a formidable translator but he was greatly helped by another early sinologist and translator for the *Repository*, the former Pomeranian saddle-maker and employee of the Netherlands Missionary Society to the Far East, the Reverend Gützlaff.

Karl Friedrich August Gützlaff, known as Charles to his British and American friends, was a missionary-doctor and diplomat-interpreter, and later an employee of opium-dealers, who came to China on the *Lord Amherst*, the same British ship that had brought the first plenipotentiary of the East India Company to Shanghai. The *Lord Amherst* first visited Fuzhou where her captain managed to sell some goods and Gützlaff, calling himself Guo Shila, distributed Christian tracts to what he claimed were "eager and grateful readers", though there is no independent confirmation of this. Gützlaff had first been posted to Java where he had learnt Cantonese and several other Chinese dialects and then to Bangkok in the Kingdom of Siam where sadly both his wife and son died in childbirth while he was working together with her on a Khmer/Lao-English dictionary. In mourning, he went in 1832 to Macau where he started printing Bibles and publishing the Chinese-language monthly journal *Dongxiyang kao meiyue tongjichuan* (the Society for the Diffusion of Useful Knowledge's *East-West Monthly Examiner*) that was launched in 1833 and continued, with a gap of several years, until 1838. However, funding for the journal was constantly short until William Jardine offered him a job as a translator with his opium-clippers, which Gützlaff pretty quickly accepted.

It was difficult to avoid the fact that there was an obvious contradiction in Gützlaff as he was a man of God but also a translator for Jardine Matheson's opium- smuggling expeditions along the China coast. In selling opium and Christ simultaneously, Gützlaff looked like a hypocrite to many observers. However, others, downplaying his day job, saw him as an effective missionary whose achievements included handing out Christian tracts in Korea while on the *Lord Amherst* voyage and founding the Chinese Union which despatched Chinese

Christians to spread the Word in the country's interior. To be fair, Jardine had been honest with Gützlaff and told him that opium would be the principle cargo to be traded and offered the missionary "...a sum that may hereafter be employed in furthering your mission ..." as well as further offering to fund the struggling *East-West Monthly Examiner* for six months. In his writings, the good Reverend made no mention of the opium that was being slipped ashore illegally. Perhaps Gützlaff agreed with Jardine who saw little wrong with the opium trade declaring it, "the safest and most gentlemanlike speculation I am aware of". Not much opprobrium had stuck, and clearly Bridgman and Morrison thought him honourable enough to contribute to the *Repository*, while Gützlaff was popular and well enough known to get a very small street named after him later in Hong Kong. Indeed, at times the workaholic Gutzlaff contributed so much to the *Repository* that it almost read like his daily diary and some described him as too self-promoting and a "bubble of self-glorification".[12] Gützlaff remarried after meeting Mary Wanstall who ran a school and a home for the blind in Macau. When her young cousin, Harry (later Sir Harry) Parkes — then a 16-year-old who had just arrived in China but who was later to rise to the heights of British consul to Guangzhou and Shanghai and then become minister to Japan — met him, he described him unflatteringly as "short and square"; and William Hunter, a young American working for Russells, noted that the Pomeranian appeared to have a rather Chinese appearance.

For the *Repository*, the involvement of Bridgman, Morrison and Gützlaff was a coup as they were generally regarded as the three leading men of learning in Guangzhou to actually understand the Chinese language at the time and to be able to best interpret the edicts of the court in Beijing. But other contributors to the *Repository* had far more bizarre reputations. The eccentric George Francis Train, "Citizen Train", had made his fortune in his youth by developing real estate in Omaha before going to England and Australia to make more money and then to China where by his mid-twenties he had made his third fortune in the China trade and wrote up his experiences for the *Repository*.[13] Thought to have been the model for Phileas Fogg in Jules Verne's *Around the World in Eighty Days*, he later returned to America where he used his fortune to support Susan B. Anthony and Elizabeth Cady Stanton and the cause of female suffrage. He also championed the 1893 Chicago World Fair, wearing a white suit and red Turkish fez to drum up support for the exposition. The last years of his life were mainly spent on a bench in Madison Square Park where he refused conversation with all adults and held impromptu services for his self-proclaimed Church of the Laughing Jackass.

At its peak the *Repository*'s circulation reached approximately 1,000 copies an issue, which proved that it was clearly being read significantly beyond the local English-language market in the Factories and Macau. One admirer went as far as to write what, at the time, was perhaps the highest praise a publication could receive — that the *Repository* "... would be considered good even in England".

Covering the Napier Fizzle and the First Opium War

As the opium trade with China prospered, merchants such as Jardine, Matheson and Dent became extremely rich but they still felt keenly that the onerous restrictions placed on them by the Qing needed to be jettisoned. Jardine and Matheson were rarely in the same place at the same time and invariably one, first Matheson and then Jardine, stayed in London to lobby Parliament for a more forward China policy and for the flag (i.e. gunboats) if necessary to follow trade in the way it had done so decisively in India. Matheson was not much liked in Parliament. For example, Benjamin Disraeli's 1845 novel *Sybil* contains a barely disguised reference to the Highlander: "... a dreadful man, richer than Croesus, one McDrug, fresh from Canton with a million of Opium in each pocket, denouncing competition and bellowing free trade". Jardine, also a Scot but a Lowlander, was not much liked either, especially by the Tory Prime Minister Sir Robert Peel who personally disliked the opium trade.

The British had been trading opium for a long time by now and it had dealt with Britain's balance of payments crisis with China but, as Beijing banned the trade, turning the merchants into smugglers, something had to be done. By the 1830s this situation was increasingly deemed intolerable by the merchants, but the problem was to find an excuse to force China to open its markets. London was also more than aware of the importance of opium, even if it felt a little squeamish over the trade at times. As classically educated men, they knew that a declining Roman Empire had partly beggared itself by exporting hard currency East to buy frivolous spices and silks; some offset was required by the more fiscally prudent British Empire. By the late 1830s the opium trade was "the hub of British commerce in the East".[14] By the end of the decade, fully a sixth of British overseas trade was with China and nearly two-thirds of that trade was in opium. As late as 1880 the *China Mail* in Hong Kong would oppose the overnight abolition of the trade on the grounds that it was worth £9 million to India and the removal of that income would throw the economy of the Raj into chaos.

Still, in general, relations between merchant and missionary remained cordial in the run up to the First Opium War in 1839. Writers in the *Repository* could frame arguments such as the following without raising much ire:

They (*the Chinese*) are sensitive of their incapacity and weakness, their empire is in so crumbling a state that they dread danger beforehand ... We must practise on their fears. The mere presence of our cruisers on their coast would sufficiently alarm them, however friendly might be our conduct ... .[15]

Writers for the *Register*, *Press* and *Repository* called for demonstrations of force by the Royal Navy to pressure negotiations and a treaty with the Chinese favourable to British merchants. This sort of strident talk regularly appeared in the missionary-run *Repository*, but it was clearly the voice of Jardine, or someone close to him, whose support of the missionaries' activities meant he had some influence with them. The merchants called in their own newspapers for Parliament to emulate the spirit of William Pitt the Younger who (as well as creating the institution of the Press Gallery in the House of Commons) had led Britain through the Napoleonic Wars and the Battle of Trafalgar and had forced union with Ireland — all events that inspired the British merchants to both new heights of patriotic strength and ideological expansionism in the face of Napoleon's Continental System of economic warfare. As a response, Lord Napier was despatched to the East in 1834. But the merchants were to be largely disappointed by Napier's arrival. He was formal British aristocracy whose ancestors had been titled under James I for, among other less useful things, discovering logarithms, but he knew nothing of China or the Chinese. Napier arrived in Macau and from there journeyed to Guangzhou but he achieved little and died not long after arriving. He, therefore, left us without his impressions of China but with his sole published book on a subject far closer to his rather stay-at-home heart than the China trade — the rearing of mountain goats.

Napier, or "Laboriously Vile" to the Chinese, was a major disappointment to the likes of Jardine as their favoured strategy of gunboats was the one thing Parliament had ordered Napier unable to authorise; William Hunter described this period as "the Napier fizzle". In the end, the best Jardine could do was argue that Napier's diplomatic failure meant little more than the correctness of his gunboat policy. He argued in this way in the pages of the *Register* where a Dr. Thomas Colledge M.D., who occasionally turned his hand to journalism on Jardine's behalf, wrote up the meetings between the Chinese and Napier. "Laboriously Vile" was portrayed as largely ineffectual, misreading the Chinese and the political situation while Jardine was eulogised as the most trusted and canny foreigner on the China coast. Colledge was yet another multi-talented and multi-tasking foreigner in Guangzhou. A British missionary, former Honourable Company employee and eye surgeon, he was — like Morrison (who died the same month as Napier), Gützlaff and Bridgman (who provided personal religious instruction to Napier in China) — a classic of those of a religious bent who often found common cause with the opium- smugglers of the time and the British government. Colledge was also Lord Napier's personal surgeon and therefore his accounts for the *Register* were presumably eye-witness ones. The *Register* also saw an opportunity to advance the Jardine agenda by hinting darkly that those advocating surrender rather than gunboats, namely to the pro-Jardine faction their arch rival Dent, were cowards and traitors.

Eventually Henry Temple (Lord Palmerston) was to become the merchant's man in London with his track record of not shirking from threatening the use of force in the national interest, which he did repeatedly in Turkey, Afghanistan, the Middle East and, ultimately, in China. Many missionaries were still able to stand, apparently comfortably, with the merchants in the triple goal of the supremacy of Britain over all others in the China trade, the supremacy of Christianity over all alternatives in religion and the supremacy of the British nation over all others in all regards — trade, religion, flag — and just to make sure, with the Royal Navy to safeguard and protect it all. British naval superiority was to be witnessed at the Battle of the Bogue Forts in January 1841. This battle at the structures that guarded the approaches to Guangzhou was the first clash between China and the West, and it registered with the public at home due largely to an amateur artist with the Royal Navy, Lieutenant Skinner, whose drawings of the action were published as coloured mezzotints by Ackermann and Company, London's most famous publisher of original prints and illustrated books. Skinner's stirring pictures of British forces taking on the Chinese Imperial Army accompanied reports in the newly established *Illustrated London News* that portrayed the war as a crusade to bring the benefits of English free trade and mercantilism to the despotic Orient.

By 1836 the *Register*, *Press* and *Repository* were all discussing what war between Britain and China would mean in terms of trade after the failed Napier mission and the Bogue Forts firefight from which the British had easily emerged victorious with their armour-plated ships. It was almost as if the Jardine line of an inevitable clash to open up China had been accepted by the entire foreign community, with just a few wayward dissenters. Maurice Collis described the attitude of all the papers and all the authors, both named and, as was often the case, anonymous, as "amused contempt" for the Chinese, with the *Repository* describing the abilities of the Chinese Imperial Navy as a "monstrous burlesque".[16]

At the time, however, missionaries were not the generally annoying interferers they were later to be perceived as but rather co-conspirators in the great mission to civilise China and make a lot of money along the way: trade, religion and flag remained close and invariably intertwined. However, over the period of the Opium Wars the English-language press in China was to divide in two with missionary-funded and written papers on one side and more commercially minded publications on the other. Likewise their views diverged and the missionaries largely found themselves writing for themselves rather than the wider audience they had enjoyed in the heyday of the *Repository*.

By the summer of 1839 the British had been expelled from their Factories and were sheltering on Macau where the *Register*, *Press* and *Repository* had all relocated their presses too. Fears of further Chinese reprisals meant that many sailed rather hastily for Hong Kong with a host of small boats ferrying families across the straits. The *Repository* was by now openly lambasting the British government for not having stepped in with the fleet and thereby having reduced the British to such ignominious measures that could achieve nothing but undermine the country's prestige in the eyes of the Chinese. War was to follow with the Battle of Chuenpee that somewhat reasserted British power under the command of Captain Charles Elliot, who had earned a positive reputation as a protector of slaves in British Guiana and was known to dislike the opium trade, but he didn't seem inclined to show the same leniency to the Chinese.

Until the summer of 1840 the *Repository* had nervously hoped that all-out war could be avoided and had reported the arrival of Honourable Company armed steamers with 4,000 Irish, Scots and Indian troops — all, as Maurice Collis commented, over "a mere customs dispute". The Chinese commissioner in Guangzhou, Lin Tse-Hsu, was reported in the pages of the *Repository* (one of the only papers to ever try and really see his point of view at the time) as declaring of the advancing British fleet: "English warships are now successively arriving at Canton, and though it is certain that they will not venture to create disturbances, nevertheless, like rats they will enter all the ways in order to protect those base followers who sell opium". For the *Repository*, a crucial moment had arrived: should it support the Chinese and oppose the opium-dealers or support the policies of the mother country and Britain's merchants? Yet again they chose Mammon and the flag without too much introspection.

The situation in China also attracted the interest of the foreign press, particularly in other parts of the British Empire. The English language *Japan Gazette* covered the developments while the *India Gazette*, a British-run publication in the Raj, wrote as follows about the Sack of Chusan in July 1840:

> A more complete pillage could not be conceived than took place. Every house was broken open, every drawer and box ransacked, the streets strewn with fragments of furniture, pictures, tables, chairs, grain of all sorts — the whole set off by the dead or the living bodies of those who had been unable to leave the city from the wounds received from our merciless guns ... The plunder ceased only when there was nothing to take or destroy.[17]

The Anglo-Chinese War, which became known as the First Opium War, had basically been the Battle of Chuenpee that, by and large, was not a major press event. However, the outcome was crucial for British expansion and also the further weakening of the Qing dynasty: cession of Hong Kong to the British crown (a victory for the *Register* which had called for Hong Kong to be a British port back in 1836) as the major British trading base in southern China, substantial indemnity payments and trade on an equal footing to be reopened at Guangzhou.

The situation rumbled on with the appointment of the dashing former spy Sir Henry Pottinger as chief superintendent of trade to Hong Kong residents and eventually more fighting erupted. The young Harry Parkes was to accompany Pottinger in his expedition up the Yangtze and, after having taken part in the capture of Zhenjiang and the surrender of Nanjing, witnessed the signing of the Treaty of Nanjing on board the British warship *HMS Cornwallis* in August 1842. The Treaty basically assured the British of everything they had wanted since Lord Macartney's failed mission 50 years earlier, and without explicitly mentioning opium. As well as the so-called "barren rock" of Hong Kong, Britain obtained her desired treaty port rights in Guangzhou, Xiamen, Fuzhou, Ningbo and Shanghai, as well as receiving indemnity payments and also reimbursing Pottinger the not inconsiderable cost of sending his fleet to China. The formal creation of Hong Kong and the new "treaty ports" where foreigners enjoyed special rights and trading privileges, particularly Shanghai, meant a major change in Britain's role in China. The development of the country following the treaty was to determine the rise of the press on the China coast while the continuing and structural weakness of the Qing dynasty led to a period of intense internal disturbance across the vast Chinese hinterland.

The opium-smugglers had, by and large, had their way and their own press had influenced British politicians and the public immensely. Jardine died in 1843 but Matheson took over his seat in Parliament, holding it for 25 years in total. He also became chairman of the P&O shipping line and the second-largest landowner in Britain, bought the Isle of Lewis in the Scottish Highlands, spent over £500,000 building a castle on it and became an octogenarian. The opium business lasted even longer, and by the 1880s the British were shipping in 100,000 chests, or 6,000 tons, of opium a year.

Hong Kong — A Colony in Need of a Press

Macau had started publishing Portuguese-language newspapers early and they reflected both missionary concerns (Catholics in this case) and internal Portuguese political tensions.[18] In September 1822 Major Paulino da Silva

Barbosa, the head of the Portuguese Constitutionalists in Macau, and briefly the governor, launched the weekly *Abelha da China* (*The Bee of China*) printed on a small press in St. Dominic's Church on Senado Square in the heart of the enclave. The paper was short-lived, folding the following year when Barbosa left office, but it did provide some commentary and analysis of affairs in China by foreigners for a readership consisting primarily of Macau's missionary community. The *Abelha da China* was mainly a vehicle for Barbosa to attack the Portuguese Monarchists in Macau. They replied with their own publication, the *Gazeta de Macao* in 1824, and in the 1830s the *Boletim Official do Governo de Macau* and *O Portuguez na China* were launched. The trend continued into the 1840s with the launching of *A Aurora Macaense* for several years and *Solitario na China* and *O Procurador dos Macaistas*.

Within a year of formal British administration, Hong Kong got its first newspaper —*The Friend of China* (formally *The Friend of China and Hongkong Gazette*) — which declared, "we inscribe Free Trade on our banner and that it may wave triumphant we shall insist on the permanent occupation of Hong Kong …".[19] Prior to this, everything the few early residents had read had been published in either Macau or Guangzhou. Soon after the *Friend of China*, the colony rapidly got a bewildering range of publications given its relatively small population: *The China Mail* in 1845; *The Daily Advertiser* in 1870; *The Hongkong Daily Press* in 1871; *The Hongkong Telegraph* in 1881; *The Hongkong Times*; *The Hong Kong Mercury and Shipping Gazette* in 1886; and what was universally considered the most boring newspaper ever to be published in the colony, *The Hongkong Government Gazette*. Most focused on trade and issues related to the growing foreign presence and business dealings in Guangzhou, while *The Hongkong Government Gazette* dealt mostly with local issues affecting the colony. Such a range of newspapers was actually quite impressive for a European and American community in the colony that numbered significantly fewer than 3,000 potential readers.

The most interesting of these newspapers was probably the *Telegraph*, an evening paper owned and edited by the scandal-mongering Robert Fraser-Smith who was described by the well-known Hong Kong University professor H. J. Lethbridge as "atrabilious" (i.e. irritable as if suffering from indigestion).[20] Fraser-Smith held court daily at the Hong Kong Hotel, the colony's social centre, conveniently situated adjacent to his editorial offices on Pedder's Hill. He was a hard drinker and inveterate gambler, and most of his staff, invariably Scotsmen, followed his example. He was also a reckless editor and constantly involved in libel actions, most of which he managed to defend by arguing his opponents into submission, but in 1890 he was finally sentenced to six months' imprisonment for libelling a foreman in the Public Works Department, having suggested he had committed rape. He remained seemingly unrepentant and the day after his release from Victoria Gaol was seen avidly betting at the Happy Valley racecourse.

Fraser-Smith featured heavily in the rather odd tale of His Majesty the King of the Sedangs who arrived in Hong Kong in 1888 with three personal servants and 13 Chinese employees and sparked a long-running war of words between Fraser-Smith and his arch-rival George Murray Bain, the editor of the *China Mail*. The king was in fact a Frenchman called David de Mayréna who took up residence in the Hong Kong Hotel and made Fraser-Smith's acquaintance. The two soon became good mates and drinking companions. The king proceeded to parade around town in a costume of Ruritanian proportions and dramatically sporting a long Annamite sword worn in a sash. After meeting the governor of Hong Kong, Sir William Des Voeux, the king awarded him the Grand Cordon de l'Ordre de Sedang. Predictably it was all a scam to get investors to hand over some cash and, while many were somewhat dubious, they weren't quite sure enough of their geography to question the king more closely.

De Mayréna had a reasonably good background but had ended up a penniless swindler in Asia, conning money out of gullible merchants with tales of expeditions to find gold, treasure and other loot. He had ventured into a remote part of Vietnam where the Sedangs lived and, in an amazing true story similar to Kipling's *The Man Who Would Be King*, he really had been anointed their king and made his local mistress the queen.[21] His royal palace was a basic hut miles from anywhere but with a very impressive flag fluttering above it of de Mayréna's own design. Eventually Bain got to the truth and "outed" de Mayréna as a fraud in the *Mail*, largely by translating articles about the self-proclaimed king's similar escapades in Hanoi and elsewhere in French Indo-China from the *Courier d'Haiphong*. Fraser-Smith, as part of his ongoing war with Bain and the *Mail*, and perhaps also out of friendship with de Mayréna (and probably for the sheer hell of it) staunchly defended the fraudulent king in the *Telegraph*. Eventually the king of the Sedangs quit Hong Kong for Europe with a second-class steamer ticket in a false name. He had raised no money, paid for no drinks and given the rivals Bain and Fraser-Smith something else to argue about in their papers for months, while the entire staff of the *Telegraph* were made "chevaliers" of the kingdom of Sedang, which left Hong Kong's reading public to enjoy all of the shenanigans immensely.

Fraser-Smith and his fellow Scotsman Bain continued to argue incessantly with each other. Bain railed at Fraser-Smith and the *Telegraph* from his Wyndham Street office round the corner from Pedder's Hill and the *Telegraph*'s offices. Though different in temperament — Bain was a respectable and pious teetotaller while Fraser-Smith was anything but — the two towered over the colony's newspaper business, which suggests that J. S. Thomson was right when he wrote in his book *The Chinese* in 1909 that "... the newspapers of the Treaty Ports were generally set up by the Macanese and edited by Scotchmen".[22] The tradition of Scotsmen and Macanese in the newspaper business was to continue as Shanghai and the other treaty port presses got underway. As a final irony, when Fraser-Smith died in 1895, J. J. Francis, the barrister who had attempted to prosecute him for libel many times, became the paper's publisher and appointed the more pro-Chinese Chesney Duncan as the *Telegraph*'s editor.

Fun as the *Mail* vs *Telegraph* spats were, ultimately more important in terms of commenting on Britain's opium trade and commercial policy after the founding of the colony was *The Friend of China*, which was published weekly on Thursdays from March 1842. The first issue was really nothing more than a long and indulgent editorial appealing for "patronage and support" and firmly identifying the newspaper as a voice of the British Empire in the East. The stated aim was to open China to free trade. *The Friend* stood stoutly for Mammon at a time when it was far from certain that Hong Kong would survive and thrive as a commercial centre. Due to the involvement of the Quaker-founded Society for the Suppression of the Opium Trade, *The Friend* did stand against opium, but it noted Matheson's departure for London and hoped that Jardine would relocate the firm's factory to Hong Kong as soon as possible. Apparently the opium business wasn't ultimately that repellent. *The Friend* was influential; it advocated that Hong Kong's capital be called Victoria, as it was, rather than the suggested Queens Town. Perhaps most interesting was *The Friend*'s regular *On Dits* column that repeated gossip heard around town, mostly about Chinese officials, and also frequent letters from concerned yet eminently respectable Hong Kong residents mainly complaining about drunken sailors getting rowdy. *On Dits* was a little more caustic than today's rather tamer and more libel-aware press in mixing news with gossip: one entry wrote: "The Hon'ble Lieutenant Governor Caine, goes to England next mail — The Colony will gain something by his absence".[23]

However, one thing the early Hong Kong press agreed upon was that, despite the brothels, misbehaving soldiers, opium-dealers, pestilence and interminable heat, the colony's development was to be vigorously supported. When in 1848 a writer for the *Dublin University Magazine*, who may or may not have actually visited, wrote an article critical of Hong Kong's establishment, climate and society, *The Friend* was extremely swift to rebut the "misconceptions" and defend Hong Kong.[24] Given Hong Kong's emergence as a potentially great *entrepôt* and crossroads of trade, this need for a vigorous defence by the local press may seem a little extreme. However, in the colony's early days after the Nanjing Treaty, the economy slumped and Hong Kong became little more than a storage depot for opium that had previously been stored at less cost on vast floating hulks. It was a "barren rock" indeed. Hong Kong was seen as worthless, and a costly burden rather than a glittering prize. In the London music halls the comedians sang "You may go to Hong Kong for me", meaning rather you than them in what many perceived to be little more than a fetid death trap of disease. There was of course some truth in all this. Hong Kong did not boom instantly, or live up to the hopes the Guangzhou merchants had initially had for it and it was certainly an unhealthy place, with the wonderfully misnamed Happy Valley being the major malarial pit of the island.

But, success or failure, the press in Hong Kong, Macau and Guangzhou was performing a useful function. In his classic book, *Orientalism*, Edward Said wrote that key to the Western study and reporting of the Orient has been a need to increase knowledge to consolidate power:

> … knowledge of subject races or Orientals is what makes their management easy and profitable; knowledge gives power, more power requires more knowledge, and so on in an increasingly profitable dialectic of information and control. [25]

Interestingly, and perhaps ironically, it was to be the missionary-run *Repository* rather than any of the merchant-funded newspapers that was to increase this body of knowledge from close to scant to something approximating useful in the first half of the nineteenth century. The often understated *Repository* brought together a vast array of knowledgeable contributors and also dipped into the raw Chinese texts and commentaries while the merchant press, in an often foghorn-like manner, was largely fixated on the state of trade and the need to influence London to give better support to business interests. The *Press* and *Register* tended to assume and pontificate while the *Repository* investigated and enquired, while also dabbling in not a small amount of proselytising. With the foundation of Hong Kong as a crown colony and the emergence in importance of the China coast treaty ports, events within the Middle Kingdom were to come to prominence and create a need for knowledge among Westerners in excess of what they had ever needed before as they engaged China to a greater extent than previously through the new treaty port system.

2
Civil and Other Wars — Rebels, Mercenaries and More Dope

"It is the destiny of Shanghai to become the permanent emporium of trade between China and all the nations of the world."

Editorial, first edition of the *North China Herald*, 3 August 1850

"Impartial, not neutral"

The motto of the *North China Herald*

Live from the Heavenly Kingdom

The foreigners who had arrived to claim their rights in the treaty port of Shanghai had barely begun to get to work when the Taiping Heavenly Kingdom suddenly appeared in revolt and threatened the very existence of the Qing dynasty in 1851. The Taiping were both mysterious and an immediate object of fascination for the foreign press and its readership. The Taiping's charismatic leader Hong Xiuquan was born a Hakka, encountered Christian missionaries, converted, declared himself a brother of Jesus, allowed only female disciples in his personal bodyguard and led an uprising that engulfed China in a massive civil war that threatened to create a theocracy and led to approximately 20 to 30 million deaths. This loss of (Chinese) life counted for little in the foreign press compared to the rebel threat to Shanghai and the stability of Yangtze trade. Reporters and readers alike were shocked by Hong's bizarre millennarial claims; he treacherously draped himself in imperial yellow which was supposed to adorn only the Manchu elite, cut off his queue, the symbol of male Chinese subservience to the Manchus, and let his hair flow free. Many were alarmed by the seeming readiness of so many Chinese to follow his charismatic lead; and with hundreds of thousands being subjected to Taiping rule and forced conscription as his armies swept across the country, and hundreds of thousands more facing starvation as the conflict ravaged the farmland, threats were posed to foreign interests in China. The Qing court felt no less perplexed and threatened than the foreigners by the sudden emergence of this strange Taiping phenomenon.

However, others saw the Taiping as genuine Christians, a potentially progressive force and an ideological ally against the sclerotic Qing dynasty. Initially there was considerable interest and sympathy for them among many missionaries, with the letters page of the newly launched Shanghai-based *North China Herald* containing a steady stream of letters from them in support of the uprising, accepting Hong's Christianity at face value while noting his proscription of opium use on pain of death in rebel-controlled areas. Also, some diplomats saw in the Taiping a possible antidote to the endemic corruption of the Qing.

The Chinese Evangelization Society and the China Inland Mission (CIM) published the *Chinese and General Missionary Gleaner* from 1851. It later changed its name and continued as just the *Chinese Missionary Gleaner* and often ran pro-Taiping letters from its missionary subscribers. Though published in London, it was widely read by missionaries in China. Over time, missionary attitudes to the Taiping were to change though one notable man of God held out longer than most — Issachar Jacox Roberts, the Southern Baptist preacher from Tennessee who had originally taught Hong Christianity in Guangzhou. Roberts wrote in the *Gleaner*: "Behold, what God hath wrought! Not only opened China externally for the reception of the teachers of the gospel, but now one has risen up among themselves, who presents the true God for their adoration, and casts down idols with a mighty hand, to whom thousands and tens of thousands of people are collecting!"[1] Roberts seems to have been most pleased with his pupil's zeal and urge to proselytise and, acting like a doting parent who can see no wrong in his child, was not overly concerned about either the manner of Hong's crusade or its finer theological points.

Against this backdrop, the Small Swords, a triad group rejected by the Taiping for its use of opium, threatened Shanghai in the general atmosphere of chaos after the Taiping had launched their uprising. In September 1853 the Small Swords occupied Shanghai's walled Chinese city and held it until February 1855. This prompted large numbers of Chinese refugees from surrounding areas to flood into the adjacent foreign concessions, which increased the population dramatically and added strains on the Settlement's welfare resources, prompting the formation of the Shanghai Volunteer Corps (SVC). A nervous foreign community followed events, increasingly alarmed at the advances of the Taiping. Foreign nerves were to fray further soon after with news of the Indian Mutiny in 1857. The British Empire and imperial trade seemed to be in peril and vulnerable; and it appeared that relying on native troops was definitely not going to make anyone feel any easier in the offices of Whitehall or the bedrooms of foreigners from Bombay to Beijing.

When the Taiping came to threaten Shanghai, the city moved beyond the hastily formed SVC as Chinese politicians and merchants established the Foreign Arms Corps. American high school drop-out Frederick Townsend Ward, a New England ship hand and mercenary, first commanded the troop, which became widely known as "The Ward Corps" (and later as "The Ever Victorious Army"). The Ward Corps received its first real baptism of fire in April 1854, when, operating with British and American naval parties, and unexpectedly reinforced by the Small Swords (a sort of "my enemy's enemy is my friend" moment), they dislodged a large force of the Imperial Army from a threatening position near the western boundary of the foreign settlement (known as the Battle of Muddy Flat [2]) in an attempt to remove them to a safe distance. They went on to some victories and some defeats over the coming years and won themselves both supporters and detractors among the foreign press.

Much of the early writing on the Taiping followed on from the end of the First Opium War through to Lord Elgin's mission to Beijing in 1857. British consular official Thomas Meadows noted the rebels' antique weaponry and their apparent lack of organisation. However, it also had to be noted that the Qing forces — the "Demon Imps" as the British troops dubbed them — had little more advanced weaponry and that the rebels had won the vast majority of engagements between the two armies. In the *Repository*, Bridgman described the Taiping as like a "new race of warriors", while the missionary and sometime-columnist and commentator with the new *North China Herald,* Walter Medhurst, noted the cruelty exhibited on both sides in the conflict. The *Herald* itself often seemed to just find the whole uprising a bothersome bore. By the late 1850s, its editorial pages were bemoaning both the incessant drunkenness of British troops passing through Shanghai, a theme in the China coast press that didn't go until way until the troops did, as well as the "fungus" of the Taiping rebels on Chinese society.

But it was the aforementioned diplomat Meadows who attracted most attention for his views. He was a striking individual: broad-chested, heavily bearded, standing in excess of six feet tall and married to an illiterate Chinese woman, before such inter-racial unions were frowned upon by the Foreign Office and would lead to the curtailment of several promising careers. He was the prime example of a group of foreign observers who were, initially at least, sympathetic to the Taiping. Their support derived from their observations that the Qing rulers were irredeemably corrupt, arrogant and incompetent, unlike the missionaries who saw, or at least hoped for, some sort of commonality of religious belief.

Meadows's views were taken seriously as he was a well respected sinologist who had studied Chinese in Munich before joining the British consulate in Guangzhou in 1842 where he had witnessed the First Opium War.

Overall the *North China Herald* (of which more later) came out as neutral. It did not heap praise on the Taiping but neither did it overtly support the Ward Corps, calling them a "gang" and a "disgrace", believing that the involvement of an ostensibly foreign- manned force of Americans, British and Filipino Manilamen as well as assorted other "drifters" would needlessly bring the wrath of the Taiping down on Shanghai and thus disrupt business. The *Herald* didn't support the Imp forces either. Some did note that much of this indignation at the Ward Corps and the corrupt Qing court was a little rich coming from a bunch of opium-dealers, imperialists and land-grabbers. Much of the generally pro-British *Herald*'s problem with the Ward Corps was Ward himself who was being accused of encouraging British soldiers to desert and join his better-paying mercenary force, which also offered greater looting and pillaging opportunities to keen young fighting men. Ward came to distrust and dislike the British press, and the British in general, and they returned the compliment in the pages of the *Herald* and the *Hongkong Daily Press*.

Still there were others who championed Ward, even at this early stage when his unpopularity was at a height within the diplomatic, business and missionary communities. One such person was Daniel Jerome Macgowan, an American Baptist missionary and physician, as well as a champion of the introduction of the telegraph in China. Macgowan argued in various China coast newspapers that Ward's men largely refrained from plunder, a far from correct assertion. It was also the case that while the *Herald* raged against Ward editorially, it also printed many letters from Shanghailanders (as foreigners resident in Shanghai dubbed themselves) supporting him. However Ward's reputation sank miserably when the Taiping routed his mercenary forces at Qingpu, near Shanghai, in 1860, forcing him to skulk away looking for additional men, money and arms. The *Herald* celebrated his overwhelming defeat in a distinctly uncharitable manner, reporting that he was not, "… as was hoped, dead, but severely wounded with a shot in his mouth, one in his side, and one in his legs …", before demanding he should be publicly punished, as if being shot three times was not admonishment enough.[3]

Then, in 1860 eyes turned from the Taiping-ridden flats of eastern China and refocused first southwards on Guangzhou and Hong Kong where opium was again a spark for war and then northwards to Beijing and Tianjin when Britain's Lord Elgin marched on the Qing capital. The *Herald*'s editorial writers continued to demand sanctions against Ward while the letters page contained more than one letter that pointed out appositely that Elgin was proceeding to Beijing to secure Britain's trading rights in China, while Ward was fighting to defend the government Elgin was supposed to be meeting and dealing with as well as to protect Shanghai, one of the treaty ports designated in the treaties Elgin wished to ratify. Were not the two things really one and the same, namely defence of trade? Of course they were, but it was to take the Second Opium War, the Elgin Mission and a major change in Sino-foreign relations for the English-language press in China to come round to that way of thinking.

Opium Again — Over to Our Correspondent Karl Marx

Nothing feeds the public's hunger for news quite as much as conflict and the Second Opium War was also when foreign commentators started to pay more attention to events in China and the discussion of China overseas in forums such as the British Parliament took a heightened precedence. During the First Opium War opposition had been muted in the British press and was limited largely to Chartist papers and the radical *Northern Star*, along with some vocal parliamentarians such as William Gladstone.[4] Most of the press and politicians had chosen to wrap themselves in the Union Jack. Those who opposed the first war were part of the government that succeeded the Whigs in June 1841 but they carried on the policies of the former government anyway; continuity of policy and the primacy of trade triumphed.

The Second Opium War, or the Arrow War, began in October 1856 when the Chinese arrested a suspected pirate ship, the Hong Kong-registered *Arrow*. The acting British consul, Harry Parkes, tried unsuccessfully to intervene and eventually appealed to Sir John Bowring, Hong Kong's governor. Bowring declared the arrest an insult to the flag and demanded the release of the ship and an apology. The Chinese released the crew but refused to apologise. Bowring ordered Admiral Seymour's fleet to bombard Guangzhou conveniently ignoring both Parliament's attempt to ban such gut-reaction gunboat responses and the news that the *Arrow*'s registration had lapsed at the time of its seizure. However, Bowring was let off the hook when Prime Minister Palmerston decided the *Arrow* incident was effectively an act of war that required British prestige to be maintained with military force and intervention as well as, as suggested by the historian of empire Niall Ferguson, to maintain the financial benefits of the opium trade to the British administration in India.[5] Consequently the red-faced and thickset Lord James Bruce, the eighth Earl of Elgin, was sent to China to sort out the mess.

One foreign commentator on the Arrow War worth mentioning, though he never visited China, was Karl Marx who commented frequently on China in his regular articles for the *New York Daily Tribune* between 1853 and 1860. Marx and Engels had considered China the "oldest and most unshakeable empire of the world", but believed it to be isolated and rotting. However, China's confrontation with the West in the form of the Second Opium War and the Royal Navy's return to Guangzhou meant they felt compelled to fit China more neatly into their world-view. For Marx, foreign incursions and the outbreak of the Taiping Rebellion indicated China's lack of stability. They concluded that, under pressure from industrial capitalism, China would move on from feudalism to capitalism and ultimately socialism.

In January 1857 Marx questioned Admiral Seymour's actions in Guangzhou, declaring that: "... the British are in the wrong in the whole proceeding". However, his was not as much of a firebrand position as might have been expected. The *Times* had written, "... there are, indeed, matters in dispute, such as whether the *lorcha (Arrow)*...was carrying British colours, and whether the Consul was entirely justified in the steps that he took". Indeed the editorialists at the *London Daily News* were far harsher on Seymour than Marx was, asserting:

> ... [a] monstrous fact, that in order to avenge the irritated pride of a British official, and punish the folly of an Asiatic governor, we prostitute our strength to the wicked work of carrying fire and sword, and desolation and death, into the peaceful homes of unoffending men, on whose shores we were originally intruders. Whatever may be the issue of this Canton bombardment, the deed itself is a bad and a base one — a reckless and wanton waste of human life at the shrine of a false etiquette and a mistaken policy.[6]

As it turned out the British government had been advised by the attorney general that Bowring's decision to shell Guangzhou was illegal but they opted to back him anyway.

Most of Marx and Engels's articles dealt with the run-up to and then the conflict that became the Second Opium War as well as the Taiping Rebellion. They were clearly against the opium trade. To them the Opium Wars were caused by, "... English cannon forcing upon China that soporific drug called opium", which again was not a massively revolutionary opinion for the time, as the lord chancellor had already taken Palmerston's cabinet to task over opium and the war. However, Marx's views on matters Chinese got a wide readership; as well as in the *Daily Tribune*, they were reprinted in a range of other American and German papers including *The Free Press, Das Volk, The People's Paper, Die Reform* and others. Not that being widely circulated, or even read, apparently really bothered Marx and Engels: "Mere potboiling ...", wrote Engels of the more than 500 articles he and Marx wrote for the *Daily Tribune*, "... it doesn't matter if they are never read again".

Marx wrote from his cramped living room in Soho's Dean Street in London though some booked passage and travelled to China to investigate for themselves. George Wingrove Cooke was the first special correspondent to China for the London *Times* and became well known for his reporting on the Arrow War and for his descriptions of Ye Mingchen, the governor-general of Guangdong and Guangxi, whom he eventually accompanied into exile to India. Cooke provided the most immediate and authoritative account of events in China yet to appear in the Western media.

Into the Valley of the Shadow — Lord Elgin and a Dead War Correspondent

The Arrow War marked another issue that was to raise its head again in the twentieth century — the physical safety of journalists in China. With the Arrow War it became apparent that the press could both report in some depth on China and also influence events. It was the London *Times* that was to first coin the term "Opium War" and what, at base, the dispute came down to, namely the ability of the foreigners, particularly the British, to open up China to trade and to do this using the commodity of opium and enshrined in the 1842 Nanjing Treaty. The follow-up Tianjin Treaty of 1858 after the Second Opium War granted 10 more treaty ports and opened up substantial inland trade and missionary opportunities. It was hailed as a great victory in Britain. *The Graphic*, a British magazine which carried regular images of China and Chinese life, commissioned the Shanghai-based artist Wu Youru, whose work often appeared in early Chinese newspapers, to provide an illustration — *Signing of the Tientsin Pact*.

The 1860 Anglo-French expedition, better known as the Elgin Mission, to Beijing to enforce the 1858 treaty terms was a gruelling slog with clashes at the Taku Forts that guarded the mouth of the Peiho River and other points along the way. Elgin, Parkes and the French noble Baron Gros all knew that to an extent they were in a race against time as pro- and anti-war forces in Beijing argued about how to deal with the approaching delegation, which was accompanied by a sizeable force of British, Indian and French troops. Elgin, who apparently spent much of the trip reading Darwin's recently published *Origin of Species*, was keen to avoid conflict if at all possible. Also along on the trip were Thomas Bowlby, the popular London *Times* correspondent, as well as the mission's official photographer, Felice Beato, who had previously accompanied the British to the Crimea and India and who published his photos in the *Illustrated London News*.

Bowlby had been born into an army family in Gibraltar that later became prosperous timber merchants in England and he subsequently became independently wealthy after rather unconventionally and slightly confusingly marrying the very rich sister of his father's second wife. He had previously been Berlin correspondent for the *Times*. However, he had managed to lose most of his matrimonially acquired fortune through a bad investment in a railway scheme. He had then moved to Smyrna in Greece where he became involved in another less than stellar railway project before signing back on with the *Times* to cover Elgin's Mission. Readers were thrilled by his account of the disastrous start to the journey with the sinking of the steamship carrying the Elgin party at Malabar off Ceylon (now Sri Lanka).

The *Times* had previously sent its reporter William Russell to the Crimea as probably the first-ever official war correspondent and then to Lucknow where he had seen first the Indian Mutiny and then British troops loot the city. Russell's reports had been extremely popular — hard-hitting, graphic and filled with gore — and significantly boosted the paper's reputation and circulation. They hoped to repeat the success in China and the *Times*'s High Victorian editor, John "J. T." Delane, the man who turned the *Times* into the thundering voice of the British establishment, despatched Bowlby as the sole reporter on the trip.

Despite the dramatic dipping in the Indian Ocean, the party had eventually reached the mouth of the Yangtze on 29 June and proceeded to Shanghai. Bowlby spent 30 June writing a report in time to catch the evening mail ship as the expedition moved on and eventually landed near Tianjin and the Taku Forts, not far from Beijing. Bowlby covered the whole journey, continuing to write despatches which were eventually published in October and November. After Tianjin was occupied, the army prepared to finally march on Beijing, believing the capital to be poorly defended. A small party preceded the main force under a flag of truce to negotiate for Elgin's arrival, with Bowlby accompanying Parkes and Elgin's private secretary H. B. Loch (formerly of the East India Company and the Bengal Cavalry) in the advance group along with some Indian sepoys and British soldiers. Things turned decidedly nasty when Parkes had a disagreement with a Chinese general who promptly took them all hostage. Bowlby was among those kidnapped and was held in Beijing's Yellow Temple together with some of the French and British soldiers guarding the party. All were starved and tortured. Parkes and Loch were later released, but Bowlby and several others died after about a week of incarceration and mistreatment.

Elgin infamously responded to Bowlby's death by torching Emperor Hsien Feng's Summer Palace, as well as permitting a general looting spree which resulted in a Pekinese dog from the Summer Palace being delivered to Queen Victoria. She named it "Lootie", which perhaps best indicates the low level of official condemnation Elgin could expect in London for his ransacking actions. When asked why he had burned the Summer Palace to the ground, Elgin ("a dour little Scotsman", according to the sophisticated and cultured Italian Minister to Beijing Daniele Varé[7]) replied: "What would the *Times* say of me if I did not avenge its correspondent?" Bowlby's remains were laid to rest in Beijing's Russian cemetery with full military honours. This was at least the second torching that the *Times* had goaded. During the Indian Mutiny and fighting which followed in Peshawar, the paper's editorialists had demanded that "… every tree and gable-end in the place should have its burden in the shape of a mutineer's carcass", and the British army complied by burning villages and hanging mutineers from trees in reprisals, presumably to the satisfaction of the *Times*.

Photographing China — Beato, Thomson, Floyd and Miller

Photography had come quickly to China, promoted by foreigners who accompanied military missions and then stayed on to cater for the growing number of tourists visiting the treaty ports, as well as a new plethora of Chinese studios which had often been established by the former Chinese assistants of the foreign photographers. However, the idea that photographs could be reproduced in papers was still technically some time in the future. *The Illustrated London News*, *Times*, *Graphic*, *Pall Mall Gazette* and most other British newspapers and periodicals were all running drawings by the 1860s while the more serious papers featured lavish maps too. Reports from China relied largely on wood engravings and lithographs which were either commissioned or copied from photographs in China and then mailed to England.

Illustrations and reproductions of paintings had proved remarkably popular with the reading public and were able to stir up some useful emotional patriotism. For example, Lady Elizabeth Butler's emotive 1842 painting *The Remnants of an Army* which depicted Dr. William Brydon, the only survivor of the British retreat from Kabul, staggering dramatically into Jalalabad on horseback barely alive, had become a fixed image in many people's minds of that particularly disastrous piece of British imperial history. Butler's painting was in many ways little more than imperial kitsch but the public liked it, apparently interpreting complete unmitigated disaster as a triumph of British pluck and resolve among the heathen. Other images were also popular. In 1858 *The Illustrated London News* carried engravings of the Happy Valley racecourse in Hong Kong and later reproduced somewhat exaggerated paintings of Boxers during the 1900 Siege of the Legations and was to reproduce William Alexander's drawings again and again for years. Indeed, *The Illustrated London News* had started earlier than most by using photographs from Felice, or Felix, Beato who was one of the pioneers of photography in China and had accompanied Elgin to Beijing.

Beato was the most important of the early photographers in China. While it is thought that a couple may have worked in China before him, including a Russian and another European, they remain anonymous. Their work, if it was indeed pre-Beato, is also decidedly more amateurish. In Macau, the Parisian Daguerreotypist Jules Itier was taking photographs in the 1840s when he was employed as chief of a commercial mission to China. His photos included one of the signing of the Treaty of Wangxia in 1844[8] in Macau. Still, the question of who brought photography to China remains open. Photographs have appeared of a highly professional nature that apparently pre-date Beato's in 1860 and also reveal what appears to be the inside of the Qing court in the Forbidden City. Authentication, however, remains elusive.[9] Meanwhile, Milton Miller was photographing in Guangzhou between 1861 and 1864, producing a series of portraits using the collodion wet-plate process that reduced exposure times from minutes to seconds and then printed in monochromes that were later colour-tinted by hand. What is known is that by being the official photographer hired by the British for Elgin's Mission, Beato became the first war photographer to work officially in China.

Beato, who later became a naturalised British subject, was one of two Italian brothers, or at least is assumed to be so: Beato described himself as a Venctian but others questioned this claiming he was from Corfu. He had worked around the Mediterranean in partnership with the pioneering British photographer and engraver James Robertson in the 1850s after meeting him in Malta. Robertson married Felice's sister and probably taught the two Beato brothers photography. They formed a partnership named Robertson & Beato and Co., the "and Co." being the other Beato brother Antoine. They took scenic pictures in Greece, Turkey and Egypt (where Antoine was to stay on) and gained some notoriety for capturing the Crimean War in 1855. Beato then travelled to India, where he photographed the Indian Mutiny, reaching Lucknow in March 1858 a few weeks after the capture of the city by British troops and taking over 60 pictures there. He then dissolved the partnership with Robertson and moved to China where he stayed until 1862 before moving on again, this time to Japan, where he accompanied the 1871 American expedition to Korea. Still obfuscating where exactly he originally came from, Beato was appointed Greek consul-general for Japan in 1873, a strange job for a Venetian. He stayed in Japan until 1884 when he went to Africa to photograph the Sudanese colonial wars in 1885 before finally heading to Burma where he opened a furniture and curios business.

Beato's accumulated lifetime work was stunning: his beautiful landscapes and portraits of the country and people captured images of Japan, China and India as well as other places perfectly; and, of course, there was also the war photography. That he took so many photographs over such a long period of time has meant that a great legacy and body of work exists. Largely we have Beato's utter lack of commercial good sense to thank for this. He saw his photography as a source of steady income to support his main interest, which was in accumulating enough capital to invest in various commercial and property-related schemes in the hope of making his fortune. Fortunately for history, he was not a wise investor and consistently lost heavily, which meant he had to unpack his camera once more and take on another commission.

Beato was not slow to sell his photographs. For instance, the American expedition he joined some years after working with Elgin left Korea on 3 July 1871. However, before that, on 28 June, the *Shanghai Newsletter* had announced a sale of photographs portraying the event. Beato had managed to secure passage to Shanghai, develop his photographs and get them on the market in around 20 days. By 22 July the *New York Times* was running an advert describing and listing 47 views available in a bound volume while the 1 August edition of *Far East* magazine described a sale of Korean photographs taken by "Mr Beato and Mr Woolett" (Beato's assistant). By 5 July, presumably with his business done and sales made, Beato left Shanghai and returned to Yokohama where he sought to further capitalise on his fame by opening "F Beato & Co., Photographers" with his assistant Woolett, a staff of four Japanese photographers and his brother-in-law James Robertson.

But this was later. Before that the British had found themselves in a problematic relationship with Beato. They hired and fired him several times, believing he liked the blood and gore a little too much. In the Crimea, Lucknow and then in China on the Elgin Mission, he exasperated British officers by insisting on positioning the Chinese dead in gory poses for hours at a time in order to capture his stunning images. Long exposure times meant the dead bodies had to be propped up and left for some time while the picture was taken. This all proved too much for one British officer who got fed up with this and fired him.

Other photographers followed Beato to China in the nineteenth century, including John Thomson who had been an apprentice in a leading Edinburgh opticians and scientific instruments maker and had also studied chemistry. In 1862 he left Scotland to join his brother in Singapore and travelled to Malaya and Sumatra before going on to photograph India and Ceylon. In 1865 he sold his studio in Singapore and went to Bangkok, before moving on once more to photograph Laos, Cambodia and Saigon. After a spell recovering from "jungle fever" in London, he embarked for Asia a final time, eventually settling in Hong Kong in 1868, setting up a studio and marrying. From there he started travelling to Guangzhou to take photographs and then on to Shanghai. This led to longer photography expeditions through the interior of China, sometimes with other people for company and sometimes with just his dog Spot and a dozen or so bearers to carry his cumbersome photographic equipment and supplies. Thomson was perhaps the most prolific of the European photographers in China in the late nineteenth century, though there were others such as William Pryor Floyd who was working in Macau and Hong Kong in the 1860s and 1870s and Milton Miller who was also active taking photographs in Hong Kong and Guangzhou in the 1860s.

It's worth noting that Beato, Thomson, Floyd and Miller were not like the later photographers who roamed around with their cameras nonchalantly slung around their necks: on average they needed 15 to 20 bearers to carry their equipment and had to develop on-the-spot in makeshift darkroom tents. The long exposure times and the novelty of the technology ensured that crowds, which were not always friendly towards the photographers, would gather wherever they set up: Thomson recalled being stoned and attacked by mobs while taking photographs inland. The bearers were quick students and many of them promoted themselves and became the first generation of Chinese photographers who were to go on to supply the foreign press and visitors with photographs. Many of these Chinese photographers became extremely well known and highly regarded in their own right.

Ever Victorious Mercenaries

The Elgin Mission, the death of 13 of his party, the burning of the Summer Palace and the resultant looting meant a change in just about everything diplomats, missionaries, businessmen and the press had thought about China and the Taiping pre-Elgin. Opinion shifted even though some influential commentators in Shanghai, such as Meadows, were still leaning towards the Taiping. The reasons for swinging away from the rebels in 1860–61, or at least from assuming neutrality, towards supporting the maintenance of the Manchu court and a resumed Ward Corps varied somewhat. For the *North China Herald*, the major factors that started to move the paper against the rebels were the threats of attacks on Shanghai and disruptions to the Yangtze trade. For the diplomats, it was the departure of Meadows from Shanghai to be replaced by the more conciliatory Walter Medhurst, as well as the arrival of Anson Burlingame, the very capable American minister to China. This marked a more active American diplomatic engagement than previously and Burlingame also, somewhat later, became very friendly with Ward.

Diplomats of all countries read the tea leaves to try to understand the series of palace coups in Beijing with the death of the debauched Emperor Hsien Feng and the rise of the scheming Empress Dowager Ci Xi. For the missionaries, who had perhaps been staunchest in supporting their apparent co-religionists, the statements of Issacher Roberts, Hong's original teacher and supporter, had an important impact. Roberts had stormed out of Hong's camp in a huff, declaring the whole Taiping project abominable and Hong irrational. The disappointed Baptist circulated a stinging critique of the Taiping's leadership, theories and organisation to the newspapers which reprinted it widely, thus sealing the fate of the Taiping with most of their remaining Christian supporters.

Attitudes continued to change. By as early as January 1861 the *Herald*'s editor, Charles Spencer Compton, was writing that the Taiping represented religious despotism and a fledgling theocracy. Both American and British diplomats, led by minister extraordinaire Frederick Bruce (Lord Elgin's brother who had just taken up residence in Beijing) seemed to be onboard to defend the Qing, along with the bulk of the press and the acquiescence of the missionaries. The Taiping movement was bereft of friends and a somewhat unholy alliance of the business-friendly press and politically calculating diplomats — who arguably didn't want a speedy end to an uprising that was neatly forcing more policy changes from the Qing than the last century of diplomacy had managed — set about resurrecting the Ward Corps to take up the fight they were reluctant to. And this time there was the added bonus of Britain desperately wanting to neutralise rising French influence by keeping them out of the struggle. But where was Ward?

He had seemingly disappeared. Yet as a Taiping force neared the strategically crucial Woosong Fort that marked the junction between the Yangtze and Huang Pu Rivers which, if taken, would cut off Shanghai's sea access, a mixed foreign-Chinese force of troops suddenly appeared bearing Ward's flag and routed the rebels. Somewhat later in early 1862, when the journalists at the *Herald* could hear the Taiping guns in nearby Songjiang again, they waited to see what would happen. Ward pulled a brilliant victory out of the bag despite overwhelming odds, and finally the *Herald*, Ward's old nemesis which had once been upset that he hadn't been slaughtered on the field of battle, was forced to admit that he had commanded a well-trained regiment to a brave victory. From that point on, the *Herald* treated Ward with respect and higher regard. So too did most of the overseas press and even the *Times* poured scorn on the few pro-Taiping supporters left in the British Parliament. There were no more calls for Ward's imprisonment or expulsion from China as there had been previously in very vitriolic language. The *Herald* and Ward were never to be the best of friends and Ward would never lose his distaste for either the Shanghai press or the city's foreign business community, but they could at last agree on a common cause — the defeat of the Taiping Heavenly Kingdom. So too could the Qing court with even the government-run *Peking Gazette*, which was roughly the size of a pamphlet, lamenting the inability of Li Hongzhang's Chinese troops to back up effectively and consolidate the victories achieved by Ward's mercenaries.

The Shanghai Explosion — The *North China Herald*, Its Editors and Competitors

In 1850 the Shanghai press had arrived around the same time as the Taiping. Small broadsheets had existed previously but the launch of the *North China Herald* under the proprietorship and editorial control of Henry Shearman marked the arrival of a real newspaper for the Settlement. When it was launched on 3 August, the *Herald* was just a folio sheet of four pages produced from cramped offices on Hankow Road. However, it was able to devote enough space to the arrival of the American clipper *Sea Witch*. It detailed all the passengers aboard — an essential service as people worried endlessly about the safety of their nearest and dearest arriving by sea — and listed all the 157 full-time foreign residents (including 14 ladies) then in Shanghai, most of whom, one assumes, knew each other anyway. The first edition included both details of local organisations such as the Shanghai Pirate Suppression Bureau and profiles of local Chinese officials: the imperial governor of Jiangsu, Hsueh Huan, was said to be a "cunning commissioner"; Wu Hsu, Shanghai's *taotai*, was "an extraordinary man"; and China's Bismarck Zeng Guofan was "strict and a harsh disciplinarian". There was also a popular column of "Phrases in the Shanghai Dialect" that included the essential and immortal British phrase rendered into Shanghainese dialect — "Make a cup of tea and bring it". However, the *Herald*'s editorial policy was clear from the start:

> It is the destiny of Shanghai to become the permanent emporium of trade between it and all the nations of the world. To aid by his humble efforts in effecting this grand object will be the one great aim of the editor's most strenuous exertions.[10]

Although there were fewer than 200 resident foreigners, this was apparently enough to justify building a racetrack and a press, before they had even formed the Municipal Council. The launch of the *Herald* precipitated a small flood in the 1860s as the Shanghai media started to explode with a wide variety of publications appearing. They weren't all initially successful and, in fact, most failed pretty quickly. The *Shanghai Daily Times* had a brief existence from mid-1861 to April of the following year but went bankrupt rather swiftly. The proprietors, Messers Wynter and Company, declared excitedly that it would be "the same size as the *Herald*", which wasn't much of a marketing ploy even by the standards of 1861. However, the paper might have lasted had not Mr Wynter absconded without a trace along with 4,500 *taels* — the rather lucrative total sum of annual subscriptions raised for the new venture. The other partners lost heart as well as their stake, and decided to cut their losses by calling it a day.

The Shanghai Recorder was another morning paper that didn't last long. It was launched in 1862 but its stock was sold off by auction five years later to pay mounting debts. During its brief tenure it was edited for a time by John Bowker, a Briton who had been born in Newfoundland, the son of a Royal Navy family. He had planned to keep on editing the newspaper following a brief home leave to England but he died on the ship during the voyage, and the paper never really got over his loss and folded. 1867 was a year of severe depression in Hong Kong and Shanghai as the after-effects of the American Civil War hit trade; as well as the *Recorder*, Dent and Company, the long-established trading firm, and long-time rivals of Jardine Matheson, failed.

Nevertheless, would-be media tycoons persevered. C. Treasure Jones, a one-time editor of the *Friend of China*, launched a daily paper, the *Evening Express* in 1867 that continued for several years. A year later the *Shanghai Evening Courier* was launched with Hugh Lang as editor and featured a range of contributions from Shanghailanders expounding their, often rather strident, views on trade, Shanghai's development and China in general. However, as most resident Shanghailanders knew each other in the close world of the Settlement, they really didn't need to read each other's views as well.

More specialised publications appeared, such as *The Cycle*, a political and literary review which came out as a Shanghai weekly in 1870 but it only lasted until June the next year. Its editor was Dr. R. A. Jamieson and it was supposed to be the official organ of the Customs Service, a subject perhaps not exciting enough to readers not intimately concerned with tariffs, duties and the minutiae of the customs and excise world. Jamieson was relatively well known in Shanghai as a practising doctor who also worked without payment at the St. Luke's Clinic maintained by the American Episcopal Church Mission, as well as working for the Royal Commission on Opium in Shanghai.

The *North China Herald* fought back against these new rivals with the launch, in 1867, of the *North China Herald and Market Report*. The *Supreme Court and Consular Gazette* was also launched in 1867, though it was soon merged into the *Herald* as the rather long-winded *North China Herald and Supreme Court and Consular Gazette*. This was published weekly, and its roll call of editors included Henry Shearman, Samuel Mossman, R. Alexander Jamieson, R. S. Gundry, G. W. Haden, F. H. Balfour, J. W. Maclellan, R. W. Little, H. T. Montague-Bell and the rather hardline and long-serving O. M. Green — a roll call that if nothing else proves that initials were popular in late nineteenth and early twentieth century Shanghai. They spanned many decades, with Green still being at the paper long after it became the *North-China Daily News* in the late 1920s and lasting through to 1930 when he retired.

Shearman was not perhaps the likeliest of newspaper proprietors as he was Shanghai's auctioneer, but he remained editor until his death in 1856. As well as being an auctioneer, he was the local representative for an invention called Pulvermacher's Patent Portable Hydro-Electric Chain for Portable Use, a product that has long since slipped into obscurity to the point that nobody seems quite sure what it did, though according to its advertising it was a "magneto-electrical machine that can cure many diseases". What is remembered is that Shearman's initial idea at the *Herald* was largely to further British interests and the Empire in Shanghai. As he put up the money for the *Herald*, he got to be the editor despite his apparent total ignorance of the rules of English grammar and lack of funds for any sub-editors which made some of the early issues a strange and disjointed read.

The *Herald* may have been the best there was, but it was not exactly current with the news. The inaugural issue on 3 August led with the breaking news that Queen Victoria had given birth to Prince Arthur (the Duke of Connaught), an event that had actually occurred three months earlier, on 1 May. Otherwise, the main story was a notification that due to the roof collapsing at the Holy Trinity Church, services would be held temporarily in a go-down along Suzhou Creek, which must have tested the faith of some of a congregation unused to gathering to pray in damp warehouses. Publication was a little erratic, with Shearman apologising for one late issue by blaming the fact that his compositor had food poisoning. For several years, circulation never got above 200 copies and all Shearman needed was a hand-press to crank out the weekly issue when his compositors troublesome guts allowed.

Shearman did, however, manage to gather around the paper an interesting group of proto-correspondents and commentators, including the well-known missionary Walter Medhurst and John Bowring, then British consul general in Guangzhou before he became far better known as the governor of Hong Kong. Medhurst was a well-known but tragic character in Hong Kong and along the China coast. After working for many years in Asia, he had returned to England to enjoy his fortune, became happily married and had a young son who was at school in Guernsey. Tragically, the boy died after accidentally ingesting strychnine in a chemist's shop. A year later the boy's mother, distraught at his death, died and in his grief Medhurst quit Britain once again to become a founder of the British North Borneo Company and moved to Hong Kong in 1882. He was to become well known for the system of emigration from China he organised, recruiting men into the North Borneo Company's territories. While in Hong Kong he became a regular contributor to a variety of newspapers in the region, particularly the *Herald*.

Shearman also laid down the policy that while, in general, the *Herald* represented London's world-view, it would not be slow to criticise British officials in China, which the paper considered as "supportive admonishment". He advocated neutrality between the Western powers and the Taiping rebels when they threatened Shanghai and maintained that the Chinese should deal with the threat and only if they were unable to do so should outside forces be brought to bear. When the *Herald* carried sketches from the 1854 Battle of Muddy Flat, both Chinese and foreigners were shown as equally determined and organised, which contrasted with the usual Western imagery of noble foreign troops facing evil, but rather shambolic hordes of Chinese. After Shearman's death, the paper's editorship passed to the missionary J. Mackrill Smith, the executor of Shearman's estate and a man of God rather than a man of the press.

Mackrill Smith was hopeless and as soon as he had executed Shearman's will, he promptly sold the paper and handed over swiftly, and one imagines gratefully, to the rather aristocratic Charles Spencer Compton, a descendant of an English Civil War hero and family of long-upstanding High Tories. Compton was far from the most enervating and exciting editor a fledgling paper could hope for even by the rather dour standards of the time. However, he did manage to make the publication the official paper of record in China with permission to adorn the cover with the royal coat of arms in 1859, following the proclamation from the British consulate in Shanghai that the *North China Herald* is, "to be considered the official organ of all notifications proceeding from Her Majesty's Legation and the Superintendency of Trade in China". Compton also presided over the paper during the worst of the fighting around Shanghai during the Taiping rebellion. He disliked the Qing government for the usual reasons most foreigners did, considering them corrupt, arrogant and unfit to rule, but he disliked the Taiping equally as a threat to free trade.

However, if nothing much else, Compton was a stout defender of his writers. When the now forgotten, but then quite famous, Ali-Ben-Sou-Alle (really the composer Jean-Baptiste Soualle) arrived in Shanghai on his world tour to perform a musical on something called a Turkophone, a sort of early saxophone, he got a good review. Some vehemently disagreed with the paper's music critic in praising the performance. After publishing several letters of differing opinions, Compton waded in with a stern note to readers that they should respect the judgement of their trained and experienced music critic in the matter of Mr. Ali-Ben-Sou-Alle and his Turkophone and submit to his better judgement. There was an end to the matter. Compton also attacked poor sanitation in the Settlement and defended the judges who sentenced drunken British prisoners (as ever, mostly sailors and soldiers) to road building duty on Nanking Road while many readers thought, misbehavers or not, the sight of white men doing manual labour in China would weaken the position of the British in Chinese eyes.

In 1861 Compton was succeeded by Samuel Mossman who had a background as a published author but he didn't tally long at the *Herald* (little more than a year). He merits mention as he bequeathed the motto "impartial, not neutral" to the *Herald* and subsequently the *North-China Daily News*. It was grand-sounding perhaps, but under Mossman's reign the paper was still only between four and eight pages and had a circulation of not much more than 500 copies.

In 1863 R. A. Jamieson, who had previously edited the failed *Cycle*, took the reins. Jamieson presided over the transformation of the paper that saw it emerge as a daily in 1864 and be renamed the *North-China Daily News*. His three-year tenure as editor also coincided with the foundation of the International Settlement as the Americans merged their more unruly concession in with the British. Jamieson didn't flinch from tricky local stories. For example, he followed Robert Hart, the Ulster-born autocratic head of the Imperial Maritime Customs Service, through the courts as a witness to arms-dealing; catalogued the many infidelities of Henry Burgevine, Ward's second-in-command; and examined the shifting fortunes of the mercenary war against the Taiping. As a classical scholar, Chinese speaker and all-round intellectual, Jamieson was seen as the editor who brought the best and most in-depth coverage of Chinese affairs to the paper. Having done this, he promptly handed over to an India Hand, R. S. Gundry, who was perceived as a more solid man of Empire.

Despite being more knowledgeable about India than China, the dapper and rather intense Gundry was the first editor of the paper to occupy the main chair for a whole decade and also to insist on being made part-proprietor as a condition of his accepting the post. Gundry had been privately educated in England and Brussels before joining *The Calcutta Englishman*. The paper then decided to send him to China as a war correspondent and he also frequently wrote for the London *Times*, and so he wasn't totally unknown in Shanghai when he joined the *Herald*. Gundry followed the general line laid down originally by Shearman of advocating a policy of China dealing with its own affairs where possible, though like many others he thought China incapable of emerging as a major power and ridiculed the establishment of the Chinese Republic in 1911, expecting it to quickly descend into just another dynasty. He extended the *Herald*'s remit again by adding to the weekly *Herald* and the daily *North-China Daily News* the weekly *Supreme Court and Consular Gazette* which had first appeared in 1866. Merging the papers saved effort on all sides as both were fighting it out for the same limited pool of subscribers and advertisers — circulation wars among a small pool of potential readers killed many an early China coast newspaper. Gundry was far from flamboyant but was reliable. He was an inveterate committee man who served on numerous boards, including being president of the China Association; and, as one of Shanghai's most prominent Freemasons for many years and a founder of the Shanghai Freemasons, he got to lay the foundation stone for the Masonic Hall on Canton Road in the 1860s. When he left China in 1878 he was reputedly one year away from being made Grand Master of all the British Empire. He got some consolation for missing this great honour (at least for a Freemason) by being given the choice of either a knighthood or Companionship of the Order of the Bath and he opted for the latter as he considered it a greater honour.[11]

Gundry's retirement threw the *Herald* and the *North-China* into a quandary for a while. D. W. Haden occupied the editorial chair for a couple of years but unfortunately upped and died to be succeeded by a Mr. Thirkill of whom little is known except that he stepped down after a couple of months to allow Frederick Balfour to take over the paper.

Balfour was decidedly more interesting. He was a sinologist and a prolific writer and was extremely well known in Shanghai. He introduced his famous "sketches", sort of small *vignettes* of Chinese life, into the paper that were later published as his partial memoirs called *Leaves From My Chinese Scrapbook*. In 1884 he published a version of the *Taoist Texts, Ethical, Political, and Speculative* that put him into a long-running conflict with the noted translator H. A. Giles. The two had been good friends but Giles firmly considered his own translation to be the better and more authentic. A fierce argument ran backwards and forwards in the letters pages of the *China Review* for some time in the mid-1880s but they retain absolutely none of what may have been their original fascination and look more like petty squabbling over details by half-hearted adversaries with little better to do with their time than have a little spat in the quiet of treaty port China. Balfour later got involved in a newspaper venture called the *Celestial Empire* and patched up his friendship with Giles who encouraged him to complete his memoirs which he later did in a second book of reminiscences after he had retired to Surrey.

Despite his somewhat quarrelsome nature, Balfour did turn the paper into a more rounded publication in the four years he edited it. When he departed, the paper went through another spate of quick turnarounds until R. W. Little took over and shook it up once again. In terms of impact on Shanghai, no other *Herald* or *North- China* editors come close to Bob Little. He was already notorious for having persuaded the Shanghai Municipal Council (SMC) to replace its rather erratic gas- and oil-fired streetlights with electric ones in the early 1880s. To show that electricity would be better, Little exhibited a sample light on the band stand in the Bund Public Gardens, which was greatly admired and visited, showing just how exciting life could be in Shanghai in the 1880s! He then formed an electric light company, won contracts from some Chinese houses, the Shanghai Club and some residences in the French Concession and eventually the SMC for some of Shanghai's street lighting. He had to battle hard to electrify Shanghai as many people feared being killed by electrocution and the local gas company naturally was keen not to lose its monopoly. Even when he managed to persuade the SMC, his system was initially not very reliable and was more expensive than gas and the machinery frequently broke down. To be fair, he was a bit ahead of his time: the Chinese word for electricity, *dianqi*, was only introduced around 1851. However, Little knew his way around the machinations and procedures of the SMC as he had been an energetic former chairman of the council, pushing through a new waterworks and sorting out the always-fraught issue of land regulations. Through perseverance, by the end of the 1880s Little was lighting up the Bund (most notably for Queen Victoria's Jubilee in 1887), Nanking Road and Broadway and a decade later the SMC took over Little's electric company to wire up the whole Settlement. Electricity bills to households and businesses soon became a major source of revenue for the council.

Both before, during and after his tenure as editor of the paper, Little was a well- known man about town in his trademark straw boaters, a fixture of the Amateur Dramatic Club and a regular at the Shanghai Club's *tiffin* hour where he would dramatically march in for a drink still wearing his editor's green-lined sunshade. "Uncle Bob", as he became known in his later years, was famous for knowing everyone and for never having a harsh word said about him. He had originally come to Shanghai around 1866 and was to stay for 40 years until 1906 when he died. He had been a sub-editor at the *Herald* before rising to become editor and was to take the paper through the turn of the century, seeing off the fair amount of competition that kept on coming.

The Competition Mounts

The Americans in Shanghai were determined not to let the British totally dominate the local press. Accounts differ as to who was the first American correspondent to reach the city, but the *New York Tribune*'s Bayard Taylor seems the likeliest candidate, having arrived in 1853 and sent back copy to Manhattan via clipper ship. But Taylor, a Pennsylvanian, was a very temporary sojourner who roamed far and wide in Asia and stayed in Shanghai just long enough to catch up with commodore Perry's expedition to Japan later the same year. Others were looking to establish a more permanent media presence. The American Civil War had delayed several planned launches in the 1860s. However, once the war between the states was concluded, they got back to business. A group of American investors launched the *Shanghai Newsletter For California and the United States* in October 1867, which soon became less confusingly known as simply *The Shanghai Newsletter*.

Into the 1870s investors still thought that Shanghai's press was a good bet. In 1873 a rival had entered the field called the *Shanghai Evening Gazette*, but a fire at the paper's premises meant publication ceased after the 18th edition. *The Shanghai Evening Gazette* was re-launched in 1874, though it was soon incorporated into the *Shanghai Courier*, which had been launched in 1868 and lasted until 1875 when its editor and proprietor Hugh Lang died. Previously, in 1871, Lang had launched a weekly edition of the *Courier* called the *Shanghai Budget and Weekly Courier*. With Lang's death, the proprietors of the *Evening Gazette* bought the paper and the newly amalgamated *Shanghai Courier and China Gazette* was launched under the editorship of F. H. Balfour who had dabbled with the *Herald* previously. The investors behind the *Courier and Gazette* also funded the launch of another weekly paper in 1874, *The Celestial Empire*, run by a Portuguese Shanghailander Pedro Loureiro. Balfour took on the editorship of both papers: the early Shanghai press was nothing if not incestuous. The *Gazette* lasted until around 1911 while the pro-Japanese *Shanghai Times*, founded by Willis Gray, took over the weekly *Celestial Empire*, appointing a Japanese manager and editor and taking a controversial pro-Japanese stance on issues from the start that lasted through to the end of the Second World War.

In 1875 the first editors of the American-funded *Shanghai Newsletter*, John Thorne, Howard Twombly and J. P. Roberts, left to launch a new weekly called *The Commonwealth*, but it lasted only six weeks. Displaying more longevity was *The Shanghai Mercury*, which was launched in 1879 by J. D. Clark (who was also known as a very good cartographer), John Reddie "J. R." Black and C. Rivington, the last becoming the paper's first editor. This publication survived and used *The Celestial Empire* name for its weekly edition and lasted, in one amalgamated form or another, through to the 1930s as the *Shanghai Mercury and Evening Post*. The paper also started a reasonably successful book and map publishing business. Clark regularly issued maps of Shanghai and China's provinces as well as a series of books on China, including Macanese-Portuguese historian C. A. Montalto de Jesus's popular *Historic Shanghai* (1909), an account of the city from the arrival of the Royal Navy till 1900. Montalto de Jesus was a spicy and gossipy writer who later described Macau as a "den of vice", a continuing image for the Portuguese enclave in the China coast press.

Of the three founders of the *Mercury*, J. R. Black was by far the most interesting. He had come to Shanghai from Japan where he spent the 1860s as chief editor of the *Japan Herald* and also for a while published *The Japan Gazette* in Yokohama. It was a limited market to say the least — at most, 500 foreigners lived in Yokohama's foreign settlement at the time and the *Japan Herald* never managed a circulation of more than 200 copies. Black had first visited China as a businessman in 1864, when the Qing army was busy recapturing Nanjing from the Taiping who were slaughtering everyone in sight and the prospects for trade didn't look so hot. He was offered the job of chief editor of the *Japan Herald*, and he jumped at the chance to get out of civil war-ravaged China and shipped back to Yokohama. He then also got involved in the *Japan Gazette* which was a messy business as it supported one *shogun* over another and Black could never quite work out why the paper was favouring one warlord rather than another.

In 1870 he branched out on his own, funding and launching *Far East*, a fortnightly English paper in Japan that consisted of editorial, news and entertainment but also included "articles with pictures for the family" to target foreign residents better. The coverage included Japan, China, Korea, Taiwan and other countries in the Far East and Black wanted Japanese people as well as foreigners in Japan to read the paper in the hope that the combination might provide a sizeable enough readership to make a living. It didn't, and so he also started publishing *Nishinshinjishi* (sub-headed *The Reliable Daily News*) to attract a Japanese readership. Black's publication was not popular with either the Japanese government or particularly many readers, but the censors never quite managed to shut it down. Eventually the government bought him out and he headed back to Shanghai, where he launched the *New Series of the Far East*, which lasted from July 1876 until November 1878 and then became involved with *The Shanghai Mercury*. Black's involvement with the *Mercury* didn't last long either: he got sick, went back to Yokohama and died there in 1880 at just 53, never having managed to launch a successful publication.

Like the Americans, the French weren't about to cede the Shanghai newspaper market completely to the British. Consequently *Le Nouvelliste de Shanghai* was launched as a weekly in late 1870, but it lasted for only a couple of years before being succeeded by *Le Courrier de Changhai* in 1873, which itself only lasted a pathetic three issues. The collapse of the first French papers was actually due to their vicious internal rivalries. The somewhat more radically minded *Progres* first appeared in 1871; but shortly after, *Le Nouvelliste* and the ensuing price war between the papers largely ruined them all. Despite these initial failures the French press persisted, with *L'Echo de Shanghai* appearing for a few months as a daily paper in 1885. However, it was not until the launch of *L'Echo de Chine* in 1895 that the French found a regularly published and reliable paper for their interests in Shanghai. *L'Echo* was to continue publishing successfully for several decades as the French newspaper of record in Shanghai and its sales were boosted in no small part by a growing French community and also the influx of French-speaking White Russians to Shanghai in the early twentieth century.

What the vast majority of these English and French newspapers appearing in the mid- to late-1800s showed was that Shanghai and the other treaty ports were still small enough places for most newspapers to remain, by and large, one-person mouthpieces. Also, the missionary-run press was waning and becoming internalised in the face of the supporters of trade rather than conversion. The popular press now largely reflected the business community's viewpoint, as did the newly formed SMC. Shanghai's destiny would not be controlled by either the military, empire administrators, men of diplomacy or men of God, but rather by Shanghai's own peculiar mix of rapacious, freebooting capitalists with a media to represent their interests and concerns.

The new Shanghai media's attitudes to the Opium Wars and the Taiping were typically reflective of business. Prescott Clarke and Frank King wrote in their 1965 *Research Guide to China Coast Newspapers* that, until the late 1860s, the Shanghai papers were, "… one man affairs … directed by an editor of limited experience supported by an inadequate staff and dependent upon a narrow range of news sources"; and as a much later biographer of Townsend Ward, Caleb Carr, put it, "… most of these editors were more interested in grinding axes than in cultivating journalistic integrity, and commentary tended to degenerate into gossip-laced feuding".[12]

Despite this, and the fact that the *Herald* and its competitors rarely put out editions with more than eight pages or had more than a few hundred subscriptions, these papers, particularly the *Herald*, became highly influential in Shanghai, China and far beyond. For the consulates, the *Herald* was the organ of public notice and the paper of record; and it was also the main vehicle for advertising in the Settlement and was read for news of events, and with the lack of many other sources, in Hong Kong and Singapore as well as in London. *L'Echo de Chine* performed a similar function for the French Concession and in Paris. Limited readerships perhaps; one-man mouthpieces invariably; and biased always — but these papers still influenced decision making in London, Paris and Washington over the future of the Shanghai Settlement.

From *Hua* to Chinese Gordon

After the victory at Woosong, the Ward Corps, whose soldiers carried banners with the character *Hua*, Ward's Chinese name, managed to continue to rout the rebels from their bases around Shanghai's perimeter. Overall, Ward was generally successful with his slightly undisciplined ragbag of mercenaries who required endless drilling.

He got several serious beatings and a lot of wounds while having the romantic, but not wholly accurate, sobriquet "The Ever Victorious Army" (EVA) attached to his force. Finally, though, his luck ran out and he was killed in action near Ningbo in September 1862, just two months shy of his 31st birthday. The hard-drinking American from Carolina, Burgevine, who had himself been a journalist briefly in New York before being fired for rather dimwittedly writing a defence of slavery on the eve of the American Civil War, briefly took over command before handing over to Crimea and Second Opium War veteran Major Charles George Gordon, whose aggressive campaign finally broke the Taiping by May 1864.

The EVA was subsequently disbanded and the rebellion ended entirely a year later. Gordon had made a study of the Chinese fighting man during his first visit to China as a soldier on the Elgin Mission, which he later published in the *China Mail*. He saw the Chinese Imperial Army as hopelessly corrupt and believed that to defeat it you had to force them into pitched battles and not allow them to exercise their advantage with hit-and-run attacks.[13] He also knew Shanghai and its environs well: as an experienced cartographer he had surveyed the entire 30-mile radius around the city and knew the ground better than anyone. The handover to Gordon was generally welcomed in the press both in China and in England in influential publications such as *Punch*. After Ward's death and the six-month period of loose leadership of the EVA, the fickle press, led by the *Herald*, started to turn against the EVA, once more describing them as a "rabble" who lacked the real hallmarks of a military organisation. But Gordon was universally liked, despite being rather prudish and stand-offish: and, of course, he went on to even greater military heights, moving from being dubbed "Chinese Gordon" to "Gordon of Khartoum", until the Mahdi in Sudan managed to achieve what the Taiping hadn't and slaughtered him in 1885.

As the century's end loomed, the foreign treaty ports were peaceful and becoming firm bastions of trade with their own established papers and press barons, while the European powers continued to clash with China, exciting journalists.

3
Boxers and Treaty Porters — Headlines Change History

"No exaggeration is it to say that the eyes of the world are upon China, it is equally safe to say that, whilst all is open and may be seen, little is understood."

Edwin Dingle, *Across China on Foot* (1911)

"The modern newspaper has taken the place of the old-time ambassador."

Opening editorial of the first edition of
the *South China Morning Post*, 6 November 1903

Mohawk Morriss — Shanghai's First Press Baron

In the half century since it had been launched, the *North China Herald* had gone through a number of incarnations: it had become the *North-China Daily News*, had merged with subsidiary publications and had no fewer than nine editors. However, the major change that was to dictate the future direction of both the paper and the Shanghai press in general was the take-over of the business in 1880 by Henry Morriss. The paper went through a few changes of ownership. After the death of Shearman, the founder, it was sold to Edwin Pickwood, who had served as the first-ever secretary of the SMC and who listed himself on the Shanghai voting roll as being a gentleman of St. Kitts, West Indies. Edwin died in 1866 while on a visit to England and his stake was taken over by his widow Janet. Then the business became a family affair. In 1880 Morriss married Edwin and Janet's daughter, Una. Henry was already a successful businessman in Shanghai and Janet asked him to sort out the company, which he did by buying it. Morriss was a hands-on but supportive proprietor and also one of early Shanghai's great characters.

He had come out to the East in 1866 to work for the British-run Agra Bank, which had opened a Shanghai branch after being successful in India. His brother was already in situ in Shanghai as head of the Hong Kong and Shanghai Bank and Henry soon made a substantial fortune as a bill-broker, investing his profits in land around the racecourse, an area that became known as Morriss Village or Morrissville. Marrying Una propelled him up a social rung and helped to consolidate his not inconsiderable assets which allowed him to get into the newspaper and publishing business. His wealth also allowed him to indulge in his major passion — horse racing. His penchant for horses and his tradition of giving many of them American Indian names led to his nickname: the "Mohawk Chief".

Mohawk Morriss was a force to be reckoned with in the newspaper business. When the paper's oldest advertiser and one of the longest-established British firms in Shanghai threatened to pull all its advertising from the paper due to an editorial it disagreed with, Mohawk stood firm and told the advertiser that he should feel free to take his advertising elsewhere should he wish. With the *North-China Daily News* having little effective competition, the advertiser shut up.

Reporting on Small Wars

China was involved in a number of wars in the last part of the nineteenth century and, to be fair, none of them greatly excited the Western press, or even the treaty port and Hong Kong press. Indeed, in Hong Kong, the newspapers, notably the *China Mail* and the *Hongkong Telegraph*, appear to have preferred to rage against each other's editorials rather than report the wider regional news. The *China Mail* set itself implacably against any social reform in the colony while the *Telegraph* championed change, after a fashion. The *Mail* had been one of the few public supporters of William Caine, Hong Kong's first magistrate, the fifth governor of the colony and a ruthless flogger while being an implacable opponent of people such as Governor Sir John Pope-Hennessy who outraged the paper's colonial sensibilities by having the temerity to abolish flogging and appoint a Chinese to the Legislative Council in 1880. Pope-Hennessy earned the ire of many Brits but the Chinese liked him, awarding him the Cantonese appellation "Number One Good Friend". Later, after a change of editor, the *Telegraph* was to jettison its more progressive and liberal stance and assume a far more staunchly colonial line too. Still, whatever the internal and incestuous machinations of the Hong Kong press, events were continuing and wars still breaking out that needed covering.

In 1894 the Sino-Japanese War over Korea attracted more foreign war correspondents than the previous Franco-Chinese War had. Many understood the war's relevance to Sino-Japanese relations and, when Japan sank China's Northern Fleet and inflicted a humiliating treaty on Beijing, 50 years of harsh animosity between the two was unleashed. One correspondent to cover the war was Arthur Cunningham of the *Hongkong Daily Press*, who later founded the *South China Morning Post* in Hong Kong. Cunningham considered the Chinese army to be fine soldiers who had been let down by their government which, steadfastly refusing to spend much money on armaments, left them armed with paper bullets and shells filled with sand — the corruption of the Qing was blatantly on show. However, his reports from the front never got prominence in Hong Kong as for much of the war the colony was in the grip of its first major outbreak of bubonic plague as well as its worst typhoon season for decades, both events that rather focused people's attentions closer to home. Another correspondent who came to cover the conflict was James Creelman, an American who worked for Joseph Pulitzer's *The World*. Creelman reported on Japanese massacres in Manchuria and Korea, calling them an "unrestrained reign of murder".

Creelman, a Canadian, had been an apprentice in the print shop of *Church and State*, the newspaper of the Episcopalian Church, before going to work on a wide variety of papers including the *Brooklyn Eagle*, the *New York Herald*, the *Sunday Herald*, the *Paris Herald* (where his interview subjects ranged from Leo Tolstoy to Pope Leo XIII) and the *Herald's* late edition, the *Evening Telegram*. He then worked briefly for the *Illustrated American* and *Cosmopolitan* before, in 1894, being hired by Pulitzer's *New York World* to cover the Sino-Japanese conflict. Accompanying the Japanese army, he reported on the aftermath of hostilities at Pyongyang and the Yalu River naval engagement, and scooped an interview with the king of Korea. At one point, he disappeared and was reported in *The World* to have been beheaded by the Chinese but, fortunately for him, the story was false. However, it was Creelman's coverage of the Battle of Port Arthur and his claims to have witnessed atrocities committed by Japanese soldiers, with whom he had initially sympathized, that gained him substantial attention.

Despite the general European view, which assumed that China would easily defeat Japan, the war ended badly for the Chinese and proved to be a significant nail in the coffin of the ailing Qing dynasty, with the loss of Taiwan to the Japanese being a particular blow that was to resonate through history. Many of the foreigners following the war were stunned by Japan's show of strength. However, the most important outcome of the war from a foreign perspective was that it kicked off the "scramble for concessions", with Japan taking Taiwan, Germany grabbing Qingdao, Russia getting Port Arthur and Britain, keen as ever to contain Russian expansionism (and at American prompting), the nearby port of Weihaiwei.

To date much of the news and writing about China from China had not been by professional journalists or committed authors but by a mixture of army and navy men, diplomat-scholars, amateur hacks, moonlighting "stringers", missionaries, merchants, and early sinologists and their wives. The *Times* used a rather bored and underemployed bank manager as a stringer in Hong Kong who sent them unverifiable stories from all over a China he never visited, while the Associated Press (AP) in Hong Kong relied on the services of a Portuguese attorney and his teenage son for news. Impressionistic writing and merchant- or missionary-generated news about China was about to be displaced by news written primarily by professional journalists. The Boxer Rebellion was to change perceptions and reporting radically as events in China commanded space, became sensational and required "eye-witness" reports by "real" correspondents. By and large, the day of the missionary or the merchant dominating the press as "amateur" journalists was over. The foreign correspondents, along with a new strident generation of press barons in China in the mould of Mohawk Morriss, were about to ascend; and the ailing, scapegoat-searching, Qing dynasty was about to provide them with the story of the century right at the start of a new one.

"All Foreigners in Peking Dead" — How a Headline Became an Invasion

A new century of foreigners reporting on China began on the morning of 5 July 1900 with the *New York Times* headline: "All Foreigners in Peking Dead". The paper followed this up a couple of days later with an account of the rumoured massacre of Beijing's foreign community by the anti-foreign Boxer movement and the arguably even more alarmist headline: "Foreigners All Slain After a Last Heroic Stand — Shot Their Women First". Readers were naturally shocked. Soon afterwards, in August, a multinational rescue force, including 20,000 British, French, American, Russian and Japanese troops, forced the Boxers onto the retreat, relieved the besieged legations and found 70 of the several hundred trapped foreigners dead, but most alive. The foreign troops then went on a rampage and looting spree through the imperial city and their governments demanded massive indemnity payments from the Qing. These were traumatic events indeed for the foreigners trapped in the city's Legation Quarter, but the *New York Times* had got it wrong. It was a shaky and confused start to a century of reporting on China that was often to be equally as shaky and confused, but with moments of brilliance and enlightenment thrown in for balance.

Technology often defeated the demands of factually correct journalism as much as the eternal desire by editors, subs and newspaper proprietors (as well as titillated readers) to get a good story. "If it bleeds it leads" was a well, if not better, understood slogan in 1900 than it is even today. Despatches were mailed with significant time-lags or telegraphed at great expense; sub-editors or fact-checkers could not, of course, simply call or email the writer. Still, the foreign press corps was not totally cut off: Hong Kong had been connected to the imperial telegraph system in 1862; the first Trans-Siberian telegraph line connected Europe and China in 1872; the first telephone appeared in China in 1879; and in 1880 the Chinese authorities had hired the Danish Great Northern Telegraph Company to construct a line connecting Shanghai and Beijing.

Stories invariably arrived in scant shorthand and were unverifiable. They were then jazzed up by foreign editors who rarely left their New York offices except for coffee and doughnuts or their Fleet Street haunts except for tea and sticky buns, let alone got out into the field. Mistakes occurred and rectification and/or apology could take months. The effect on public opinion was dramatic. An erroneous account of a massacre could lead an outraged readership to demand revenge, action and gunboats from their Congressmen or MPs; and executive decisions could be taken, troops despatched and ambassadors recalled before the truth fully emerged. Such was the case at the time of the Boxers.

Perhaps if the foreigners hadn't been quite so closeted in the walled Legation Quarter, they would have been more aware of the fury building up outside their privileged little world. The China Hands, as normal, failed to predict the uprising as the Boxers rallied across the country stoking anti-foreign and anti-Christian sentiment and opposing technological advances such as railways and the telegraph — both foreign intrusions that offended the gods and caused crop failures, droughts and floods as punishments from on high. It was also largely true that the foreign press corps missed the rise of the Boxers, cloistered as they also were in the Legation Quarter, well away from the vicious reprisals starting to take place against the inland missionaries, Chinese Christians and Qing officials considered to be too friendly to foreigners. Heads rolled, European as well as Chinese, but this rarely appeared in the papers. After rampaging across northern China, the Boxers rounded on Beijing. A nervous and indecisive Qing court threw in its lot with them and an attack on the legations became inevitable. The middle and southern provinces of China were largely appalled by the action of the court and suppressed their own nascent Boxer movements, realising that eventually foreign reprisals would humiliate the government. By the middle of June the legations were under siege and the city's foreigners trapped in the British Legation. As the siege set in in Beijing, the Boxers became front-page news.

The Boxers were officially "The Society of Harmonious Fists" and their fearsome reputation and anti-foreign ideology was to make them fodder for the foreign press. The term "Boxers" was first applied to them in despatches from inland missionaries working as stringers for the *North-China Daily News*, which used the term in its early reports on the rise of this new phenomenon. Then the *Peking and Tientsin Times* started using the term, followed by the *Hongkong Telegraph*, and soon everyone else had picked up the sobriquet. But it was the *North-China* that was really the first paper to warn the world about the Boxers. Its practice of using in-country stringers meant that, on 10 May 1900, the paper ran a piece by a stringer writing under the title of a "native correspondent". He was apparently a Chinese official of good standing in the foreign community and long trusted as a reliable source. The anonymous writer talked of a "great secret scheme" afoot in China that foreigners were unaware of. He named the leaders and their aims, noted that the dowager empress would do nothing to restrain them and that many in the Chinese upper classes had been trying to warn their European "friends" of the coming problem but had been mostly laughed off and not taken seriously.

By June 1900 things were clearly becoming more worrying. The *North-China Daily News* in Shanghai was still leading the pack, being the first to report the killing of a "European Minister" in Beijing on 14 June from unconfirmed Chinese sources. The world press reported the story on the 17th, naming the victim as the German minister Baron von Ketteler, who was widely considered the most odious and condescending of all the senior Europeans in Beijing at the time. Strangely, von Ketteler was not killed for another four days, on 20 June. Clearly von Ketteler's murder was premeditated and rumours of the planned killing of a senior European diplomat had been flowing around Chinese Beijing and reached the ears of the *North-China*'s "native" stringers who assumed, rightly as it transpired, that the target was the generally loathed von Ketteler and got an accidental scoop.

The first half of July 1900 saw the world's press carry a succession of increasingly alarming reports regarding the fate of foreign Beijing. Actually, most of these stories did not come from Beijing but from Chinese sources in distant Shanghai, and they were not confirmable. The official line of the Chinese government was more conciliatory — Chinese officials attempted to reassure the foreign public while an appeal, supposedly from the emperor to Queen Victoria, the Russian czar and the emperor of Japan, asked them all to try to sort out the situation. This appeal from the emperor was odd, as surely his own people had better contacts with the Boxers than the royal families of London, St. Petersburg or Tokyo; and some also noted that the appeal was issued on 3 July, a day of particularly ferocious attacks on the legations.

Yet the *New York Times* and a host of other leading newspapers were to get it wrong. How did this happen? On 16 July Beijing made the front-page of the London *Daily Mail*. That the *Mail*, run by the strident pro-imperialist Alfred

Harmsworth (a.k.a. Lord Northcliffe), would highlight such a story and run it so quickly without due care and attention was not surprising for a newspaper that declared: "If Kipling be called the Voice of Empire in English Literature, we may fairly claim to be the Voice of Empire in London journalism". The *Mail's* special correspondent in Shanghai, a man by the name of F. W. Sutterlee, filed the story headlined "The Peking Massacre". The story affirmed what had been a whirling rumour for days, quoted anonymous Chinese sources and contained a mass of supposed detail. It was accepted as the complete truth by the *Mail*'s editor, shocked the readership and was then repeated by papers around the world. The article described the events in the legations on the nights of 6 and 7 July. The Boxers had apparently brought up heavy artillery and bombarded the foreign quarter. Ammunition had run low and on the morning of the 7th the beleaguered foreigners had rallied for a final defence. They had been overrun and, according to the *Mail*, everybody found alive was "… put to the sword in a most atrocious manner". As the story was retold and reprinted, it grew with descriptions of women and children being slaughtered after their men had been shot and hinting that women may have been raped. These supplementary gory stories were not verified. Peter Fleming, a London *Times* journalist who later wrote a book on the siege (a historical reconstruction — he wasn't actually there) believed that most of these additions were echoes of previous newspaper stories about the Siege of Tianjin. Beijing—Tianjin? Did anyone in Fleet Street care that much? It appeared not.

So the *Mail* story snowballed and expanded with the details becoming ever more bloodthirsty and horrific and designed to outrage public opinion, which was a *Mail* speciality. At the same time, doubting the story was deemed unpatriotic. The *Times* thundered from London: "It would be foolish and unmanly to affect to doubt the awful truth". If anyone did doubt the story and its sources, it appears they valued their manliness higher than the truth and kept quiet. Of course, the inevitable demands for retribution and vengeance flowed. By 23 July London was rehearsing for a memorial service for the "Europeans Massacred in Peking" at St. Paul's Cathedral. But at the same time as editors were running stories complimenting the organisers on their selection of appropriate psalms, doubts did start to creep in.

Editors, particularly at the *Mail*, naturally didn't like the idea that they might have got something so significant so wrong. However, the release by the State Department in Washington of a coded message from its legation calling for relief troops, but indicating that most people were still alive and barricaded inside the British Legation, cast major doubts on the *Mail*'s story. The editors held off as they clearly had a vested interest in the massacre and, as a group, did not relish looking unprofessional and foolish; and they had also booked St. Paul's at considerable expense and, perhaps more importantly, a non-refundable deposit. By early August a host of legations had managed to send out telegrams, including the British, which the *Mail* could hardly dismiss so easily. The papers had to backtrack, with the *Spectator* writing in a typically non-explicit apologetic mood: "Europe has been greatly surprised this week and also relieved".[1]

Henri Cordier, who published a book that was to become a standard work on the era, attacked the *Mail* for having used an unnamed source for such a major story, and suggested that the *Mail*'s "Special Correspondent" could have been a practical joker. The *Times* was most outraged and started a brief round of in-fighting on Fleet Street, demanding that the *Mail* defend its story and the decision to publish. In response, the *Mail* prepared a dossier of details and the *Times* declared this to be satisfactory. The *Times* and the *Mail* appeared to be off the hook and largely were, except with their Beijing correspondent Dr. George Morrison who later railed at the paper's managing editor Moberley Bell for participating in the "whitewash".

Morrison confirmed that the *Mail*'s special correspondent was F. W. Sutterlee, the manager of Keen Sutterlee and Company of Philadelphia, who Morrison believed was a swindler and a fraud (Morrison did actually have a good track record of spotting frauds in China). Sutterlee had moved to Tianjin and gone into business with a certain Louis Spitzel after the bankruptcy of Keen Sutterlee. Spitzel was wanted by Scotland Yard, having absconded from Britain. Sutterlee and Spitzel, according to Morrison, had established a new firm called Taylor and Co., along with another man called Baker who had previously forged certificates for Sutterlee as part of a long-running fraudulent scam. He claimed that these men had been gunrunners and arms traders in Manila and Hong Kong during the Spanish-American War, supplying the Philippine insurgents, and in the process had repeatedly swindled both the Chinese Customs at Guangzhou and the American consulate in Singapore. Morrison further claimed the American consul in Singapore was in on the swindle. Sutterlee then ended up living in Shanghai at the swanky Astor House Hotel where he made some extra cash as the *Mail*'s special correspondent.

The absolute truth of Morrison's detailed assertions is not known, though later in 1906 Sutterlee was to resurface as the managing director of the American Chinese Company. However, the point in broader historical terms is that the report the *Mail* printed, and was then reprinted around the world, did more than anything else to set in train a series of actions by the Great Powers — the Eight Power Allied Army relief force; strong public condemnation and demonising of China and the Chinese; and eventually the savage looting of Beijing by the soldiers that was unstoppable by the time the veracity of the report or the discussion of its authorship came up. Despite mostly attacking the sacking of

Beijing in print, it has to be noted that not a few journalists also took part in the looting spree.

The *Mail* didn't remain cowed by its sloppy journalism for long, if at all. In 1901 it was offering readers a special publication — "The *Daily Mail* Map Of The War in China — following the Boxer Rebellion of 1900 against the foreign powers in China and consisting of a linen-backed, folding map housed in a fine red hard cover; the map itself is divided into a main map (showing Treaty Ports, railways and sea routes), two smaller maps and a diagram of Peking". They'd got it wrong but that wasn't going to stop them making a few quid with a souvenir map.

If the British public was concerned about and scared of the Boxers, one reason was the British press's portrayal of them. Representations of Boxers were highly dramatic, not a little bloodthirsty and tended to overemphasise the average Boxers' height and physique. Most of the artwork was drawn by professional artists already in China such as Sydney Adamson and Henry Savage Landor, or by those who were able to get to China quickly such as Fred Whiting and John Schonberg. Photography was possible as Kodak were selling their cameras to a growing legion of people who were taking what were already known as "snapshots", but they were not readily or easily reproduced in newspapers at the time. In addition, several military officers, such as Francis Gordon Poole, found a profitable side-line in sketching, writing or photographing what they were observing in the heat of battle. This was by now an established tradition: in the early 1870s, *The Graphic* had carried mildly exotic illustrations of foreigners gambling with pig-tailed Chinese and young women with fans in Macau that greatly titillated its English readership.

Gordon Poole and others found a ready market for their illustrations in New York and London. Adamson, a Dundonian, was a particularly well-known war artist while Savage Landor, an extremely stiff-upper-lipped Englishman, had already made a reputation working in Korea before attempting to reach Lhasa despite official government disapproval from London and Beijing. He went anyway, believing firmly that an English gentleman had the right to get his throat cut wherever he damn well pleased. He nearly got his wish, being captured and tortured by the Tibetans to discourage similar attempts: they tied his arms behind his back; put him on a half-wild horse; sat him in an infamous "torture saddle" that had spikes sticking into his back; and forced him to ride many miles, during which he was slowly ripped to pieces. He survived the Boxers, angry Tibetans and the "torture saddle" before being, rather anticlimactically, run over by a London bus in 1924.

Morrison of Peking — The "Canny Scot" from Australia

Clearly the Boxer Rebellion of 1900 was by far the biggest story to come out of China in the living memory of the foreign press corps. For them it eclipsed the Opium Wars as this time foreigners were being killed while previously it had been Chinese. Still, not a single reporter in Beijing got a scoop on either the rebellion or the dramatic siege that ensued and became instantly legendary. Missing the scoop was particularly galling for one correspondent, the most famous one in China at the time — Dr. George Ernest Morrison. G. E. Morrison, otherwise known as "Morrison of Peking", who became so famous that one of the major thoroughfares in Beijing was named Morrison Street.[2]

Morrison was caught napping by the Boxers, as he was out of town on a snipe-hunting expedition. As a man who believed his own vainglorious press, he was extremely angry to have missed the scoop. Later during the siege he was to reassume his great stature after reading his own obituary and being reported dead by his employers at the *Times* before resurrecting himself and announcing to the world that he was alive after all. This was thrilling stuff and great reading, but it didn't cover up the fact that he had missed breaking the biggest story of his career. Neither was his misreported death in China a first: James Creelman had that honour only a few years before, being reported as beheaded only to reappear with his head firmly intact. His paper had had to apologise to its readers for the error and, perhaps more importantly, to Creelman too. Typically the *Times* spun the resurrection of its greatest foreign correspondent as a victory, conveniently ignoring the fact that he had missed the start of the action and that they had misreported his death.

Morrison carried a certain amount of weight from the moment he assumed the post of *Times* Beijing correspondent. He had been hired in 1895 by the gruff, chain-smoking Moberley Bell who presided over the *Times* empire at London's Printing House Yard and had persuaded Morrison to go to China while the man himself had wanted to be posted to the Kingdom of Siam (Thailand). Bell wanted him in Beijing because Morrison had already made a small name for himself by travelling to China from his native Australia (though he was often known as the "Canny Scot" as he had spent time in Edinburgh). As a younger man, Morrison had canoed across Australia, been speared through the nose in Papua New Guinea (which had to hurt) and then been reported dead before reappearing. He had spent time with slavers in the Pacific, moved on to study medicine in Edinburgh, qualifying as an M. D., worked as a doctor in North Africa and then came to the China coast. In Shanghai he decided to walk to Burma; he did so and got a best-selling book out of it that made him a minor celebrity.[3]

In the same year as he hit the bestseller lists, Bell introduced Morrison to Valentine Chirol, an ex-Foreign Office official, who worked for the paper's foreign department. Chirol then brought along the leader writer (and later editor) of the *Times*, the monocle-wearing George Earle Buckle. The paper was a little lost on China at the time. Japan had intervened in Korea, then a vassal state to China, inflicted some devastating military defeats and seized Taiwan and Port Arthur. The French, Germans and Russians prevented the Japanese making more gains and forced them to relinquish Port Arthur. In return, China had reportedly granted Russia various rights, including a railway concession in Manchuria which would shorten the route of the Trans-Siberian Railway. "Great Game" politics had crossed the Himalayas and come to northern China, and London feared for its vaunted position as the supreme foreign power in China and the gunboat-laden de-facto military guarantor of the Yangtze delta.

Despite this, the readers of the *Times* were not well served on what was happening. For China news they had to rely on a part-time stringer — Mr. T. H. Whitehead, a bank manager living quietly in the sleepy backwater of Hong Kong and rather remote from Manchuria and Beijing, though enjoying a little top-up to his regular salary courtesy of the *Times*. Whitehead had cabled London a story on the supposed Sino-Russian treaty that proved to be false. Bell, spitting teeth at the loss of face, decided it was time for a full-time Beijing correspondent. Britain's greatest newspaper would no longer rely on a moonlighting bank manager for China news. Morrison was a seemingly ideal candidate. He had just come back from China, had a glowing reputation from his book and had already been to Yunnan, then the subject of growing interest to British merchants looking to penetrate China's vast interior; the British had already annexed Upper Burma in 1886. The easiest way into Yunnan was via Morrison's preferred destination of Thailand and so a compromise was reached.

In November 1895 Morrison set sail for Burma, Thailand and Indo-China, the idea being that he would report the situation there and then proceed to Beijing to start work. Effectively, this began the age of the modern China correspondent with a permanent *Times* bureau in Beijing. It also started an age of China correspondents confusing their reporting duties with their relationship with governments and intelligence agencies and of China correspondents occasionally becoming a little vainglorious. Morrison was to write for the *Times* on his travels, but he was also told to monitor the activities of the perfidious French in the region. He was under no illusion that these reports were simply for the eyes of the *Times*'s readers: Whitehall, the Foreign Office, the Chinese Consular Service and the India Office were also interested. Where foreign correspondents went and wrote, increasingly the Great Powers, and their intelligence services, would follow (and at times guide) their movements.

For his part, Morrison, who was no dupe, knew the business he was in from the start. He was a solid "Man of Empire" and more than aware that Europe now controlled something approaching 85% of the world's surface. Sir Thomas Sanderson, the British undersecretary for foreign affairs, got involved when he wrote to Moberly Bell acknowledging the usefulness of the information Morrison was gathering in Thailand and Indo-China. Sanderson, known as "Lamps" due to his thick spectacles, saw all his despatches. Morrison filed stories to the *Times* as well as notes of his observations from locations as varied as Saigon, Phnom Penh, Siem Reap and Angkor Wat as well as Battambang in Cambodia. Paris also had a pretty clear idea of what Morrison was up to and made sure the interpreters they gladly provided him with reported back on his movements to the local *Sûreté*. Anglo-French tensions were relatively high and the Mekong Crisis of 1893 was still fresh in everyone's memory, as was the fact that France and Britain had nearly gone to war over Thailand. Morrison, virulently pro-British and pro-Empire as always, urged London to stand firm against creeping French expansionism.

Word of Morrison's mission was also passed around the British in the region. In Bangkok he stayed for a fortnight with the British Chargé d'affaires Maurice de Bunsen and carried letters of introduction from the India Office, the Foreign Office and the Colonial Office. He then left Southeast Asia and headed into Yunnan and China proper, eventually arriving back in Bangkok and de Bunsen's hospitality almost exactly a year after he had left London. In the interim Bell had sent a letter to Bangkok instructing Morrison to head straight to Beijing and start reporting immediately. Chirol, in Bangkok on a world tour before becoming the *Times*'s foreign editor, delivered Bell's instructions to Morrison personally. Morrison sailed for Hong Kong and then Shanghai before finally reaching Beijing in March 1897. At the time he wrote: "My new life is about to begin". It was also the case that a new chapter in foreign reporting from China was about to commence.

Within a few years Morrison was to rise to national attention through the pages of the *Times*, and to be known by officials in most European foreign offices and the American State Department for his role during the Boxer Rebellion and the Siege of the Legations. Though missing the start, Morrison had smuggled himself into the British Legation and then been promptly immobilised by a gunshot wound in the thigh and was unable to send any despatches to London. As the *Times* was also under the impression that the legations had fallen to the Boxers and all foreigners had been slain, it printed his obituary, which was so laudatory Morrison felt the paper should raise his salary if he was regarded so highly. He was alive but stuck, fuming, on a mattress in the legation hospital.

Morrison might have missed the start of the siege and early opportunities of filing back to London but his fame was spreading. Following the Boxers, Beijing returned to a sort of normality, albeit with a vastly enlarged foreign troop presence. The next major event to attract international press interest was the murky death of the emperor followed swiftly just a day later by the Empress Dowager Ci Xi. The whole event took on a slightly tabloid aspect when Duan Fang, a provincial governor, allowed the press to photograph the funeral cortege and sold some photos of the funeral ceremony himself, a moment of paparazzi speculation for which he was dismissed. However, Morrison managed to be out of town when the empress dowager died too. He was on yet another of his regular hunting trips, just as he had been when the Siege of the Legations began.

Morrison missed the two biggest scoops of his career but his reputation just kept on growing regardless. In London the *Spectator* had hailed his despatches from the siege claiming: "Gibbon could not have told the story better". Morrison's reaction is not known but one can imagine his ego was thrilled at being compared to the great chronicler of the Roman Empire, though he also probably considered it a just and fitting acknowledgement of his skills. After all, were his op-eds in the *Times* not laid out in bold, upper case and a large font size as "DR MORRISON ON CHINA"? They were indeed. All this raises two problems: first, the need to recover from history the two men who covered for Morrison for many years and suppressed their own reputations and careers as sinologists, writers and journalists so that the often pompous Australian could flourish; and second, the need to recover for posterity the many other journalists in Beijing at the start of the twentieth century who have been largely obscured and forced to remain hidden in Morrison's shadow.

Morrison's Crutches — The Titled Hermit and the Cynical Ulsterman

Morrison was able to retain his reputation with the *Times* and its readers largely through the efforts of two men: J. O. P. Bland and Sir Edmund Backhouse. They both supplied him with information, sources and translations (Morrison never learned to either read or speak Chinese); and, on occasions, they even wrote his despatches for him. Morrison was to be mentioned by name in Parliament and in the official Chinese court circulars while Bland and Backhouse, though both notorious and well known for different reasons in China and among the burgeoning foreign press corps, were to remain distinctly in Morrison's shadow as far as the international reading public was concerned.

John Otway Percy "J. O. P." Bland was one of several high-profile Ulstermen who had made a career in China in the late nineteenth century and whose number included notably Sir Robert Hart, the famous inspector general of the China Imperial Maritime Customs Service (known simply as the "IG") and his successor, and brother-in-law, Boyd Bredon. Hart was famous throughout China for his rigid, efficient and largely incorruptible customs service and his sizeable personal brass band — a rather ostentatious perk. He became a close adviser to the Chinese government and was instrumental in founding the Chinese Postal Service as well as the Chinese Lighthouse Service. Hart had offered Bland a job in China in 1883 as his secretary and, in 1896, Bland also became the secretary of the Shanghai Municipal Council. After serving the Chinese government for 13 years in various roles, including helping to negotiate some railway loans, Bland was awarded the Order of the Double Dragon. Morrison had met him and hired him as an occasional correspondent for the *Times* in Shanghai. Bland went on to work for the British and Chinese Corporation, a large financial firm, but remained a contributor to the paper.

Bland was a major figure at the time, writing for the *Times*. Though with hindsight he was overshadowed by the arch-self publicist Morrison, his writing can be seen to be fresher and more insightful than his more esteemed colleague's imperial bluster. Edwin Haward, an India Hand who served for many years as one of the more enlightened editors of the *North-China Daily News* in the 1930s, commented in the *Kipling Journal* (the organ of the Kipling Society in England): "We in China have often longed for someone to do for us what Kipling did for India. Mr J. O. P. Bland's charming pen has gone nearest to fulfilling these aspirations, and quaintly enough its wielder would shake hands with Kipling in the refusal to abandon old political deities". [4]

Bland reported on the daily events and machinations in Chinese politics and provided a vivid portrait of Chinese life; and he also was a keen sportsman. His 1909 book *Houseboat Days* is one of the more interesting British-penned memoirs of China. He was a cynic about most things China-related including those who wrote about the country, noting: "Remembering all the tomes on China which burdened our shelves even before the days of travelling MPs one wonders, as the stream of books rolls on, what and where are the people who buy them?". Despite this, Bland contributed his own tomes to the crowded shelf space. He still kept writing for the *Times*, supporting Morrison, though the pair's characters were completely at odds. Morrison was aggressive and arrogant while Bland was considered expansive and sociable; and, though they maintained a professional relationship as was required to get the job done, they came to dislike each other intensely. Indeed Bland was moved from Shanghai to Beijing in 1907 to cover for Morrison who was awarded the grand title of correspondent-in-chief of the *Times* in China. While Morrison roamed far and wide, usually hunting, Bland and his friend Backhouse kept the paper supplied with despatches. A lifelong Tory, Bland disliked what he considered to be Morrison's dogmatic approach to political questions and staunch unquestioning support for British imperialism. Bland, a supporter of peaceful trade with China, also considered Morrison superficial and vain in his claims to be the ultimate interpreter of China and the Chinese without being able to speak the language or having any real sympathy with the culture.

What became increasingly clear was that Bland's value to Morrison was as a translator and interpreter of events in China which the chief correspondent was unable to decipher himself, while Morrison's greatest asset to the *Times* was to understand British imperial aims in China and articulate them in solidly Empire rhetoric. As Hugh Trevor-Roper said in his biography of Backhouse, "China, in England, was not news. The penetration of China by foreign powers was".[5] Later, in a 1912 profile of Morrison, the *New York Times* was to sum up his dual position of foreign correspondent and agent of British aims in China as follows:

> Nominally, he has been the correspondent of the London *Times*, but really the unofficial representative of the British government in China, with more influence and more power than the accredited Minister of Great Britain to the Chinese Court.[6]

Bland and Backhouse had met in 1899 when, while Backhouse was researching for Morrison, a rabid dog had bitten Backhouse and Morrison had sent him to Shanghai to recuperate. Bland liked him immediately and was impressed by his scholarship and grasp of Chinese. Backhouse perhaps eroticised writing about China more than any other foreigner. His 1943 memoir, *Decadence Mandchoue*, which was written in his elderly years, was deemed too steamy and pornographic to be printed in England: homosexuality, sadomasochism, bestiality and his (rather far-fetched) claim to have bedded the empress dowager were a bit too much for refined English tastes. However, the French obliged, French publishers, and presumably readers, being less easily affronted by such practices than their English neighbours. Though from a wealthy and influential English family, Backhouse had not been above a little looting in Beijing after the relief of the Siege of the Legations, getting himself arrested by some Russian soldiers who were aggrieved that he was looting on what they considered their patch.

Bland and Backhouse became well known for a biography of the empress dowager they wrote together. The book was extremely influential in shaping foreign opinion of the empress and the last years of the Qing dynasty. However, others called them a pair of demented British propagandists. Their 1910 book *China Under the Dowager Empress* was certainly a mix of canny observation along with Backhouse's gossip and rumour collection. A later biographer of the empress, Sterling Seagrave, was to describe the book as a "... bloodthirsty caricature" that mixed, "Western fantasy and Chinese pornography". Certainly the book contained allegations of her murdering enemies with poisoned cakes, protecting false eunuchs and indulging in wild sexual romps in the imperial palace — romps Backhouse claimed to have been invited to, attended and happily participated in. Earlier though, many had relied on Bland and Backhouse's book as a source. For example, Pearl Buck relied heavily on it when writing her long fictional biography *Imperial Woman* in 1956 and the popular Italian diplomat-author Daniele Varé called it a *"magnum opus"*.

Backhouse is one of the most enigmatic foreign characters in Chinese history. He claimed to have saved the diary of His Excellency Ching Shan that formed the backbone of *China Under the Dowager Empress* from a fire at the nobleman's house at the end of the siege. Morrison considered this nonsense and a fabrication and thought Backhouse probably invented the diary with the aid of his Manchu teacher. This does seem more likely, though some thought it less important; Varé, for instance, declared: "If the Diary is apocryphal, it is a real work of art".[7] Bland seemed to believe Backhouse's story, or at least to go along with it in the interests of book sales and profits. It was Bland who deposited the original document in the British Museum for all sinologists to examine, which many did, and the debate raged over steamed spectacles for decades.

Backhouse maintained a close relationship with Morrison, and by the end of the Siege of the Legations he was Morrison's translator. The two would work late into the night, with Backhouse translating court documents as Morrison scribbled despatches. Backhouse remained a largely uncredited source for Morrison but he appears not to have minded this too much as Morrison allowed him the free time (though apparently not wages, but rather patronage) to pursue his scholarly studies, learn Manchu dialect and Mongolian and venture out on his night-time excursions into the underbelly of Beijing. Morrison also got him the post of professor of law and literature at the newly founded Peking University. Bland and Backhouse, though often competing with each other, had a common love of laughing at Morrison behind his back, knowing that his supposed infallibility on all things China was largely the result of their knowledge and research. They knew best that the Morrison reputation was largely a myth.

But the situation couldn't last and, as the relationships of the three men started to unravel, Morrison turned nasty. When in 1909 an article perceived by the English press to be by Morrison, but actually by Bland, was praised, Morrison was furious and Bland was left feeling cheated of his due respect. Things reached a head when Morrison returned to London and tried to discredit

Bland. However, Valentine Chirol at the *Times*'s foreign desk was no fool and knew that, despite his popularity with the public, Morrison was not as great as the readers, or the man himself, thought and stood by Bland. Bland stayed and, at least in public, Morrison's reputation with the public as the great "Morrison of Peking" remained intact; and it remained so until his death in 1920, despite several serious errors of judgement on his part later, such as becoming an adviser to China's would-be dictator Yuan Shih-kai.

In Morrison's Shadow — Those Crowded Out of History

Rarely has a major historical event been so identified with one journalist as the Boxer Rebellion was with Morrison. Arriving late or not, he still became the major articulator of the rebellion and the siege to the world, or at least to the British Empire. However, of course, other reporters were there whose reputations have not loomed as large as that of Morrison. Luigi Barzini, a well-known European war correspondent for Italy's *Corriere della Sera*, whose articles were also often carried by Britain's *Daily Telegraph*, also covered the siege as well as eight other wars, including the subsequent Russo-Japanese War of 1904–05. During the siege, Barzini wrote some excellent on-the-spot reports, including spending time with 100 Cossacks who were confronted by 2,000 sabre-wielding Boxers. But he has largely been lost to history and, rather than being dubbed "Barzini of Peking", he became a confirmed anti-war agitator and immigrant to America.

Unlike the rather aggressive Morrison, Barzini did not like what he saw in Beijing where he also reported from inside the legations and accompanied the elite *Bersaglieri* Italian light infantry that formed part of the international rescue mission, or later on the Chinese battlefields of the Russo-Japanese conflict. He became one of the first "anti-war" war correspondents, claiming that he had never seen "… any glory in war, no heroics, only slaughter". He later tired of conflict and launched into a series of more peaceful journalistic adventures, such as driving over 7,000 miles from Beijing to Paris with Prince Scipione Borghese. Barzini and Borghese won the race, despite a spectacular crash off the side of a bridge. Barzini then emigrated to America, while Borghese became a leading fascist, founding the Italian-American newspaper *Corriere d'America* in 1923. However, the paper was a short-lived venture, as the combined effects of America's 1924 Immigration Act, followed by the Wall Street Crash and the Great Depression, cut off the influx of Italian immigrants and, bereft of readers, it ultimately failed and Barzini returned to Italy.

The Russian press was in town but it took a slightly different line from either

Morrison's imperial outrage or Barzini's pacifist horror. In 1900 St. Petersburg was highly sympathetic to the Qing dynasty. In 1896 Russia had signed the Li-Lobanov Treaty with China which formally allied the Romanovs with the Qing. Russian public opinion was not much vexed by the siege as it seemed to be aimed at the Western European powers and not Russia. Czarist troops did participate in the relief expedition but many in St. Petersburg were in a state of conflict and reluctant to become involved. Prior to, during and after the siege, the Russian press continued to be sceptical of the Western Powers' aims in China in what was for many of the major papers an extension of the "Great Game". The mood was summed up by editorialists and popular cartoonists such as S. F. Sokolovskii (a.k.a Soré) whose cartoons regularly appeared in the St. Petersburg-based *Novoe vremia*. One popular Soré cartoon showed a Chinese with a large bill to pay watching some fat Europeans enjoying their loot and was captioned "Someone's pulling a fast one", referring to the onerous reparations the Western powers forced the Chinese to pay, while the editorial writer railed: "Europe is paying the price in China for its sins".[8] Conservative columnist Prince Vladimir Meshcherskii commented: "What a cruel irony this confrontation is for the Europeans now, after they condemned the Middle Kingdom's millennial somnolence for so many years".[9] In a left-right alliance, *Novoe vremia*, along with the ultra-conservative *Grazhdanin* and the progressive daily *Rossiia*, had little sympathy for the Western Europeans. Many editors were openly supportive of the Boxers and their grievances, while others, such as the journalist, historian and popular novelist Aleksandr Amfiteatrov, echoed official diplomatic and court opinion in St. Petersburg, going as far as to compare the Boxers' resistance to the Western powers with Russia's 1812 stand against Napoleon — London was now what Paris had been and both were "people's wars". [10]

Pricking Foreign Pomposities — The Shanghai Satirists

Though the Boxers, the siege and Morrison have come to dominate, and somewhat overshadow, the history of early twentieth century foreign journalism in China, there was a lot else happening and it wasn't all in Beijing. Of course, the foreign diplomatic community remained there and had been deeply affected by the tumultuous events. However, in Shanghai, where diplomats were scarcer and businessmen more common, the issues of the day were different. Commerce ruled Shanghai from the start and what passed for local politics was ultimately at the service of the China traders. The Shanghai-based satirist Jay Denby lampooned the SMC for its pro-business stance and dominance by the *taipans*, the new class of commercial bosses. Denby wrote:

A *taipan*, let me explain, is a red faced man (the redder the face, the *taipanner* the *taipan*) who has either sufficient brains or bluff to make others work for him and yet retain the kudos and bulk of the spoils for himself.[11]

Denby, a Brit, was popular (though perhaps not with the hideously self-important *taipans*) for his dissections of Shanghai society, its cliques, ridiculous social pretensions and haughtiness. His view of Shanghai was captured in his 1910 book *Letter From a Shanghai Griffin*, "Griffin" being a word in Shanghailander slang meaning a new arrival, and referred to both people and horses. The book was illustrated by the Shanghai artist and cartoonist H. W. G. Hayter who was also the editor of *The Eastern Sketch* which described itself as an illustrated weekly and was modelled on *Punch*. The *Sketch* would often devote a whole front cover to one of Hayter's cartoons; that is to say, the slightly sarcastic-looking Hayter would magnanimously award the cover to himself. However, he can perhaps be forgiven as before the *Sketch* few English-language publications in China featured cartoons, but after the success of the *Sketch* hardly a newspaper, Chinese or foreign, dared not have cartoons, so popular were they with readers. Launched in September 1904, the *Sketch* hit the Shanghai streets every Sunday morning for 30 cents. It was considered extremely hard-hitting and vicious towards its targets, but it could get away with it as winning a libel case in the treaty ports at the time was a decidedly tricky business. One novel component of the paper was that it reprinted cartoons from the Chinese language press with the captions and punch lines translated into English.

As well as Hayter and Denby, another satirist lampooning foreign society was B. L. Putnam Weale who waged a one-man campaign against Sir Claude MacDonald, the British ambassador during the siege. MacDonald apparently attempted to have Putnam Weale arrested for looting, an act that earned MacDonald Putnam Weale's eternal ire. Putnam Weale did loot, but only in the Russian zone where he was safe from arrest by the British and Americans and considered his actions fair game and not the business of the officious British ambassador.

Of course "Gunboat" MacDonald has gone down in history as the stout defender of the legations and the epitome of English reserve and cool under fire (not least due to his portrayal by David Niven in the 1963 film *55 Days in Peking*). Putnam Weale's 1921 book *Indiscreet Letters from Peking* was a satire, but at the time it was often read as a true record of the siege as he was actually one of the besieged. Certainly, MacDonald was rather pompous in an officious British way (as was his aide Sir Henry Bax-Ironside, known by everyone as "Iron Backside") and was an easy target for any satirist, his enormous waxed moustache making him a heavenly gift for the cartoonists. Even Morrison, who would have rather cut off an arm than criticise England normally, described MacDonald as the "type of military officer rolled out at a mile a time and then lopped off in six foot lengths". Despite this, little anti-MacDonald rhetoric or mockery ever got back to England where his reputation as a strong defender of British personages, property and interests remained firmly intact in the public mind.

Putnam Weale was a pseudonym for Ningbo-born Bertram Lenox Simpson and his *Indiscreet Letters* was marketed at the time as "Being the notes of an eyewitness, set forth in day to day detail the real story of the Siege and sack of a distressed capital in 1900 — 'the year of great tribulation'". Later Peter Fleming, who identified himself clearly with the ruling classes Putnam Weale enjoyed satirising, described the book as a "rather odious work".[12] A former employee of the Chinese Maritime Customs Service, Putnam Weale wrote ten books as well as numerous articles for a variety of publications including the *Peking Gazette* (he was a good friend of its Trinidadian-born editor Eugene Chen), *Asia* magazine and the *Daily Telegraph*; and he went on to become chairman of the *Far Eastern Times* syndicate and editor of the English-language *Peking Leader* before getting himself caught up in Chinese politics, working for the political section of the office of the Chinese president. He could never resist an intrigue and involved himself in the dark machinations of warlord politics, eventually getting himself brutally butchered on a Tianjin street in the 1920s, probably in revenge for some prior indiscretions. His killer was never identified or caught.

Other cartoonists and artists were supplying both the local English-language press and selling their drawings overseas too. Sir Leslie Ward, an accomplished sketch cartoonist who used the pseudonym "Spy", produced a range of paintings of Chinese statesmen for *Vanity Fair*, including one of His Excellency Guo Songdao, the first Chinese ambassador to Britain. Hayter, Denby and Putnam Weale were to be the height of satire until a later generation came along in the 1930s who continued the tradition of satirising the eternally pompous and aloof foreign Shanghailander society.

German Communications

English dominated the foreign press but there were other languages represented and other foreigners too, such as the French and Americans (as seen previously) and also, importantly, the Germans. The *Ostasiatischer Lloyd* was the oldest German-language paper in China and had been founded in 1889 in Shanghai as a daily edited by Herr von Gundlach and later by Bruno Navarra and then, from 1900 to 1917, by Carl Fink who changed it into a weekly when it became generally regarded as the best German newspaper in the Far East. Its readership covered all the German communities in China and across Southeast Asia. The *Ostasiatischer Lloyd* was later joined by the *Pekinger Deutsche Zeitung*, which was launched in 1901.

The ever-entrepreneurial Fink then launched an illustrated monthly magazine *Der ferne Osten* in 1904, which the *North-China Daily News* reproduced in English translation, but it only lasted a few issues as the minutiae of German China coast society perhaps predictably failed to interest greatly the largely English readership of the *North-China*. However, Fink was one of the most important Germans in China in the first years of the century and was also instrumental in establishing the German news service for East Asia — *Deutscher Nachrichtendienst fr Ostasien*. German newspapers internationally and in Berlin all took feeds from Fink's agency. He was also an early example of a foreign journalist who became intricately involved in Chinese politics and not just as a casual outside observer. *Shiwubao* (also called *Shiwu Ribao* and later *Zhongwai Ribao*), the major publication of the nascent Chinese reform movement at the end of the nineteenth century, was linked to a German firm run by Fink, which was able to protect the paper from a certain amount of censorship and repression.

German correspondents also launched a newspaper for northern China, the *Tageblatt fr Nordchina*, which was published in Tianjin; and there was a smaller publication called the *Brigade-Zeitung*, which was specifically produced for the German military railway guards stationed in northern China until 1906. In addition, Qingdao, the major German interest in China, had five papers: the *Deutsch-Asiatische Warte*, a weekly which lasted until 1906 and featured a cultural supplement *Die Welt des Ostens*; *Altes und Neues aus Asiens drei Kaiserreichen*; the *Tsingtauer Neueste Nachrichten*, a daily that was launched in 1905 and lasted until 1914 edited by Fritz Secker; and the *Kiautschou Post*, a daily that ran between 1908 and 1912. Meanwhile *The Hankow Daily News* was published in English but edited for many years by a German. The China coast press was becoming truly multilingual.

The Arrival of the *Post*

At the same time, the press in Hong Kong was growing but it wasn't exactly a boom time: by the early 1920s the combined circulation of English-language papers in the colony was barely 5,000 daily. The *South China Morning Post* was founded in 1903 and published its first edition in November, declaring itself the colony's first "modern newspaper". The press was also becoming a force for social progress in Hong Kong by making suggestions that influential citizens of the colony adopted. Hong Kong's *China Mail* first proposed combining the existing medical and technical colleges to form a university for the colony, an idea the Parsi businessman Hormusjee Mody took up at the insistence of prominent businessman Paul Chater and bequeathed its major building to the new Hong Kong University. Unfortunately, Mody died before the university building was completed.

The *South China Morning Post*, or the *Post* as it quickly became commonly known by everyone, was to outlive its major competitors, the *Hongkong Telegraph*, the *Hongkong Daily Press* and the *China Mail* to become regarded as one of the best papers in the Far East. The *Post*'s launch wasn't popular with the competition. As the *Hongkong Telegraph* noted, "Hongkong's troubles are to be increased by the addition of a new daily newspaper with the voluminous title of *The Morning Post of South China* ... We sympathise deeply with Hongkong. It will soon be as bad as Shanghai in this respect".[13] The paper's founders —Arthur Cunningham who had covered the Sino-Japanese War for the *Hongkong Daily Press* in 1894 and the Australian-born Chinese political activist Tse Tsan-tai — begged to differ. The *Post* marked somewhat of a sea change in Hong Kong, declaring in its opening editorial on 6 November 1903:

> The modern newspaper has taken the place of the old-time ambassador. The cynic has said the ambassador is sent abroad to lie for the good of his country. The newspaper is sent abroad to tell the truth for the good of humanity. Whereas the ambassador, by means of weary months of negotiation, may make or prevent a war; a newspaper by means of a few trenchant articles, so be that they have truth behind them, will rouse a public to resent aggression, so to reform abuses, to mould the policy of governments. Such is the power of the modern newspaper.[14]

Tse Tsan-tai, who had been baptised James See, was a particularly transnational character for the times. Born in Grafton, Australia, to a family of Chinese merchants, he moved to Hong Kong in 1887 to study at Queen's College and was one of the founders of the Literary Society for the Promotion of Benevolence (*Furen Wenshe*). In 1895 Tse and his colleagues aligned themselves with Sun Yat-sen's *Hing Chung Hui* (Society for the Restoration of China), though Tse and Sun soon fell out. Tse recalled Sun as "... a rash and reckless fellow. He would risk his life to make a name for himself. Sun proposes things that are subject to condemnation — he thinks he is able to do anything — no obstructions — 'all paper!'".[15] Though history has crowded out Sun's detractors in the early days before he rose to power, there are many and his nickname was the "windbag". Later, in the 1930s, a heated debate would arise in Australia when some prominent overseas Chinese campaigned to have Tse recognised as the true father of the Chinese Republic, thereby arguing for the demotion of Sun.

Tse pushed hard for social change in Hong Kong, arguing that the Chinese community should elect the Chinese representatives on the Legislative Council rather than having them nominated by the governor, as well as inventing an advanced steering system for airships. He campaigned against superstition, *feng shui*, footbinding and opium smoking, while promoting religious tolerance, railways and mining, and calling for the protection of China's heritage. He had corresponded with Morrison since the 1890s, was friendly with the *Hongkong Telegraph* editor Chesney Duncan and also knew Cunningham well when he was the editor of the *Hongkong Daily Press*. In 1901 Tse worked briefly for the *China Daily*, the newspaper of the Society for the Restoration of China. As well as being a prolific journalist and newspaper proprietor, Tse also authored about half a dozen books on subjects ranging from ancient Turkestan to solving unemployment, to why typhoons occur. He was nothing if not a multi-tasker.

Tse and Cunningham appointed Douglas Story as the paper's first editor. Their founding aim was to present the viewpoint of both the British colonial regime and the business community and promote the cause of republicanism in China. This was a tricky project and wasn't an easy balancing act. Story only lasted a year, claiming that he didn't like Hong Kong because people took too many holidays and played too much sport. However, he was a staunch supporter of self-government for Hong Kong and considered the governor's post unnecessary. Transition from a crown colony to a self-governing colony would allow Hong Kong to flourish and also allow for greater Chinese involvement in affairs. Although in a seeming contradiction to opposing crown colony status, he also staunchly defended the rights of British trade in China and spoke out against what he saw as American encroachment on British business interests — Washington's "Open Door" policy.

Despite all this, the *Post*'s early survival was far from sure. Within a few years at the turn of the century several new papers, as well as the *Post*, appeared in Hong Kong along with the nearby *Canton Daily News*, which sought to compete with the rather larger and well-established *Canton Chronicle*. It seemed that, although the market was already crowded, investors thought newspapers were a potentially profitable investment, but this wasn't initially the case. Despite the rather vague claims from the backers of the *Post* that investments in the paper would earn returns of anywhere between 12% and 200% a year when they issued $150,000 worth of shares at $25 each, three years later shareholders had received no dividends and the shares were valued at just $18. The *Hongkong Telegraph* gloated over the *Post*'s initial financial woes, noting both the difficulty of the English- language newspaper business in Asia and remembering the early days in the Canton factories: "Conditions in the Far East have changed since the time when anybody could come along with a hand press and start a paper …".[16] Despite this gloomy prognosis, the *Post* persisted and ultimately outlasted all the competition.

The *Post* survived its early traumas. Various acting editors ran the paper until 1910 when Angus Hamilton was appointed, but he lasted only a few months. Hamilton, an English correspondent of aristocratic background, had started out working on the *New York Evening Sun* which sent him to Korea. He then found work as a war correspondent for the *Times*, covering the defence of Mafeking alongside Baden Powell before moving to the *Pall Mall Gazette* where he covered the Siege of the Legations, the wars in Somaliland and those between the Balkans and Macedonia at the turn of the century. Then, job-hopping again, the *Manchester Guardian* hired him to report from the frontlines during the 1905 Russo-Japanese War, and he also visited Afghanistan before finally being hired by the *Post*. Though an immensely talented man, he was also troubled and restless. He lingered in Hong Kong for only a short while before heading to India and then becoming a reporter for Britain's Central News Agency in the Balkans where he was twice captured by the Bulgarians and severely tortured as a Turkish spy. He travelled to America to give a series of lectures on his experiences around the world, only to discover he was a poor speaker, nervous and attracting small audiences. Considering himself a failure, in dire financial straits, suffering from ill-health courtesy of his Bulgarian torturers and unsure of the future, he cut his throat in a New York hotel room.

As the immediate terror of the Boxers receded, China found itself faced with new challenges — a continually ossifying Qing court that had caused the humiliation of China, as a result of which the country had to accept a greater foreign presence on Chinese soil. At the same time, other rising powers chose China as a battlefield for their grievances.

4
The Vultures Descend

"You see a thing in China and you think that you understand it. You fix it in your mind and tell yourself that you have absorbed it, whatever it may be, and that you now have the final thought and word and correct meaning. But after a little time you find, by a peculiar process of Chinese national twisting and shifting, no matter, what you see, hear, think, believe, your final thought and word and correct meaning are changed completely."

Edwin Dingle, *China's Revolution* (1912)

"I am disgusted! I'll never go to a war between Orientals again. The vexations and delay are too great."

Jack London

A Foreign War on Chinese Soil

The major event to consume foreign correspondents in China after the onslaught of the Boxers was the 1904–05 Russo-Japanese War. Characterised by some as a rehearsal for the First World War, with trenches and sword-wielding cavalry going up against machine guns, China was not a combatant, but the conflict was fought largely along its borders and a fair amount of it on Chinese soil in Manchuria. It should have been an instructive conflict for European generals and politicians, giving them some indications, which they largely ignored, of how brutal and efficient modern warfare was becoming. It should also have raised alarm bells among the Chinese about the rise, regional ambitions and military prowess of Japan that many intellectuals absorbed but the Qing court singularly failed, or chose not, to appreciate. Some papers had predicted the clash. In 1903 the *Times* correspondent in Seoul reported deteriorating Russo-Japanese relations and the *Hongkong Telegraph* voiced its agreement with

London's opinion, but it was Shanghai's *North China Herald* that got the scoop on the start of the conflict proper. The *Herald*'s editor Bob Little personally received a telegram announcing the closure of Vladivostok port, which meant that the paper was the first to proclaim the start of the conflict and launched the ensuing media scrum to cover it.

The newspapers and fledgling wire services were desperate for additional correspondents and persuaded many foreigners in China to switch professions and take up the pen. Willard Dickerman Straight was one such person. An orphan, he had attended Cornell before being appointed to work as personal secretary to Robert Hart at the China Imperial Maritime Customs Service. He had many friends in Beijing's foreign press corps and, as a part-time artist, had illustrated J. O. P. Bland's rather forgettable 1902 book *Verse and Worse* (most of which fell firmly into the latter category). However, despite being well known for having become wealthy by the time he was 30 and reputedly "earning as much as the President of the United States", when the Russo-Japanese War broke out he signed up as a correspondent with Reuters and headed off to northern China and Korea. His despatches caught the eye of the American State Department and he was soon persuaded to change jobs once again, becoming the personal secretary to the American ambassador in Korea while still covering the Japanese annexation of Korea as a freelancer. He was later to return as American consul-general in Shenyang and reacquainted himself with Bland, illustrating the latter's rather better book *Houseboat Days*. Straight eventually left China after the Nationalist revolution in 1911. His departure was not a comment on the rise of the Republic but rather that in 1906 at a Beijing dinner party he had been introduced to Dorothy Payne Whitney, heiress to the Whitney fortune, and they had fallen in love and decided to marry. This meant that he, rather fortuitously, no longer had need of employment, having made a fortune and then married one. Still, it seems that the press had got into his blood and he and Dorothy subsequently established the *New Republic* together in 1914.

The new correspondents also included some who had actually been around in Asia for a while but opted to trade professions. Many fancied a life of adventurous reporting and newspapers believed that it was easier to train someone to write a despatch than to educate them in China's myriad ways and language. In 1891 James Ricalton, a school teacher from Maplewood, New Jersey, with a penchant for travel to Russia and the Far East, resigned from his regular job to become a photographer and war correspondent. For 15 years he photographed and recorded events, including the Boxers, the lavish Delhi Durbar that installed Edward VII as emperor of India and then the Russo-Japanese War. Ricalton's real passion was photography but he also wrote despatches to accompany his images. Indeed, as well as arguably being the first real photojournalist to operate in China, he also staged the first moving picture show in China, presenting a programme of Edison films at Shanghai's Tien Hua Tea Garden in 1897.

This occasional-correspondent life was a feature of the time and gained momentum with the Russo-Japanese War, as did reporting with wireless despatches. The *Times* got the scoop on the opening clashes of the conflict from its special correspondent Lionel James who reported the first months of the war from the first-ever wireless station used by a war correspondent anywhere. James, who had previously covered the Boer War, transmitted from a specially chartered ship in the Yellow Sea to a cable station at the British enclave of Weihaiwei, which gave the *Times* and the *New York Times* the chance to publish reports the next day. It was a short-lived venture as James was forced to abandon his enterprise as a result of Russian paranoia and concerns from the British Admiralty of reprisals by the Japanese with whom James had struck a special deal. Though James survived the pioneering experience unscathed, his less fortunate assistant, Yei Theodora Ozaki, was largely unable to assist due to constant and terrible sea-sickness.

As well as the hastily recruited reporters, there were also some big names around. Chicagoan John Foster Bass, brother of the New Hampshire governor Robert Bass, went to cover the war with his sister Gertrude, but he later sent her to Shanghai for safety while he followed the frontline troops. Bass became a noted war correspondent and went on to cover the First World War while Gertrude, later known as Gertrude Bass Warner, became famous for her Asian art collection and portrait photography of Japan and China.

And then there was Jack London. Though the American was later to become known for his novels and short stories, he was also present for the Russo-Japanese War, reporting for the Hearst group. He was just 28 but had already published his classic story *The Call of the Wild* in 1903. London was one journalist who didn't mind the harsh conditions in Manchuria, having just emerged from the Yukon, but while in Japan and Korea he did suffer from bouts of debilitating depression that laid him low for days at a time.

London was one of a group of American journalists who travelled together from San Francisco to Yokohama on the *SS Siberia* specifically to report the war. They called themselves the "Vultures" and included Richard Harding Davis, a correspondent of rather aristocratic manners who was more used to socialising with admirals, generals and statesmen than roughhousing with hacks. He was something of a contrast to the more down-at-heel London, as was Frederick McCormick, *Collier*'s magazine's extremely literate war correspondent who travelled with the Russian side.

London travelled all the way to Pyongyang where he sent out his first scribbled notes on rice paper covering the initial land clashes and smuggled out photographs from the Japanese front at Chemulpo (Inchon), a major staging-post for Japanese ground forces in Korea. For this he was arrested and subjected to hours of rigorous interrogation by the Japanese who suspected him of being a Russian spy. After some arguing back and forth, Harding Davis and Lloyd Griscom, the US minister to Japan, managed to secure his release. Back at large, London used his sailing skills to hire a boat and catch up with the Japanese First Army, which was moving north over treacherous, icy mountain passes towards Manchuria where he was to see the fighting around Pyongyang and the assaults on Russian fortifications in northeast China. He managed to get himself arrested again and was forced to enlist Harding Davis's support to secure his release twice more. London went on in his career to cover other wars and revolutions but never in Asia, after declaring of his experiences in the Russo-Japanese War: "I am disgusted! I'll never go to a war between Orientals again. The vexations and delay are too great".

Harding Davis — London's multiple saviour from Japanese jails, or potentially a firing squad — was a novelist and playwright as well as a war correspondent. He was to inspire a series of sketches by the immensely popular American illustrator Charles Dana Gibson while also churning out pulp fiction for *Collier's* and *Scribner's* magazines to pay for his lifestyle. While not off chasing wars, he was usually to be found at his private table at Delmonico's in Manhattan. He was a muscular Christian, student football and tennis star at Lehigh University and, as most who knew him agreed, a terrible snob. He was also the son of Clarke Davis, the managing editor of *The Philadelphia Inquirer*, though Harding Davis always worked for his father's competition the *Philadelphia Record* before moving to the *Philadelphia Press* where he interviewed Walt Whitman and other luminaries. From Philadelphia he moved to the *New York Evening Sun*. By the time he reached Manchuria he had already covered the Boer War and Teddy Roosevelt's dramatic charge up San Juan Hill in 1898. China was not to be his last posting either as he went on to cover the First World War where he was caught behind German lines near Brussels.

Harding Davies was notoriously competitive, whether in ensuring the success and good reception of his theatrical plays, on the tennis court or arguing for the prominence of his by-lines. Immediately upon arrival in Japan, he launched a spat with the resident Tokyo correspondent of *Collier's* over who should be the lead reporter. However, he was also among friends: he had travelled to Japan with his wife and there found his old friend Bass, with whom he had previously covered the Greco-Turkish War of 1897. At first, in effect, Harding Davies and Bass could get no news as all the reports from the station closest to the front in Yantai were censored by the Japanese authorities and useless. Rather than join the first batch of foreign correspondents who went to the front, both reporters remained in Tokyo after they discovered that the closest anyone was allowed to get to the fighting was three miles away. However, they did eventually reach Manchuria and the frontlines.

As well as the American Vultures, the British press corps was well represented. Ellis Ashmead-Bartlett, an experienced British war correspondent, reported as an "embedded" reporter with the Japanese forces for the *Daily Telegraph*. He was the eldest son of the Brooklyn-born Sir Ellis Ashmead-Bartlett MP who moved to England where he did remarkably well: he became Lord of the Admiralty and was viewed as having become "more English than the English" (not always considered as a compliment). With his father, Ellis had spent time with the Turkish army in the Greco-Turkish War and served as a subaltern in the Bedfordshire Regiment during the Boer War. His despatches from northern China were widely read, along with those of his colleague, Bennet Burleigh, the paper's famous special war correspondent who was based in Tokyo during the conflict.

Others "embedded" themselves with the Russians in China. These included Maurice Baring, an Englishman of letters, dramatist, poet, novelist, translator, essayist and travel writer. A former diplomatic official, he had become a correspondent after finding himself bored rigid in Whitehall. He took up a recommendation from his friend Count Alexander Benckendorff, the Russian ambassador to London, and followed the Russians for the *London Morning Post*. Like Ashmead-Bartlett, Baring had an illustrious father, the banker Baron Revelstoke. He trailed the czar's army kitted out in his trademark straw boater, a permanent fixture since his mildly eccentric Cambridge days. He spoke fluent Russian but in Manchuria he reportedly came to be fond of the Chinese and found he could write strong prose too. After witnessing a battle he wrote of the casualty-strewn battlefield:

> He was lying with brown eyes wide open and showing his white teeth. But there was nothing grim or ghastly in that smile. It was miraculously beautiful ... a smile of radiant joy and surprise, as if he had suddenly met with a friend for whom he had longed, above all things, at a moment when of all others he had needed him. Near him a Russian boy was lying, fair and curly-headed, with his head resting on one arm, as if he had fallen asleep like a tired child overcome with insuperable weariness, and had opened his eyes to pray to be left at peace just a little longer.[1]

Obviously members of the Russian press corps turned up but they found themselves in trouble and intrigue pretty quickly with their own compatriots and government. The newspaper *Novi Krai* had been established in the Russian enclave of Port Arthur. It survived the siege of the city during the war and, when the town fell to the Japanese, the presses and staff decamped for Shanghai before eventually re-establishing operations in Harbin and re-launching the paper. Despite being owned and run by Russians, the paper managed to annoy St. Petersburg by effectively accusing General Anatoly Stoessel, the Russian "defender" of Port Arthur, of cowardice and fleeing the town leaving it, and its Russian inhabitants, to an uncertain fate while also severely mistreating the town's Chinese residents. Then in May 1905 the paper's proprietor Colonel Artemieff was summoned to St. Petersburg for a personal audience with the czar which was believed to be about the paper's rather too detailed coverage of the war and the several "stormy" interviews Artemieff had conducted with Stoessel which had shown the czarist general in a bad light. Afterwards he returned to continue running *Novi Krai* in Harbin with his editors Messers Veroshkin and Tchernikofsky, the latter of whom was well known to the Shanghai press corps as the former telegraphic correspondent of Moscow's *Ruskoe Slovo*. The paper had clearly angered officialdom in St. Petersburg which, though apparently aware of Stoessel's poor leadership, had still publicly backed and decorated him. In March 1906 all three men suddenly disappeared and *Novi Krai* was suppressed. Nothing further was ever heard of any of the three journalists and the paper never resumed publication.

The conflict between the Russians and the Japanese in the Chinese far north had seen more journalists arrive in China than any previous single event and it affected many of them deeply. Originally from a long-standing newspaper family, the muckraking American reporter Charles Edward Russell came as the *New York Herald*'s correspondent. In his time Russell penned several pro-socialist books and was as well known as his muckraking contemporaries such as Upton Sinclair who had been inspired by Russell's articles to write *The Jungle*, his condemnation of the Chicago meatpacking industry. Russell wrote:

> I question much if any of the correspondents that followed the Russo-Japanese War are enthusiastic supporters of the theory that modern war has been humanised ... I was in Japan just after the close of the war, and saw some of the remains of Japanese soldiers brought home for burial, an arm or a foot or a cap (being all that could be found after the shell exploded), and there was nothing about these spectacles that appealed much to one's senses as remarkably humane.[2]

In China, reporting the Russo-Japanese War, Russell moved from being an impartial observer to becoming a dedicated pacifist and socialist for the rest of his life. Many of the press corps who travelled to Manchuria saw the writing on the wall for the mechanical future of war and were disturbed, but the politicians and the Qing dynasty all seemingly took far less notice.

Photography and the Russo-Japanese War

As it was for modern warfare, the Russo-Japanese War was revolutionary for modern photography. While stereoscopic slides had been about during the Boxer Rebellion and the Spanish-American War, the Russo-Japanese War was perhaps their major introduction to mass appeal. Arguably the strongest images of the war came from the Russian "Photographer to the Czar" Sergei Mikhailovich Prokudin-Gorskii. He was both the official photographer for the Russian side on the Manchurian battlefield and for the Trans-Siberian Railway project.

The war was photographed in graphic style — which showed clearly that by 1905 editors understood the value of gory pictures — with images of Shenyang and Port Arthur sent around the world. Self-taught photographing brothers Elmer and Bert Underwood produced box sets of stereographs from the war, including a striking shot of Japanese soldiers carrying out an execution. Jack London and James Ricalton sent photographs, which demonstrated that war correspondents were now sending images as well as text and pioneering photojournalism in China. Ricalton sent back amazing shots for the time and was given virtually unparalleled access for a foreigner to the Japanese forces. Herbert Ponting, an Englishman who had emigrated to America in his early twenties, went to the war as *Harper's Weekly*'s correspondent and later returned to travel around Japan, India, China, Korea, Java and Burma. He too sent back pictures as well as text. Ponting was later the official photographer on Scott's British Antarctic Expedition.

The Russo-Japanese War was also the first time spies posing as journalists used photography. Some were found to be smuggling secret reports in microphotographic form and the war provided evidence of the increasingly shady links between journalism and espionage. The Russians later revealed that they had obtained information on Japan's strategy, including the plan for the major offensive in Manchuria in March 1905 that Jack London witnessed, through a Tokyo-based French correspondent, a Monsieur Balais of *Le Figaro*. Through the mysterious Frenchman, Russia found out in August 1904 that Japan would attack Shenyang, which was under Russian control at the time, as early as January 1905. Alexander Pavlov, a senior Russian diplomat in Korea, had apparently hired Balais who had begun his espionage career in Shanghai a couple of years earlier. Balais sent around 30 reports to Pavlov in Shanghai by regular sea mail.

Film cameras were also in evidence now too. George Roberts filmed the Russian army marching from Siberia to Manchuria, securing notable images showing the beheading of a Chinese bandit, while Joseph Rosenthal filmed on the Japanese side for the Charles Urban Trading Company. Rosenthal had already filmed the Boer War, travelling with Lord Roberts's column, as well as the American occupation of the Philippines. At the same time, correspondents also did deals with local photographers, even buying pictures from the photographic unit of the Japanese Imperial General Headquarters and from Japanese photographers such as Koson Ohara who produced prints similar to those that had proved popular during the earlier Sino-Japanese War.

After 1905, wherever foreign journalists were to be found in China, photographers would also be constantly present, and shortly after that newsreel cameramen also. The China story was now to be one of text and images together.

Donald of China —"He Could Not Be Fooled"

Arriving in China just before the Russo-Japanese War, William Henry Donald was one of the most connected men in China. One journalist described him as "a man who could not be fooled", though he has gone down in history primarily for his role in advising Chiang Kai-shek and being a close confidant to Madame Chiang rather than for his extensive journalism and writing on China. Born in Lithgow, New South Wales, he had learned his trade on his local papers and the *Sydney Daily Telegraph*. Donald ("Will" to his family, "Don" to his close friends and "Bill" to acquaintances) had been a get-ahead young journalist but was best described as ambitious but poor. When he ventured to China he was so poverty-stricken that he had to work his passage as the cook's helper aboard a ship that eventually docked in Hong Kong. There he got lucky and landed a job on the *China Mail* and had become the paper's managing editor by 1903, chiefly on the grounds that he claimed at the interview to be neither a drinker nor a smoker, both far from entirely truthful statements.

He soon acquired a reputation for being tenacious. He was sent to Beijing to secure an interview with a senior minister in the imperial court. Refused admission to the palace, he was chased away by angry guards. However, he managed to scale a wall and get into one of the imperial gardens, but again he was expelled by guards. Finally he plonked himself down on the wide marble steps leading up to the palace and refused to budge; and he remained there for several hours while the guards fretted over how to deal with this determined but obviously simple-minded foreign devil. Eventually a fat mandarin appeared, asking what exactly this stubborn barbarian wanted. Donald told him and also berated the much older and more senior man about the poor treatment the Chinese government was dispensing to a representative of the foreign press. The apparently mild-mannered and forgiving mandarin found the young foreigner interesting enough to hire him as an adviser. Only later, after accepting the impromptu job offer, did Donald find out that the fat work-offering mandarin was actually the minister he had originally been sent to interview. When not advising mandarins, he kept his hand in by covering the Russo-Japanese War and sending despatches to various international newspapers from the front.

Donald always wrote, though he spent much of the rest of his career briefing, advising and being interviewed by foreign correspondents in China and practising the art of what is now called "spin" for his bosses. He was clearly happier as an adviser at the heart of the action than as a hack on the fringes, but he never quite lost the desire to pick up the pen occasionally. He was hired by the viceroy of Guangzhou as an adviser in 1905 and befriended the legendary Hainan Christian convert and wealthy Bible publisher Charlie Soong in 1911, becoming an uncle to the three Soong sisters and liking Mei-ling the best — a choice that was to have dramatic implications later when she became Madame Chiang Kai-shek. He never made any significant financial profit from his time in China as he accepted only reasonable salaries even when he advised people with clearly louche and corruptive tendencies such as the drug-addicted Young Marshal Zhang Xueliang (who Donald persuaded to go into drug rehab accompanied by his favourite concubine). Not that he didn't live well — while advising the Young Marshal, Donald lived in an old imperial hunting lodge outside Beijing nicknamed the "temple" and hosted lavish and legendary picnics with masses of food, wine and everyone wearing formal dress.

Much later, when Chiang Kai-shek was kidnapped by the Young Marshal in 1936, Donald was by Madame Chiang's side throughout the ordeal and attempted to secure the Generalissimo's safe release. Their close relationship was seemingly sealed when, in 1937, they were in a serious car crash together and Mei-ling was hurled from the car. Donald picked her up and tried to cheer her up by singing "She flew through the air with the greatest of ease, the daring young woman on the flying trapeze". Madame Chiang, having broken a rib and having trouble breathing, was not in a humorous mood, but the pair still became solid friends due to their shared experiences over the years.

Donald cared deeply about China, despite never mastering the language or developing a taste for the cuisine — "Never touch the stuff! It ruins my stomach', he told the visiting poets Auden and Isherwood — but he could also be infuriated by its ways. Isherwood believed that Donald's lack of Chinese was his great protection in a world of plots and secrets: he heard no more than it was good for him to know to do his job. According to his journalist friend Ilona Ralph Sues, when Chiang Kai-shek once asked him how he would reconstruct China if he had total power, Donald replied:

> First, I would shoot everybody who spoke about "saving face". Second, I would shoot everybody who said *meiyou fadze* ("It cannot be done"). Third, I would shoot every damn fool in the administration.

Upon hearing this, Chiang apparently declared that he would have to build an arsenal in every village to deal with these immense problems.[3] Donald was to be a pre-eminent figure in China through to the end of the Second World War and features again more than once in this tale.

Across China with a Curious Englishman

China was on the cusp of change by 1910, but few foresaw it. However, many foreign members of the China press corps were to go through massive changes in the coming decades. But before considering the upheavals that were brought about with the collapse of the Qing dynasty, it's worth remembering Englishman Edwin John Dingle, or Ding Le Mei as he was known in Chinese. Dingle deserves a mention in any history of the foreign press corps due to the fact that, though he had become a successful publisher on the China coast, he decided that there was more money in running a religious cult. Many called him a faddist and fanatic, but he personally preferred to be known as an esoteric scholar and cartographer. He had started out as a journalist in Singapore, where his brother worked for the Harbour Board, and then moved to Shanghai to work on publications including the *China and Far East Finance and Commerce*, a distant predecessor of the *Far Eastern Economic Review*, published in Shanghai from 1920 until 1937. The publication was really a digest of market data on commodities and goods traded throughout the region. However, he also made his fortune with a cartographic business based in Hong Kong and Shanghai, mapping western China for Sun Yat-sen and studying Tibet. His contributions to cartography in China were recognised by the Royal Geographic Society (RGS) in London and his maps regularly appeared in the *North-China Daily News*. He published *Across China on Foot* in 1911, an account of his trek across China two years before which nearly killed him. While wandering in Yunnan, he claimed to have been "at the point of death" due to lack of food and shelter.

The book somewhat retrod (both literally and literarily) Morrison's trek from Shanghai to Burma; and, like Morrison, Dingle spoke little Chinese and seemingly did equally sparse pre-trip preparation which was presumably why he kept running out of food and nearly dying.

It was during his time in Tibet that Dingle became interested in alternative religions. He befriended both Earnest Holmes, the founder of the Religious Science metaphysics movement, and Paramahansa Yogananda, the founder of the Self-Realization Fellowship that practised meditation — when their guru died his followers claimed that his body did not decay. For his part, Dingle went on to found The Institute of Mentalphysics in 1927, a spiritual teaching and retreat centre in the Southern California desert (designed by Frank Lloyd Wright) teaching his own pseudo-science, Mentalphysics, which was founded on breathing techniques and known by some adherents as "super yoga". Dingle, now calling himself a Reverend, claimed to have learnt these skills, which were designed to open the consciousness, clear the body's energy centres and reconnect the practitioners with their higher selves, in a Tibetan monastery. Detractors described it all as "enlightenment by mail order": Dingle did sell lessons successfully and profitably via the postal system. He carried on writing and published a series of books including *Breathing Your Way to Youth* (1942) that apparently worked for him as he lived into his nineties while also obviously enjoying himself: another book was called *The Art of Love Making*. A start in the old China press corps could clearly lead to some interesting career developments.

With the Russo-Japanese War over, for many foreigners China started to feel cosy again after the danger of the Boxers had seemingly passed. Consequently, after the first decade of the twentieth century, most didn't realise it, few expected it and nobody predicted it accurately, but China was on the cusp of fundamental and radical change.

5
Writing in a Republic — Printing What They Damn Well Liked

"The Empire was not overthrown. It crumbled away.
We watched the afterglow, where the sun had set."

Italian diplomat and author Daniele Varè

"Those newspapers under British ownership carry nothing but advertising on the first two or three pages, followed by several pages of solid news and "leaders" (editorials), these being followed in turn by more pages of solid advertising…The news is briefly told and without guiding headlines to attract the reader…It is all very staid and austere and appears dull at first glance; only upon closer examination does the influence of such dailies become apparent."

J. W. Sanger, US trade commissioner on
the newspapers of the China coast

China for the Chinese

China was changing, and the Chinese were changing and, though generally considered hopelessly sclerotic, some elements in the imperial court were also changing. The dynasty was limping to its death but some tried desperately to modernise it in an ultimately futile attempt at last-minute regime survival. Primary among these men was His Excellency Taotai Yuen-cham Tong, better known as Y. C. Tong, who was one of the first Chinese graduates of Columbia University. Tong wanted to get out the message of his progressive faction within the court to create a channel of communication and understanding with the Western powers. To this end, he founded an English-language periodical called *The National Review*. His partner in this venture was Captain Walter Kirton, an Englishman who had seen action in South Africa and then worked as a correspondent during the Russo-Japanese War. He returned to China to work with Tong in the belief that promoting the court's progressive faction was the only way to save it from Japanese encroachment.

Kirton became co-proprietor and managing editor of the *Review* and also a major personal mouthpiece for the progressive elements in the imperial court. He, rather hopefully, claimed the *Review* had a circulation of 5,000. Tong contributed regularly and the paper's banner slogan was "China for the Chinese". Both the *Review* and Tong were to survive the Nationalist revolution of 1911 and continue publishing for some time, but Kirton was to disappear from history while Tong went on to be one of the directors of the highly influential *China Press* newspaper in Shanghai.

As China changed by 1910, the China coast press was also changing. Journalists such as the young Francis Nichols who came to China at the turn of the century to work for New York's *Christian Herald* were penetrating the interior of the country for stories. Nichols bypassed Beijing and Shanghai entirely, heading inland to report on the efforts of missionaries in the interior and the state of the country where few reporters went at the time. In the main settlements, foreign papers were getting more influential and becoming established organs of record of foreign life in China. Hong Kong was still somewhat wilder than it was to become when a certain late Victorian paternalism and development settled over it — the *China Mail* quite regularly ran reports of roaming tigers menacing farmers in the New Territories and the brothels of white prostitutes which Kipling had once turned his nose up at when visiting the colony were still busy. Beijing mostly remained home to the diplomatic community wherever the Chinese capital officially moved over the following decades, and its newspapers continued to reflect the rather stodgy day-to-day business of tracking the imperial court and helping the diplomatic community to make sense of it. A new newspaper called *Chinese Public Opinion*, launched in 1908, sought to perform just this task, declaring in its inaugural editorial:

> It may be thought by some that China is flooded with a superfluity of journalism but we can claim a separate and unique niche, for it is our privilege to put before the world in a foreign tongue the Chinese viewpoint of affairs of the day.[1]

The proprietors were correct; there was "a superfluity of journalism" and the paper didn't last long. It was soon amalgamated into the somewhat general *Peking Daily News* as readers sought more than just the court's views and, on a more mundane business level, the paper doubled its price in a matter of months rather deterring readers.

Tianjin and Guangzhou remained major centres of trade but other treaty ports had already seen their brief glory days pass and their importance diminish significantly. The successful introduction of tea-planting in Ceylon and India marginalised the importance of Fuzhou and Jiujiang and their local English-language presses shrivelled in importance as the foreign community ebbed away on the changing tides of trade. Xiamen and Shantou were still pleasant enough places to live but they were also shrinking in stature as foreign ports of interest as their tea-shipping role dwindled and the Chinese came to dominate local trade, reducing the opportunities for foreigners. At the same time Ningbo was suffering from being in the shadow of nearby Shanghai and Yantai declined as Qingdao grew in importance. However, most treaty ports kept small English-language newspapers going. For example, the *Chefoo Daily News* in Yantai survived due to a mix of contributors which included businessmen, bored housewives and missionaries. Shanghai, with its unique meeting of East and West in the International Settlement and Frenchtown, was now overshadowing all the other treaty ports. The foreign geography of China was changing even though most Englishmen, and notably people such as G. E. Morrison, still saw China and foreign interests through the prism of trade, colonialism and the supremacy of the British Empire.

Newspapers were a part of this global colonial and imperial system of acquiring and dispersing knowledge in order to enforce control. The colonial expansion of Britain, France and Japan and, to a lesser extent, Germany, America, Russia and other nations meant more newspapers. However, in Shanghai, as a new Nationalist China emerged, it was a somewhat different story. The International Settlement was growing rapidly, both in terms of its foreign population and its wealth, and also crucially in terms of its cosmopolitanism. This brought a host of new players into the local foreign media, including an increased presence for the French with the *Journal de Shanghai*, the expansion of *L'Echo de Chine* to include a sister paper *L'Echo de Tientsin* in Tianjin, and the start of a Russian language media with the likes of *Slovo* and *Shanghai Zaria*. There was also a growing number of magazines and publications catering for visitors to the city and those Shangailanders trying to keep up with the social scene — *Social Shanghai* covered nothing except arrivals/departures, history, fashions and news from the growing number of clubs and societies in the city. However, it was the upstart and precocious Americans, with a growing awareness of their national and international "Manifest Destiny", who were to come out of the shadows, get a whole new set of presses rolling and change the face of the China coast press, both in terms of the publications people read and the men and women who wrote them.

Printing What They Damn Well Liked — The *China Press*

The American Thomas Franklin Fairfax Millard, the founder and first editor of the *China Press* in Shanghai, was once asked what he thought was fit to print in his new paper, to which he gave a rather blunt but perhaps characteristically American reply: "... anything I damn well like ...".[2] This certainly wasn't the sort of thing editors of the *North-China Daily News* or the other British newspapers in China ever said. In fact, Millard was anything but blunt normally. Indeed, he was long regarded as one of the most dapper and sophisticated chaps about town. He lived in the Astor House Hotel, and was known for his snappy dress sense, Missouri accent, abilities on the dance floor and quick temper, as well as his established anti-colonial and anti-imperialist views. However, as regards press freedom, he chose not to mince his words. When a young J. B. Powell first met the life-long bachelor Millard in 1917 he described him as: "... a short, slender man weighing perhaps 125 pounds and dressed so perfectly that I wondered how he would be able to sit down without wrinkling his immaculate suit".[3]

The launching of two publications backed and conceived by Millard — the *China Press* in August 1911 and his own more personal vehicle *Millard's Review* in June 1917 — was to have a profound and lasting effect on the foreign press of the China coast. Millard started out as a drama critic in the 1890s before making his name by switching tack and covering the Boer War from the side of the South African Dutch whose cause he supported. Somewhere along the way, he picked up a serious facial scar and managed to annoy Lord Kitchener so much that the British commander had him expelled from Africa, which meant that Millard ever after disliked the British and their empire. He had come to China to report the aftermath of the Boxer rebellion for the *New York Herald* and the Russo-Japanese War, and then stayed on and established the *Press* and his *Review*. Though it came after the launch of the *Press*, *Millard's Review*, a weekly based in Shanghai, was in many ways the foremost independent journal of events and politics in China to have appeared so far — independent in that the early issues were little more than very long and opinionated (though informed) editorials from the proprietor on the state of China. Described by J. W. Sanger of the US State Department in 1921 as "aggressively American", the *Review* covered everything to do with China and awarded several annual prizes for an "authoritative list of books which might serve as a foundation for a library dealing with all phases of Chinese life, art, trade, finance, customs, politics, international relations and history". Later this authoritative list was renamed the "five-foot shelf" and was judged annually by: Dr. Wu Ting-fang, the former Chinese minister to America and a former premier of China; Julean Arnold, the long-serving American commercial attaché in China; and Dr. F. L. Hawks-Pott, the president of the prestigious St. John's University in Shanghai.

The judges' panel for Millard's "five-foot shelf" tells the story of his own approach to China. As a free-thinking American with close contact to senior Chinese officials such as Dr. Wu from an early stage, Millard was also highly regarded in America as an expert on Chinese affairs. Following the Russo-Japanese War, he had travelled round America with the cameraman and projectionist Fred Ackerman as they combined images and impressions in a joint speaking tour with an accompanying photographic show, which was one of the first of its kind. He was also a prolific writer on Chinese affairs, with his books including *Our Eastern Question* (1916) which presented a strong argument on the present and future inter-connected relations of China, Japan and America and *The End of Exterritoriality in China* in 1931 which was considered a definitive statement on the subject at the time.[4]

After Millard moved on to become an adviser to the Nationalist Chinese government in Washington, John Benjamin Powell, his former pupil at the Missouri University School of Journalism, took over. Powell, known to most people as simply "J. B.", became the chief editor of *Millard's Review* and then bought it outright in 1922 when Millard left. Powell changed the name to *The Weekly Review of the Far East* and then finally *The China Weekly Review*, which continued for several more decades before being suppressed by the Japanese. The erudite and soft-spoken Powell was from the start a first stop for many young foreign would-be journalists (mostly Americans) turning up in Shanghai, including a young Edgar Snow, a fellow Missourian, fresh off the boat from the *Kansas City Star*.

Millard's other great creation, the *China Press,* was a more general newspaper but it still aimed to change the perception of Shanghai as being cut off from the daily events in a rapidly changing China. However, resistance to the idea was strong among the local Shanghai press corps, most of whom thought Shanghai was hardly worth commenting on and felt the same about Beijing too. The Scottish journalist Richard Wood had served his apprenticeship on the *Dundee Advertiser* before coming to China in 1907 to work for the *Shanghai Mercury* and then switching over to the *North-China Daily News* around 1911. He told the newly arrived Carl Crow, who had been hired by Millard from the *Fort Worth Star-Telegram* in the summer of 1911 to help launch the *Press*: "Most of them [*the Qing court*] live in Peking and telegraph tolls are high". Wood was trying to explain to Crow why Shanghai reporters expended little effort on covering events in Beijing. When news had to be telegraphed overseas, the tolls became even higher.

The result was that the wiremen usually only sent the bare bones, the necessary details, while editors in far-flung newsrooms added the background and colour, and explained and analysed the facts. Without them, the readers of the *Times* would never have thought Morrison such a great interpreter of China. These people are largely lost to history — salaried employees who didn't get by-lines and didn't write their memoirs. They got the despatches, fleshed them out and went home to the suburbs for tea at 5 p.m.

However, despite high tolls, the telegraph system revolutionised newsgathering and dissemination from China. Missourian Carl Crow had a sideline setting up the United Press's (UPI, known as "Scripps Howard" at the time) first China bureau and acting as its correspondent. He timed his arrival well. Not only did the Qing dynasty's collapse shortly after provide him with a world-class story to start his career as a China Hand but the global telegraph network was expanding fast, particularly the network that linked the disparate British Empire with London. As Simon Winchester commented: "The British saw cables as the vital synapses of the Imperial nervous system".[5] UPI was one of several wire services operating out of Shanghai, and often with Beijing bureaus too, including Reuters, the earliest wire service, which had first established itself in the Far East as early as 1872. A few maintained stringers in Guangzhou and Tianjin as well. They could operate as the British submarine cables already extended from Singapore to Hong Kong and then under the sea and up the coast to Shanghai. The British were typically paranoid about control of their cables and, rather than place them on Chinese soil, built a relay station on a hulk and then moored it in the middle of the Min River near Fuzhou to ensure total control. Still, for Crow and others, sending cables to the wire services had to remain a sideline rather than a full-time occupation, as wage rates were very low (between $5 and $20 per article in the mid-1920s), and there were no guarantees that all articles sent would be used. If they weren't used, the stringers weren't paid.

The *China Press* was an upstart, as this was still the period of British press supremacy, before the Great War when British newspapers could still seriously run a headline "Fog in English Channel — Continent Isolated". Millard was anti-isolation and started the *Press* partly with the vision that the paper should promote contact between the foreign community and the Chinese. He went as far as to install several prominent Chinese on the paper's board of directors and actively sought to promote China stories to the front pages, adopting the adage that news about China should be treated in the same way as the big New York papers covered US news.

Like others who came into close contact with Millard, Carl Crow, virtually immediately after arriving in Shanghai, fast adopted his stance of combining a generally anti-imperialist pro-Chinese view of China with a deep belief in

America's Manifest Destiny and the "Open Door" policy towards China that saw it as America's right to exploit a free market, a theory that often trod on the toes of the Great Powers who sought to exploit their personal trade privileges for themselves. Prior to coming to the East, Crow had never really evinced any great opinions on China, the Chinese or the Far East. His pre-China journalism, on the *Columbia-Missouri Herald* and *Fort Worth Star-Telegram*, had certainly tended to champion the underdog — the pioneer against the large landowner or the citizen against the rampant town planner — in a classic American position of support for the little guy. Powell also quickly adopted Millard's pro-Chinese views and general support for the underdog. When he arrived in Shanghai in 1917, he had no experience of Asia, having come directly from Hannibal, Missouri. He spent the next 25 years in Shanghai and became perhaps the best-known journalist of his generation in China and the undisputed doyen of the inter-war foreign press corps. Like Crow before him, Powell had been recruited after he had received a cable from Millard calling for a recent journalism graduate to be sent. To say they were fresh off the boat would be an understatement; Powell had never even seen a transoceanic telegram when he received Millard's, and Crow had no idea whether he should sail across the Atlantic or Pacific from Texas to reach Shanghai. Both the "owlish-looking" and usually bespectacled Powell, who was always seen "smoking a corncob pipe" and was heavily involved in the local Good Roads Committee, and the rather overweight and genial Crow were to become legendary China Hands thanks to Millard.[6]

With his wariness of the motives of the European Great Powers and distrust of Japanese ambitions towards China, Millard was the role model and mentor for a host of Western journalists that were to act as advocates for China, as later were Crow and especially Powell. They all had different styles: Millard was reasonably academic and precise in his advocacy of China while Crow developed a more personal touch in his writing style and Powell became a wide-ranging expert on many things China-related. Peter Rand, an authority on the history of China reporting, said of Millard: "He wanted to influence American policy ...", to be precise influence it towards a pro-China and anti-Japanese stance.[7] The work of Millard, Crow and Powell was almost universally reproduced in translated form in the Chinese press in Shanghai.

Millard also began a tradition of the American reporter in China as being influential back home, perhaps not to the level that Morrison had achieved in England but still important. Later American politicians were to listen closely to the advice of many American reporters like Crow and Powell but Millard had, virtually from the start of his China sojourn, been influential and been consulted by America's great and good, up to and including President Teddy Roosevelt.

The three also became the nucleus of "Show Me" state journalists that became known as the "Missouri News Colony", or the "Missouri Mafia", in the Far East, or (as the British hacks dubbed them) the "Corncob Cowboys" — an appellation the Missourians surprisingly didn't like much. They were one of the recognised groups of foreign journalists congregating in Shanghai, and to a lesser extent Beijing, before the First World War that included the large British contingent of "Fleet Street Transplants" and a smaller caucus of Australians. Millard had founded the *Press* with Benjamin "B. W." Fleisher, another Missourian who went on to establish the *Japan Advertiser* in Yokohama in 1909, where Crow and several other Colony members were later to work. The *Press* remained a major employer of young American journalists. It was the first port of call for a young Harold Isaacs, the son of a New York real estate magnate who was later headhunted by the left-leaning Agnes Smedley to work on the communist-funded *China Forum* and later described by the judge of the American court in China as an "obnoxious young Bolshevik".

From the start, the *China Press* broke the mould of English-language newspapers on the China coast. Many of the initial journalists were, like Crow, not dyed in the wool China Hands but neophytes from America and not subject to the established British-style rules of the Shanghai press. In design terms, the *Press* looked startlingly different to a 1911 Shanghai audience used to the English style of newspaper design with the front page filled with adverts. The *Press* believed in running news on the front page and hoped that the major news stories would be from China rather than England or the British Empire as was standard. The hard core of the established foreign press corps, the transplanted Fleet Street types, openly mocked Millard's ambitions and both Millard and Crow recalled that late at night when news was slow they had their own severe doubts about whether the enterprise would work. It seemed the reading public agreed with them as initially sales were sluggish. However, history was on the side of the *Press* and its founding team. It was to be a real revolution that brought the *China Press* to readers' attention and China to the front pages of the world's newspapers too.

Rebels and Revolution

Though the Americans had burst upon the scene with their new concepts, designs and energy, they were far from getting it all their own way. The *North China Herald* still held sway and the paper had now been in business continuously for over 60 years. Rather than cower in the face of the new competition from the *China Press*, the paper struck back with the appointment of O. M. Green as editor. He was perhaps the paper's most strident and opinionated (some would say hardline) leader in its history and was to serve as editor through to 1930 and remain active in writing about China until after the Second World War. Green was a forceful apologist for the British position in Shanghai and continued his advocacy of British superiority long after he left the paper and the city.

Against this entrenched British presence, the outbreak of the 1911 revolution saved the *Press*. In general everyone got the news wrong. Shanghai panicked when tales of a massacre in Nanjing filled the papers, when in fact it had been in Hankou. Carl Crow dashed up to Nanjing to find a gin-sodden stringer in an apologetic mood because of his gaff. When the troop garrison at Hankou revolted, sparking the Nationalist revolution, Millard and Crow dithered about whether to describe it as a "minor revolt" or a "revolution". Rebellions happened frequently and were usually put down quickly, so the tendency was not to exaggerate for fear of looking foolish later when everything came to nought. Eventually they decided this was the real deal and despatched Crow by steamer up the Yangtze to Hankou.

Their timing and connections were perfect and the *Press* managed to scoop all the other foreign publications with news of the rebellion, the fall of the Qing and the rise to power of Dr. Sun Yat-sen. The *Press* won out as from the start of the paper Millard had appointed the highly-connected Dr. Wu Ting-fang to the board. Dr. Wu smoothed Crow's passage, introduced him around and translated for him. When Dr. Wu was appointed head of the Nationalist delegation to the meeting to sort out the terms for the dissolution of the Qing dynasty, the *Press*'s access only improved. When he was appointed minister of foreign affairs in the first Nationalist government, once again the *Press* had unparalleled access; and from the moment Sun Yat-sen arrived back in China to lead the take-over of power the *Press* had access to him via Dr. Wu. This insider position meant that on 4 January 1912 the *Press* was the first English-language publication to publish a summary of Dr. Sun's first proclamation in which the provisional president explained his plans for the government and then again the formal proclamation on 6 January that announced the establishment of a republic in China.

The *Press* continued to get the scoops throughout the first months of the new government, such as the decision to inaugurate the new capital in Nanjing, the first in-depth interview with Dr. Sun and the formation of a republican army. The paper had by far the best team covering the revolution: as well as Crow, Edwin Dingle was commenting in the paper in a regular column which tracked the progress of events. As Crow managed to get scoops on statements from Sun and Wu, Dingle in Nanjing secured scoops from one of the leaders of the Wuhan Garrison revolt, General Li Yuanhong. Of course, Crow and the *China Press* weren't the only members of the foreign press corps covering the revolution. Richard "Dick" Wood, who had set Crow straight about how things worked in the China coast press when he'd first arrived, was covering the engagements between rebels and imperial troops around Nanjing. He filed thrilling reports from armoured troop trains travelling back to Shanghai. Also, Bill Donald was covering the story as the *New York Herald*'s China correspondent. The *Herald* was the only US paper to maintain a full-time reporter, rather than a stringer, in China at the time and had a reputation for international coverage.

But the Republic's honeymoon didn't last long. The rise of China's "strongman" Yuan Shih-kai, his ousting of Dr. Sun and his pretence to a republican throne that soon emerged as more of a military dictatorship saw the China coast English-language media by and large revealing its true political colours. While the pro-Sun *China Press* was extremely wary of Yuan, the British-controlled papers showed their visceral distrust of republicanism and anything that rocked the status quo. To them, Yuan's rise marked the end of the brief republican experiment, the possible establishment of a new dynasty and all a jolly good thing too in their general opinion — a strong man was needed, don't you know. The *North-China Daily News* declared in 1912:

> Republicanism in China has been tried and found wanting. The Mercantile classes and the gentry of China are weary of it. A coup d'état should be brought off, for we all know that nothing succeeds like success.

A large dose of wishful thinking was going on here. It was not at all apparent that either the Chinese mercantile classes, all the gentry or the Chinese masses were fed up with republicanism, and wanted Yuan or his sort of heavy-handed leadership; and rather than bringing any restoration of order, Yuan moved towards an ever more dictatorial style of government, with what appeared to be daily increases in ermine and braid and imperial-style celebrations.

Despite being generally anti-republican, the British-controlled press was not very keen on Yuan personally. It raised quite a few eyebrows therefore when Morrison of Peking became Yuan's personal adviser, which showed once again his grossly overrated reputation for interpreting events in China. Morrison's original contract with Yuan stipulated a five-year term for his post, but China's strongman was not to last that long. As he increasingly adopted the trappings of a new emperor, China's so-called "Second Revolution" broke out when some provincial warlords and military commanders challenged Yuan in July 1913. Warlord after warlord seized territory and the initiative flowed away from Yuan. By June 1916 the short, squat Yuan, referred to by some in the press as "China's Machiavelli", was relying increasingly on military dictate to govern China, had lost any popularity he had with the people and then died in his bed of natural causes. Sun was recalled to power but China had already descended into the chaotic warlord period that lasted for the next couple of decades, forcing the Nationalists to reassert control across the country by force later. Morrison had backed the wrong horse and looked ridiculous to many in the foreign press corps for his bad choice of boss. It was effectively the end of Morrison of Peking being influential in Chinese affairs.

Eyes West — The First World War

Despite the Nationalist revolution and the excitement over the rise and fall of Yuan and then Sun's return, the onset of the First World War saw foreign newspapers lose interest in China while the local foreign press also naturally concentrated on events in Europe as invariably increasingly demanded by their readers. Things were so altered by the war that the *Hongkong Telegraph* even shortened its coverage of horse racing, its major selling point in many readers' eyes, to give more coverage to the war in Europe.

One outcome of the onset of war was that many German-owned newspapers were closed. The *Hankow Daily News*, published in English but edited by a German, was shut as were the German newspapers in Qingdao as the Japanese occupied the German-controlled treaty port. The *Ostasiatischer Lloyd*, the largest German paper in China, had problems and its editors launched another daily, the *Deutsche Zeitung fr China*. When China entered the war in 1917 on the Allied side, the German press was totally suppressed. At the onset of the conflict the Germans responded by buying an interest in other papers. The *Times* reported that German buyers had acquired the *Peking Gazette* in October 1914, which meant that the nearest wholly British-owned newspaper to Beijing was now in Tianjin.

During the war locally there were also several smaller and often satirical publications. *The War* was published three times a week in English and found both Chinese and foreign readers, with most of the news coming from Germany via America. There was also *Wau Wau*, a Shanghai-based satirical weekly modelled on the Munich paper *Simplicissimus*, a bright, graphic-heavy and liberal-intellectual publication which supported Germany.

The war also forced the traditional united front by the foreign powers in China to fracture. Dr. Gilbert Reid, the New York-born editor of the *Peking Post* that aimed squarely at the foreigner market (its front page always carried adverts including a regular one that stated simply, but to the relief of many a homesick ex-pat presumably: "Just Arrived — Cheese") was called before the American

Court in Shanghai for allegedly libelling President Wilson. The American diplomatic authorities also threatened Reid with prosecution in America if he continued to edit the German-funded and politically inclined *Post*. It was true that Reid had penned an editorial praising Germany and critical of America's entry into the war in the summer of 1917 which had led to a stern letter from Dr. Paul Reinsch, the American minister in China, reminding Reid that the US had broken diplomatic ties with the Kaiser. Reid, who was also a clergyman and self-taught in Chinese, was well known in Beijing. Since his arrival in 1882, he had written a well-received book on China and also had the dubious honour of being the only American to have been wounded in the Siege of the Legations, having been shot in the leg. He continued to be a thorn in the side of the Americans and the British. The latter formally complained to the Chinese government when it publicly celebrated Reid's 60th birthday despite his being declared *persona non grata* by the Allied Powers, which technically should have included China. Eventually the American Court deported him to Manila for the duration.

For the foreign correspondents, wiremen and stringers in China, the war years were frustrating. They felt more than ever that they were living in a remote outpost, and some like Dick Wood enlisted and left China for the trenches of Europe. He joined the Black Watch, where as Captain Wood, he won the Distinguished Conduct Medal, Military Cross and the Military Medal, but he was twice injured and never fully recovered from his wounds. Later Wood put his experiences in Nanjing in 1911 and Europe in 1914–18 to good use by tracking the various warlord battles around the country and sizing up the relative strength and merits of their opposing forces for the readers of the *North-China Daily News*. However, nothing could shift the growing and incessant carnage in the European trenches from the front pages. Western readers had temporarily lost interest in China and it would not return until the bloodletting in Europe was over.

The Mandarin of Journalists — The Most Influential Newspaper North of Shanghai

In the initial months of the Great War, the political line of those English-language papers published in the treaty ports was often very different from the spin the readers in Europe were receiving. The fact was that, for many treaty porters, the war in Europe initially seemed quite distant. The deaths and numerous personal tragedies were yet to hit home, and the general enormity of the war and the scale of the slaughter was yet to sink in and absorb people totally as no other world event had in living memory. This was still the period when people believed that it would all be over by Christmas. In Tianjin the British community still patronised and enjoyed the excellent ice creams at Kiesslings on Victoria Road (soon to be optimistically renamed Woodrow Wilson Street) and coffee at Bader's Café, both German-run institutions in the city's German Concession. When the *Peking and Tientsin Times* published articles about the early months of the war, the paper's editor received a number of letters from its British readers complaining about his overtly anti-German tone. For many in Tianjin and Beijing, the threatened and much rumoured resurgence of the anti-foreigner White Lotus Society and a possible Boxer revival were perceived as more real threats to all foreigners than Germany and the Germans. For a while at least, until the propaganda kicked in and the horror of the war became too obvious to ignore, the foreign community banded together as it traditionally had — against threats from China and the Chinese, rather than from each other.

Since its creation as a treaty port, Tianjin had enjoyed a flourishing English-language press. Apart from the Beijing newspapers, there was little competition north of Shanghai: *The Chinese Times* had been launched in 1886 in Tianjin but it was a famously boring read. Alexander Michie, a man whose entire life was connected with the China trade and who was an intrepid traveller across China, edited the paper throughout the 1890s while also acting as the local agent for Jardine Matheson. He hired an interesting range of correspondents, including Charles Stewart Addis who became one of the first Western bankers to live in Beijing when he was posted there as acting agent for the Hong Kong and Shanghai Banking Corporation. Addis opted to continue his banking career over pursuing journalism and eventually became the director of the Bank of England, which probably indicates he made the right choice. However, it was to be the *Peking and Tientsin Times* launched in 1894 that was to become the most famous newspaper in Tianjin and second only in China to the *North-China Daily News* in reputation and stature. The paper lasted until the 1930s and was generally regarded as the most influential English-language paper north of Shanghai, with a circulation of about 1,000 daily. The paper's inaugural edition stated:

> The difficulty of establishing an acceptable newspaper for Western readers in this part of the world, is undoubtedly great ... The foreign communities are small and scattered, with means of intercommunication hardly equal to those which existed in Europe three centuries ago. In the interior there are no posts, either to convey news or by which to distribute it when printed ... We bring these facts to the minds of our readers in order to dispose them to deal leniently with the *Peking and Tientsin Times* as a vehicle of what we Westerners understand by "news".[8]

Henry George Wandesforde ("H. G. W.") Woodhead had arrived in China in 1902 and previously been the editor of the *Peking Daily News* (which included the old *Chinese Public Opinion*) whose header stated "Impartial But Patriotic" and always started with the latest imperial edicts. Woodhead was to rule the roost at the *Peking and Tientsin Times* as well as becoming the most well-known and influential foreigner in Tianjin for several decades. The paper invariably reflected his strident opinions on China and the world and from the start promised to "… be essentially British", a virtue Woodhead staunchly upheld.[9] Much later, in 1936, *Time* magazine described him as "hard hitting" and "suave", though the *China Weekly Review* opted for "die-hard", which was not meant in an overly complimentary way.[10] He was a long-time friend of former *Times* war correspondent Henry Thurburn Montague Bell, who had covered the Boer War and then became a long-standing editor of the *North China Herald* and the *North-China Daily News*. He was also a prolific editorialist, was well known as a China Hand in Beijing, Shanghai and Tianjin and wrote the 1929 book *Extraterritoriality In China: The Case Against Abolition*, which was really just a collection of his articles expressing his trenchant views on the subject from the paper. This title also pretty much summed up Woodhead's political attitude to both China and the Chinese which accounted for the uncomplimentary opinions of people like Powell who were anti-extraterritoriality. H. T. Montague Bell was also well connected in London due to his being the brother-in-law of the editor-in-chief of the *Times*.

In the 1920s Woodhead launched a campaign to try to stop Britain from spending its Boxer Indemnity monies (the reparations forcibly paid by the Chinese government to Britain and other foreign powers after the Siege of the Legations) on promoting education in China as he believed that the schools and colleges of the country were little more than breeding grounds for revolutionaries and anti-foreign, anti-extraterritoriality sentiment. When it was reported that a Chinese mob had stormed the British Concession in Hankou and that the British government had seemingly caved in and handed the territory back to China, Woodhead fumed that "The principle of extraterritoriality is at stake" and urged Britain to remember the Treaty of Tianjin that guaranteed the treaty ports system and to oppose the government.[11] On another occasion, he declared that Britain should have conquered China rather than India in order to ensure the country was well run. He regularly fulminated against America for its "Open Door" trade policy towards China which, he believed, would undermine Britain's "Most Favoured Nation" status — a status it has to be said which had been forced at gunpoint on the Chinese. Brian Power, a young boy in Tianjin at the time recalled: "When Woodhead spoke Washington trembled … By the time Woodhead's outbursts reached England, Whitehall, too, must have trembled".

This was probably overestimating Woodhead's influence somewhat but, on the other hand, he was equally tough in criticising many foreign businessmen, accusing them of becoming wealthy off the back of child labour and low wages. He also had a major influence on Tianjin's civic life. He had urged the formation of the Watch Committee, an ad hoc group that sought to patrol and protect the foreign concessions, and he was a founding member of the Tientsin Club, which provided him with a lavish send-off dinner when he finally left the city.

Woodhead remained a vibrant and dedicated editorialist, moving on in the 1930s to be an editorial associate of the *Shanghai Evening Post and Mercury* and editor (from 1934) of the quarterly journal *Oriental Affairs*. Power recalled that foreigners in the city were "stunned" when Woodhead announced his departure to Shanghai. Tributes to the great editor, which resembled obituaries, poured into the paper. Power believed that, despite his "Bully Pulpit-style" of editorialising, Woodhead's lasting impression on Tianjin was his defence of the rights of car drivers. He accused the Chinese of being "primitive" for opposing the rise of the car. It seems that an unresolved incident between Woodhead and a rickshaw puller after a collision was the cause of his repeated diatribes against Chinese car drivers.

Woodhead and the *Times* did provide work for some young reporters who would later become better known. In 1921 a young Owen Lattimore passed through. His parents were living in Tianjin but were about to move back to America. Lattimore met Woodhead who offered him a job at the paper which the young American accepted as he thought it would give him an opportunity to develop his literary interests. However, he was to be disappointed as he was given few opportunities to investigate and write stories of his own, spending most of his time proofreading. He lasted a year before returning to work for his old employers, the traders Arnhold and Company, on a larger salary and at their Tianjin branch before becoming one of America's foremost China Hands and experts on Mongolia. After Lattimore, a young Israel "Eppie" Epstein, later to become a senior member of the Communist Party of China and remain in Beijing supporting Mao and the revolution, started his journalistic career on the paper in the 1930s when he was barely 15 years old. Epstein had been born in Poland but his family escaped from the Russian Revolution and fled to Tianjin where he attended American-run schools before becoming a cub reporter.

Woodhead appeared all-powerful in Tianjin between the wars, though he did have some competition. The *North China Commerce* newspaper was established in 1920 as an English-run weekly but didn't last long while the American-owned *North China Star* was also published in Tianjin. Ohio-born Marshall Sprague graduated from Princeton with a degree in English and wanted to dedicate his life to writing and jazz. In 1933, he moved to Tianjin where his sister was living and got a job as a local reporter on the *North China Star*, which was still going strong as an "aggressive, newsy, and enterprising"[12] publication, which ensured that Woodhead didn't have the entire market to himself. Indeed, the American State Department estimated the paper's daily circulation in 1921 as 2,500, more than double Woodhead's *Peking and Tientsin Times*, but also noted that the *Star* was far less influential than Woodhead's paper which to men like Woodhead was what really counted.

Proliferating at the Fringes — News from Nearly Nowhere

New newspapers kept appearing along the China coast, though some lasted longer than others. Guangzhou's only surviving English-language daily, despite numerous attempted launches of competitors, was the *Canton Times* which, as well as serving the city's foreign community, was subscribed to by many republican-minded Chinese who could read English. The *Tsingtao Times* was the German Concession's only English newspaper and survived both the German occupation of Qingdao and most of the Japanese occupation too until full-scale war broke out in the late 1930s and it was closed. In the main, the paper kept out of the local political spats, preferring to cover the growth of amenities and the growing economic prosperity of the Shandong seaside resort.

Hankou had a small press that included the *Central China Post* while New Yorker Bruno Shaw was the founder and publisher of the better-known English-language daily *Hankow Herald*. He was a journalist in China throughout the 1920s and 1930s and was general manager of the small Trans-Pacific News Service, a Chinese information newswire he founded that reported on local affairs from the end of the First World War onwards as well as stringing for AP. The more remote press didn't pay well. For example, A. Cecil Taylor worked for the *Hankow Herald* but had to teach English to make ends meet, which was a common practice for inland journalists.

The missionaries who had done so much to pioneer the English-language press in China kept launching new papers. *The Chinese Recorder and Missionary Journal* was still alive but, perhaps in a move aimed at not alienating the less pious reading public, it changed its name to simply the *Chinese Recorder* in 1910 and lasted till 1939. Others remained more overtly religious, such as the *China Christian Advocate*, the official organ of the China section of the East Asia Central Conference of the Methodist Episcopal Church and of the China Mission of the Methodist Episcopal Church for South Shanghai. The *Advocate* was read wherever American Methodist missionaries were found in China (and there were a lot of them). Like many missionary papers, it was edited and staffed mostly by the missionaries themselves in their spare time. For instance, Lyman Hale supervised mission schools and churches in Wuhu, Nanjing and Shanghai in the inter-war period and, while stationed in Zhenjiang, served as mission supervisor and treasurer as well as the editor of the *Advocate*; and he also contributed articles about missionary life and activities to a range of papers, including the *Shanghai Times* and the *China Christian Conference Bulletin*. The *Advocate* dealt with matters spiritual in the widest sense, from reprinted sermons to articles detailing the changes in China during and after the fall of the Qing and the rise of the Republic. The missionaries remained a prolific bunch: a list of in-country stringers for the Shanghai, Beijing, Tianjin and Hong Kong papers reveals plenty of missionaries working as occasional correspondents.

Journalists were clearly starting to become involved in politics, their communities and the running of the treaty ports. J. O. P. Bland had been secretary of the SMC between 1896 and 1906 before being hired by the *Times* and he later caused a ruckus by arguing that the council had failed to retain its temporary control of the northern Chinese suburb of Zhabei during some riotous disturbances in 1913. The energetic J. B. Powell was later to become a scourge of the SMC's Good Roads Committee and also led demands for a clean-up of the dirty and malodorous Suzhou Creek, something that was not to happen for another 70 odd years. Newspapers also caused minor spats in Shanghailander society which reflected their growing role as social spaces. In 1918 Joseph Ezra, part of the rich and powerful Ezra family in Shanghai that was linked to the Sassoons and had interests in oil, property and construction, was summoned to court after having reportedly assaulted Gordious Nielson, the Danish proprietor of the *Shanghai Gazette* which had printed something Ezra didn't like much and took violent offence to.

Elsewhere consolidation was occurring. After having lampooned its launch in 1903, the *Hongkong Telegraph* was merged into the *South China Morning Post* in Hong Kong (where newspapers always appeared to be far more businesslike than in the treaty ports) when Jardine Matheson's wealthy Eurasian comprador Robert Hotung sold a controlling interest in the *Telegraph* to Dr. Joseph Whittlesey Noble in 1916. Noble, from Pennsylvania, was Hong Kong's second registered dentist who had been in practice in the colony since 1887, meaning that the *Post* held the dubious distinction of being the only newspaper in the world to be owned by a dentist.

Arthur de Carle Sowerby — Naturalist, Adventurer and Editor

If H. G. W. Woodhead ruled the roost in Tianjin, then a strong contender for his equivalent in Shanghai was Arthur de Carle Sowerby. Sowerby was a prolific author and the founder and editor of the *China Journal of Science and Arts*, which was usually known simply as the *China Journal*, in 1912. To readers of the *Journal*, he came across as a sinologist with a particular interest in the flora and fauna of China. But Sowerby was much more than just a birdwatcher with an interest in plants. Indeed, the *Journal* was viewed as an intellectual high point in the China coast media and continued to be highly regarded. For example, the great Cambridge sinologist Joseph Needham regularly referred to the publication when compiling his multi-volume and ground-breaking *Science and Civilisation in China* in the 1950s.

Sowerby had been born in Taiyuan, the capital of Shanxi province in 1885, where his father was a British Baptist missionary who later became the personal tutor to the two sons of Yuan Shih-kai. The Sowerbys were a family of naturalists, collectors, artists and publishers stretching back centuries in England, although Sowerby might not have been around at all if his father hadn't taken the wise decision (in hindsight) to take a furlough in England in 1900 when the Boxers killed most of the foreign missionaries in Shanxi. After attending Bristol University, running away to sea and sailing to Canada, he returned to China and began collecting specimens for the Taiyuan Natural History Museum. He then joined the staff of Tianjin's Anglo-Chinese College as a lecturer and curator of that city's Natural History Museum. He was also a member of an expedition to the Ordos Desert in southern Mongolia in 1907, where he collected mammals for London's Natural History Museum on an expedition organised by the Duke of Bedford; and he then joined American millionaire Robert Sterling Clark's 1908 expedition to Shanxi and Gansu. Thus began a long association between the heir to the Singer sewing machine fortune and Sowerby, with the multi-millionaire financing several collecting trips in China, and to Bali and Java, that included Sowerby and Roy Chapman Andrews, the man who found the Gobi Desert dinosaur eggs.

During the 1911 revolution, Sowerby led a foreign-organised relief mission to evacuate a British and a Swedish missionary in Xian who had been cut off by bandits, the despatches of which provided thrilling entertainment to the readers of the *North-China Daily News*. According to the account of one mission member, second lieutenant Denver-Jones, when they encountered the bandits: "We expected to be fired on at any moment and probably would have been had not Sowerby with his usual coolness and courage, ridden up to the muzzles of their guns and convinced them that we were on a peaceful errand. It was one of the bravest things I have ever seen". Sowerby then donned a regular British army outfit during the First World War when he served in France as a technical officer with the Chinese Labour Corps, the so-called "Coolie Corps", clearing the killing fields of the Somme. He rested up for a year in England after the war and then returned to Shanghai, though he found time to write his five-volume *magnum opus*, *The Naturalist in Manchuria* (1922).

In between these adventures, he also found time to correspond with Morrison of Peking and to write over half a dozen books to make some extra money. After the war he settled in Shanghai and established the *China Journal*, which he edited until 1941, contributing a wealth of articles, sketches, zoological illustrations and photographs to the well-regarded publication. The *Journal* was co-founded with the enterprising missionary and newspaperman John Ferguson who edited the magazine with Sowerby for many years from offices on Shanghai's Museum Road next to the offices of the Royal Asiatic Society's Shanghai branch, of which Sowerby was a leading member. After Ferguson's death, Sowerby continued as advisory editor with Bruno Kroker as the editor. The *Journal* covered a multitude of subjects, from Sowerby's articles on the nature of China and gardening columns to business and engineering news. Contributors were equally many and varied and far too numerous to list, but they were invariably of a high calibre and experts in their fields, but with a popular touch in their writing. Typical of the type Sowerby recruited was Stuart Lillico, the long-time editor of the somewhat obscure *Hawaiian Shell News*, who perhaps typifies the sort of arcane and rather specialised people Sowerby liked. However, though having an intimate knowledge of molluscs which Sowerby thought Shanghailanders should share, Lillico had also written a popular travel guide to Asia. With this sort of twin ability to be both highly specific and also to write for a wider audience, he was the *Journal*'s perfect contributor, writing as easily and as knowledgably about shells as he did about Tibetan Lamas and Singapore's architecture.

Sowerby was very political. He was a sniper for the SVC during the Shanghai riots of 1925. He had orders not to shoot Chinese rioters but rather to pick off any policemen who were seen to be wavering on the line. In the end, all stood firm and he never needed to pull the trigger. He was also seriously right-wing and acted as a replacement leader of the Shanghai *Fascisti* for a time and became a committee member of the British Residents' Association, which had been formed in 1931 to represent British Shanghailander interests against the SMC, and to lobby against any reforms to the extraterritoriality laws. He stood on this platform in the 1932 SMC election, which brought him into conflict with those of a more liberal position such as J. B. Powell. This earned Powell the dislike of Sowerby. Though rather reactionary politically, he was also seen by many as socially a bit radical — he married three times in addition to constant rumours that he had had a number of children by a Chinese woman in Shanxi.

Though they supported different causes, the likes of Millard, Crow, Powell and Sowerby were all foreign journalists in China who came to identify themselves with Chinese causes and sensibilities of one kind or another. Before the Nationalist revolution, the vast majority of writers and correspondents in China had seen the Middle Kingdom and the Orient as "other" and a region and culture that needed to be "enlightened" by the West. However, 1911 marked a significant break from this period, with Millard, Crow, Powell and others starting a process of identification and understanding with the Chinese Republic and many, such as Woodhead and Sowerby, resolutely resisting change and staunchly defending concepts such as extraterritoriality. After the First World War there was no longer a uniform template for the typical member of the China press corps.

The Qing were officially gone, and only the remnants of the imperial family left isolated and bereft in the Forbidden City (apart from a healthy annual stipend from the new government). Yuan Shih-kai was dead and numerous warlords were jockeying for position across the country, but in the wake of the First World War the masses were to make their voices heard on the streets and journalists found themselves engaged personally in the intense mass struggles that were shaping the new nation.

Elijah Coleman Bridgman (1801–1861)

Karl Gützlaff (1803–1851)

Robert Morrison (1782–1834)

William Milne (1785–1822)

1. The Men of God and the *Chinese Repository*.

2. Morrison of Peking outside his house in Beijing.

3. Tom Millard — the most prominent and knowledgeable of the Missouri News Colony in Shanghai who found a host of Missourians jobs on the newspapers of the China coast.

4. Arthur de Carle Sowerby and his wife Alice photographed in 1917. His *China Journal of Science and Arts* was a highly respected Shanghai publication for decades.

5. The original *North-China Daily News and Herald* offices that housed the papers until 1921 when a yet more splendid building was constructed that quickly became known as the "Old Lady of the Bund".

1850-1924

N**O OTHER JOURNALS** attempt such a complete presentation of all phases of contemporary life in China.

Exclusive contributions from special correspondents in practically every city and town of importance in China.

NORTH-CHINA DAILY NEWS

NORTH-CHINA HERALD

SHANGHAI

6. The British-controlled *North-China Daily News* was, for a century, the most powerful English language newspaper in Asia.

7. The press corps were also part of the wider foreign community. Here H.G.W. Woodhead (back row far left) and W.V. Pennell (second row fourth from left) of the *Peking and Tientsin Times* are photographed at the 1934 Parents vs Tientsin Grammar School pupils annual cricket match.

NOW READY
CHINA YEAR BOOK,
1924-5

Edited by

H. G. W. WOODHEAD, C.B.E.

PRICE $15.00

The new Issue of about 1,200 pages, contains the following Chapters :

1. Area and Population
2. Geography
3. Geology
4. Fauna
5. Flora, Forestry and Reforestation
6. Climate and Meteorology
7. Mines and Minerals
8. People and Language
9. Manufactures
10. Education
11. Public Justice (With Translation of Regulations Relating to Criminal Procedure)
12. River Improvement and Harbour Works.
13. Communications—Railways
14. Communications—Post Office, Telegraphs, Wireless Telegraphy
15. Shipping
16. Chinese Customs Tariff
17. Customs Revenue and Trade Statistics
18. Products—General Pastoral and Agricultural, including Exports
19. Opium
20. Greater China—Mongolia, Tibet, Manchuria, Turkestan
21. Summary of Medical Events in 1923
22. Religions
23. The Chinese Renaissance
24. Labour
25. Commerce
26. Currency, Banking, Weights and Measures
27. Finance
28. International Issues (Including the Lincheng Outrage, the Gold Franc Controversy, Weihaiwei Negotiations, The Trade Mark Law, Sino-Russian Negotiations)
29. Defence—Army and Navy
30. Who's Who
31. The Chinese Government (Including New Constitution)
32. Miscellaneous
33. Summary of Events in China in 1923-4 (With comprehensive Index and Railway Map)

ORDER FROM YOUR BOOKSELLER

8. H.G.W. Woodhead, the long serving editor of the *Peking and Tientsin Times*, was also the editor of the annual and widely read *China Year Book*.

9. Suzhou-born Roy Anderson divided his time between consulting to American corporations in China, advising war lords, acting as a go-between for the Chinese government and writing for the *North-China Daily News*.

10. Missourian Carl Crow arrived in 1911 to witness the Republican revolution and stayed until forced out by the Japanese in 1937. He became one of the best-known journalists, authors and businessmen in Shanghai.

11. Edna Lee Booker was one of the early "Girl Reporters" in the old China press corps — arriving just after the First World War. Here she is travelling in a palanquin to cover the 1926 kidnapping of a several hundred foreigners and Chinese during the so-called "Lincheng Outrage".

THE CHINA ILLUSTRATED REVIEW

Meets a long-felt need on the part of those interested in events and politics in the Far East. Edited and printed in the same offices as the PEKING and TIENTSIN TIMES, it gives a more comprehensive and reliable survey of events in the Far East than any other paper. The illustrations deal chiefly with events in the Far East, and picturesque scenery in China and Japan.

Proprietors:
TIENTSIN PRESS, LIMITED,
VICTORIA ROAD,
TIENTSIN, NORTH CHINA

12. The *China Illustrated Review* was one of a number of English language publications in China that combined news with photography, travel tips and social events.

13. The White Russian Sapajou was Shanghai's most prolific cartoonist between the wars producing a daily cartoon for the *North-China Daily News*. Here he draws himself at work.

14. The *New Yorker's* Emily Hahn with her largely uncontrollable gibbon Mr. Mills.

15. The dashing *Times* Special Travel Correspondent Peter Fleming with his typewriter and pipe somewhere on the road to Kashgar in 1935.

16. J.B. Powell (with binoculars), one of the most respected members of the old China press corps and the editor of the *China Weekly Review*, watches the Japanese attack on Shanghai in August 1937.

> **THE FAR EASTERN REVIEW**
> FINANCE—ENGINEERING—COMMERCE
>
> To obtain China Trade, and Knowledge of the Far East
> THE GREAT HIGHWAY IS
> **THE FAR EASTERN REVIEW**
>
> The only Engineering Publication in Eastern Asia.
>
> SUBSCRIBE FOR IT
> STUDY IT
> ADVERTISE IN IT
>
> *It Will Pay You*
>
> FOUNDED IN 1904
>
> 16 JINKEE ROAD SHANGHAI

17. *The Far Eastern Review* became a prominent right wing publication based in Shanghai. After the Japanese annexation of Manchuria in 1931, it became an outright supporter of Japanese policy.

18. Shanghai radio announcer Carroll Alcott angered the Japanese so much with his broadcasts after the attack on Shanghai in 1937 that he was forced to move around the city in body armour, with a pistol and two bodyguards to avoid assassination.

19. In 1938 many journalists converged on Hankow as the Japanese invasion progressed. The self-styled "Hankow Last Ditchers" included Anna Louise Strong (second from left) and Agnes Smedley (far right). Here they are pictured with their landlord Bishop Logan Roots (left), Frances Roots (second from right) and deputy commander-in-chief of the Communist forces Peng Dehuai.

20. Polish-born journalist Ilona Ralf Sues with Eight Route Army Commander Zhu De at his Shanxi headquarters.

21. Many of the relationships between the press corps and the Communists were cemented in Hankow in 1938. Here Ilona Ralf Sues (back row third from left) and Agnes Smedley (middle row second from left) pose with, among others, Mao's number two Zhou En-lai (front row second from left).

22. Intrepid newsreel cameraman Harrison Forman filming for *The March of Time* in Shanghai in 1940.

PEKING AND TIENTSIN TIMES

(Established 1894)

The leading daily newspaper of Northern China, British Owned and British Edited.

Entirely independment in its views and criticisms, the "Peking and Tientsin Times" is by far the most influential newspaper in the district.

Proprietor:
TIENTSIN PRESS, LTD.
Victoria Road
TIENTSIN, NORTH CHINA

23. The *Peking & Tientsin Times* was known as "the best newspaper north of Shanghai".

24. Newsreel Wong's controversial picture of a baby among the rubble of Shanghai's railway station in September 1937. The photo sparked a controversey over its authenticity but was seen by nearly every newspaper reader in the world.

25. Madame Chiang Kai-shek, Ernest Hemingway and Martha Gellhorn chat happily together in Madame's garden in the wartime capital of Chongqing in 1941. Hemingway described their trip to China as an "unshakeable hangover".

26. *China Press* Journalist Malcom Rosholt inspects bomb damaged buildings in Shanghai in 1940.

27. Rosholt, a popular member of the Shanghai press corps, relaxes in a sampan on the Huang Pu River.

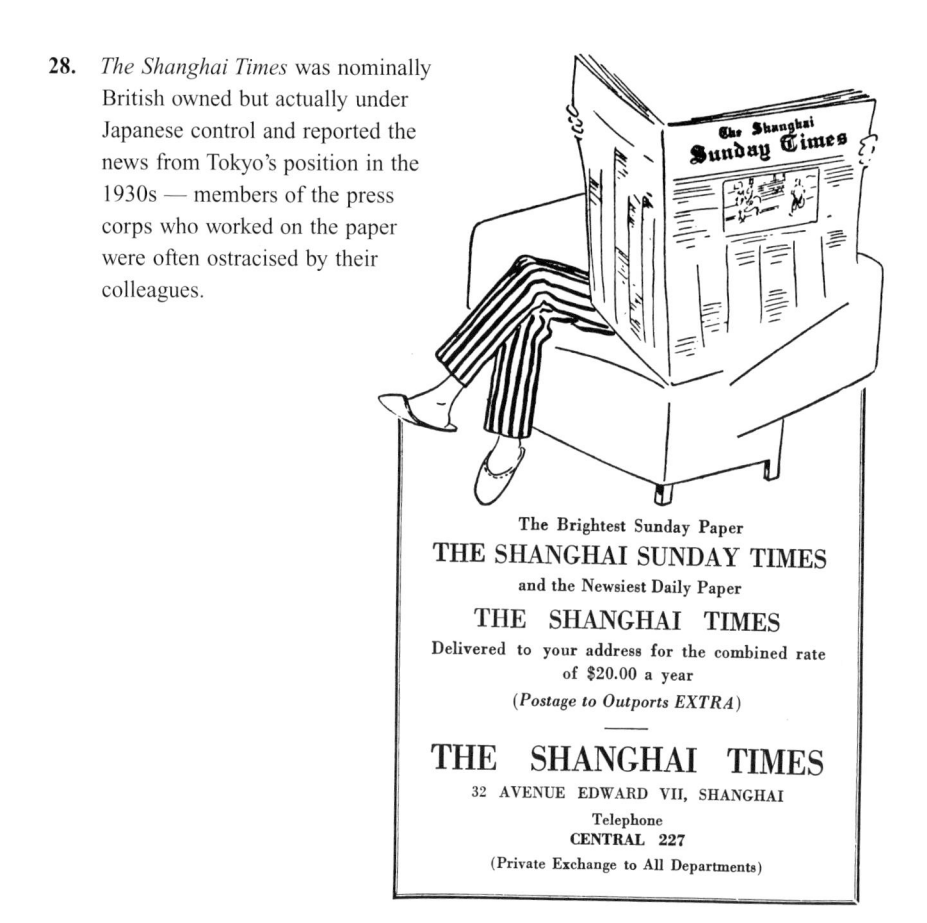

28. *The Shanghai Times* was nominally British owned but actually under Japanese control and reported the news from Tokyo's position in the 1930s — members of the press corps who worked on the paper were often ostracised by their colleagues.

The Brightest Sunday Paper
THE SHANGHAI SUNDAY TIMES
and the Newsiest Daily Paper
THE SHANGHAI TIMES
Delivered to your address for the combined rate of $20.00 a year
(*Postage to Outports EXTRA*)

THE SHANGHAI TIMES
32 AVENUE EDWARD VII, SHANGHAI
Telephone
CENTRAL 227
(*Private Exchange to All Departments*)

29. *Time-Life* proprietor Henry Luce (here with his wife Claire Booth Luce) felt a deep connection to China and the Chiangs. He would not tolerate any criticism of them in his publications.

30. The press corps relaxes — from left to right, James Bertram, Edgar Snow, Helen Foster Snow, Rewi Alley and Evans Carlson on a break in the Philippines.

31. "Amateur War Correspondents" — Auden and Isherwood leave London for a whirlwind tour of the China front in 1939.

32. After the war Senator Joseph McCarthy hounded many of the old China press corps. Here Owen Lattimore, one time reporter and later noted Sinologist, testifies before McCarthy's House Committee on Un-American Activities in Washington D.C.

6
The Roaring Twenties — Substituting Action for Talk

"Newspaper work in those years was a continuous series of stirring adventures, wide travel, and a widening circle of acquaintance with men who were making history in the Far East."

New York Times correspondent Hallett Abend

"China is a tough proposition; it will either make you or break you. Don't close your eyes to anything, open 'em wide, and your mind too."

Gordon Lum, Chinese tennis champion and nephew of a warlord, offers some advice to a newly arrived foreign journalist.

Blood on the Streets — The Foreign Press Corps Engages

Decades can be messy things; the 1920s in China really began on 4 May 1919 with China's disappointment following its betrayal at the Versailles Peace Conference. Despite President Wilson's pledge that every country would be represented, China was not. The Great Powers and America did not apply any more than cursory pressure on China's behalf and Japan retained the "special rights" it had snatched from the Germans in Qingdao and Shandong. The seats at Versailles reserved for the Chinese delegation were never occupied and the Chinese decided not to sign in protest against the clauses in the treaty agreeing to the transfer of German leaseholds to Japan. On 4 May, angered at the betrayal and fired up with a justified nationalist fervour, radicalised students staged large-scale demonstrations across China. These were the first mass protests in modern Chinese history and in many ways set the hallmark for the 1920s as a decade of domestic protest and internal unrest — what became known as the May Fourth Movement.

Several key figures supported the Chinese position, not least Dr. Paul Reinsch, the US minister to China. Reinsch, who was pro-Chinese, had been angered by Japan's 21 Demands on China during the war and was a friend of American journalists such as Carl Crow and Roy Anderson. He felt personally compromised by America's lack of support for China in Paris despite Wilson's pledges and resigned in 1919 to take up a post advising the Chinese government in Washington. Also prominent was Bill Donald, who was briefly editing the *Far Eastern Review* and penned a lengthy editorial sympathetic to the May Fourth Movement. Others were also inspired and radicalised by 1919, such as the pioneering American missionary Frank J. Rawlinson, who developed a brand of liberal Protestantism after becoming involved in the May Fourth Movement and the connected New Culture Movement. Rawlinson had been born into a Plymouth Brethren family but arrived in China in 1902 as a Southern Baptist missionary and remained based in Shanghai for his entire career until his death in 1937. After becoming radicalised, he split with the Southern Baptists and joined the American Board of Commissioners for Foreign Missions. In 1914 he became the editor of the interdenominational *Chinese Recorder*, which under his tutelage reflected his liberal and often outspoken views forged in 1919.

But perhaps the best foreign chronicler of the May Fourth Movement was Pennsylvanian native and Harvard graduate Rodney Yonkers Gilbert, who had come to China as a medicine salesman in 1912 before becoming a long-standing Beijing-based reporter for the *North-China Daily News*. Gilbert had covered the May Fourth demonstrations in the city and attended the lively and raucous meetings held at Peking University. He seemed to be broadly supportive of the student's anti-Japanese stance, or at least applauded their decision to organise and take action, writing: "The advertisement given to this gathering inspired the local students to do something on their own account, and whatever one thinks of the action they eventually took they certainly deserve full credit for being the first in China to substitute action for talk".[1]

However, Gilbert was an extremely contradictory character. His initial enthusiasm would later become tempered with cynicism. He concluded his 1926 book *What's Wrong with China*, which was widely read at the time, with the passage: "We have therefore to be grateful to the firebrand element in China which is driving furiously on towards the complete ruin of China as a nation, the utter collapse of foreign trade with this bad-boy people, and very possibly the martyrdom of those of us who are foolish enough to live in China: and out of great weariness of the spirit and something like Petronian good cheer in the face of what is coming, our toast is: 'More power to their elbows!'"[2]

Gilbert had partly made his name with some excellent mood pieces which included an acclaimed essay *Concerning Camels*, a lyrical account of departing from Beijing with the great camel trains bound for the Silk Road and life outside the Great Wall when the "Outer" in Outer Mongolia really meant something and fascinated many readers. As a committed writer on Asian affairs, Gilbert went on to pen many more articles, a book *Unequal Treaties: China and the Foreigner* published in 1929 (with a foreword by Mohawk Morriss) and an historical novel set in China.

Gilbert was in Beijing while Joseph Washington Hall was in Tianjin watching the action. Hall came from Kelso in Washington State and worked for the American Legation's espionage service in Shandong from 1916 to 1919. He left the service in time to observe the student protests in Tianjin, which he supported, as a journalist. He freelanced for Powell's *China Weekly Review* and as a Beijing correspondent for the *China Press*. From the start, the swarthy Hall, whose bright red hair invariably stood bristlingly up on end, was intensely politically engaged in his subject matter and came to represent the cause of China against Japanese encroachment. He followed the numerous warlord battles across northern China in the early 1920s and was falsely reported dead at least twice. As Upton Close (his pen name derived from the fact that he always signed his telegrams to the *Review* with "up close" to hide his identity from the censors and indicate to Powell his proximity to the frontlines), he became a major advocate for Chinese territorial integrity in the 1920s. In this sense he was one of a growing number of the foreign press corps who would overtly identify themselves with the causes of progressive China more directly after May Fourth and often mix reporting with commitment.

Hall was to move on from freelancing to specialising in longer, more descriptive, pieces. In the early 1920s he travelled with the International Famine Relief Commission to Henan province and visited the site of a major earthquake in remote Gansu, which registered 7.8 on the Richter scale and killed an estimated 200,000 people. The epicentre was so remote that there was not even a telegraph station from which to send his despatches, and Hall was left "trucking" them out by mule. The Gansu earthquake also occasioned his first, and much praised, longer descriptive piece — *Where the Mountains Walked* for *National Geographic*. He then, like many of the press corps before and after him, briefly left journalism to become a foreign affairs adviser to a warlord, Wu Peifu, the "Jade Marshal". While working for the warlord, Close was severely injured and had to return to America where he lectured for a time and eventually became a radio broadcaster.

As the decade developed, those with a close and personal knowledge of China became important figures in developments and dabbled in the press. Bill Donald, who was dubbed "China's number one white boy" by H. B. Elliston, the editor of the *Saturday Evening Post*, was increasingly making a name for himself as a fixer, as was his best friend Roy Anderson. The supposedly unflappable American China Hand Anderson was an old acquaintance of both Donald and Carl Crow. They had all met originally in 1911 when Anderson was working for Standard Oil and he was described by Crow as "the most interesting character I ever knew".[3] Anderson had also been a Shanghai-based journalist for some time on the *North-China Daily News*, writing under the pseudonym Bruce Baxter, as well as being an old friend of Powell and submitting the occasional op-ed to the *Review*. Crow and Powell got to spend time with Anderson again throughout the 1923 Lincheng Outrage, when bandits ransacked the famous *Blue Express* train, the incident that became the basis for Josef von Sternberg's 1932 movie *Shanghai Express*. Anderson took on the job of hostage negotiation on behalf of the Chinese government, Powell was a hostage and Crow was representing the American Red Cross during the ordeal that ended with Anderson securing the safe release of the hostages, to wide acclaim.

Anderson was a mysterious though well-known figure at the time and was arguably one of the most knowledgeable and passionate of all the foreign China Hands. Born in China, the son of the founder of Suzhou University, and educated in the US, he spent all his life in China after returning in 1902. According to *North-China Daily News* journalist George Sokolsky's prominent obituary of him, he spoke eight Chinese dialects while Crow described him as "... always at heart a Chinese and thought like one".[4] He was a tall, portly man with a clipped bristly moustache who invariably wore khaki, a pith helmet and riding boots. He had been an early convert to the cause of Chinese nationalism and had served with the Nationalist army. He also acted occasionally as an adviser and trusted middleman to foreign businesses, including Standard Oil and several mining companies that were looking to secure contracts in Yunnan. Unfortunately, he died prematurely of pneumonia in 1925 (on the same day as Sun Yat-sen) at the point when President Coolidge was reportedly considering appointing him America's minister to China.

Anderson was gold-dust to the China coast press as he was one foreigner with versatile linguistic skills who moved among the Chinese community and found out more than, the invariably monolingual, foreign reporters could. At best, foreign newspapers in Shanghai in the 1920s had one or two Chinese journalists on their staff though many, such as the *North-China* apparently, had none, at least in the newsroom. And yet they often had very accurate reports of events in the Chinese community. How so? They achieved this through the so-called "police reports" compiled by the Shanghai Municipal Police (SMP). Whenever a meeting or gathering occurred, the SMP would send along one of its Chinese detectives who would report back in English. These reports were almost universally "leaked" to the press, with reporters told to change the text so as not to make the copying too obvious. Of course, while this meant that foreign journalists and their papers could cover local events, they were at the mercy of the SMP's interpretation of what was going on. The SMP was as capable of starting whispering campaigns against journalists it didn't like, that is left-wing ones, as it was of favouring its friends with advance peeks at its reports.

Out with the Old, In with the New

May Fourth was to usher in a new and chaotic decade in China's history and also a new crop of reporters, correspondents and writers. The old guard was depleted: Morrison had left China and was on his deathbed and he would die shortly after May Fourth; and at the *North China Herald* and *Daily News*, Mohawk Morriss had died in 1918 and control of the company had passed to his sons, while the hardliner O. M. Green was in the editor's chair and saw the paper successfully through its 70th anniversary in 1920. The paper continued to grow in power and circulation under Green's editorship throughout the 1920s, with a Sunday edition being launched in 1929. In commemorating its diamond jubilee in 1924, the paper was wealthy enough to open rather grand premises with gold mosaic ceilings at No. 17 The Bund, which became known, rather quickly, as the "Old Lady of the Bund". The constantly running presses annoyed the clerks in the Chartered Bank next door but those eager for news could collect the day's first editions at 3 a.m. from the front door. The glorious new building included the motto "JOURNALISM, ART, SCIENCE, LITERATURE, COMMERCE, TRUTH, PRINTING" carved on the front of the building. The paper's reception was on the ground floor while the editorial offices took up the whole of the fifth and sixth floors, and above were two luxury apartments.

However, the paper still had an often slightly "Parish News" feel to it at times. For example, in 1923 the start of horse racing in Chongqing was reported in the *Herald* via a chummy letter from the clerk of the course that amazed sophisticated Shanghailanders with tales of horses that could walk up and down stairs.[5] Indeed, Chongqing was long considered a strange place by Shanghailanders. At around the same time, foreigners in Chongqing started publishing *Babylon of Babylon* which comprised all the local news written in Old Testament biblical language, presumably to provide some amusement during the long nights. Throughout the 1920s, the *North-China* and the *China Press* fought a circulation war. The *North-China* could claim to be the oldest and most influential paper on the China coast, but the *China Press* outsold it with a daily circulation of approximately 4,500 compared to the *North-China*'s 3,500, according to a survey by the US State Department.

Mohawk's son Harry Morriss took over the day-to-day management of the paper leaving the editing to Green. Mohawk's other two sons left Harry largely to the newspaper business. Gordon Morriss preferred dealing in gold bullion and made only the occasional foray into the newspaper game; and Hailey Morriss, the black sheep of the family, had been sent home to England where he became involved in several scandals involving questionable young ladies that got him into the *News of the World*. Harry was known to be shy and withdrawn and reluctant to talk about anything personal. His three passions were business, horse racing and the violin, of which he was apparently an accomplished amateur player. In 1926 he used his wealth to build the art-deco style Morriss family compound known as Shanghai's "San Simeon" that occupied a full block in the densely-populated French Concession, as well as to develop horse breeding in China and to establish his own stud at Cheveley, near Newmarket. He was a top owner at the Shanghai Race Club and his horse *Manna* won both the Two Thousand Guineas and the Epsom Derby in 1925 where the betting was more ferocious than usual as bookies in England took hundreds of bets from Shanghailanders sure that their local boy's horse would win. When the news came through that *Manna* had won, the bar at the Shanghai Club on the Bund was drunk dry.

Another *North-China* rival, the *Shanghai Mercury*, celebrated its golden jubilee in 1929 proving that, though not as illustrious or strong-selling as the Old Lady of the Bund, it was still around. It had changed hands several times and was now controlled by the Cumine family who also owned several successful property and architectural businesses and were very rich. Eric Cumine was also a stalwart of the Shanghai Race Club and the paper's tipster as well as occasional cartoonist. Despite being wealthy, Eric had a taste for the slightly odd and, as well as drawing cartoons, was known in Hong Kong in the 1960s for having invented and championed something called "the Hong Kong Necktie", now sadly long forgotten.

Stories were breaking thick and fast as things changed. In Guangdong the rebellious Chen Jiongming's administration was breaking relations with Sun Yat-sen. Sun wanted to unify China through the use of military force if necessary and crush the warlords, while Chen advocated peaceful unification by drawing up a federalist constitution. After returning from Fujian with the Guangdong Army in November 1920, Chen had immediately embarked upon a programme to make Guangdong a model province. Rodney Gilbert interviewed him for the *North-China*, which meant that the split between Chen and Sun, a split that threatened to destabilise the fragile government, became public via the English-language press.

This new flood of China stories with international relevance — would China fragment and self-destruct or not? — also meant that the wire services were growing. The early wires relied on the fledgling telegraph network but then in the 1920s things took another technological leap when a certain Mr. S. T. Dockray of the Marconi Wireless Telegraph Company was despatched from the company headquarters in Chelmsford, England, to install three 25kW telegraphy transmitters in China. Dockray arrived in Shanghai with his equipment and then journeyed overland to Urga (now Ulan Bator) to install the first transmitter. Satisfied with its installation, he headed to Beijing to begin transmissions. However, there was no signal, so he returned to Urga to find the transmitter vandalised by Mongolian warlords who were trying to oust the Chinese government from the region. The Marconi man was shot at, captured, discovered that most of his local staff had been murdered and was then charged with being an English spy. From there things got worse. Dockray eventually fled Urga and reached Manchuli where he was quarantined in a cattle truck due to raging bubonic plague. Eventually he reached Beijing, where he was, quite rightly in most people's opinion, awarded the Chinese Order of Chao Ho for meritorious conduct. Later in 1920, the Urga region was subdued and Dockray returned to repair his transmitter.

However, he had established only a single transmitter and two more were needed. The second was to be at Urumqi and so he set out with a caravan of 1,200 camels, 468 ponies and 117 bullock carts carrying the equipment required to what was then Turkestan. Warlords were a problem again but he got the transmitter up and running by 1922. The last station was in Kashgar and this involved crossing swollen rivers on makeshift rafts but the final transmitter was in place by May 1923. The quickest way back was actually through India, then by boat from Calcutta to Shanghai and finally overland to Beijing again. When he finally arrived back he threw a switch and was, we can safely assume, immensely relieved to find all three transmitters working and the age of reporting by wireless begun.

The wires were to employ as many characters as the regular newspapers. David Fraser was Reuters' Beijing correspondent through much of the 1920s but he was much better known to many foreigners in China for his horse *Bengal*. Fraser, who clearly had other sources of income apart from his salary from Reuters, had become a very successful horse owner at the Beijing and Tianjin races. He bought a horse in 1923 from the then legendary Duke of Mongolia, Frans August Larson, a failed Swedish missionary who was given a Dukedom by the Mongolians for negotiating with the Chinese on their behalf and basically stopping a Chinese invasion of their territory. Larson had been taken to a spot on the Chinese-Mongolian border and told that all the land he could see in every direction, plus all the land for one day's ride beyond, was to be his fiefdom. Given the lack of obvious business opportunities in the area, he started dealing in the stout Mongolian ponies that were raced by foreigners at tracks across China. Fraser bought *Bengal* from Larson and it was to become the most successful winner in the history of the Shanghai Race Club before being sold to Frank "One Arm" Sutton (who had lost his appendage in the First World War to a Turkish hand grenade at Gallipoli), the Eton-educated military adviser to several northern Chinese warlords. *Bengal* was traded on once more to a mystery Hong Kong buyer, who, it turned out, was really the Shanghai tycoon Sir Victor Sassoon whose stable ran the horse to many more victories at Happy Valley.

While Fraser was running Reuters in Beijing, the eternally boyish-looking Christopher Chancellor was running the Reuters bureau in Shanghai. He stayed in the post for eight years and was later to become chairman of Reuters worldwide after the Second Word War when he turned the company into a truly global organisation, for which he was eventually made Sir Christopher Chancellor. The wires quickly proliferated. By 1928 the recently appointed *New York Times* China correspondent Hallett Abend, a failed fiction writer and Hollywood gossip columnist in the silent film era who had taken up journalism and come to China, was amazed that several thousand words he had filed with the radio station in Nanking had all arrived in Shanghai within an hour.[6]

Increasingly newspapers and magazines wanted photographs and so the number of freelance photographers was growing too. Donald Mennie travelled up the Yangtze to the famous Three Gorges and published a book of highly aesthetic photogravures taken during winter when the waters were lower and the landscapes more spectacular. He also published *The Pageant of Peking* in 1920 for which B. L. Putnam Weale provided the text. Mennie was actually rather wealthy and could take his time with his photography, having been the director of the pharmacy chain A. S. Watson in China. Others specialised to a higher degree, such as architecture specialist Osvald Siren who conducted a survey of Beijing's city walls for the Chinese Ministry of Works in 1920 and published his photographs in various papers. Other photographers produced books even if their work would never make it into most papers. German-born Heinz von Perckhammer had arrived in Macau in the early 1920s. He took many photographs of China but specialised in Chinese female pre-pubescent nudes and, while not acceptable to most papers, he did manage to get a few published in the more risqué French magazine *Voila* in the 1930s.

Others found themselves in interesting predicaments that led to articles. Kidnapping was in vogue. Carl Crow, J. B. Powell and Roy Anderson had been embroiled in the1923 Lincheng Outrage. Also present there were the First World War veteran, cameraman, AP reporter and occasional *China Press* writer Colonel Lloyd "Larry" Lehrbas (much later to be appointed General Douglas MacArthur's press aide in the Second World War); *Shun Pao* Sunday editor

Kang Tung-yi; and Roy Bennett, yet another graduate of the Missouri University School of Journalism, who happened to be passing through Shanghai on his way to the Philippines to start work on the *Manila Bulletin*. Crow, Powell, Lehrbas, Kang and Bennett all wrote up the hostage crisis for different publications.

The late 1920s and early 1930s saw more journalists arrive on both the local press and as foreign correspondents. The Chinese-language press started to expand as a by-product of the May Fourth Movement. This happened to an extent in Beijing but most noticeably in booming Shanghai where Europe's post-war recovery was driving demand, and both foreigners and Chinese were making fortunes and crying out for Western products on which to spend their new-found wealth. Advertising rates soared and newspaper profits were healthy.

Some foreigners participated actively in the attempts by the Chinese press to avoid the censors and stay in business. Carl Crow, by now running a highly successful advertising company in Shanghai and making vastly more money than he had as a reporter, stepped in to become a board member on two newspapers — one in Tianjin and another in Jinan. He became the nominal owner and chairman of the board of both the Chinese-managed daily papers. As he was an American citizen, this made them technically foreign publications, as the American and British consulates in Shanghai only required proof that 51% of the paper's stock was in foreign hands. He never wrote an editorial or even visited the offices of either paper and admitted that "… he had no more to do with the management of the paper than with that of the London *Times*". In fact, he didn't even draw a salary and his only contribution was to eat the sumptuous banquets the editors of both papers provided for him as thanks.

This was not an unusual tactic to combat censorship. Of nine Chinese newspapers in Shanghai surveyed by British Intelligence in 1918, seven were registered with the Japanese consulate and others with the French authorities, though their shareholders were mostly Chinese. The *Sin Wan Pao* (*Xinwenbao*), which Crow estimated to have a circulation of 10,000 copies daily rising to 35,000 when it ran a particularly sensational story, had been technically founded and owned by an American missionary Dr. John Calvin Ferguson who played an intimate role in the paper's management and editorial policy while also contributing articles to missionary-targeted newspapers such as the *Chinese Recorder*. Ferguson's *Sin Wan Pao* was registered at the American consulate in Shanghai and other papers were under Italian or Portuguese protection, as well as Japanese (which would later become a problem for them). Crow noted that the two papers he helped were just two of half a dozen that approached him for assistance.

"A Hermetically Sealed Glass Case" — The Shanghai Mind

Beijing remained a romantic and often overwhelmingly sensual experience for many foreigners, often with a little whiff of scandal or intimated sex involved while Shanghai increasingly gave way to more obvious and public pleasures. Shanghai was brash and showy where Beijing remained somewhat Victorian and discreet. Increasingly Shanghai was consolidating its position as the centre of English-language newspapers as well as being the major place to hear foreigners express their views on China — loudly and often bellicosely. However, some wondered what views exactly were being expressed, aside from the regular letters in the *North-China* from outraged readers about various grievances, including whether or not the Chinese were allowed to use the Bund public gardens, a vexed question the paper's letters page and regular editorials constantly debated back and forth from the 1880s.

Despite publications with a distinctly pro-British bent, such as the *North-China*, which was seen locally as the mouthpiece of Whitehall, Albion and the British Empire, those arriving in Shanghai from London found them somewhat different in slant. Arthur Ransome, who arrived after a stint covering the Bolshevik Revolution for the English newspapers, didn't see the British-controlled press in Shanghai as particularly British at all. He wrote in the *Manchester Guardian*: "The Chinese naturally turn to these papers and judge England and England's policy by what they find there. It is impossible to persuade them that what they find is an expression not of the British but of the Shanghai mind".[7] He found the British community in Shanghai to be somewhat different from their peers in other far-flung outposts of empire who held tightly to the mother country: "The Shanghailanders hold that loyalty begins at home and that their primary allegiance is to Shanghai ... Shanghailanders of English extraction belong, if they belong to England at all, to an England that no longer exists".[8] Ransome's comments reflected the growing divergence of official British and British-Shanghailander opinion. Others noted a similar condition among Shanghailanders. As the sinologist and former Chinese Maritime Customs Officer L. A. Lyall commented: "The British residents in Shanghai are the spoilt children of the Empire. They pay no taxes to China, except that landowners pay a very small land tax, and no taxes to England. Judges and consuls are provided for them; they are protected by the British fleet, and for several years they have had in addition a British army to defend them; and for all this expenditure the British taxpayer pays".[9]

Commentators like Ransome clearly saw a difference between England and Shanghai and believed that by the mid-1920s a clearly identifiable and myopic Shanghailander mindset had emerged and was dominating the press and its editorials. He was to coin the term "Shanghai mind" and refer to the International Settlement as a "hermetically sealed glass case". This notion of the treaty ports seeing things slightly differently was not totally new; as noted before, the British-run *Peking and Tientsin Times* had been chastised by some of its British readers for being too anti-German in 1914. They, after all, lived in a relatively small community side-by-side with Germans and saw themselves as having far more in common with them than with, say, the Russian and Siberian riff-raff on the edge of the European settlement and certainly little in common with the Chinese.

The Shanghai mindset was to remain important not only in determining much of the foreign experience in China in the first half of the twentieth century but also in how China was portrayed to the outside world, given that so many of those who wrote articles or staffed the wire services that pushed out information on China to everyone else had that mindset. It was also a mindset that some vocally opposed after the likes of Ransome identified and defined it. *Bon vivant* Chicagoan and minor celebrity John Gunther was a globe-trotting foreign correspondent for the *Chicago Daily News* and author of the widely read *Inside Asia* (1939) along with "Inside" books on most other continents. He visited Shanghai in the 1930s and vocally proclaimed his dislike of the Shanghai mindset, which persisted through to the Second World War when arguably things changed as the horrors of war kicked in. Others, such as the journalist Carroll Alcott, didn't consider the Shanghai mindset a problem and thought it essential to reporters working in the city, seeing it as reflective of the International Concession being the world's "most cosmopolitan village".

Still, what the existence of a particular Shanghai mindset indicated was that the city was emerging as a distinct culture, the infamous transnational blend of East and West with commerce, trade and the making of large amounts of money and personal fortunes as the ultimate goal rather than defending the Empire, which was always supported in public though never quite with the same verve and determination as the International Settlement itself was to be defended in the next two decades.

Revolutionaries with Typewriters

The May Fourth demonstrations continued in other agitational forms and inevitably some took on a socialist leaning. The USSR and the Comintern was involved in China first through Mikhail Borodin and then N. M. Roy. Though in China to foment revolution and in the pay of the Comintern, Borodin was officially a correspondent for the Soviet Russian Telegraph Agency (Rosta, and later better known as TASS). This was a rather transparent cover as everyone knew exactly what Borodin was up to. He may have been stoking revolution all day and occasionally despatching an article to Moscow, but his children spent their time being well educated at the Shanghai American School. Borodin was undoubtedly a committed communist which was more than could be said of the gang of Soviets who were sent to support him in Shanghai, many of them posing as journalists and with a large stash of Moscow gold. Most of them became corrupted by Shanghai fairly quickly and spent Moscow's money on cars, champagne and flash suits, and also sparked a mini-boom for Shanghai's prostitutes, before Borodin could think up ways to put the cash to revolutionary uses.

In Guangzhou a revolutionary government committed to federalism was in control which attracted committed as well as not-so-committed journalists. Hallett Abend had arrived in Shanghai from America only to be advised by George Sokolsky to go to Guangzhou. He did, and sailed into a firefight on the Pearl River, declaring in his memoirs: "My fifteen years in China had begun — fifteen years in which boredom was never to return".[10] Among the committed, the American socialists Rayna Samuels Prohme and her husband, the self-taught revolutionary William Prohme, had arrived to serve the cause. Rayna was from a wealthy Jewish business family and a graduate of Chicago University who had been married to Sampson "Raph" Raphaelson, a *New York Times* reporter who had sold his play, *The Jazz Singer*, and was waiting for it to be produced. Despite Raph's impending success, Rayna left him and found a new beau, the older and already divorced Bill Prohme, who had been a newspaperman on the *San Francisco Examiner* and became infatuated with Rayna. She had come to China first, only to hear that Bill was missing back in America; and she returned to find him sick and depressed in a Texas brothel, patched him up and insisted he return with her to China. After an extended sojourn in Hawaii and Japan for Bill to recover fully, they arrived in Beijing not as correspondents or even as hopeful freelancers but rather to establish an agency they called *Chung-Mei* (China-American), the aim of which was to circulate Trotskyist-inspired propaganda in China. Perhaps predictably, the venture didn't make much money, though Bill subsidised it through his job as editor-in-chief of the *Peking Leader*. Rayna wrote letters to her friend Rebecca Hourwich Reyher, who ran the National Woman's Party in America, arguing that being penniless was not so bad: "... being broke in China is different from in New York. If you are white you have to have five servants!"[11]

Bill relapsed and had to stop work, so Rayna stepped in to run the *Leader* while he recuperated. She met the charismatic Trinidadian-Chinese revolutionary Eugene Chen, at that time on the run from the warlord Zhang Zuolin, the Tiger of Mukden. He was editor-in-chief of the *Peking People's Tribune* and became her guide to, what they saw, as the imminent Chinese revolution. Life on the *Tribune* was not easy, to say the least. The "Old Marshal" Zhang Zuolin hated the newspaper and his soldiers once burst into its offices, took away one of the Chinese editors (the paper had both a Chinese and English edition) and swiftly executed him; and they then returned regularly to threaten the staff and ransack the offices. Rayna, new to China, was quickly under threat and couldn't necessarily rely on her own country to help her. Long-serving UPI Asia Hand Miles Vaughn heard a rumour that Zhang Zuolin was planning to kidnap Rayna. She laughed it off, but a combination of the fact that the American Legation was backing Zhang at the time and Vaughn's eyewitness accounts of a series of recent particularly nasty Zhang-ordered executions by garrotting finally persuaded her the time had come to move on.

However, the Prohmes (though Rayna adopted Bill's last name, it is not clear they ever formally married) became obsessed with the idea that the Chinese revolution would begin in Guangzhou and left the agency in the hands of her friends and fellow-Trotskyites Mildred Mitchell and journalist Milly Bennett before heading south to get involved. As soon as they arrived, they volunteered for the Guangzhou Revolutionary Government's Propaganda Department. They were given the task of establishing a new English version of Chen's *People's Tribune* in Guangzhou, partly to compete with the twice-weekly *Canton Gazette*, the well-established major English-language paper between Shanghai and Hong Kong. Initially, the *Tribune* was an official publication and continued after the revolutionaries all later moved on to the next site of revolutionary possibilities: Hankou. It did so well that Mildred Mitchell was told to drop the *Chung-Mei* agency in Beijing and get down to Hankou to help out as revolution was expected. Bill was despatched immediately to Hankou and Rayna was left for a time to run the *Tribune* in Guangzhou.

While the Prohmes were becoming deeply involved with the cause of the left, the list of the politically committed that arrived in China in the 1920s was growing. Grace Simons was an American who came to Beijing in 1925 with her husband Wilbur Burton, an Indiana journalist with a bit of a track record. Grace was actually Rayna Prohme's sister and they were alike: both were committed Trotskyists and both had relationships with other journalists. Simons and Burton moved on quickly from Beijing to Shanghai where Burton got a job with the *China Courier*, a newly launched morning daily, while Grace found work with the French news agency Havas. Burton was a good friend of the intrepid journalist Vincent Sheean and had already had a series of adventures in Latin America as a correspondent for the *Baltimore Sun*.

Sheean himself came to China in 1927 (when he was just 27), also intending to cover events in Guangzhou. He had dropped out of Chicago University and taken a job at the *Chicago Daily News* and the North American Newspaper Alliance. Despite his youth, Sheean had an urbane air that allowed him to charm warlords, revolutionaries and diplomats alike. He walked into an early scoop a few days after arriving when he secured an interview with Chiang Kai-shek in Nanjing. Following this, he returned to Shanghai — a city he didn't like for its all-pervading atmosphere of colonial repression and self-declared superior foreigners — and proceeded to bag an interview with T. V. Soong, Madame Chiang's brother and then China's finance minister in the middle of cleaning house financially and establishing the Bank of China. Also deciding to follow the action to Hankou, the prematurely greying Sheean (which helped him to be accepted by everyone) found the more politically committed leftists a rather dull bunch. He disliked Chen, seeing him as "venomous", as well as the overly serious Bill Prohme, who equally disliked Sheean for his bourgeois tastes which included a fondness for Scotch and Egyptian cigarettes. However, he found Rayna more bearable, intellectually rather than physically, after the *New York Times*'s Frank Misselwitz introduced them. He described himself at this stage of his life as still really a "middle class dilettante" and Rayna agreed with his assessment of himself calling him "a fence-sitter", though he loosely adopted her socialism and became rather infatuated with Borodin. However, his infatuation with Rayna was initially a rather non-committal way to enter a rather fun and loose social circle as opposed to a dedicated belief in the theory of permanent revolution. Still, what Sheean understood, despite his often flippant attitude, at least at that point in his life, was that in 1927 Hankou was the crucible for those hoping for a Chinese revolution, particularly a Trotskyist version now that their hopes of permanent revolution were fading in the Soviet Union as the brutal contradictions of that upheaval became increasingly apparent when Stalin consolidated power.

In Hankou Frank "Missi" Wisselwitz enjoyed teasing the left-leaning members of the press corps but was friendly with Rayna and described her as that "red headed gal, spitfire, mad as a hatter, complete Bolshevik. Works for Borodin" (which she did).[12] Rayna, with her beloved German shepherd Dan, arrived to reunite with Bill and work on the *Peking People's Tribune* which was now the voice of the revolutionary movement. However, in the end, Hankou's short-lived revolutionary government, which was more late-night rebellious talk than action, collapsed and Rayna moved with Chen, Borodin and others to the next hoped-for centre of revolution, Wuhan, where she continued to work closely with the two men on the *Tribune*. Bill was there too but the couple were apart increasingly as Rayna revelled in the romance of the rebellion while Bill remained a more grounded revolutionary committing such outrageous bourgeois sins as insisting on regular meal times.

As Wuhan too collapsed, Rayna decided to travel to Moscow with Soong Ching-ling (Madame Sun and one of the Soong sisters). Though she was only in China for a short time, she managed to make an impression with her fiery politics, curly mop of red hair and striking looks. Bill, known for being a bit wild, shouting a lot and having vast reserves of revolutionary enthusiasm despite regular bouts of illness, refused to tag along to the USSR and headed off to the Philippines.

Sheean travelled to Beijing by train during the troubles of 1927 as warlord violence peaked and Chiang Kai-chek launched his Northern Expedition to reunite the country. It was not an overly safe journey as, several weeks before he made the trip, Basil Miles, a London *Times* correspondent, had been murdered on the same route. From Beijing he travelled to Shenyang and Harbin in northeast China and then hopped on the Trans-Siberian to Moscow where he met up with Madame Sun and Rayna, with whom he was still completely obsessed to the point of believing she had been used by Chen and Borodin and had not actually believed their propaganda. Rayna was now separated from Madame Sun, broke and in a bad way. They talked late into the night about her decision to move to Moscow and he still refused to really believe her revolutionary views were her own, but the conversations were fruitless as Rayna was in a deep depression and Sheean was drinking heavily. She escorted him on a tour of Red Square and the revolutionary sites of the Soviet capital but she was clearly not well. A few days later, in November 1927, while preparing to enter the Lenin Institute to train as a professional revolutionary, she died of an inflammation of the brain (she had suffered debilitating headaches for years) aged just 33. To the end, Rayna stayed a revolutionary, though she died too young to see her hero Trotsky ousted and Trotskyists persecuted in Russia and the man himself assassinated in Mexico. She was attended in her last days by Madame Sun and Anna Louise Strong who was later to become well known in China for her pro-communist writing but was at the time freelancing in Moscow. Sheean and Strong escorted her coffin in Moscow as she was given an official revolutionary heroine's send-off. Despite their separation, Bill Prohme, who missed the funeral as he was stuck in Manila, never got over losing Rayna. He did eventually travel from Manila to Moscow to collect her ashes for final burial in Chicago and several years later killed himself in Honolulu on the anniversary of her death.

Others writers began their personal routes to leftist politics during this time of intense radicalisation. Maurice Eldred Votaw arrived in Shanghai in 1922 to be a journalism professor at St. John's University. He was yet another Missouri University graduate who came to Shanghai with a newly-minted bachelor's degree. He taught at the prestigious St. John's until the late 1930s, freelanced virtually the entire time for a variety of publications, including the *Baltimore*

Sun, the *North China Herald* and the college newspaper the *St. John's Dial*, and also founded and ran the Shanghai Short Story Club, a very active organisation. During the Second World War Votaw was to be a popular visitor to Yenan, the Communists' wartime base, and also covered the terrible famine in Guangdong Province.

The politically committed in the 1920s certainly formed a small clique within the wider China press corps, to the extent that they mostly socialised together. They were largely accepted as many in the wider press corps leant generally to the left though they were rarely as committed as the likes of Rayna Prohme. However, some of the press corps were life-long revolutionaries. For example, Grace Simons remained in China after her sister went to Moscow and married the English-born, South African-raised Trotskyist correspondent and activist Frank Glass — a marriage that was to become an enduring and politically committed union. Later in Shanghai, Glass was to become a well-known fixture of the Shanghai media scene, variously working for the *Shanghai Evening Post and Mercury*, the *China Press* and the *Shanghai Times*, as well as being an assistant editor on Powell's *Review* and a popular commentator for the American-owned XMHA radio station. Glass perhaps illustrated how journalists who were also committed socialists remained an integral part of the wider China press corps. Though J. B. Powell did have a distinct fondness for those who liked stirring things up a bit, he was certainly no socialist revolutionary himself. He would have known that Glass was involved in the Trotskyite Communist League of China and was also writing for revolutionary publications around the world, using the pen names John Liang, Myra Weiss and Li Fu Ren. Yet Glass always remained employed, published and respected by the likes of Powell. The Glasses later moved to Los Angeles where life was comfortable as fortunately Grace inherited a large trust fund from her mother and Frank freelanced occasionally for the *Los Angeles Sentinel* and edited *Laging Una (Always First)*, a newspaper for Filipinos in California and Arizona. They were also instrumental in a number of pro-environment campaigns, including one to preserve LA's Elysian Park, for which a statue was erected in their memory.

Big names with leftist credentials also arrived. As noted already, Arthur Ransome was not overly taken with Shanghai and Shanghailanders but he found China fascinating. The English journalist, critic and renowned children's author is now best known for his series of books following the adventures of the *Swallows and Amazons* which were first published in the 1930s. However, prior to achieving his fame as a children's writer, Ransome was a foreign correspondent and spent time in both Russia and China for the *Manchester Guardian*, the *Daily News* and the *Observer*. The *Manchester Guardian* was, of course, a left-wing paper which had originally been formed in response to the Peterloo Massacre of 1819; and the *Daily News*, which had been founded by Charles Dickens in 1834, was also considered a radical paper. Ransome chronicled his visits to Russia prior to and at the outbreak of the First World War as well as during the Bolshevik Revolution. He became close to Trotsky, and to a lesser extent Lenin, and developed a sympathy for the revolutionaries. However, he was expelled from Russia by the Soviet regime. He got out safely with the assistance of Evgenia Petrovna Shelepina, Trotsky's personal secretary, who fled with Ransome and the two eventually married.

After Russia, Ransome returned home to a not altogether welcome reception. He faced some close questioning in London from the Metropolitan Police who suspected him of being a Bolshevik agent and it took the intervention of C. P. Scott, the *Manchester Guardian*'s forceful and liberal editor, to get his passport returned. Ransome then went to Egypt for the *Guardian* in 1924 and finally to China in 1925 where, like so many others, he was persuaded to write for Powell's *Review*. It published a number of his articles between 1927 and 1929 in which he criticised the Unequal Treaties, examined why socialism appeared not to have caught on in China and provided some profiles of notable warlords, as well as his aforementioned comments on the Shanghai mind which, unsurprisingly, didn't endear him to all Shanghailanders.

Ransome had arrived in the International Settlement at an uneasy time, a period that spurred his particular interest in warlords, a subject he was to write about extensively. Throughout his time in Russia and China, British Intelligence kept a watching brief on him, concerned about his political leanings but particularly interested in Evgenia who was believed to be involved in smuggling diamonds from Moscow to Paris to help fund the Comintern. Ransome's time in China was clearly to stay with him and later one of his *Swallows and Amazons* series —*Missee Lee* (1941) — was set on the China coast, with the children falling foul of pirates.

Most of the foreign correspondent community and old China Hands didn't take Chiang Kai-shek's launching of the North Expedition in 1926 overly seriously and, in general, did not think it would achieve its objective of unifying China once and for all under the Nationalist *Guomindang* (KMT). This opinion was to change as Chiang swept northwards. Charles Dailey of the *Chicago Tribune* wrote: "He (*Chiang*) is advancing with his right flank protected by the fountain pen of Eugene Chen and his left by the pistols of Two Gun Cohen". In other words, Cohen provided the muscle while Chen provided the PR.

The thin, British-accented Chen was a shadowy figure who rose to prominence in Shanghai. Having been born in the British West Indies of a Cantonese father and a black Trinidadian mother, he was to be foreign minister of China four times. After an English education, he briefly practised as a barrister in London's Inner Temple, where he developed his reputation for being a "master of the stinging invective ... who thought and wrote in headline slogans ..."[13] before returning to Trinidad. However, he soon emerged in China as a legal adviser to the Ministry of Communications. Unable to read, write or speak Chinese, Chen founded the *Peking People's Tribune* (later *Gazette*) in 1914 and published caustic editorials against the pro-British *North-China Daily News*. He also raged editorially against Yuan Shih-kai and for his tirades was thrown into jail in 1916, though as a British subject he used the extraterritoriality laws he often criticised to quickly secure his release. Leaving jail, he moved to Shanghai and became a personal adviser and private secretary to Dr. Sun, a position he held until Sun's death. The *Peking Gazette* under Chen's editorship was a vociferously pro-republican newspaper. In a rare example of one journalist praising another in China, B. L. Putnam Weale declared in the preface to his 1917 book *The Fight for the Republic in China*:

> The writer desires to record his indebtedness to the columns of the *Peking Gazette*, a newspaper which under the brilliant editorship of Eugene Chen — a pure Chinese born and educated under the British flag — has fought consistently and victoriously for Liberalism and Justice and has made the Republic a reality to countless thousands who otherwise would have refused to believe in it.[14]

Chen didn't rest on his laurels or allow the authorities to intimidate him. He went on to found the *Shanghai Gazette* and continued to attack British interests in his clipped British accent, for which he was thrown into prison yet again for his trouble. In 1919 he was a delegate to Versailles where he tried to assert China's cause. Later on he continued to agitate against the British in China with some success, including forcing a deal whereby London returned the British Concession in Hankou to China. At times when Chen was being held at his majesty's pleasure, the *Gazette* was edited by C. H. Lee, another ethnic Chinese of Trinidadian birth. Also adding to the mystery around the *Gazette* was the mysterious involvement of George Sokolsky, the man who had advised the newly arrived Hallett Abend to head to Guangzhou.

Sokolsky was a famously enigmatic figure in the foreign press corps. The son of Russian-speaking Jewish immigrants to America, he had studied at Columbia University's School of Journalism from which he had nearly been expelled as a radical. Aged 24, he returned to Russia in 1917 and edited the *Russian Daily News,* an English-language newspaper in Petrograd, but when the Bolsheviks ousted Kerensky he became disillusioned with the revolution and moved on. He arrived in China in 1918 and promptly married a Chinese woman, joined the editorial staff of the *Shanghai Gazette*, which put him in close proximity to Sun, and became involved in the May Fourth demonstrations as a courier between Sun and the students. Sokolsky left the *Gazette* pretty quickly after a row with C. H. Lee, but he stayed close to Sun and wrote for a wide range of newspapers including the *North-China*, the *New York Post*, the *New York Times Magazine*, the *Philadelphia Ledger* and Ben Fleisher's *Japan Advertiser*, as well as stringing for the *St Louis Post-Dispatch* and the London *Daily Express*. Sokolsky had close connections to the left and was one of the first journalists to know about the formation of the Chinese Communist Party in 1921. He often appeared in the *North-China* as an editorial writer, under the pseudonym "G Gramada", reporting from Guangzhou and Shanghai regularly throughout the 1920s until he left China in 1931 to return to America where he became decidedly reactionary, totally disavowed his leftist past and earned a good living as a popular right-wing columnist in New York. At his height, his column was carried by an estimated 300 papers and he was also doing a weekly radio broadcast for the rather reactionary National Manufacturers Association. He then became a close friend of Joe McCarthy in the 1950s (McCarthy called him "Sok"), favouring him despite Sokolsky's rather late conversion to anti-communism.

As well as C. H. Lee and Sokolsky, Chen was also to provide work for a number of other journalists, both Chinese and foreign, and revolutionaries and those not politically aligned but useful. C. H. Lowe was educated at missionary schools and then attended Boone University in Wuchang, a college set up by the American Church Mission. There they taught him English and he wrote his first articles for the *Boone Review*. He saw the May Fourth Movement from Wuchang and was then accepted into Chicago University where he continued to write and contribute to the *Chinese Students Monthly*. After returning home and teaching for a while, Lowe became involved with the *Hankow Herald* and, around 1926, the *Peking Leader*, which had "Independent, Liberal, Constructive" as its slogan. It later became the *Peiping Chronicle* and had a circulation of around 1,200 when the Northern Expedition advanced and the government moved its headquarters in Guangzhou up to Wuchang and then Hankou. As Wuchang and Hankou became newsworthy, Lowe was appointed special correspondent for both the *Herald* and the *Leader*. He was well placed. As the leaders arrived in the city, he scooped the first interviews with Madame Sun, Borodin, the minister of communications Sun Fo and the minister of justice Xu Qian.

Lowe was also able to cultivate a contact with Eugene Chen, at that time the minister of foreign affairs in Wuhan. Despite having moved into government, the impeccably dressed Chen who always had his hair heavily "brilliantined", making it shine like a mirror, constantly felt the lure of the newspaper business and was considering restarting the *People's Tribune* that had been forcibly closed down by the vicious warlord Zhang Zuolin. Chen liked Lowe and vice versa and in 1927 Lowe moved jobs to work on the restarted *Tribune* based in Hankou's former German Concession.

There he was sent to interview the visiting US senator for Connecticut, Hiram Bingham. Lowe was refused permission to board the ship on which Bingham was staying. The senator later met another *Tribune* reporter and it was clear that the ship's commander was happy to let a Western, but not a Chinese, journalist on board. Meanwhile the government moved on from Hankou to Nanjing as the Northern Expedition rolled on and the *Tribune*'s staff were told the paper was relocating to Shanghai. However, the KMT right-wing was resurgent, the left was purged and the *Tribune* never did resume publication. For his part, Lowe remained partially in the newspaper business sending despatches from Shanghai to the *Honolulu Star-Bulletin* in the 1930s, the *Shanghai Evening Post*, the *North-China* and the *China Press*, as well as being a founding contributing editor of the influential journal *The China Critic*.

As the leftist government in Hankou collapsed and Chiang asserted total control by viciously purging the KMT and locating the government in Nanjing, the *Hankow Herald* was also left rudderless and in need of a new editor if it was to survive. The successful applicant was Edward Hunter, a career foreign correspondent and no leftist. After getting his start in America by writing for various New York and Philadelphia newspapers, he moved to Asia. He first worked for the *Japan Advertiser* as the paper's news editor and then went to China to work on the *Hankow Herald* and *Peking Leader*. Hunter took over the *Herald* after the left-leaning government had been dissolved and activists like the Prohmes, Chen and Borodin had all fled the city. After reorienting the newspaper's political line to suit the KMT, he went to Beijing to take over as managing editor of the *Peking Leader*. Hunter was to move again in 1931 to the Hearst newspaper syndicate to cover the Japanese occupation of Manchuria.

Even those who were not avowed leftists managed to fall foul of Chiang and the KMT. Former *Peking Leader* news editor Hallett Abend was appointed as the *New York Times*'s north China and Manchuria correspondent in 1927, while Missi Misselwitz (yet another Missourian) acted as the paper's Shanghai correspondent when the veteran journalist Frederick Moore returned to America to act as an adviser to the Japanese government, a post he would hold until 1941. Misselwitz had big boots to fill. New Orleans-born Moore was a China press corps legend who had been the AP correspondent in Beijing since 1910 and during the First World War and the managing editor of *Asia* magazine in 1917–18. Abend was relatively new to China but positively ancient for a foreign correspondent, having already turned 40 when he arrived. During his time Abend roamed across China as well as covering events in Beijing and Shanghai, and he was to spend a great deal of time in northern China covering the Japanese incursions into Manchuria. He was accused of being soft on Japan by some other correspondents. However, he was generally pro-Chinese, particularly after he witnessed Japanese atrocities in the city of Jinan in 1928 where, during Chiang's Northern Expedition, the Japanese had run riot throughout the town, killing trapped Nationalist soldiers and civilians alike.

Being a leftist journalist or newspaper was guaranteed to get you into trouble with the government, but life was also difficult for decidedly non-leftists too in the 1920s.

Bans — Fun with the Censors

The government took exception to a wide range of foreign correspondents in the 1920s. The *North-China* was often openly hostile to the government. It was a supporter of extraterritoriality and constantly worried about the loss of Great Power privileges and rights if Chiang should decide to continue his Northern Expedition into the treaty ports, which seemed a distinct possibility to many; and the paper was also often perceived to be sympathetic to Tokyo, in line with British Foreign Office thinking at the time. In 1929 the paper was subjected to a postal ban by the government, largely as a result of articles by Rodney Gilbert and George Sokolsky. Following this, in 1930, the paper's editorial line changed noticeably when the staunchly pro-British O. M. Green was rather controversially replaced as editor by Edwin Haward, the well-regarded India Hand who had worked on the *Civil and Military Gazette* in Lahore (Kipling's old employer). The paper became more pro-government and also more objective in its reporting of issues involving tricky topics such as extraterritoriality. The Old Lady of the Bund's change of heart was due to Haward's new editorial decisions as well as a broader change in the sensibilities of the foreign population in China who increasingly decided to live with the Nationalist government rather than oppose it. Haward may have been more a man of India than China but he knew his stuff and had also been a long and close friend of J. O. P. Bland. Though the *North-China* was hardest hit, both the French-owned *Journal de Pekin* and Woodhead's *Peking and Tientsin Times* suffered various penalties, from being denied the use of the mail system to all copies circulated outside the foreign concessions being seized and burned by Nationalist officials.

However, few journalists were as directly targeted by the Nationalists as Hallett Abend. He had made multiple enemies in the Chiang clan through various actions, including the perhaps unwise decision to punch Chiang's son on the nose and accuse the Generalissimo of suffering from unbridled ambition. The government tried to discredit him with Adolph Ochs, the publisher of the *New York Times*, and attempted to deport him several times. They were unsuccessful, but the Chinese telegraph offices were ordered not to handle his despatches and he had to resort to the rather roundabout method of sending them to the *Times*'s Tokyo bureau for forwarding to New York. Despite the government's intense dislike of Abend, extraterritoriality meant they couldn't expel him and, as he was the representative of a highly influential paper, he was still invited to the regular tea and sandwiches briefings for foreign reporters held by Chiang and Madame Chiang in Nanjing. However, he could never be sure if the two shots fired at him while in a rickshaw in Beijing, or, several years later in 1934, an attempted stabbing at Shanghai's North Railway Station, were random attacks or botched assassination attempts. Other correspondents also found themselves the subject of intense lobbying of their bosses by the Nationalists, if not assassination attempts. For example, Charles Dailey, the *Chicago Tribune*'s Beijing correspondent was contacted by his bemused editor who had been deluged with sacks of mail denouncing Dailey in what appeared to be an orchestrated campaign similar to that organised against Abend.

White Russia and Japan Find a Voice

The end of the First World War and the Russian Revolution had seen large numbers of anti-Bolshevik White Russians move to northern China before filtering out across the country and, in particular, going to Shanghai where passports, visas and official papers were less of an issue. Naturally, wherever they settled they needed something to read in Russian. *Evreiskoe slovo*, a Russian monthly aimed at the Jewish community, was launched in Harbin where many of the White Russians initially settled in 1918; and the *Russian Daily News* also appeared in Harbin in 1918. Russian readers had a wide choice from *Shanghai Zaria* and *Slovo* (*Word*), both based in Shanghai, to *Rubezh* (*Border*), a Harbin-based weekly that regularly included popular stories that were mostly rather melancholy memoirs of pre-Bolshevik mother Russia that appealed to the traditionally gloomy and introverted Russian literary soul in exile.

The other group that was growing in number in China in the 1920s was the Japanese. Their numbers grew for a variety of reasons, including the growing expatriate Japanese business community in Shanghai and other cities, spreading Japanese commercial interests and, of course, Japanese meddling in northeast China. Most Japanese passing through or living in Shanghai eventually found their way to Uchiyama Kanzo's bookshop, which had opened in 1916 and remained in business until the late 1930s. Uchiyama sold Japanese-language books and magazines and was also popular with some Chinese intellectuals who at the time saw Japan as an example of a strong Asian nation that could provide a potential model for China. Uchiyama had grown up with a wide appreciation of Chinese culture and was a practising Christian who hoped to develop better Sino-Japanese cultural relations. He was also a publisher, putting out a few journals, including one he coproduced under the auspices of the Chinese Drama Research Society that served as the mouthpiece for a literary and cultural group he set up. The group met regularly at his shop which, in the mid- to late-1920s, was the major sales point in Shanghai for Japanese magazines and journals.

Uchiyama himself was a correspondent of sorts who wrote articles on Chinese life, politics and culture. His first essay, called *Twenty Years Living in Shanghai*, was published in *Kaizo* in 1934. He went on to publish more articles in the journal in the late 1930s, including *Random Prattle About Shanghai* and *Lively Discussions About Shanghai*. But, despite being seen as broadly pro-Chinese, it was nearly impossible for any Japanese to be too sympathetic and Uchiyama failed to condemn absolutely Japanese aggression in China, seeing Tokyo's action more as a nuisance in daily business life rather than a significant threat to the peace and stability of China, let alone an abuse of China's sovereignty. Uchiyama always preferred discussion of culture and the arts to politics, which was a policy one could still just about follow in China in the 1920s. However, this was not the case in the 1930s when the anti-Japanese backlash forced him to shut up shop despite his personal sympathies.

Left and right, English and other languages, new publications run by foreigners and others in English — like *The China Critic* journal, run by Chinese intellectuals — politics and East-West relations were already becoming increasingly blurred in the 1920s. They were to become yet hazier in the 1930s with foreign writers backing the KMT and others intrigued by communism, while some stuck firmly to the line of supporting foreign influence in China which often tipped over into support for Japan. The China press corps was about to become even more multi-layered, complicated and cosmopolitan in the most tumultuous decade of the twentieth century.

7
The Decadent Thirties — Celebrities, Gangsters and the Ladies of the Press

"... Shanghai, this electric and lurid city, more exciting than any other in the world."

J. G. Ballard, *Empire of the Sun,* describing Shanghai in 1937

"Years ago a speck was torn away from the mystery of China and became Shanghai. A distorted mirror of problems that beset the world today, it grew into a refuge for people who wished to live between the lines of laws and customs — a modern tower of Babel."

Opening on-screen introduction to Josef von Sternberg's film *The Shanghai Gesture* (1941)

The Squire of Nettlebed and Kini the Swiss — Fleming and Maillart

As the clouds of revolution and war gathered, the rash of new visiting journalists and correspondents descending on China continued with many not intending to stay long. Ada Chesterton came to China with impeccable Fleet Street training in the early thirties and recorded her impressions of the country while Gerald Yorke of Reuters came initially for a brief visit, ended up staying two years and found both a country in flux and a new interest in mysticism. After leaving China Yorke pursued his mystical interests and became the *Frater Voto Intelligere* of the Hermetic Order of the Golden Dawn (a sort of more mystical version of the Masons). However, among the brief sojourners of the early 30s, Peter Fleming, special travel correspondent of the London *Times*, who combined features and political reportage with travel writing, stands out as the most worthy of note.

The dashing Fleming was from good stock — wealthy Scottish bankers who had made a fortune in Dundee jute, founded a bank and invented the investment trust. His father, Valentine, had been a barrister and MP for Henley, but he was killed in action in 1917 and was posthumously awarded the Distinguished Service Order. Winston Churchill wrote his obituary. The Eton- and Oxford-educated Peter was also incidentally the Squire of Nettlebed, a charming village in the Chilterns where the family's 44-bedroomed estate Merrimoles was located, and was known as the "smarter" brother of James Bond and *Chitti-Chitti-Bang-Bang* creator Ian. The handsome, though incredibly shy, Peter was also glamorous, eventually marrying the English film star Celia Johnson. He had worked as the literary editor of *The Spectator*, often under the by-line *Strix* (the Latin for a screech owl), contributing to the magazine for over 40 years. He then specialised in travel, traipsing ill-prepared across Brazil in search of the hapless and long-lost explorer Colonel P. H. Fawcett. He didn't find him, but returned safely, wrote it all up as a bestselling book — *Brazilian Adventure* — and made his name. After a few months at *The Spectator*, he was given leave to head to Manchuria and immediately started filing stories, one of the first being an in-depth examination of duck fighting in southern China.

In *One's Company*, the story of his 1933 trip via the Trans-Siberian Railway to China, Fleming appeared flippantly detached from events and characteristically scathing while able to cope adequately with deprivation: that, due to a childhood illness, he had no sense of smell or taste arguably helped. For him, Beijing was "lacking in charm", Harbin was a city of "no easily definable character", Changchun "entirely characterless" and Shenyang "nondescript and suburban", while even innocent little Yingkou up on the Korean border was "decaying". Eventually Fleming arrived in Chengde, a city he finally liked, though largely due to its resemblance, in his eyes at least, to Windsor! Fleming liked these strange comparisons, presumably thinking it would help his readers in England to visualise China better; he compared Beijing with Oxford for some reason![1] He did manage to meet a few notables but, it seems, did not learn much. His interview with Chiang Kai-shek apparently left him none the wiser and he only managed to think of three questions to ask China's leader at a crucial time in the nation's history. He hadn't expected to actually meet Chiang, typically not really having made any preparations beforehand, but when Fleming turned up at Chiang's retreat in Kuling, Madame Chiang wondered who this strange foreigner was lurking outside their house and invited him in. Fleming was infamously clueless about politics. He predicted that Japanese soldiers would wipe out the bandits and restore peace in five years, when in reality five years later they were busy bombing Shanghai and raping Nanjing; and he also predicted that the Communists would never successfully take power in China. This last belief caused no end of misinformation as when he made it to Shanghai — a city he didn't write about at the time, believing that it had been "overdone" by previous sojourners — he was hailed as something of an authority on the Communists, as he was one of the few correspondents at that time to have met one. However, he did make one very pertinent comment that seems to have drawn him back: "In China there is always something worth watching". But if *One's Company* is anything to judge by, he didn't seem to actually find that much.

After a brief experience working for the BBC, he soon realised he wouldn't advance in the corporation: his accent was deemed too posh even for the BBC in the 1930s! His thoughts turned to the East once again. In 1934 he returned on a trip financed by the *Times*, through Russia into China and then back out via Chinese Turkestan and into India. For part of the journey, he was accompanied by the intrepid female traveller Ella Maillart, whom he had met in a London nightclub and dubbed "The Swiss". He flippantly said "see you in China" and then did indeed bump into her in Harbin completely by accident later. Together they travelled 3,500-miles from Beijing to India via Turkestan mainly on horseback and camel, along with a Mr. Yao of the China Central News Agency. The trip was of interest to the *Times* as no foreigner had recorded crossing Turkestan since Owen Lattimore nearly a decade previously, as visas were almost impossible to get and the area was plagued by ongoing civil wars and competing warlords. Fleming and Maillart undertook the journey without the knowledge of the Chinese government which was not keen on issuing passes for foreigners to travel in the disputed and chaotic region. Still they went, with Fleming in many ways epitomising the understated travel writing of the English in the 1930s while Maillart epitomised the newly independent women travellers of the period — an odd mix.

Ella "Kini" Maillart reputedly hated writing but loved travelling and undertook the former only to fund the latter. Born in Geneva of Swiss and Danish parents, she was technically an ethnologist specialising in Asia. Despite being a woman, she was a perfect travelling companion for the manly, rugged and outward-bound Fleming as she had, among other things, founded the first Swiss women's hockey team, sailed for Switzerland in the 1924 Paris Olympics, competed in international ski races and, aged 20, sailed in a small boat across the Mediterranean and up the Atlantic to England — all this just to prove to her family that she was over her regular bouts of childhood illness.

After traversing the Soviet Union, Fleming arrived in Harbin where he bumped into Maillart who was working as a special correspondent for *Le Petit Parisien* and they decided to take their trip across China to India without much thought. However, after deciding on the epic trip, Fleming took off for the comfort of the Keswick family (the controllers of the Jardine Matheson empire) houseboat in Shanghai to enjoy some *taipan* comforts. As 1935 dawned he travelled to Beijing to meet up with Maillart for their grand trek, after he had already been travelling for four-and-a-half months. Maillart, a bit of a linguist, immediately got them business cards printed up with Fleming becoming Fu Leiming (learned engraver on stone) and Kini as Ma Naya (horse of international goodwill).

Despite their different characters, Fleming and Maillart got on pretty well. She was an inveterate and educated traveller with more experience of western China and Central Asia than Fleming could claim. They both watched fascinated as Mongol tribesman slit the bellies of sheep to take out their still-beating hearts and visited an opium den to try to find a cure for her sore throat, or at least that was their excuse. Maillart thought Fleming smart and admired his ability, due to his lack of taste or smell senses, to eat anything and indeed he lived happily on Tibetan *tsamba*, parched barley meal not much liked by many foreigners. Their joint trek was recorded later by Fleming in his witty *News from Tartary* and Maillart published her version of the trip as the rather more serious *Forbidden Journey*. Unlike Fleming, Maillart was an able photographer who recorded the trip with her camera too. The pair got what they both, and presumably their readers too, wanted — bandits, warlords, beggars and some pretty rough living. The trip culminated in their arrival at the British consulate in Kashgar whereupon Fleming was annoyed that the Piccadilly-bought tropical suit he had saved for the occasion (and carried the entire way!) had somehow turned green and that he had to present himself to the British consul "disguised as a lettuce, looking like something that had escaped from Devil's Island … and letting down the British Raj".[2] He was also keen to contact staff at the *Times* who had no idea where he was for six months — and they cabled back to Kashgar, "ALL IMMENSELY RELIEVED YOUR REAPPEARANCE".

Inevitably Maillart and Fleming had on occasion rubbed each other up the wrong way on such a long and arduous trip. Fleming moaned about Maillart's tendency to never stop chatting; and Maillart was annoyed by Fleming's flippancy, stinking pipe and, what seemed to her, his rush to finish the trip and get back to Scotland before the end of the grouse shooting season, a comment in which there was some truth. Fleming thought that, given the circumstances of travelling in Turkestan, Mongolia and Tibet, they should have either fallen madly in love or murdered each other. Instead they managed to get along and Maillart commented: "How do you expect me to fall in love with a man who, in deepest Central Asia, complains every morning that he hasn't got his *Times* to read?" It was effectively a travel marriage of convenience by two loners, given that Fleming had written a book called *One's Company* and Maillart had made her name with a book entitled *Turkestan Solo*. One good thing to come from the trip was that a worried Celia Johnson, back in England, had found out that

Fleming was travelling with "The Swiss". Before leaving for China, he had joked with Celia about Maillart's beauty. Celia decided in secret to marry Peter, unaware that he had not felt anything for Kini beyond a sense of adventurous kinship, had described her as "not my cup of tea" and had indeed pined horribly for Celia throughout the trip. Still, he always retained a soft spot for Maillart (they met regularly for lunch in London for the rest of their lives) who on their trip had lived up to her motto "Nobody can go? Then I shall go".

In any book about foreign correspondents, the question inevitably arises of who is the closest to Evelyn Waugh's bumbling correspondent William Boot in his satirical novel *Scoop*, based on Waugh's stint as a war reporter for the *Daily Mail* in Abyssinia. The truth is that among any group of foreign correspondents, particularly those covering wars, there will invariably be one William Boot, sent by Lord Copper, the arrogant and ignorant owner of the *Daily Beast*, to cover the war in the fictional East African country of Ishmaelia. Fleming was undoubtedly the Boot of the China press corps. He was constantly striding around in his immaculate outfits from Piccadilly, rarely aware of what was going on in wider Chinese politics, bereft of pertinent questions when stumbling across an important personage and largely reliant on other journalists and the authorities to shuttle him from one place he failed to appreciate or understand to another. Indeed, in many senses Fleming out-Booted Boot.[3] He was also a sight to behold. Aside from his immaculate attire and creating the image in his books of travelling light, he always carried with him a typewriter, a box of books, a gramophone, multiple bottles of brandy and his essential supplies of potted grouse and Stilton from Fortnum and Mason. Fleming was to return to China later for more Boot-like adventures.

The Ladies of the Press and Shanghai's Gangster No. 1

The 1930s was a period when women appeared increasingly as part of the China press corps, both as locally based correspondents, writers and freelancers as well as brief sojourners. The years after the First World War had seen a few pioneers such as Edna Lee Booker who became a "girl reporter" on the *China Press* and the Shanghai stringer for the International News Service (InterNews) and shared a house with Nora Waln, an up-and-coming novelist who subsidised herself by being a roaming correspondent for the *Atlantic Monthly*. Booker was the sole woman working for the *Press* but she claims to have been welcomed warmly by the paper's city editor, the redheaded Irishman J. Edward Doyle. She was hardly a novice as she had worked previously for both the *Los Angeles Herald* and the *San Francisco Call Bulletin*. Dinty Doyle was sparing but precise in his advice to her — "The only order I received regarding my copy was that American prestige must be upheld" — regardless. "Face!"[4] Booker, determined to be a war correspondent, never let her gender dictate what she could and couldn't write about. She famously disregarded the advice of the old China Hands at the *Press* and, heading north, got the first interview ever given to a woman by the Old Marshal Zhang Zuolin, at the time China's most feared warlord. She trumped this feat by then accompanying Upton Close to an interview with the warlord Wu "Jade Marshal" Peifu, while he was preparing to do battle with the Old Marshal, and so became the first woman to interview him too. Booker was to go on to get a remarkable number of scoops, including being in Guangzhou when Sun Yat-sen's government fell and he was forced to flee on a gunboat. Booker caught up with the boat, was hoisted aboard and got an interview with Sun and the last-ever interview with Wu Ting-fang who was to die two days after their meeting.

Other early "girl reporters" included Louise Blakeney, who edited the *North-China*'s woman's page, and San Franciscan Elsie McCormick who specialised in vignettes of Shanghai life for the *China Press* in the 1920s and later wrote for the *New Yorker*. McCormick was also well known for her widely-read and amusing *Unexpurgated Diary of a Shanghai Baby* and had accompanied Upton Close to cover the 1920 Gansu earthquake. There was also the New Yorker Irene Corbally Kuhn who went on to become a local radio star and J. B. Powell's wife Margaret who was, from 1921, the *Weekly Review*'s editor in charge of local news and "women's interests". Still, women were definitely a tiny minority of the arriving foreign correspondents. In the 1930s, more came, some of whom were primarily politically motivated, such as the aforementioned Rayna Prohme, Anna Louise Strong, Agnes Smedley and Mildred Mitchell. But not all were overtly politically committed by any means.

Alexandra Roube-Jansky arrived in Shanghai from her native France in 1936 as a stringer for *Paris Soir*. She combined a louche and busy social life with her reporting duties and photography for *Paris Soir* magazine. Roube-Jansky was to be a major interpreter of Shanghai's vibrancy and decadence to the French reading public in the 1930s and indulged in it herself wholeheartedly with some highly erotic writing that embarrassed more than one of her Shanghai lovers. By contrast, Russian-born Iustina Kruzenshtern had moved to Harbin as a refugee when she was three years old. She worked for various Russian émigré periodicals in Harbin before moving to Shanghai in 1930 to work jointly for *Shankhaiskaia Zaria* and the *North-China*. She stayed until the 1949 revolution and then went to the USA to work for the *Voice of America*. Indeed, the *North-China,* despite being seen as a hard-drinking masculine environment, did actually employ some women over the years, such as Marguerite Yancey, who went on to become a lieutenant in America's Women's Army Corps (WAC) in the Second World War.

The *China Press* was arguably more female-friendly than the *North-China* in the 1930s. Miriam Griffith, a Californian, edited the *Press*'s woman's page for some years, which by 1930 was featuring full-colour drawings of the latest season's fashions. Her colleague Malcolm Rosholt remembered her as a good writer who could hold her own in the overwhelmingly male environment of the paper's office. She left the *Press* to marry a German national and moved to Berlin where he became a Nazi. She left him in disgust, returning to Shanghai, where she eventually committed suicide. When Griffith left Shanghai, Nevada Semantza replaced her as the woman's page editor. The tradition of the inter-office romance at the *Press* was upheld: among other office romances, Carl Crow had married another employee Mildred Powers in 1912. Semantza married the city editor in 1932 and they moved to California. After Semantza, the woman's page was given over to Au Huna Tong, a petite Chinese woman journalist and then again in 1934 to Betty Wang, both Chinese journalists who trained in America.

Other women freelanced to keep themselves occupied and while their husbands were out of town on business. New Yorker Su-Lin Young was an exquisite woman who roamed around the crowded newsrooms of Shanghai picking up freelance work. She was the young wife of the handsome Chinese-American explorer Jack Young and had been raised in a wealthy and pampered Manhattan household. Jack and Su-Lin had married in the mid-1930s. Despite being short, thin and having luxuriant shoulder-length hair, Su-Lin accompanied Jack and his younger brother Yang Tilin (who adopted the English name Quentin after a Roosevelt) on several panda hunts and expeditions, including an arduous nine-month trek into Tibet where she was in charge of preserving their botanical specimens for delivery to American clients. Prior to the expeditions with her husband, the most arduous experience of Su-Lin's life had been as a camp counsellor in New Hampshire. Despite being an American citizen, she was awarded the title of China's first woman explorer. When Jack and Quentin were away having adventures, Su-Lin often stayed in Shanghai freelancing for the *North-China* and Sowerby's *China Journal*, where her newly acquired botanical experience and travels to Tibet were useful. She was also something of a socialite and the husband and wife explorers made a dashing couple around town. Even Emily Hahn, the most social of Shanghai socialites, described her as "glamorous".[5] She was certainly one of the few daughters of a Manhattan nightclub owner to scale peaks in Tibet, track bears and build yak dung fires.

Others didn't have husbands to worry about and struck out for China fuelled by their own wanderlust. Polish-born Ilona Ralf Sues was to be one of the more eccentric journalists of any gender ever to arrive in China. As a player on the fringes of the League of Nations in Geneva, she had decided that the prioritisation of the welfare of the whale over Manchuria was seriously wrong and headed east. China had first grabbed her attention when she had worked for the League's Anti-Opium Information Bureau, basically a private lobby group that sought to influence League opinion on the opium issue. She hoped to hold nations to their pledges to stamp out the illicit trade but was frustrated in her efforts: as one commentator said at the time, trying to completely suppress the opium trade was like "… trying to catch a million fleas with teaspoons". Opium and the League were where thinking on Manchuria met for Sues. The Japanese were annexing Manchuria and using it as a production and distribution base to flood China with cheap morale-sapping narcotics. Limit Japanese expansion in northern China and you would deal a major blow to the dope trade. As the League was supposed to be dealing with the Japanese incursion into Manchuria and had been entrusted with the global fight against opium, the intersection of the two fell at the League's door. Yet, as Sues found to her frustration, the League was taking neither question seriously. She became disenchanted at the appeasement of Japan and the inability to tackle the illicit dope traffic seriously. She decided the Great Powers were tolerating Japan's Manchurian annexation in order to gain some arm sales and she walked out of the whole business in disgust. She took Chinese lessons and decided in 1936 to set out for China, writing later in her memoir: "I sold my couch, bought a Leica, packed my three Cs — Cat, Camera and Continental typewriter — and set out as a freelance journalist".[6]

Sues arrived in Guangzhou where a mutual friend introduced her to the highly amiable Alfred Lin who was covering Chiang's "pacification" of the rebellious southern city as a young correspondent for Reuters. Lin got Sues an appointment with Colonel Li Fang, the new Guangzhou mayor's secretary who in turn got her in to see Chiang's newly appointed mayor Tseng Yang-fu, a Pittsburgh-educated engineer who had flirted with journalism while studying at Yenching University where he had edited the student newspaper. Sues was also extremely lucky to meet T. T. "Francis" Yao, the director of the official government Central News Agency who was also in town to co-ordinate Chiang's propaganda effort. Yao took Sues on an unparalleled VIP tour of the city's new political establishment: the Guangdong Reconstruction Commission building, the Government Cement Works, the Government Textile Mills and a host of KMT-run kindergartens were the rather boring attractions highlighted on the official grand tour at the time. However, Sues did get a good story that summer when she witnessed the official launch of the Chiang's Confucian-authoritarian New Life Movement that spearheaded the suppression of such fatal vices as flies, mahjong and open collars.

Sues moved on to Shanghai where she knew some long-term missionaries and one of them introduced her to Bill Donald, "a bewitching talker", who was now the Chiang's *major domo*. Sues described Donald at their first meeting as "volcanic", talking up a storm but refusing to discuss the situation in China vis-à-vis opium. She recalled him as, "… tall, broad shouldered, with a strong ruddy face and curiously streaked grey hair, a wilful chin, a determined mouth and extraordinary, world-conscious eyes that look right through people and things and cannot be fooled" [7]. This was a more flattering physical description of Donald than usual.

Actually Donald's stance on opium was interesting. He had told Chiang that it was a curse on China and that as the man with the army he should suppress it totally and brutally. Donald had an agreement with Chiang (which the boss occasionally decided to forget) that, though he advised him, he was free to criticise him in the press: in this way Donald was both adviser and commentator. Donald hoped the knowledge that he could attack Chiang would both ensure Chiang's honesty and also safeguard his position of journalistic liberty and trustworthiness with the press corps. Unconditional independence was paramount to Donald, though most who knew him would have seen it as having different limits to Donald's own opinion of his freedom to criticise. On this issue Chiang had roundly ignored Donald's advice and established an organisation to regulate opium sales to "better control them" and also earn some much-needed revenue. Donald had gone ballistic and written a number of scathing articles in the English-language press in which he criticised Chiang in no uncertain terms. Madame Chiang had translated them to the Generalissimo who was not happy but didn't kick Donald out.

Sues initially stuck to reporting the situation with opium and revealed such tit-bits as number one gangster Du Yue-Sheng (Big Eared Du) and the Green Gang's involvement in the drug trade and the fact that Shanghai Customs was seizing illegal morphine shipments that were destined for New York and the notorious Lepke-Buchhalter gang and Murder Inc. She also found that the Shanghai Opium Suppression Bureau was being run by Big Eared Du and that all narcotics seized were turned over to him for destruction; in other words, the Chinese Maritime Customs was turning over dope to China's biggest dope dealer who had once been a fearsome dope addict but had cured himself — using heroin tablets! She also met with Henry Hollssen, a Norwegian known as "Denmark's Globetrotting Journalist", who was not based officially in Shanghai but visited it regularly. He was particularly keen on researching the opium business; its links to the criminal underworld; the lives of addicts; and just what was so attractive to people about the "Big Smoke". Hollssen would prowl the streets of Shanghai's Zhabei district in search of back-street opium dens, planning his great exposé of the opium trade.

Eventually Sues's articles about opium came to Du's attention and he summoned her to a meeting. People had been summoned by Du before; some came back, some didn't. Sues's religiously-inclined friend, Aimée Millican, advised her to ask Du to repent his sins while Donald told her she had to go as refusal could end up being interpreted as an insult. The police advised her bluntly and presented her with her rather limited options; don't go and he will have you shot or go but refuse to write laudatory articles and he will have you shot. Sues arrived at Du's large Frenchtown mansion where she courageously peppered the gangster with questions about Shanghai's opium trade. For his part, Big Eared Du predictably wanted Sues to write glowing portraits of him for the foreign press. The gangster remained calm and told her everything was under control and he was head of the Suppression Bureau, a fact that had thrown the League's Anti-Opium Information Bureau into an impotent fury but that seemed highly amusing to Du. Less amused was Sues's policeman friend who had been waiting for her to report back after the meeting. She decided instead to head out for a stiff drink, only turning up later to meet her, by then, nerve-shredded acquaintance who had assumed that she had been shot and dumped in the Suzhou Creek.

Mickey Hahn and Mr. Mills

However, of all the women to join the China press corps, perhaps none was as notorious as Emily Hahn. Hahn had travelled extensively before arriving in China and she was to travel extensively afterwards too, though it is with Shanghai she will probably always be most associated. Arriving in 1935, almost by accident and not intending to stay but just to get some new dresses made, she hung around, freelanced occasionally for the *North-China* and contributed a number of pieces to the *New Yorker* that have become perennial favourites for capturing the flavour of old Shanghai. She got tight with all the right people — Sir Victor Sassoon, the rich owner of the Cathay Hotel, as well as Madame Chiang. She had enchanted many men, including Sassoon and the intellectual, poet and dapper man-about-town Zau Sinmay (Shao Xunmei).

To say that Hahn was from a varied background would be understating it. She was the first woman to gain a mining degree from Wisconsin University, a Wild West trail guide, a Congo explorer, a London literary scene habitué, an author of a book on the art of seduction and an Oxford student; and, while in Shanghai, she reputedly occasionally hosted Mao and Zhou En-lai in her apartment. She was certainly not a typical *North-China* freelancer. Emily, or "Mickey" as she preferred to be known, was a hit with her big dark eyes, frequent smile, husky voice, large rear-end and fashionably bobbed hair. She was half tomboy and half *femme fatale* and most men seem to have found her irresistible, even with all the other attractions on offer in Shanghai in the 1930s. Though some tried, few could dismiss her as just another "Shanghai babe" or "girl reporter" as she was clearly a thorough journalist, a quick wit and a widely read author.

Mickey also had two monkeys: the monkey on her back that was her opium addiction and the monkey on her shoulder that was Mr. Mills (technically a gibbon and therefore an ape, Mickey would castigate anyone who insulted him by calling him a mere monkey). Mills ensured her an instantly memorable entrée into Shanghai high society with his fondness for urinating or masturbating in public. As well as writing some of the most evocative and descriptive prose on Shanghai in the late 1930s, Mickey managed to also become a writer who had a foot in both camps — the International Settlement social whirl of Shanghailander life and the *avant garde* Chinese life of the city. These two coexisting worlds that all too infrequently met and impinged on each other were the inspiration for Hahn's writing. She was prolific across her lifetime and turned out over 50 books, including memoirs, biographies, journalism, travelogues and children's books, most of which were rushed and written in difficult personal and political circumstances.

On the Chinese side of her life, she became notorious for her affair and marriage, as a concubine or second wife, to Zau, who was then a well-known Shanghainese poet inspired by the European Decadents of the nineteenth century. This didn't necessarily make for great poetry in Chinese but was certainly an interesting experiment in modern Chinese writing and was symptomatic of the Shanghai mixture of Eastern and Western influences that so defined the modernist character of the city during the 1930s. The French- and English-educated Zau published a range of *avant garde* magazines and literary journals in English and Chinese inspired by the likes of Baudelaire, Rimbaud and Mallarmé as well as the English Decadents. He was also inspired by the opium pipe, to which he introduced Hahn. A concubine, an opium addict and an *avant garde* publisher, she had crossed the line into modern Chinese culture in a way no other foreign journalist managed in China between the wars. Most wouldn't have really wanted to either, but Hahn felt it essential to immerse herself. What she got, among other things, was her addiction to opium that led to a need to cure herself and subsequently one of her best pieces for the *New Yorker* dealing with addiction and cure: *The Big Smoke*.

The other side of her was pure Shanghai sojourner and she excelled at both being a central part and simultaneously critic of the excesses of Shanghailander society. Hahn chronicled the late and long dinners, the endless rounds of drinks and parties and the decadence of Shanghai shortly before its fall while personally exceeding most of these excesses. The image of her swanning around parties at Victor Sassoon's with Mr. Mills, complete with his own ape diapers, remains one of the enduring images of old Shanghai as does, for some who knew her anyway, her tendency to answer the door completely naked without any idea who her caller was. She also retained a long-term close relationship with Madame Chiang (who, were she not China's first lady, apparently fancied herself suited to a literary career) to whom she became both biographer and confidante.

When Shanghai fell to the Japanese, Hahn managed to get to Hong Kong where she was able through pure chance to escape internment by the Japanese. Technically (perhaps, perhaps not) married to Zau, the Japanese classified her as Chinese and so not liable for internment. However, they demanded proof and Mickey didn't have a marriage certificate. Quite by chance she bumped into an old Shanghai friend in Hong Kong who was willing to swear an affidavit that Zau and Mickey were married and so she stayed out of Stanley internment camp. Still, the Japanese couldn't really work her out. While accepting her marriage in Shanghai, they were bemused by the fact that she had started an affair with the already married Charles Boxer who, as well as being a leading Portuguese scholar, British peer of the realm and Japan Hand, also happened to be the head of British Intelligence in the colony. Boxer and Hahn had fallen for each other over legendarily long drinking sessions in Hong Kong. When the Japanese invaded, British women were evacuated to Australia, including Boxer's wife Ursula, known as the most beautiful woman in the colony. As his marriage disintegrated, Hahn found herself pregnant to Boxer, but with him under armed guard in a Japanese-controlled hospital and her stuck on the outside foraging for food while trying to complete a long book on the history of the Soong Sisters that had involved trips to Chongqing and close contact with all three women. The Japanese were bemused and eventually asked Hahn what was going on? — Zau, Boxer, the baby? She confessed that she was a "bad girl", while a sympathetic Japanese soldier patted her back and told her that no, she was indeed a good girl.

Good or bad, Hahn carried on writing, carried on getting more and more pregnant and carried on smuggling food into Boxer under the noses of his guards. Rumours abounded about the period and continue to. Why did Boxer leave Ursula for Mickey? How did she get round the Japanese guards to feed Boxer? How did she stay out of the camps and eventually manage to get herself and her baby daughter Carolla repatriated to America? Those who disliked Mickey and her relationship with Boxer and considered her a bad girl suggested she had a large rear-end and had slept with the Japanese to win favours for herself and Boxer. Those who warmed to her dismissed this gossip as nonsense. Either way

Mickey and her baby got back to New York, Boxer followed some years later and their reunion at the New York docks made front-page news, while her writing on the International Settlement became an enduring testament to the last glorious days of the old Shanghai.

The Revolving Doors of the *China Press*

The local English-language press continued to develop its own star writers as the *China Press* passed its 20th anniversary in 1931 as an employer of just about every budding hack that passed through town and the *North-China* had been in business for over 80 years and was infamous for its boozy newsroom — "the Norsh Shina Daily Newsh" as the office wits dubbed it. The *Press* particularly offered opportunities for young would-be newspapermen and women turning up in Shanghai, as well as old hacks looking for a soft posting at the tail end of their careers. Most papers were relatively sedate by Fleet Street or New York standards, with daily siestas, office bars and generous expense accounts. However, the reporting was arguably more hard-boiled than either Fleet Street or New York. When the American reporter Carroll Alcott arrived in Shanghai in 1928, he saw a woman beggar run over by a fancy limousine on the Bund on his first day and was horrified. He had no idea that such tragedies were commonplace and that local journalists prided themselves on being inured to such events: "I could picture the headline: 'MILLIONAIRE'S CAR KILLS AGED WOMAN AS SHE SCOOPS DINNER FROM THE STREET'. Later I learned that Shanghai newspapers were not deeply interested in events of that sort".[8]

The *Press* was now under the control of Chinese interests but was still largely staffed and edited by Americans. The *Shanghai Times* was also still in business and its overtly pro-Japanese line was still considered questionable by most of the foreign press corps.

There were few newspapers that hired as many foreign journalists as the *Press*. The tradition had started when Tom Millard hired Carl Crow, J. B. Powell and others. The world over, newspaper work, despite a veneer of glamour, remains mostly about routine and deadlines. Crow, working on the nightshift at the *Press* in 1911 when news was slow, was left at 2 a.m. wondering what the next day's headline would be — there had to be one, news or no news. It was similar for those who followed Crow, with the bulk of the work being the endless round of SMC meetings, court reports, police bulletins, community events, sports results and shipping announcements. Yet a significant number of unique characters were to work on the paper in the 1930s, lifting it above the routine.

In the early 1930s the *Press* was the employer of talents such as Frank Tillman Durdin, a Texan who had worked on the *San Antonio Express* and the *Los Angeles Times* and who had planned to study music in Europe but jumped ship in Shanghai on the way and stayed at the *Press* for seven years. Others that formed a clique at the paper included Malcolm Rosholt, as well as Earle Selle who was the city editor in 1931. Selle, a stickler for accuracy and grammar, was an old-school hack who gave new hires on their first day a copy of the annual report of the Chinese Maritime Customs and told them to summarise it for an article. If they could make sense of it, précis it down and turn out something printable, they were invariably allowed to stay. Another of the *Press* clique was Jim Hammond who succeeded Selle as the *Press*'s city editor in 1933. He was originally from Elcho, Nevada and stayed in Shanghai until 1939, when he was eventually forced out by the Japanese.

Alexander H. Buchman joined the *Press* in 1934 as a feature writer while also stringing for Havas and travelled extensively in China. A refugee from the Great Depression, he arrived in Japan having travelled in "Filipino" class for $80. (He wanted to travel in steerage, but the shipping line didn't permit "white people to do that".) However, he was moved along by the authorities who suspected him of being a communist after he spoke out about the invasion of Manchuria. Actually they were right, despite his being the son of a wealthy family of musicians, intellectuals, and businessmen from Cleveland, Ohio and having trained as an aeronautical engineer. In Shanghai he became friendly with the confirmed Trotskyite journalists Frank Glass and Harold Isaacs and got involved with the Chinese left opposition. When the Japanese invaded Shanghai, Buchman moved to Hong Kong to work for Eastman Kodak, a job he enjoyed as he had long been an amateur snapper and his pictures appeared regularly in the *Press*. Buchman roamed around Shanghai after the Japanese invasion with a camera concealed surreptitiously in a special pocket in his jacket, the lens peering out through a buttonhole while an extension trigger ran around his neck and into his pocket. He eventually made it back to America in 1939 and then, like many others including Isaacs, went to Mexico to meet his political idol Trotsky, bizarrely got a job as one of the revolutionary's bodyguards and also snapped some amazing pictures of the exile at work and play.

Malcolm Rosholt's friend George Moorad was one of the few *Shanghai Times* writers to be generally welcomed in foreign correspondent society. Most were ostracised due to the *Times*'s pro-Japanese slant that was more a product of the controlling interests of the paper than many of the journalists themselves. Moorad had previously worked on the *Press* but he had moved to the *Times*, much to the dismay of many close colleagues who liked him. He stuck it out at the *Times* until the war when the pro-Japanese stance of the paper finally became too much for him and he returned to America. But he turned straight around and headed to Cairo as a CBS correspondent in 1943 where he died in a plane crash over Bombay aboard the same plane as another well-known Shanghai journalist H. R. "Red" Knickerbocker who also perished. Although Moorad was considered a political reactionary by some in the press corps, he remained well liked by many and, in the face of the mounting Communist victory in 1949, staunchly supported the KMT. Moorad was not alone in moving from the *Press* to the *Times*; William Fisher did the same and was also still liked among the press corps. Fisher later became internationally famous for scooping an interview in India with Gandhi and then covered the Japanese invasion of Burma in 1942 for *Time-Life*.

Others were firm favourites among the corps, such as La Selle "Lu" Gilman, a Nebraskan who joined the *Press* in 1933 as a 25-year-old feature writer and eventually became city editor. He later moved to the *Shanghai Evening Post and Mercury*, which was being edited by the acerbic and also immensely popular Minnesotan Randall Gould, and then left China to join Earle Selle on the *Honolulu Advertiser* where he wrote a regular column of society goings-on called "Port and Off Port" that tracked the comings and goings of the rich and famous in Hawaii. He covered the Pearl Harbour attack, wrote his Honolulu war diary and also published four novels, including *Shanghai Deadline* in 1936 about being a Shanghai newspaperman.

The *Press* turned out a surprising number of great feature writers. One of the best regarded at the time was Patrick "Pat" McGrady from Seattle. McGrady, like many others, covered the visit of the aviator Charles Lindberg to Shanghai and wrote the story of the first of the American military personnel to be killed in China by the Japanese — Robert Short of Tacoma who was shot down in a dogfight over Suzhou during the First Shanghai War of 1932. The Chinese were astonished by Short's action and gave him a hero's funeral which was delayed for a month so that his mother and brother could attend, along with half a million Chinese who gathered along the route of the procession to remember "Short La".

Among the characters at the *Press* were a few with problems ranging from money to depression to women, but that didn't necessarily stop them being good reporters. For instance, Herbert Lewis, known simply as "Herb" to most people, worked at the *Press* for much of the 1930s as the editor of the commercial pages though mostly he sat around the office cracking jokes. When Lewis left Shanghai, many a tear was shed, mainly by his vast number of creditors who were left with no forwarding address and his worthless chits unpaid. Lewis was a good friend of another troubled character, Wilbur Burton, Grace Simons's husband, a heavy-footed bear of a man who was the *Press*'s night editor for several years in the thirties. Burton enjoyed a good adventure and in 1932 he,

Till Durdin and Rosholt went out to Kiangwan in the Shanghai suburbs where various warlords had been scrapping with the Japanese and each other. Wandering around following the intrepid Burton in the dark, Durdin and Rosholt heard repeated pings. It took them about 20 seconds to realise they were being shot at and to jump back in their car and head for the safety of the *Press*'s traditionally well-stocked drinks cabinet to recover from their near miss. Burton worked from 10 p.m. to 2 a.m., made up the front page and got to choose the all-important daily headline. He was a man of fixed ideas and regularly told Rosholt that he only cared to live to 55. Rosholt thought nothing much of it at the time, assuming it was wee-small-hours chatter over yet another whisky and soda, but he found out later that Burton, back in New York, committed suicide on his 55th birthday.

Victor Keen's problem was women, though he was always admired for pushing out hard-hitting stories that often attacked Japanese military aggression against China despite the interminable crises in his love life. After graduating from Colorado University, Vic Keen had been a correspondent for the *Japan Advertiser* and the *New York Herald Tribune* before moving to the *Press*. As a fun-loving, wise-cracking hard drinker, he relished the social whirl of Shanghai. He had married during a day off from reporting the Japanese bombing of Shanghai in 1937 and seemingly lived amicably with his wife, but in fact they were estranged though they remained on good terms. Keen kept a White Russian mistress who bossed him about, spoke no English and generally was perceived by his friends to make his life a misery. His wife not only continued to cover for him with the *Press* when he left town on trips to the interior but also took care of his mistress who, being of former czarist Russian high-society stock, was completely unable to help herself. Having ended up in Shanghai after being raised in some luxury in imperial Russia, the poor woman was unable to cook, clean or support herself at all.

The *Press* also maintained a few correspondents in other parts of China who reported in regularly. James A. Mills was covering western China reporting from Chengdu and Kunming with stories, features and photography, while Sammy Chang (Chang-ling Chu) was for many years the *Press*'s man in Shantou. Chang had been educated in America but was a Shantou native. He came to Shanghai to act as managing editor briefly during the 1932 Shanghai War and became involved in the armistice negotiations in the spring of that year. Sadly, he was shot in the back and killed while dining at a restaurant on Nanking Road in July 1940 by a hit man from Wang Jingwei's pro-Japanese puppet government. Wang, it seems, had taken offence at an editorial Chang had written.

There were also a number of "unofficial" *China Press* correspondents. Just as traditionally the *North-China* had reduced costs but earned itself a name for national coverage by relying on inland missionaries to send in the odd story, so the *Press* used its contacts too. The main one throughout the 1930s was E. O. Scott, one of Shanghai's leading funeral directors who specialised in dead foreigners. In return for some advertising, Scott would write the obituary pages — after all he knew who had died, what of and when, and was in contact with their families — and it seemed a natural fit. Scott also heard first if foreigners were murdered which always made a good news story.

The *Press* had a long tradition of employing English-speaking Chinese journalists. In part this connection went back to the Missouri School of Journalism which had from the start helped train Chinese journalists who then returned to China joining the Missouri news colony and picking up work on Missouri alumni-heavy publications like the *Press* and Powell's *Review*. For example, Missouri alumnus Woo Kyatang (K. T. Woo) had made a name at the *Press* with his scoop on Ruth Harkness, the female explorer and panda hunter, and later became managing editor of the paper. He had grown up in a newspaper family in Shanghai and, after studying journalism in Missouri, had married his fellow-student Elizabeth Hart; the couple had eloped to Illinois, as inter-racial marriages were still illegal in Missouri. Woo stayed in Shanghai until the war and then later became the editor of the *Hong Kong Standard*, known as the *Tiger Standard*, a paper established in 1949 by Aw Boon Haw, the founder of the fabulously wealthy Tiger Balm pain-relieving ointment empire. Also, K. S. Chang was a popular sports editor of the paper during the 1930s. He had graduated from Shanghai's prestigious St. John's University and was instrumental in arranging many sporting events in the International Settlement, including a baseball game when a team of visiting Americans including Babe Ruth and Lou Gehrig gave a demonstration in Shanghai as an extension to their Major League All-Star Tour of Japan.

Hawthorne Cheng was another long-time Chinese member of the *Press*'s staff who preferred to work on the night desk and knew Rosholt, Lewis and Burton from the early morning shifts. Cheng's initial skill was in translating stories from the Chinese newspapers that might be suitable for the *Press*. The Chinese papers usually had much more racy and juicy stories than the English press. Even by the 1930s, this situation hadn't changed much. It seemed that Western sensibilities remained intact in public and in print whatever shenanigans went on at night in Frenchtown and along the notorious Blood Alley bar and hookers' street. In 1912 Carl Crow had had trouble publishing a story in the *Press* about a senior eunuch in the Forbidden City who had had access to the bedchambers of most of the women of the Qing court. After his death it had been revealed that the man had not had the necessary removal of his most crucial appendage and had indeed scandalously masqueraded as a eunuch for decades and could potentially have contaminated the imperial bloodline. This had been considered a little too much information for the delicate sensibilities of most Shanghailanders then and Crow had had to tone it down. By the 1930s Hawthorne Cheng and Rosholt were still unable to run a story from the Chinese press about a woman who had cut off her husband's penis after finding out he had had a string of affairs. The Chinese papers delighted in the story but the *Press* feared the reaction of its apparently more easily offended readers. Consequently Rosholt and Cheng got to enjoy the story as did Chinese- language readers while *Press* subscribers remained in blissful ignorance of such goings-on.

A popular face was Clarence Kuangson Young, a dapper, good-looking and sharply-dressed Chinese with a penchant for well-cut Western-style suits and gold-rimmed glasses. The almost universally liked Young, known by most simply as "C", was the paper's new CEO. C worked closely with KMT-insider Hollington "Holly" Tong and also created an inner core of colleagues to guide the paper's direction and style. This included F. L. Pratt, an older journalist with a long history of working in Australia and John B. Pratt (no relation), an American who had worked for the older Pratt for many years. They were immediately, and perhaps predictably, known as the "Two Pratts".

However, Young's work for the *Press* was only half his life. In late 1937 when the Chinese army was forced to retreat from Shanghai, Young uncharacteristically didn't turn up at work for several days. Throughout November nobody was sure of their CEO's whereabouts or if they did know they weren't saying. It was a mystery. By chance Malcolm Rosholt was visiting Paris that December and heard through the grapevine that Young was living in the French capital. He sent his boss a note asking if he would like to meet at a café; and in return he received an invitation to Young's substantial and well-furnished Parisian apartment for dinner. Rosholt, who had known C reasonably well in Shanghai, was somewhat surprised by the opulent surroundings, the fashionable and rich Parisian couples that composed the other dinner guests and Young's fluency in French. It transpired that C had been sent urgently to Paris on the direct orders of Chiang Kai-shek to secure additional supplies of armaments for the Chinese army.

Young continued to work for Chiang in a number of roles. In 1940 Chiang sent him to Manila as China's consul general for the Philippines. He stuck to his post even after the retreat of General MacArthur to Australia and the surrender of the American troops. He apparently had the chance to leave with Macarthur's party for Darwin but insisted on staying at his post. The Japanese arrested the entire 25-strong staff of the Chinese consulate and demanded to know where the consulate's money was. Young told them, truthfully, that there was none. The Japanese army machine-gunned the entire staff and buried them in a shallow grave. After the war Chinese investigators located the grave and identified Young by his trademark gold-rimmed glasses.

Affectionate Cartoonists — Sapajou and Schiff

In the 1930s cartoons became a major art form and way of communicating in the Shanghai press. The two greatest exponents of this art form were Sapajou and Schiff. Sapajou's distinctive line drawings revealed Chinese daily life and idiosyncrasies as well as the decadent life of foreign Shanghailanders in the 1930s. Sapajou was the *nom de plume* of Georgii Avksentievich Sapojnikoff, a graduate of the Aleksandrovskoe Military School in Moscow, a lieutenant of the Russian imperial army, an aide-de-camp to the czarist General Horvath while he was overseeing the completion of the trans-Siberian railway and a veteran of the First World War where he was wounded on the battlefield. Invalided out of the army, he enrolled in evening classes at the Moscow Academy of Arts to study drawing. The tall, thin and bespectacled Sapajou always limped and walked with a cane as the result of his injuries during the war, but he had maintained a pretty good social standing in imperial Russia by marrying a daughter of a general.

Thousands of Russians escaped to Shanghai after the 1917 revolution, and by the 1930s more than 20,000 Russians lived there. Sapajou and thousands of his compatriots made their homes in Shanghai, which as an open city accepted just about anybody without a passport or visa requirements. In Shanghai Sapajou continued doodling and drawing local scenes both as a cartoonist and an accomplished water colourist.

This idle sketching started a new life for him. He worked for many of the major Shanghai newspapers, as a commercial artist for a range of companies including Carl Crow Inc. and on special commissions such as Crow's books. In 1925 he joined the staff of the *North-China*. In his memoir of Shanghai and its newspaper business, Englishman Ralph Shaw who himself worked as a reporter for the *North-China*, described Sapajou as "the star of the office".[9] For 15 years Sapajou published a daily cartoon in the newspaper and in 1937 the *North-China* published *Shanghai's Schemozzle*, which consisted of two collections of his cartoons reflecting the contemporary situation in the city, together with comments from R. T. Peyton-Griffin, the long-time author of the humorous and gossipy "In Parenthesis" column. As he was always asked how it was possible for Sapajou to produce a complex cartoon on the deteriorating situation in Shanghai on a daily basis, Peyton-Griffin wrote:

It would never do to give trade secrets away ... or at least all of them, ... but this one may be mentioned. At the mention of the word "cartoon," Sapajou sits, looking far away into the distance and meditates. Suddenly he makes a stabbing motion in the air with his pen. An idea has been speared for treatment. Hence a cartoon.[10]

Though he mixed with Shanghai's foreign elite as a member of both the exclusive Shanghai Club and a regular at the French Club, Sapajou remained involved in White Russian community affairs and was a director and shareholder of the Shanghai-based Russian publishing house and newspaper *Slovo*.

As he was both a refugee and somewhat sympathetic to the Chinese situation, Sapajou became a natural supporter of the underdog. Though his cartoons often made fun of Chinese manners and customs, they were never malicious. He developed a style of simple cartoons that commented succinctly on the day's events both poignantly and humorously. He never shirked from pricking the pomposities of the more gauche and ridiculous Shanghailanders, the most venal politicians, the most deadly gangsters or the militarism of the Japanese. For the readers of the *North-China*, he was simply a part of Shanghai life and a much-enjoyed ritual when turning to the newspaper.

Sapajou's rival was Friedrich Schiff, known by everyone simply as "Schiff". He was a satirical cartoonist, an accomplished draughtsman and a noted post-impressionist painter; but cartoons paid the rent, though some of his thoughtful watercolours were used as covers for the *China Journal*. Schiff was descended from a long line of skilled Viennese artists, his father having been a well-known portrait painter who had been commissioned to paint no less a personage than Emperor Franz Josef. Schiff moved to China where he started his career by providing illustrations to Kelly and Walsh, the largest English-language book publishers in China at the time. He then provided cartoons for the *Tientsin Times* but it was in hedonistic Shanghai that he found his *oeuvre* and started to satirise the foreign community. Unlike Sapajou, who favoured line drawings, Schiff also worked regularly in colour. His most famous cartoons are perhaps those accompanied by satirical ditties such as *Miss Shanghai*: "Me no worry, me no care! Me go marry a millionaire! If he die, Me no cry! Me go marry another guy!!" and another cartoon of young street beggars chasing a sailor shouting "No papa! No mama! No chow chow! No whisky soda! Please pay cumsha!"

Sapajou and Schiff captured in their cartoons a new Shanghai of modernist architecture, avant-garde styles, high fashion and jazz. They also captured a Shanghai riven by political splits and threatened by Japanese aggression, and where the poor and marginal rubbed shoulders with the fabulously wealthy and influential. The Shanghai that Sapajou and Schiff represented was entering other artists' imaginations too, both foreign and Chinese. In 1935 Shanghai-based cartoonist Zhang Leping created his popular *San Mao* (*Three Hairs*) character — a young Chinese boy-tramp who gets into trouble around Shanghai — and it remained popular until after the Second World War. Zhang credited both Sapajou and Schiff as being among his inspirations.

In the 1930s, China was perceived by an increasing group of reporters as a fascinating land of travel and adventure, or perhaps just a better place to be than depression-ridden Europe or America. China was both a potential cradle for revolution and a symbol of the downward spiral of world events. That the foreign press corps should ultimately have become so political was in this light no great surprise.

8
The Dirty Thirties — Left Wing, Right Wing, Imperialists and Spies

"Living on the rim of a volcano"

J. B. Powell on life in China in the 1930s

"While in an international and undamaged quarter,
Casting our European shadows on Shanghai,
Walking unhurt among the banks, apparently immune

Below the monuments of an acquisitive society,
With friends and books and money and the traveller's freedom,
We are compelled to realize that out refuge is a sham."

W. H. Auden and Christopher Isherwood, *In Time of War* (1939)

Forming Cliques and Taking Sides

For the foreign press corps, China in the 1930s, and particularly Shanghai, was a mixture of hedonism, excess and privileged extravagance in a world pitched into deep depression on the one hand and sliding into polarised politics and conflict on the other. The China press corps was, like its colleagues around the world, forced to take sides. Some did so willingly and others found themselves slipping into activism. This was the "dirty thirties" of fascism vs socialism, war vs peace and civilisation vs barbarism; but, for those with jobs and money in a relatively cheap country like China, it was also, of course, a time of opportunity and possible excess. It was also a time when journalistic cliques multiplied in China based on politics as well as location. There were clearly groupings of like-minded leftists and communist sympathisers as well as those more closely associated with the ethos of the ruling treaty port powers, some hardline right-wingers and a few out-and-out fascists. Geographically, Hong Kong had a distinct press corps to itself as invariably did Shanghai and Beijing. Each had its own different mindset. Hong Kong's was rather introverted and concerned more with local minutiae than the coming global storm; Shanghai remained preoccupied with business and commerce for as long as Japanese war planes allowed; while Beijing focused on diplomatic comings and goings. Also, Nanjing, which for much of the decade was technically the capital, had its own press corps that was generally perceived to be more relaxed and at ease in Chinese society than that in Shanghai. The rest of the Nanjing foreign community was mostly made up of academics and diplomats and so did not, according to Ralph Sues, include the "exclusive and rapacious types" that congregated in Shanghai.[1] Things got increasingly and noticeably cliquey in the corps.

Others just turned up without any particular agenda, stumbled into journalism almost by accident and often ended up writing some of the best reports on the deteriorating situation. Englishman Ralph Shaw had trained as a cub reporter in his native Derby before joining the army and shipping out to Shanghai. He managed to get out of the military, which didn't suit him much due to the low pay and early nights, and land a job with the *North-China*. If we know anything about just how much sex was available and enjoyed in the International Settlement in its final days before the Japanese takeover, it is largely thanks to Shaw's remarkably frank and graphic memoir *Sin City* which combines political analysis and newsroom memories with a long list of sexual escapades and encounters. Shaw chronicled long nights in the notorious Blood Alley bar street, knee-tremblers in the cinema and his patronage of gangster Big Eared Du's Silver Taxi Company, which basically provided fellatio on four wheels. It is also thanks to the oversexed Shaw that we know the two greatest typos ever to appear in the *North-China's* headlines. The first was a report about Harry Morriss who had entered his racehorse, The Knut, in the big Autumn Champions Sweepstake at the Shanghai Race Club. The Knut won but the headline the next day read "THE KUNT WINS AUTUMN CHAMPIONS". The second was a report of a football match, part of which read: "Then Loh, the Lido outside-left, dropped a great shit right in the goalmouth". Sub-editors, editors and typesetters were hauled in and questioned but the final blame could never quite be apportioned.

Shaw started at the *North-China* in 1937 and stayed through to 1949, turning his cub reporting skills into a good job and a rather satisfying life in Shanghai. Others took journalism-related posts to gain some freedom. The Institute of Pacific Relation's journal, *Pacific Affairs*, happened to need an editor in the summer of 1933. H. G. W. Woodhead recommended Owen Lattimore, one of his former cub reporters at the *Tientsin Times*. The IPR approved, and Lattimore accepted. The position suited the budding China Hand's ambitions perfectly.

He could do his editing from whatever base he chose and have time to carry out his own travel, research and writing.

The China press corps of the 1930s was certainly a mixed bunch who arrived for different reasons, pursued different aims and objectives and, perhaps most importantly, came to radically different conclusions about the country, its development and future. Among all the cliques that formed, perhaps the one that was to involve the most people and to have the most lasting effect was those that made an overt shift to the political left during the decade.

The Parlour Pinks

The so-called "parlour pinks" of the press corps came from a wide variety of backgrounds, countries and original political starting points. Some were of a previous generation and not really as "red" as their detractors liked to paint them. Grover Clark, a long-term resident of Beijing, had been the editor of the *Peking Leader* and owned the company that published it. Many in the newspaper business derided Clark for everything from being American, a prejudice that simmered in the non-American press corps pretty much constantly, obese and having no journalistic background (he had been a university professor) to the fact that most of his stockholders were missionaries. Others were jealous of his access. Randall Gould working in Beijing for UPI in the 1920s, having moved from the *Japan Times* in Tokyo, recalled that Clark would breeze into important briefings for the Beijing diplomatic corps simply by wearing a shiny top hat, looking more like a diplomat than a hack and strolling past the minders charged with keeping out the newspapermen. However, the most damning indictment against Clark, who did hire real "reds" like Rayna Prohme and C. H. Lee as well as those less politically-inclined such as Hallett Abend briefly, was that he was a closet "parlour pink".

In reality, Clark was quite the opposite of a politically committed leftist and was taking considerable sums of money from both China's foreign minister Wellington Koo and Feng Yuxiang, a warlord known as the "Christian General" who dominated parts of north China at the time and was known for his pro-Soviet leanings. The money was "donated" on the understanding that no news in the *Leader* would be critical of either of them. When Abend was left briefly in charge of the paper while Clark visited America, he found the editorial board consisted of the president of Yenching University, the secretary of the Peking YMCA and the head of the missionary-funded Peking Language School — a strange cabal of revolutionaries. News of the deal with the Christian general leaked out, leading to Clark being accused of being a "parlour pink", especially by the *Leader's* rival paper, the Japanese controlled *Peking Standard*. The slur hit home. Clark became *persona non grata* in the foreign community and Abend recalled former acquaintances ostentatiously ignoring him on the street. Clark did indeed play at warlord politics, which could be a dangerous business as Putnam Weale had discovered when it got him killed. While friendly towards the Christian General, Clark wrote a number of *Leader* editorials in which he repeatedly attacked another warlord, the widely detested Zhang Zongchang who was known as the "Dogmeat General". This was nearly the end of Clark. When he attended a press conference to meet the warlord Zhang Zuolin, only to see another, his enemy Zhang Zongchang, stride into the room, Clark turned pale then green, assuming he would be shot dead. Fortunately, however, the Dogmeat General didn't read English and nobody had had the guts to translate Clark's editorials to him. Clark survived the warlord but not the opinion of the Beijing foreign community.

Clark was wrongly labelled a leftist while others in the press corps had backgrounds that suggested they should be on the right but took a different course. New Yorker Harold Isaacs was the son of a property magnate who had studied the writings of Tom Millard at college and subsequently drifted to the left and became what was then often known as a "snob-Bolshevik". He was generally considered talented but was also a committed Trotskyite and had married his childhood sweetheart, another Trotskyist with a background in journalism, Viola Robinson. Lifelong Trotskyist Frank Glass was the best man at the wedding, making it a truly Trotskyist China press corps nuptials, including several toasts to the old Bolshevik himself. Isaacs, having arrived in Shanghai in 1930, became the city editor of the *China Press* but a year later he told the paper that he wanted to take an extended trip to western China and a leave of absence was granted. The management's sole condition was that he never return! The *Press* was controlled by pro-KMT interests and Isaacs had made it clear he didn't much like the KMT. It was well known that leftists could probably get a job on the *Press* if they kept their heads down, and could always pick up work on the *China Weekly Review*, as J. B. Powell, whatever his own politics, never bothered much about his staff's ideological leanings. Isaacs did travel to the western provinces and, on returning to Shanghai, launched his own publication *The China Forum*, a monthly periodical that, after his printers refused to touch it, he and his wife produced on a hand-press he had picked up cheap somewhere. It lasted for just over a year until the Japanese invasion when the Shanghai authorities declared a state of emergency and banned it.

The *Forum* was politically charged railing against extraterritoriality and the KMT, regularly alleging that foreign imperialism, in the form of the SMP, Special Branch and British Intelligence, was intent on smashing communism in China. This was a not wholly untrue assertion by any stretch of the imagination. Naturally, in return, both the US consulate and the Special Branch in Shanghai took a special interest in Isaacs and the *Forum*, earning him the special enmity and attentions of Patrick T. Givens, the Irishman who ran the Shanghai Special Branch for much of the 1930s and was caricatured in Hergé's *Tintin and the Blue Lotus* as cruel and close to the Japanese. Givens was also lampooned by Isaacs for being awarded a medal by the Chinese military for, according to Isaacs, "excellent" work in hounding down communists and suspected "reds" and bringing them to "justice", which in the vast majority of cases meant death.[2]

At the time Isaacs was still sympathetic to Stalin and not aligned with the Trotskyists such as Glass. However, he broke with the Stalinists in 1932 when they ordered him to print articles attacking Chen Duxiu, the de-facto leader of China's Trotskyists. As the *Forum* was produced at the height of his flirtation with Stalinism, it had included a special issue devoted to "Five Years of Kuomintang Reaction", which did not endear him much to the government. He then read Trotsky, socialised with his sympathisers in the press corps and embraced their cause.

Small politically committed publications like the *Forum* controlled by one or two people and expressing the, usually left-wing, views of the proprietors regularly came and went in the early 1930s. As well as *The China Forum*, a radical French lawyer based in Shanghai called Destrées launched the short-lived leftist journal *La Vérité* which delivered tirades against the hopelessly corrupt and compromised French officials who ran the city's French Concession. Also, Edgar Snow, the leftist "mishkid" Ida Pruitt and Snow's wife Helen (who often wrote under the pseudonym Nym Wales but was known to friends simply as "Peg"), as well as some Chinese leftists formed the Beijing-based semi-monthly periodical *Democracy*.

After *Forum* collapsed in 1935, Isaacs sold his hand-press and went to Beijing to continue researching his planned book about the events in Guangzhou in 1924.[3] Then he fulfilled one ambition by travelling to Norway to visit the exiled Trotsky. In one sense, the meeting apparently did not go well as shortly afterwards Isaacs publicly broke with the Trotskyist movement. However, in another sense something approaching common ground must have been found as the exiled Bolshevik supplied a foreword to the first edition of Isaacs's book, a foreword omitted from later editions due to political considerations among the American reading public rather than the author's continually evolving politics. Isaacs eventually left China and headed back to New York to work for Havas.

Trotskyists were prominent but Stalinist sympathisers were around as well. Israel Epstein was later to become an immortal of sorts in Communist China but in the early 1930s he was hanging around Shanghai living a hand-to-mouth existence by freelancing. Max Chaicheck, a former editor for J. B. Powell's *Review*, who worked on the *China Press's* sports desk, took pity on him and passed him some work while he also freelanced on an occasional basis for the Russian newspaper *Zarya*. Epstein eventually landed a more regular assignment with UP, a job that took him to Hankou and Hong Kong. Chaicheck may have hired Epstein but shared none of his politics. He later changed his name to Milton Chase, became night editor for UPI in Shanghai and eventually returned to America after Pearl Harbour and worked for the Office of War Information (OWI) China desk in San Francisco with Owen Lattimore and Carl Crow.

Other Stalinists visited briefly and penned their remarks on China. Victor Yakhontoff, a former czarist general, had been military attaché at the Imperial Russian Embassy in Tokyo and then a member of the Kerensky cabinet, but he had somehow reached an accommodation with Stalin's regime. He visited Shanghai in the mid-1930s, where he talked with a few foreign newspaper correspondents. Then he published a book entitled *The Chinese Soviets* that the Kremlin hailed as "authoritative" and followed that up with *Russia and the Soviet Union in the Far East*. Yakhontoff largely managed to survive and thrive by spending most of his time as a propagandist for the USSR in the USA in the 1930s (i.e. he wasn't stupid enough to go back to Moscow during the purges and let himself get arrested and shot) which brought him into contact with another Stalinist who covered China briefly at the time, Harry Gannes. Gannes was a "foreign expert" for the *Daily Worker*, the newspaper of the American Communist Party, of which he was a member. He wandered around the world in the 1920s and 1930s covering wars and revolutions in Abyssinia, Spain and China, which led to him arguing for the Comintern's Popular Front strategy for China. In general, the Stalinist sympathisers spent much of their time taking pot shots at the Trotskyists and vice versa, each labelling the others as spies and *provocateurs*. After news of the purges in Moscow filtered out and forced divisions everywhere from Republican Spain to the Chinese Communist Party, those on the various schisms of the left in the China press corps started butting heads ideologically too.

As well as the revolutionaries, there were also overt reactionaries though these were far fewer in number. Several worked on the *Shanghai Times* but, as has been shown, there were some journalists there who, despite the paper's pro-Japanese bent, were friendly with their colleagues on other papers. As a new arrival in Shanghai, Hallett Abend had taken a job with the paper but soon resigned as he didn't like the low pay —without, so he claimed, actually realising that the paper, despite having a nominal British owner, was actually under Japanese control. Others had a longer history of being pro-Japanese, were committed to supporting Japan and were generally despised. One such person was George Bronson Rea.

Rea was an American who ran the right-wing monthly *Far Eastern Review* which he had founded in Manila in 1904. Carl Crow, in a document on the Shanghai press prepared for the US State Department[4], identified him as a right-wing element with strong pro-Japanese sympathies as far back as 1919 when Rea had got into a heated argument over the Versailles Peace Treaty with Chinese officials and subsequently openly and determinedly transferred his loyalties from Beijing to Tokyo. The *Review* eventually moved from Manila to Shanghai to be under Japanese protection. Crow had assumed then that Rea and his publication were financially supported by Tokyo but he had no proof. For a time Bill Donald had agreed to edit the *Review* but he also resigned in 1920 over Rea's overt pro-Japanese stance. Then Carroll Lunt, who was best known for publishing an annual *China Who's Who*, edited the *Review* for a while but a falling-out rapidly ensued there too. J. B. Powell had attacked the *Review* in 1922, claiming that it had a "… policy differing from ours (*The Weekly Review*'s) by about 100 percent".[5] By the early 1930s the links to the Japanese military's Propaganda Department were even more overt and well known as the *Review*, almost alone, championed the Japanese annexation of Manchuria and the creation of the Manchukuo puppet state with the former boy Emperor Pu Yi as its de-facto ruler.

The annexation of Manchuria in 1931 was the major issue that allowed the reactionaries to be identified. Rea was one example who nailed his colours to the mast with his book *The Case of Manchukuo* (to use the Japanese name for Manchuria was to identify your loyalties clearly), and several journalists joined the pro-Japanese *Manchuria Daily News*. But most of the press corps saw the annexation of Manchuria as both a harbinger of future troubles and the tipping point in their political sympathies. Consequently Manchuria, its fate and fortunes, became a subject of much interest to the China press corps and many travelled north to see what was going on.

In the Cockpit of Asia — With the Press Corps in Manchukuo

The hapless "Last Emperor" Pu Yi had been bandied from pillar to post since 1924 when Chiang Kai-shek had brought pressure to revise the Agreement, the so-called Articles of Favourable Treatment, that preserved some privileges, an income and access to the Forbidden City, which Pu Yi wasn't actually allowed to leave, and required the imperial family to surrender the imperial seals. After surrounding Beijing in November 1924, the Christian general had ordered the abolition of the imperial title and the eviction of Pu Yi (who liked to use the

English name Henry) and his followers from the Forbidden City. Pu Yi sought asylum with the Japanese, a decision that was to marginalize him for the rest of his life, while the Japanese sensed a publicity coup and embraced him warmly. Pu Yi was later to describe the decision as "entering the tiger's mouth". Several months later he and his entourage were transferred to Tianjin's Japanese Concession, a move Pu Yi called his "flight to freedom" at the time. In fact, he was swapping one cage for another. When he arrived at Tianjin railway station under Japanese escort, a group of specially invited foreign and Chinese dignitaries was assembled to greet him, including Woodhead of the *Tientsin Times*. Woodhead could never get enough of being considered a scion of respectable local society or of trumpeting his own belligerent views on the situation at any given time. He was fulsome in his praise of Pu Yi, unsurprisingly given that in the past he had warmly welcomed Yuan Shih-kai's treachery against Sun Yat-sen. However, Woodhead evoked a general opinion in the China coast English-language press of favouring Pu Yi and being generally anti-republican. Certainly the letters pages and social column of the *Tientsin Times* were filled with admiring letters from readers praising Henry Pu Yi and his social whirl about town. It is unclear how much of this was genuine support for the last emperor, now in his twenties, and how much was a combination of Woodhead's judicious selection of letters, Japanese *agents provocateurs*' writing in (a common tactic used by the Japanese in the 1930s to influence the press) and something finally happening to spice up Tianjin's rather lacklustre social circuit. Woodhead took the whole thing a stage further when Pu Yi's bodyguard and Japanese Secret Service operative Colonel Doihara became involved with the British Municipal Council's Watch Committee. Woodhead declared rather bizarrely to the readers of the *Times*: "Colonel Doihara is the Lawrence of the East", presumably a reference to Lawrence of Arabia and also a reference presumably lost on many people at the time.

Naturally the Japanese eventually called in their favour and told Pu Yi he would become emperor of the newly annexed territory of "Manchukuo". Pu Yi agreed, desperate to wear a crown again and surrounded by bad advisers, flunkies and Japanese secret service operatives. With the annexation and the planned coronation, an influx of journalists was inevitable.

The foreign press corps had been interested in Manchuria since the Russo-Japanese War. In the 1920s foreign correspondents still journeyed to the area occasionally. Chicagoan Paul Randall Wright had spent 1918–19 as the staff correspondent for the American Expeditionary Force in Siberia and the Russian Far East during the ill-fated Wars of Intervention after the Bolshevik Revolution. He then roamed around Manchuria, Shanghai, Japan and the Philippines between 1926 and 1930 for the *Chicago Daily News*. Wright covered the Northern

Expedition as well as the subsequent fighting between the Nationalists and the Communists. In 1929 he had spent some time in Manchuria, sponsored by the Carnegie Endowment for International Peace, reporting from Harbin, Shenyang and Dalian. He found himself constantly bumping into other curious members of the press corps.

Reporting from Manchuria in the early 1930s was not without its hazards. H. Hessell Tiltman, a British journalist for the *London Daily News* and three-time president of the Tokyo Foreign Correspondents' Club, became well known for covering Japan's latest outposts as its expansionist policy advanced. He was arrested by the Japanese secret police, the *Kempeitai*, in Manchuria for spying and bizarrely charged with "taking a photograph without a camera", an accusation neither the journalist nor anyone else seemed to really understand. However absurd a charge, the Japanese were probably right to watch Hessell Tiltman as he probably was a spy, at least part-time. In 1934 he published his take on the Manchurian annexation in association with Colonel P. T. Etherton in their book *Manchuria: The Cockpit of Asia*. Etherton had been British consul-general in Kashgar between 1918 and 1922 where his major task had been to thwart Bolshevik expansion into either British India or Chinese Turkestan. After that he had been involved in various Balkan machinations before travelling to Manchuria. It is hard to imagine that Hessell Tiltman was not aware of who Etherton was and could not look at the "diplomatic" roles he had undertaken and add two and two together to get "spy".

Like many others, Malcolm Rosholt headed to Manchuria for the *China Press* to cover the Japanese-sponsored enthronement of Pu Yi as the new puppet emperor in March 1934. Rosholt and others were sceptical of the Japanese, wary of their advances in Manchuria and concerned about what it would ultimately mean for China. They saw Pu Yi as a largely pitiable and misguided figure. But, of course, this all depended on your politics; Rosholt's were generally pro-KMT but for someone like Woodhead they were largely informed by his overriding desire to protect and shore up extraterritoriality. The foreign community in northern China was nervous and not a little dismayed by the Japanese occupation, but Woodhead reassured them. Writing in what even he would later see as a rather reactionary tone when bombs fell on Shanghai, and the Japanese marauded and pillaged through Nanjing and seized control of the foreign concessions in Tianjin, he said:

> It is Japan's duty to keep the peace in the Far East. After constant provocation by the Chinese, Japan has at last hit back. We should be grateful that she, alone of the allies, has staved of the surrender of foreign rights. Thanks to General Tanaka's positive China policy, the abolition of extraterritoriality is now in cold storage.[6]

To some, of course, Woodhead appeared a sort of buffoonish Colonel Blimp willing to sacrifice anything and support anyone to preserve treaty rights. To others, he appeared to be a stout defender of the foreign imperial cause. He was a guest of honour at the investiture, got a private audience with the Tokyo-sponsored young emperor and was treated lavishly by the Japanese who naturally appreciated his editorials. Edward Hunter, formerly of the *Hankow Herald* and *Peking Leader*, was also in Manchuria, having joined the Hearst newspaper syndicates in 1931. He accompanied the League of Nations Mission of Inquiry to attend the coronation of Pu Yi. Always on the right politically, Hunter was now an avowed anti-communist and accused Powell's *Review* of being pro-communist and anti-American, charges he was later to repeat to Joe McCarthy's House Un-American Activities Committee in 1958.[7] The political fissures in the foreign press corps were becoming starkly evident.

The newsreel correspondents also packed their bags and headed to Manchuria. Famed self-promoter and war correspondent Floyd Gibbons arrived from an assignment in Tunis for Hearst's Universal and International News Services. Gibbons was a veteran reporter with the *Chicago Tribune* who had covered the Mexican border war of 1916, the torpedoing by the Germans of the *Laconia* (on which he was a passenger), the fighting at Belleau Wood in the First World War (where he lost his eye and took to wearing his trademark eye-patch) and the 1921 famine in Russia; and he was to go on to cover Italy's war in Ethiopia, along with Red Knickerbocker, another reporter that would pitch up in China. He became known as a fast-talking radio and newsreel commentator — NBC radio's "The Headline Hunter" — and returned to China in 1937 to film the fall of Shanghai.

It seemed the rush was on as the highly-strung little Karl von Wiegand hurried by boat, train and plane to Shenyang on orders from Hearst headquarters and Frederic Kuh, UPI's Berlin bureau manager, raced across Europe to Manchuria, while AP Shanghai correspondent Glenn Babb (yet another Missouri News Colony member) and Hallett Abend grabbed the next train north to Shenyang. Most arrived in time for Pu Yi's investiture ceremony, but not everyone in attendance at the elaborate and ornate mock enthronement was quite so serious or self-important as Woodhead and Hunter. Shenyang's Yamato Hotel became the base for most of the press corps covering the annexation and the enthronement, with over 80 of them at one point. However, according to Hallett Abend, many never ventured further than the journey between the Yamato's bar and the cocktail lounge at the nearby Mukden Club, "cabling reports claiming to be at the 'front' with the Japanese, suffering with them in the trenches … going hungry with them when no rations arrived".[8]

There was a touch of glamour too. The swashbuckling *New York Herald*

Tribune foreign correspondent and radio announcer Linton Wells and his fiancée (later wife) Fay Gillis turned up. Though not a China specialist, Wells, who was better known as a pilot, was interested in Manchurian affairs as it bordered Russia's Far East and developments there naturally interested the Soviet leaders in Moscow who were keeping an eye on Japanese movements. Fay Gillis arrived at her fiancée's side for the ceremony in a leopard skin fur coat bought in Moscow, which earned her the nickname "The Leopard Lady". She didn't need an extravagant coat to be a flamboyant character as she had formerly been an aviation correspondent in the Soviet Union after her father, a mining engineer, went to Moscow in 1930. She had achieved some notoriety as the first American woman to fly a Soviet plane and the first, and quite possibly last, foreigner to own a Soviet glider. She had become friendly with aviatrix Amelia Earhart and worked as a stringer for *The New York Times*, which sent her to Manchuria. She had met Wells just shortly before. After Pu Yi's enthronement, he proposed marriage and took her on his idea, and probably hers too, of a romantic honeymoon to cover the Italian-Ethiopian War.

A glamorous Leopard Lady and a dramatic eye-patch wearing correspondent aside, the whole investiture was one of the more bizarre events in China between the wars. A mixed bunch of reporters assembled for the elaborate ceremony, including Walter Bosshard, the pioneering Swiss photojournalist and travel photographer. He had previously been a plantation manager in Sumatra, a gemstone trader in Siam and the technical manager responsible for recording the 1927 German Central Asia Expedition through then unknown parts of the Himalayas and Tibet. His photojournalism was popular with the readers of the *Berliner Illustrierte Zeitung* and the *Münchner Illustrierte Presse*, the latter of which had despatched him to India to cover the growing unrest and independence movement where he photographed Gandhi. This was to be his introduction to the China press corps, of which he was later to become a key member.

For many, the Japanese invasion of Manchuria was the point at which they realised the true extent of Japanese aggression towards China. Some decided it was time to take a stand. C. V. Starr, Shanghai insurance magnate and the owner of the *Shanghai Evening Post and Mercury*, told his editor Theodore Olin Thackrey: "Up to now I've never tried to lay down specific policy for the *Post*, but on the Manchuria thing — I must. We are against it!".[9] It would be very hard in future for the press corps to remain unbiased about Japan's intentions towards China.

The First Shanghai War

In the early 1930s it was far from clear, despite the annexation of Manchuria and Japanese machinations in Inner Mongolia and other border regions, that Shanghai and the whole of China would be pitched into all-out war. In 1932 Malcolm Rosholt, who had recently arrived in Shanghai and was a "newbie"at the *China Press* thought the then city editor Christian Sutton slightly mad when in January he posted a memo for all the staff to see stating that "we might have a war on our hands". By 18 January, Sutton was proved right and Sowerby in his *China Journal* was accusing both the KMT and the members of the Commission of Inquiry sent by the League of Nations to Shanghai of "fiddling while Rome burns", while the League's representatives did little more than be "dined and wined by various organizations, institutions and associations anxious to secure their good graces".[10]

The 1932 Shanghai War, later of course to become known as the First Shanghai War, effectively started on 28 January after a Japanese-inspired provocation. The Chinese-run Shanghai Municipal Government tried to calm the situation and appease the Japanese but it was impossible. Japanese troops, backed by fighter planes, attacked key points around the city causing havoc and terror. However, the war boosted the city's journalist community noticeably, both in terms of the number of papers represented and the nationalities of their correspondents. There was still a recognisable corps of old-timers such as Karl von Wiegand and Victor Deen at the *New York Herald Tribune*, Hallett Abend and his long-time assistant Douglas Robertson at *The New York Times*, and the veteran Reginald Sweetland at the *Chicago Daily News*. The German newspapers took a decided interest in events with the fabulously named Mrs. Ungtaren von Starnburger and Hans Heiburg for the *Berliner Tageblatt*; W. M. Holmes for *Berlin am Morgan*; Agnes Smedley, who was yet to become notorious in China, for the *Frankfurter Zeitung*; and Dr. V. Vogel for the *Hamburg Frendemblatt*.

The French section of the press corps was boosted too, though many French newspapers kept to a tradition of employing English stringers in China. The very un-French sounding Captain J. A. Bates reported for *L'Illustration*, O. H. Champly for *Le Temps* and George Moresthe for the *Petite Parisian*; and all of them worked alongside *Le Matin*'s D'Auxion de Ruffe. Albert Londres came for *La Journal* of Paris and proved popular with the press corps, but sadly died in a fire on board his ship when returning home from Shanghai to Europe soon after the First Shanghai War. The tall, pipe-smoking and always dapper Rene Laurens was the doyen of the French press corps in Shanghai during the 1930s and a popular figure with almost everyone, not least due to his habit of buying a lot of freelance features for translation into French, which provided more than one Shanghai-based hack with some extra beer money. As well as being the Shanghai correspondent for *Paris Soir*, he edited and ran *Le Journal de Shanghai*, which he had established. The stylish Laurens, who was so well known about town that he was bestowed the immense honour of being immortalised in a Sapajou cartoon, was Shanghai-based but travelled around China reporting. In 1936 Laurens and his wife Marguerite were heading back to Paris, intending to take the Trans-Siberian Railway via Moscow. To connect with the Trans-Siberian, they took the train from Shanghai to Harbin up near the Russian border. Bandits derailed the train and Laurens was knocked unconscious; and, after a fire broke out, Marguerite was forced to drag the unconscious Rene from the train. He was badly burned and lost an eye. They did get to Paris eventually, but Rene's health never recovered fully. He was trapped in the French capital after the German occupation of France and died of TB, to be much mourned by the remaining press corps back in Shanghai.

The wires were also better staffed and flourishing during this period. Morris Harris, the *Manila Bulletin* veteran, arrived in China to be China bureau chief for AP while A. T. "Arch" Steele was based in Hankou; and the courageous but sometimes foolhardy (at least when it came to his personal safety) H. R. "Bud" Ekins and the multi-employed Randall Gould — better known as a former UPI Beijing correspondent, the China correspondent for the *Christian Science Monitor* and the editor of the *Evening Mercury* — all ran UPI. Reuters, which was the largest wire service by a significant margin, employed the long-serving Christopher Chancellor, Mike Fox in Tianjin, Jimmy Cox, Frank Oliver and Christine Diemer among others.

Though much of their work as wiremen was never to reveal their writing flare due to the nature of their brief despatches, many of these journalists were talented characters. M. J. "Jimmy" Cox covered Shanghai for a decade or so before heading to the Reuters Tokyo bureau in the summer of 1940. His spectacular timing meant that he was, perhaps somewhat predictably, almost immediately arrested by the Japanese police as a spy. No one is sure what happened, but it is believed that Cox was tortured and then either jumped or, more likely, was pushed over the balcony of a police station. Either way, he never regained consciousness after the fall and died several days later.

Virtually the entire China press corps moved to Shanghai for the duration of the First Shanghai War, which lasted through to the final end and the departure of Japanese troops in May. The corps headed out every day to watch the battles across the city from rooftops. Edna Lee Booker and the first-ever accredited American female war correspondent, the *New York Daily News*'s Peggy Hull, found a lookout post in a flour mill and reported on the conflicts while spending all day glued to their field-glasses.

Red Stars over China

Major events that obsessed the press corps just kept on coming in the 1930s. The Jiangxi Soviet of the early thirties was seen by some, such as Carl Crow and J. B. Powell, as an interesting sideshow to events in China; for others like Edgar Snow it was a promise of revolutionary things to come; and for still others, such as the Soviet reporters, it indicated revolution was imminent. The remote and seemingly inaccessible Soviet in Jiangxi was a relatively short-lived state-within-a-state founded in 1929 and led by Mao and his comrade Zhu De who were on the run from Chiang after the 1927 crackdown. However, it was organised enough to mint its own coins, adorned with a hammer and sickle. Between 1931 and 1933 Chiang's army attacked the Soviet three times and encircled it with defensive forces to stop its expansion. In 1934 80,000 Communist troops broke through Chiang's blockade, and the Red Army abandoned its Jiangxi base and began the Long March; a march only 8,000 were to complete.

The regular turnover of foreign correspondents continued as usual. Frank Smothers took over from the long-serving Reginald Sweetland as the *Chicago Daily News*'s correspondent. Smothers was to make his mark in covering the Jiangxi Soviet. He had arrived with a pretty impressive track record but not much knowledge of China. Indeed, if he knew anywhere, it was Greece where he had covered events for many years. After graduating from Chicago's Northwestern University, he had joined the *Chicago Daily News* in 1925 and, after several years covering the city's gangland violence, he served tours in Japan, England and France and also, later, covered the Spanish Civil War and was expelled from Italy on the direct orders of Mussolini himself.

Of all the politically engaged journalists who had a global impact on views and perceptions of China, Missourian Edgar Snow still stands out. He was to have a long and deep relationship with China that affected all aspects of his life; indeed in 1933 a young and attractive woman, Helen Foster, had come to Shanghai specifically to interview him and ended up marrying him and becoming Helen Foster Snow. His life was not like the austere committed leftist image that has grown up around him since. Living in Beijing in the mid-1930s, the couple attended endless dinner parties and soirees on the roof of the Peking Hotel as well as owning a Mongolian racing pony and a white greyhound called "Gobi". Still, despite having started out in Shanghai with J. B. Powell's *Review*, he had moved to the left of the traditional Missouri News Colony position and now considered Chiang kai-shek a sell-out. While always doing some journalism, long periods of Snow's time in China were spent just writing his books and travelling.

Snow will always be best known for his 1937 book, *Red Star Over China*, which had an unprecedented impact on how the world viewed the Chinese Communist movement and Mao in particular. For contemporary readers, it appeared revelatory while for modern readers it is more problematic with the benefit of hindsight. Exactly what access did Snow have? To what extent did he put his journalistic objectivity to one side when portraying the Communists? Why did he fail to address the violence and purges that marked the Jiangxi Soviet and that later proved to be indicators of the direction Chinese communism would take when in total power? What is clear is that Mao needed to get his story and cause out to an international audience and Snow, coming recommended by Madame Sun, seemed the man who could provide this much-needed exposure.

From the start Snow's access was predicated on secrecy. The meeting between Snow and Mao was brokered by Sun Yat-sen's widow Soong Ching-ling in defiance of Chiang's ban on foreign reporters contacting the Communists. After the Communist's Central Committee granted permission for Snow to visit the Communist bases, he set out with his interpreter Huang Hua and, in Yenan, worked out his reporting plan with no less a person than vice-chairman Zhou En-lai and eventually sat down with Mao for a prolonged period.

Red Star Over China was instantly popular and a best-seller: after appearing in England it went through five reprints within a month. It was translated into Chinese in 1938 by underground Communists in Shanghai, renamed *Travels to the West* to appear more like a travelogue and issued by a fictitious publisher to get around the KMT censors. However *Red Star* and Snow were not universally and uncritically popular with all on the left. For example, the British leftist Freda Utley pointed out that in the first edition of the book Snow had included some passages which were critical of the Comintern and showed the subservience of the Chinese Communists to Moscow. Utley commented: "My Hankow impression of Snow as an honest journalist was altered when he eliminated, in the second edition of his book, a number of passages distasteful to Moscow".[11]

The Strange Death of Gareth Jones

The 1930s was a time when the links between journalism in China and espionage became murkier than at any time previously. While Edgar Snow was working on the final draft of *Red Star Over China* in Beijing in early 1937, his wife Helen suspected violent threats and assassination attempts were being attempted against the couple to stop the publication of the book about which much rumour was circulating in anticipation of its appearance. Real or imagined as these threats and attempts may have been, the Snows took precautions, including have sabre-armed guards at their Beijing home. They survived, but others did not.

Briton Gareth Jones wrote features for the *China Press* and was one of its most intrepid travellers around China. He had arrived in Shanghai with an established reputation for being a fearless journalist, having published some of the first exposés of the Ukrainian famine in 1933. These articles, written when Jones was just 28, were derided by Walter Duranty, the veteran Moscow correspondent for the *New York Times*. Duranty ended up with egg on his face for swallowing Soviet propaganda, and for Jones it was the start of a promising career and soaring reputation.

In 1935 Jones headed to Inner Mongolia to do a feature for the *China Press*. As they were driving across country, Jones's Chinese driver was shot dead next to him by bandits. He was forced to lean over, gun the engine and outdistance the bandits on their sturdy and fast, but fortunately not fast enough, Mongolian ponies. Jones had been one of that British generation after the Great War who had been slightly too young to fight and felt a little left out and mildly ashamed through no fault of their own. A Cambridge graduate with a first class honours in French, German and Russian, he initially worked as British Prime Minister David Lloyd George's foreign affairs adviser. However, Jones wanted to travel further than just the stuffy corridors of Whitehall. He started writing for the *Western Mail* in his native Wales, the *Times*, the *Manchester Guardian* and the *Berliner Tageblatt*. He was also a regular contributor to the Hearst International News Service. As well as chronicling his adventures and declaring the Ukrainian famine to be the result of Stalin's policies, he also predicted the terrors the rise of Hitler in Germany would presage and revealed the ambitions of Japan's senior army commanders to annex China.

However, Jones's career was cut short. After surviving famine in the Ukraine and Mongolian bandits, he was murdered in Chinese Inner Mongolia while exposing the machinations of the Japanese army. He was killed by Chinese bandits, though most people assumed that they were linked to the Soviet secret police, the OGPU or, more likely, to senior Japanese army officers (or perhaps both, such were the strange alliances of the time). Jones had certainly made deadly enemies of both with his reporting. He was travelling in Inner Mongolia with two other people. One was a Chinese naturalised-German, Dr. Herbert Mueller, who worked occasionally as a reporter for the German news agency DNB (*Deutsches Nachrichtenburo*) but the third member of the party remains a mystery. The prime candidates appear to be the journalist Gunther Stein or the super-spy Richard Sorge, both of whom were dedicated communists. Whoever it was, it was dodgy company. The jury remains out on Mueller. Certainly it seems Britain's MI5 believed him to be a Comintern spy.

While in Tokyo briefly in the mid-1930s, Jones had been friendly with Stein, a correspondent for the *London News Chronicle*, which was long regarded as a known hotbed of Soviet spies. He had first met him in Moscow in 1933 where Stein was the *Berliner Tageblatt* correspondent and Jones was stringing for the paper. Stein was to go on to spend time in the Yenan mountain retreat with Mao during the war. His Tokyo flat was a way-station for many communists, correspondents and other interested parties heading to China, though this wasn't necessarily always a good thing; one house guest had been the greatest Soviet spy of the twentieth century, Richard Sorge. Stein himself was German by birth but had become a naturalised British citizen. He left Japan in 1938 for China to work for AP where he immediately fell in with like-minded individuals such as Agnes Smedley who was herself close to Sorge. The whole case was typical of the murky allegiances and interactions of the time. The truth about Jones's murder has never fully come out. It could be as simple as bad luck and some opportunistic but deadly bandits, but it could be a hidden tale of intrigue, espionage and double-dealing.

Where's the Generalissimo?: The Xian Incident

The Xian Incident and the kidnapping of Chiang Kai-shek in late 1936 was a major news story and a pivotal moment for China. Chiang's kidnapping by the warlord Young Marshal certainly gripped the Chinese public who largely rallied to Chiang's side. The Young Marshal had intended the action to force an alliance between the KMT and the Communists. Ilona Ralf Sues, who was in Nanjing to see the eventual return of the released Generalissimo and his wife with Bill Donald by their side, noted that the entire population of China seemed to breathe a sigh of relief at the end of the incident and that out of it was born the United Anti-Japanese Front between the KMT and the Communists. Carl Crow remembered being on his houseboat in Jiangsu and seeing fireworks let off across the countryside as news of Chiang's release filtered out.

Some correspondents had managed to get to Xian in time to cover the story. Hallett Abend had chanced upon news of the kidnapping early, having phoned T. V. Soong, Madame Chiang's brother and China's finance minister, at his Shanghai home to follow up a quick query on customs revenues. Soong tipped him off about the kidnapping and he got busy cabling New York to get in first with the scoop. Close behind Abend was Earl Leaf, a popular press corps member who had arrived in Shanghai in the mid-1930s. He worked for UPI but used to hang around the *China Press* office all the time. UPI immediately despatched him to Xian to cover the kidnapping. Leaf, who didn't speak Chinese but was known by the name of Li Fu, found a translator from the US Embassy to help him, a military attaché and language student called Joseph W. Stilwell, who was yet to pick up the moniker "Vinegar Joe" and be promoted to the rank of general.

Also up in Xian covering the dramatic events was James Bertram, a New Zealander (though often erroneously described as British), Rhodes scholar, left-winger and stringer for the London *Times*. The wavy-haired Jim Bertram, who had studied Mandarin in Beijing, was to remain in China for some years and spent time with Communist military units that formed the basis of his best-known articles and several books and also saw him move further to the left. Then just 26 years old, Bertram stayed in Xian for the full 44 days of the kidnap crisis. He made friends with two other writers who showed up in Xian that December, Edgar and Helen Snow. This friendship helped him later when, through the Snows, he landed an interview with Mao after travelling with the Communist Eighth Route Army, which was included in Mao's collected works, so pleased was the Communist leader with Bertram's opinions.[12] His leftist inclinations were partly developed from being a New Zealander in China in the late 1930s and mixing with others in the small but influential and generally leftist Kiwi community, some of whom were prominent leftists such as Rewi Alley and Robin Hyde. Bertram was to collaborate with Hyde on her 1939 book *Dragon Rampant*, though he was not wholly pleased with the outcome.

Hyde greatly influenced Bertram's evolving politics. Born in South Africa and raised in New Zealand by her socialist father, she stayed in China for only six months, breaking an extended voyage to England, but she managed, in August 1938, to found the small monthly Shanghai-based internationalist magazine *Tien Hsia* (*Common Wealth*). The pages of *Tien Hsia* were mostly filled by leftist writers, both foreigners and Chinese, though it did include more scholarly work by those not normally associated with the left, such as Charles Boxer of British Intelligence in Hong Kong and later Emily Hahn- infatuation fame. Hyde funded *Tien Hsia* with some freelance work she picked up through her contacts with fellow Kiwis such as Bertram and Alley. She did travel to the front, arguably the first white woman journalist to do so, on a pass signed by Chiang himself. She ended up doing voluntary work in a hospital in Suzhou as the city fell to the Japanese. She was having an adventure, but her family and friends in Wellington were worried as she hadn't contacted any of them since arriving in China and they assumed her missing, presumed dead. Fleeing Suzhou, Hyde walked to safety along a railway line for more than 50 miles after being beaten up by Japanese soldiers, temporarily blinded in one eye and being severely malnourished. All the way, she carried her suitcase full of notes. She eventually made it to England and published *Dragon Rampant* but wished to get back to China. She did in fact arrange a visiting lectureship at Wuhan University.

However, her always poor health deteriorated while her lifelong battle with severe depression returned with a vengeance and she committed suicide in London in August 1939 on the eve of the war in Europe.

The kidnap crisis ended eventually. Malcolm Rosholt, Jim Hammond and Till Durdin were all having a Christmas Day lunch together at Rosholt's apartment in Shanghai when the feast was interrupted by the news that the Xian Incident was over and Chiang released. Durdin suggested they should all head to the *China Press* offices and put out a special edition. They did, and it was on the streets by 7 p.m. That they decided to do it and that it sold out instantly was one indication that the kidnapping had gripped both foreign and Chinese alike for the duration of the event.

Jews and Nazis on the Huang Pu

Following the defeat in 1918 and the loss of major territorial possessions such as Qingdao, the German press in China had been minimal, though the official German news agency, the DNB, had maintained a Beijing bureau which was run for some years by the alleged Comintern spy Herbert Mueller, a wealthy lawyer and sinologist who had amassed a formidably large collection of Chinese art. In addition, from the early 1920s the Transocean News Service had been the major German-language wire service in China. By and large, the German-language newspaper business had remained quiet after the war for some time. Fritz Secker launched the *Deutsche China Post* in 1922 but it only lasted three months while in 1925 P. Kettner, a militant Protestant pastor, launched a weekly called the *Deutscher Ostasien-Bote*. As the paper was basically one long and rambling editorial by Kettner, it ceased publication mostly unlamented when he died in 1931.

By the 1930s the German press in China was changing, as was Germany itself. In 1929 the *Deutsch-Mandschurische Nachrichten* was launched in Harbin. Though there weren't actually many Germans in Harbin, there was a White Russian community that included many German speakers and plenty of them were solidly right-wing. However, this was clearly not enough, and anyway the paper had little content and consisted mostly of adverts. In 1930 it moved to Tianjin and renamed itself the *Deutsch-Chinesische Nachrichten*, but its fortunes improved only slightly. The largish German community in Shanghai also had its own newspapers, the *Deutsche Shanghai Zeitung* based in the Astor House Hotel, which began publication in 1932 as well as *Die Tribüne*.

From the end of the nineteenth century up to 1914 German papers had largely been politically neutral and aimed at informing the local German community about events in China and Asia. However, in the 1930s things changed as the press became a tool for the National Socialists. Most German nationals in China opted for a German- language newspaper as, even if they could read English, they perceived the English- language press to be increasingly suspicious of and hostile to Germany. *Deutsche Shanghai Zeitung* was founded in 1932 by Max Simon-Eberhard, a former military man. A professional journalist, Paul Huldermann, took control of the editorial side of things and in 1936 it was renamed the *Ostasiatischer Lloyd* in an attempt to take over the reputation that the paper of the same name had had before the First World War. The paper did carry some news from Germany but concentrated on events in China. The official organ of the China branch of the National-Socialist (Nazi) Party was launched in Shanghai in 1933 as a monthly called the *Mitteilungs- und Verordnungsblatt der Landesgruppe China der NSDAP*. At its height, and renamed the *Ostasiatischer Beobachter*, it reached a top circulation of about 2,000 copies, or so it claimed. The Nazis' propaganda was backed up by the Shanghai branch of the solidly pro-Mussolini Stefani Italian News Agency.

The influx of German and Central European Jewish refugees to Shanghai meant that both a press to serve this new community and a response to Nazi anti-Semitic propaganda were required. Naturally the Jews established their own flourishing press, with 16 different Jewish-oriented publications being published before 1937. The Jewish press in China had started with the English-language *Israel's Messenger* in 1904 which was set up and edited by a Sephardi Jewish businessman, Edward Ezra. It appeared fortnightly and then monthly until 1941, consistently taking a rather strident pro-Zionist stance. Ezra, an extremely rich British citizen, constantly dabbled in the newspaper business, including buying the *China Press* for a while. The Ezra family had been involved in the opium trade but switched to the construction and property business around 1900 and built a formidable residence on Avenue Joffre, as well as having an interest in the Astor House Hotel. Ezra cemented his position in Shanghai by having been born and educated in the city, marrying into the Sassoon family and serving on the SMC.

In 1931 a weekly was launched called *Die Gelbe Post* (*The Yellow Post*) that concentrated more on Jewish cultural affairs, some news and commentary. In 1938 Albert Joseph Storfer took over the editorship and eventually turned it into a daily. Storfer had been a noted Viennese psychoanalyst and a founder of, and writer for, the International Psychoanalytical Press, which published Freud's works. He was also employed by the *Frankfurter Zeitung* and had even tried, largely unsuccessfully, to make "psychoanalytical films" in Berlin. After this brief foray into movie-making, he returned to publishing, working in Berlin for the Ullstein Publishing Company. Storfer had moved around Europe through

Switzerland and Germany as a psychoanalyst and writer and, in December 1938, he emigrated to Shanghai to get back into the newspaper business and enjoy some Nazi-free nightlife. In 1939 he announced his intention of turning *Die Gelbe Post* into a weekly, then, in 1940, a bi-weekly and eventually a daily.

In 1939 a new rival entered the market with an English name but written in German: the S*hanghai Jewish Chronicle*. Under the editorship of founder Ossie Lewin and two Viennese journalists, Ladislaus Frank and Dr. Mark Siegelberg, it became the Jewish community's paper of record in China and a major challenger to *Die Gelbe Post*. It was sanctioned by the Japanese authorities and they used to it to publicise instructions to the displaced Jewish community and so it lasted through the war years and longer, renaming itself the *Shanghai Echo* and remaining in print until 1948. By 1939 around 12 Jewish periodicals were being published regularly, with a host of others that were short-lived. All could be found at Shanghai's major Jewish run bookstores: The Lion and The Paragon. Ossie Lewin particularly was a fixture of Jewish cultural life in Shanghai as chairman of the European Jewish Artists Society and an active leader of the German-speaking Zionists in the city. Frank was also well known in Shanghai, editing the *Chronicle* and also getting into some hard-fought fights with the SMC in its dying days, while Siegelberg eventually left for Australia where he founded the *Neue Welt* newspaper in Melbourne.

As well as this Jewish and naturally anti-Nazi press, there were a number of German papers that were either generally anti-Nazi or politically disinterested. One of the best known was the fortnightly *China-Dienst* launched in 1932 by Theo Eckardt, which was heavy on illustrations and had a good reputation for attracting writing from some of the best German sinologists. However, like many German papers, it was really based around one person, Eckardt, and when he died in 1937 the *China-Dienst* ceased publication. Eckardt had been a popular figure among the foreign press corps. He had come to China, via America and Japan, in 1902 as a specialist in gardening and, indeed, he was the first person to introduce carnations to China. He was a gifted linguist and had worked as a magistrate in Shanghai's French Concession before the First World War. During the war he had edited the English-language pro-German publication *The War* and, in 1918, was expelled from China. He returned in 1920 as a full-time journalist working for the Transocean News Agency. That didn't work out and he returned to Germany to work for a decade as a commercial adviser to the War Ministry in Berlin but returned once again in 1932 to set up *China-Dienst*. The tall, thin and slightly bowed older Eckardt was considered an Old China Hand by many of the younger members of the press corps and was known to always be willing to discuss China and Far Eastern matters with anyone who called on him.

Other interested parties engaged in the pro- and anti-Nazi debate too. The Russian Fascist Association launched *Nash Put* (*Our Way*) in Harbin, which viciously attacked all the anti-Nazi press as financed by Jews and was eventually closed by the Japanese authorities in Manchuria, though it later restarted on a smaller scale in Shanghai. The paper competed with *Ha Dagel* (*The Banner*) which, in spite of its Hebrew title, was the Russian-language magazine of "Manchukuo Revisionism" (i.e. pro-Japanese). The Japanese also sponsored a Russian newspaper called *Dal'nevostochnoe Vremia* (*Far Eastern Times*), based in Shanghai's Hongkou district. The Ukrainian National Committee in East Asia was also active in Shanghai and published two newspapers *Ukrains'ky I Holos Dalekomu Skhodi* (*The Ukrainian Voice in the Far East*) in Ukrainian and *Call of Ukraine* in English. Shanghai's Polish community largely lived close, culturally at least, to the Russian community but it had its own newspaper, *Echo Szanghajskie* (*Shanghai Echo*), published by the Shanghai Polish Union.

Radio Shanghai

Newspapers, journals and periodicals were all well-established media forms by the 1930s but the decade was a time of technological change when both the radio and the newsreels became forms of mass communication to stand alongside, complement and often rival the newspapers. China's first wireless station — the Osborn Radio Station, known alternatively as XRO and the Radio Corporation of China — had opened in 1923 in Shanghai. It transmitted from studios on the roof of the Dollar Building on the Bund with an initial 65-minute programme of classical and light music as well as some news. The station estimated that there were 500 wireless sets in the International Settlement though, to boost the audience, XRO's signal was transmitted to Tianjin and other major areas where foreigners lived. The station was owned and established by an American journalist called E. G. Osborn and a wealthy overseas Chinese. Sun Yat-sen declared himself a fan of the new media but there simply weren't enough listeners. Despite moving the studios to the more prestigious roof garden of the Wing On Department Store on Nanking Road and trying to organise live concerts, the station failed after a few months due to a combination of precious few listeners, government distrust and censorship.

Shanghai's second radio station — the Carol Broadcasting Station launched in 1924 from studios on Nanking Road — fared better. The station was supported by the Carol Corporation, the *Shen Bao* newspaper, the *Shanghai Evening News*, the Paris Restaurant and the Kobe Electrical Equipment Company. Others followed. In 1928 the *China Press* backed a new station, KRC, that also introduced lady broadcasters to Shanghai's airwaves as Irene Corbally Kuhn moved over to the wireless. Her first broadcast on 14 December 1928 was from the studios housed in a back room at the *China Press* offices: "… with my legs melting under me like butter on a hot stove, I had stepped up before a 'mike' and sent my voice into the air, the first woman ever to broadcast in the Orient, and probably the first feminine announcer in the business".[13]

These early foreign attempts at radio stations, and others set up by American, British, French, Italian and Japanese entrepreneurs, were not great successes but they did encourage more people to buy wireless sets and they also led Chinese entrepreneurs, as well as the government, to start stations aimed at the Chinese population that had large audiences and were both popular and commercially successful.

By the early 1930s Shanghai had a proliferating number of stations. Thirty started broadcasting in 1930–31 alone, including the Millionton Radio Station jointly run by Reuters and Millington Ltd., and by 1935 there were over 60 in operation across the city. Most were Chinese-run and light music-oriented but others were foreign-owned and ranged from music to political commentary. There was also the Christian Broadcasting Station run by Dr. Frank and Aimée Millican, an energetic husband and wife team of Presbyterian missionaries who also ran Shanghai's Christian Literature Society and regularly prayed that Shanghai's leading gangster Big Eared Du would see the error of his ways and embrace Christ. Their radio show was something different, partly because the Millicans were the nucleus of the Shanghai branch of the evangelical Oxford Group which believed in public apologies and confessions and was highly influential in founding Alcoholics Anonymous and other group therapy type organisations. The Millicans personally "shared" with their Shanghai audience to the good impression of some and the ridicule of others.

Radio first became a popular medium and then an extremely important one as the political situation worsened. Following the bombing of Shanghai in 1937, with newspapers being censored, banned or having their distribution interfered with, the radio became a way of keeping up with world events and also finding out about the local situation. The best-known station was XHMA owned by U. S. Harkson, the wealthy head of the Henningsen Produce Company of Shanghai that ruled the ice cream and candy bar business in the city and sold the concept of the Eskimo Pie to the Chinese. At first Harkson used the station to build his ice cream and confectionery empire but it soon became a proper business in its own right due to advertising revenues. Harkson was also keen for the station to be relevant to all of Shanghai's various communities and the station broadcast a wide series of programming for the Shanghailander community, including shows in Yiddish, from its studios on Race Course Road. When war broke out in 1937, Harkson handed the station over to anyone who needed to communicate with relatives, colleagues or nationals inland, and missionaries, diplomats and business people all used it as a lifeline to the outside world.

The station's star was Carroll Alcott, originally from South Dakota and a former journalist on the *Sioux City Tribune* and the *Denver Post*. He then worked his way around Asia for 15 years as the *New York Herald Tribune*'s Philippines correspondent and a reporter for the *Manila Bulletin* and finally moved to Shanghai in 1928. He freelanced, breaking some good stories, notably about the opium business, German gunrunners and Japanese aggression in China; and he had once famously dined with a warlord in Yantai while the blood of his recently executed enemies dripped from the floor above into his noodles and shredded beef. Alfred Meyer, the managing editor of the *Shanghai Evening Post and Mercury* had snapped him up to cover the Shanghai crime beat, a job Alcott revelled in, noting that a typical day involved "... as many as three murder trials, a gang shooting, half a dozen armed robberies, a jewel theft, and a couple of kidnappings".[14] In 1933, and by now one of the most widely read journalists on the China coast, he moved over to the *China Press* as its cable editor.

In 1938 Jack Horton, who ran the RCA-Victor factory in China, suggested to Alcott he might like to replace XHMA's former announcer Acheson Lucey, who had also been a print journalist on the *Post and Mercury* before trying his hand at radio. It hadn't really worked out with Lucey who was heading back to America, so a vacancy had occurred. XHMA's manager Mike Healey thought Alcott would fit right in and all agreed that it was time for Americans to respond to Japanese propaganda broadcasts on the radio. As soon as Alcott arrived at XHMA, the old China press corps network kicked in and corps members were regular guests on his radio shows. His reach was substantial through XHMA as both Shanghailanders and Chinese listened while cafes, shops, bars, hotels and casinos all kept the radio on all day for news of the deteriorating situation. The station's signal reached across China and as far as Japan, causing no end of annoyance to the Japanese authorities.

Alcott was modestly popular at first when he started broadcasting in July 1938 but as the situation worsened he became a must-listen-to radio journalist and one of the greatest enemies of the Japanese in Shanghai. He also attracted a rather large and loyal following among women listeners, receiving 500 letters a month from fans, due to his charm, though he was actually quite fat and not particularly attractive — a "great face for radio", as they say. His shows were funded entirely by advertising from brands like Jell-O, Ovaltine and Maxwell House Coffee, despite Japanese threats to punish those companies for sponsoring his broadcasts, which they regularly tried to jam. He managed to annoy particularly the sinister Mr. Suzuki, who had vowed to run him out of town, with an advert declaring: "This broadcast is brought to you courtesy of the Bakerite Company, Shanghai's leading bakers and makers of better bread. The jam tonight is courtesy of Mr. Suzuki and the Japanese Army".[15] He was also well regarded by listeners for ignoring the official Japanese press releases but obviously, for the same reason, was disliked by the Japanese military command. For the four years Alcott stayed on the air at XHMA he was extremely popular but he also lived in fear of assassination the entire time. Indeed, it didn't start well. As Alcott was a well-known Shanghai print journalist, his debut on XHMA was advertised widely around town but he was also well known for being anti-Japanese and a supporter of the Nationalist government. Three days before he was scheduled to debut on air, a bomb was hurled at the studio and though it didn't do much damage, it sent a message that Alcott's appointment was controversial with somebody.

Several other stations appeared, including some with close ties to the press. The *Evening Post and Mercury* launched XGRS and British journalists on the *North-China* were closely involved with station XCDN. Generally non-political and apparently charmingly innocent was Station XQHB run by a Mrs. Robertson from her Shanghai studios at 274 Rue Maresca, which appears to have been her kitchen. XQHB became invaluable after 1937 as people worried about friends and relatives and Mrs. Robertson broadcast personal and business messages free of charge. A pro-Nazi station appeared that put out fascist-leaning programming in German as well as a show in Ukrainian put together by Ukrainian fascists who were friendly with both the German and Russian fascists. As total war came closer and then engulfed China, radio became even more important. XQHB and XHMA remained on air as long as possible and the ever-energetic J. B. Powell also maintained a secret underground station, the Press Wireless, for as long as he could.

Always alert to the political opportunities afforded by radio, the government Propaganda Ministry established the Hankow Short Wave Radio Station, XGOW, which endeavoured to keep people in Japanese-occupied areas in touch and also broadcast in English occasionally, with Ilona Ralph Sues as its English and French language newsreader. This meant Sues was awarded the rank of colonel and the title of official foreign broadcaster. XGOW was a valuable propaganda tool, though its nightly light music show managed to anger both Sues, her Propaganda Ministry bosses and not a few listeners when the girl who played the records (and selected one from the top of the pile and then the next and so on without being able to read the labels) innocently played the Nazi anthem, *Horst Wessel Lied*, before a speech by the Generalissimo. Sues requested that the record be broken and not played again, but as is the way in bureaucracies, nobody would take responsibility for breaking government property. A piece of white tape was put across the record with the instruction in Chinese that it was not to be played for the duration.[16]

The Flicks ... the Arrival of the Newsreels

With radio becoming widespread, many were also now flocking to the cinema to watch the newsreels. One of the major improvements in newspaper technology and design in the 1930s was, of course, the use of photos that could be reproduced in good quality and quickly. What were termed "soot and whitewash" photos began to appear in newspapers and were produced in such a way as to provide stark black and white images with high contrast. Most papers in the 1930s were printed on buff-coloured newsprint, which meant that many blacks came out more greyish, so high contrast prints were essential for good reproduction on the printing presses of the time.

A number of photographers appeared who capitalised on this new demand for instant pictorial records of newsworthy events, people and local colour. Major clients such as Henry Luce and his *Time-Life* publishing empire appeared and some members of the press corps were able to supplement their incomes with photo credits. Typical of these were Wilhelm Walter whose street scenes of Shanghai and the race course in the 1930s were popular and Berliner Ellen Thorbecke's portraits of every aspect of Chinese life from beggars to sing-song girls to wandering monks, which left an excellent pictorial record. She came from a wealthy and cultured German family, married Dr. Willem Thorbecke, a Dutch diplomat to China in the 1930s, and created startling images through her keen eye and her selective cropping of her pictures to enhance their poignancy.

The arrival of the newsreels offered still more opportunities to make some money. Newsreels first appeared around the end of the nineteenth century and were pioneered in America. In August 1896 the Biograph Company used a motorized camera to make its first newsreel that, as it happened, was of the Chinese diplomat Li Hongzhang's visit to Washington. Sound newsreels appeared around 1926, though in 1922 the Mingxing Film Company, China's first film company, had been founded in Shanghai and began making newsreels of local events.

1932 heralded the start of regular newsreel coverage from China. The newsreels provided an opportunity for Chinese cameramen to find work with foreign news agencies. The famous Chinese-American Wong Hai-Sheng ("Newsreel Wong", who used the name "Newsreel" on his passport) ran the Hearst organisation's Shanghai Bureau while Paul Heis worked for Fox Movietone. Other newsreel cameramen included Captain Ariel Varges for

International Newsreel; Joe Ruker and William Jansen for Paramount; and several others who worked for Universal. Universal remained a low-budget, silent newsreel producer into the 1930s but still got critically acclaimed coverage of the Sino-Japanese conflict in 1937, much of which was photographed by Norman Alley and George Krainukov, who later changed his name to Crane.

The newsreel cameramen did more than most, including the print journalists, to bring home the reality of the deteriorating situation in China. Alley had been a long-time freelance writer who had bought a hand-held movie camera and started freelancing as a cameraman. Krainukov, a White Russian émigré to Shanghai had arrived in 1932, and in 1937 he was to largely outshine the competition with what many thought was the best footage of the carnage from the Japanese bombing of Shanghai for Universal Newsreel. There were also a number of freelancers such as Eric Mayell, who moved to Fox Movietone, and the much-admired George Lacks whose collection of Leica cameras was the envy of many in the press corps. Lacks progressed from still photography to the newsreels as the market changed and selling newsreels was found to be more lucrative than photos, while Walter Bosshard, the Swiss photojournalist, had become the main cameraman for the German Ustein Syndicate. All these men started to produce newsreels in China in the early 1930s and some of them were real veterans. For instance, Ariel Varges had taken photographs in the Balkans of Serbian troops in action in the First World War for the British Topical Film Company before coming to Shanghai as a photographer in the 1920s.

Unsurprisingly the disastrous year of 1937, when Shanghai suffered aerial bombing, was the high point of the China-shot newsreels. Alley and Krainukov got good shots for Universal, as did the American cameramen Harrison Forman for the *March of Time*. Forman and Krainukov, as well as Newsreel Wong, were all present to photograph the bombing of the Cathay and Palace Hotels on Nanking Road on Black Saturday in August 1937.

Forman was an interesting character. He was a Milwaukee native and graduate of Wisconsin University where he got a degree in oriental philosophy and later became known as "a modern Marco Polo" in America for exploring Tibet. He had started out in Shanghai selling planes as well as writing about the developments taking place among the country's young engineers and industrial designers. He sold articles to trade magazines and wrote a book called *So You Want to Fly?* He then worked briefly for the *Shanghai Times* before going on to more broad-based freelance journalism for the likes of the *New York Times*. He based himself in Chongqing which was rather unfashionable at the time, and the *Times* which allowed him to travel extensively. In 1932 he organised an expedition by motor caravan to Central Asia and was the first Westerner to drive a car to the shores of Tibet's Lake Kokonor. His Tibet travels paid off when he was hired as a consultant by the Hollywood movie director Frank Capra who was preparing to make his film version of James Hilton's 1933 book *Lost Horizon* about a plane crash in Tibet and the discovery of the magical mythical land of Shangri-La. Forman drew a salary of US$500 per week for several weeks until his contract ended. Capra never asked him one question during the whole time, so he pocketed the money and went back to his regular work.

In the later 1930s Forman was looking around for stories to cover and bumped into Malcolm Rosholt who advised him to head to Yenan to see the Communists who had pitched up there at the end of their Long March. Forman took Rosholt's advice and met up with Mao and his followers. He became friendly with them and covered their activities in some detail. When he returned to Shanghai, he picked up a camera for the first time, learned how to use it and started filming for NBC. It was the start of a whole new career that was to last for decades. He kept on travelling for his whole life, producing stunning photographs of Afghanistan in the 1960s and joining a scientific expedition to the South Pole as a cameraman in 1970.

Newsreels were not without controversy, however. One of the most famous incidents involved Newsreel Wong. He filmed the Japanese bombing of Shanghai's South Station in September 1937, a reel that included a now-famous scene of a crying baby sitting on the tracks amid the rubble of the station. The scene became one of the most celebrated symbols of the Asian conflict and over 136 million people were said to have seen it, not least due to the fact that it appeared on the cover of *Life* magazine, as well as 25 million copies of various Hearst publications and a further 1.75 million copies of other newspapers globally, including 800 American newspapers alone. The photo had a profound impact, its release leading to the Japanese government placing a price of $50,000 on Wong's head. But many people were suspicious of the photo: Wong was known to have leftist sympathies and was a close friend of Edgar and Helen Snow; and others simply remembered William Randolph Hearst's well-known phrase: "You provide the photographs, I'll provide the war". Questions started to be asked almost immediately. What was the baby doing sitting alone on the tracks inside the station building? Having taken still photographs of the baby, Wong also filmed the scene. Is it possible that the distressed little baby would have sat still for that long? Soon another picture appeared in the 21 December 1937 issue of *Look* magazine. This was of an Asian man, probably Wong's assistant Taguchi, carrying the infant. It does seem that Wong staged the photo for propaganda purposes; and it had a devastating effect too at a time when support for the Nationalist army was rising and dislike of Japan increasing. The arguments still continued over the photo, with people debating shadows, sight lines and lighting almost as much as the famed Zapruda footage of the Kennedy assassination. For his part, Wong never fully committed to either conclusively denying or admitting the rumour. He wasn't the only newsreel reporter accused of a little exaggeration in pursuit of a good story or personal image. One-eyed Floyd Gibbons, who was back in China again and now reporting for the International News Service, was accused of wrapping his head with fake bandages along with his trademark eye-patch to add to his dramatic appearance for the cameras.

There were problems with the new medium, but the newsreel cameramen did often live exciting lives in which they were exposed to danger, particularly after the conflict with Japan spiralled out of control. Concerns about bias aside, many foreigners saw the newsreel cameramen as hopelessly glamorous, largely due to the 1938 B-movie *Too Hot to Handle* in which newsreel reporter Clark Gable was working in Shanghai covering the Sino-Japanese War and met pilot Myrna Loy. Newsreel cameramen rather enjoyed this portrayal of their lives, often to the chagrin of the now decidedly less glamorous print hacks with their inky fingers and nothing more complicated than a notebook and pencil. However, very soon they, like everyone else, were about to get a nasty taste of life under fire.

9
Too Hot — China Fights for Its Life

"To Our Subscribers — The situation in the Western District may make it impossible for our messengers to deliver all newspapers this morning. Papers not delivered will be kept at this office for later delivery, or may be called for by subscribers."

The Publisher, *North-China Daily News*, 28 October 1937

There is a dry wind blowing through the East, and the parched grasses await the spark.

John Buchan, *Greenmantle* (1916)

Black Saturday — The Game Changes

The number of foreign journalists who happened to be in the vicinity of central Shanghai when the bombs fell on Black Saturday, 14 August 1937, was incredible. Chinese air force planes flew over Shanghai to bomb Japanese cruisers on the Huang Pu to prevent Japanese air raids on China, but they missed. One of their 550-pound bombs fell at the crowded intersection of Nanking Road and the Bund and two more bombs fell on the bustling Avenue Edward VII. The bombs caught crowds of onlookers gazing up at the planes and the loss of life was appalling, with 1,740 people killed and 1,873 injured. It was a Black Saturday indeed.

Carl Crow had his office windows blown out while he was crafting a report to a major advertising client, and the South African reporter Henry John May was only 50 yards away from the Great World amusement palace on Thibet Road when a bomb fell on it knocking him flat on his back in the street and killing many Chinese refugees sheltering in the building. Hallett Abend's long-suffering Scottish assistant, Douglas "Robbie" Robertson, was dining on

Nanking Road and was severely injured as the restaurant's windows blew in and he had to be evacuated to America for long-term medical treatment. Being Abend's assistant was a perilous job as Robertson's replacement, Anthony Billingham, was caught in a descending elevator at the Wing On department store on Nanking Road a week or so later when another bomb was accidentally dropped on central Shanghai. Of the 11 people in the elevator, nine died and only Billingham and the 12-year-old elevator boy were left alive, though both were seriously wounded.

Frank J. Rawlinson, the British-born liberal missionary editor of *The Chinese Recorder*, was less fortunate and was shot through the heart by a Japanese machine gun bullet as he was standing next to his wife and daughter while the bomb that fell outside the front door of the Cathay Hotel killed A. D. Williams, the British accountant for the *North-China Daily News*. Randall Gould was in his office, got out his camera and snapped the black smoke drifting across the Huang Pu towards the Bund from Pudong as the Japanese battle ship *Idzumo* pounded the wharves and factories of Zhabei and Pudong. Like Malcolm Rosholt and other keen amateur photographers in the press corps, Gould was always ready to snap away with his camera and several months later he was to photograph the immense human tide that surged across the Garden Bridge from Hongkou and Zhabei into the comparative safety of the International Settlement. His aerial shot of the crowds streaming across the bridge — "the Flight from Hong Kew" — which became an iconic and much reprinted image was taken from the window of the Shanghai Foreign Correspondents' Club on the ninth floor of the Broadway Mansions Building adjacent to the bridge.

After Black Saturday, things went from bad to worse. By October 1937 it looked as if the Chinese army was facing total defeat. Many in and around Shanghai fled into the International Settlement and the adjoining French Concession to escape the Japanese onslaught. Robert Guillain, a dyspeptic Agence France Presse (AFP) reporter who also wrote for *Le Monde*, was in Frenchtown and saw KMT soldiers surrendering to French forces rather than the Japanese: "They threw down their German guns and their helmets marked with the blue sun of the Kuomintang. Their faces shone with tears. Some shook with emotion. Others made strange cries like wounded animals".[1] Guillain roamed Shanghai throughout August 1937 before moving on in 1938 to cover the war from Japan where he witnessed the firebombing of Tokyo and stayed until Hiroshima. This wasn't entirely voluntary as Guillain found himself in Japan after the attack on Pearl Harbour and was only allowed to return to France in 1946.[2]

Others got out on the streets to report the events as best they could. UPI had to issue a memo to its reporters against foolishly exposing themselves after a machine-gun bullet bounced off Bud Ekins' tin helmet while he was out covering the fighting. Edgar Snow was reporting the fall of Shanghai for the British Labour Party's mouthpiece, the *Daily Herald*, and was so stretched he recruited his friend Rewi Alley to help out. As a veteran of the New Zealand Expeditionary Force in the First World War, he came to Shanghai in 1927 and found work as a fire officer and later as chief factory inspector with the SMC. Short and stocky Rewi (named after a Maori chief) with his famously "Romanesque" nose was a fairly indomitable character for the temporary job.

Shanghai remained a dangerous beat as the so-called Second Shanghai War saw more casualties occurring among the press corps. The London *Daily Telegraph*'s correspondent Philip Pembroke Stephens was killed by Japanese rifle-fire in November 1938 in Nantao, the old Chinese city. Harrison Forman witnessed the shooting, which occurred when Stephens climbed over a breach in the old wall dividing the Chinese city and Frenchtown. He stepped onto the platform of a water tower to get a better view of the fighting and a Japanese sniper shot him in the head, killing him instantly. Stephens was a well-liked correspondent who had given up an early career on the London stage and then a second career in the law to cover the Italian invasion of Abyssinia for the *Daily Express* and then the Spanish Civil War for the *Telegraph* before arriving in Shanghai shortly after Black Saturday. His funeral attracted most of the remaining corps left in the city to mourn the loss of a friend and discuss the worsening situation. Randall Gould, Malcolm Rosholt, James Mills and Hallett Abend were all in attendance and Abend and Red Knickerbocker were among Stephens's pallbearers.

However, Stephens's death also highlighted just how far relations had broken down between the foreign press corps and the Japanese authorities and press. Hallett Abend attended a heated press conference where the Japanese refused to accept the blame for the shooting of Stephens. The official translator and interpreter for the Japanese was Robert Horiguchi, a Japanese journalist with whom Abend had travelled in 1928 to report the massacres of civilians in Jinan, and many in the corps knew him well. Now Bob Horiguchi was pitted against his former colleagues and friends. He was later to be posted to Washington, and then, after Pearl Harbour, to Vichy France while his American-born wife and their baby son were stranded in America. On the same day as Stephens was buried at the Bubbling Well Cemetery in Shanghai, the leading Tokyo newspaper, the *Nichi-Nichi*, scandalously reported that he was not killed by Japanese gunfire but rather in a fight with other foreign correspondents.[3]

The Foreign Press Outstays Its Welcome

After Black Saturday the situation was immediately bad for the foreign press corps: even getting to China could be problematic. Hubert Renfro "Red" Knickerbocker, the roving war correspondent for Hearst's International News Service, who had already been to Ethiopia and Spain, arrived in Kobe en-route to Shanghai in 1938 aboard an American liner. When confronted by Japanese customs, the extremely tall Knickerbocker, who towered over the Japanese officials, had his camera snatched and promptly snatched it back; and the official then barked orders and a wooden crate was brought on deck. The official climbed onto the crate and slapped Knickerbocker several times around the face. Red called him a "son of a bitch" in his best Yoakum, Texas accent, grabbed him by the wrist, and lifted him into the air, leaving the startled official dangling; and he was about to throw him overboard before a bilingual Japanese businessman interceded to calm the situation. Clearly Japanese officials had been told to crack down on foreign journalists heading to China. Some decided the time had come to leave. Lists of foreigners deemed not welcome by the Japanese kept appearing and, after 25 years in Shanghai, Carl Crow and his wife packed their bags and boarded an evacuation ship for Seattle. Crow had been high on the list.

Others chose to stay and tough it out. J. B. Powell was the most famous long-term journalist who remained and found himself at the top of the most-wanted foreigners list. *Time* magazine had pointed out that "... he had been singled out as Jap 'Public Enemy No. 1' as far back as the invasion of Manchuria".[4] Characteristically, Powell had come out fighting after Black Saturday and issued a "War Edition" of the *China Weekly Review* on 21 August 1937, apologising for fewer pages due to employees fleeing, the printing plant being bombed and the office gas supply being cut off. Still Powell led with an editorial in which he called on everyone to remember one-time visitor to Shanghai, General and former President Ulysses S. Grant, as well as reprinting Eleanor Roosevelt's best wishes telegram to Madame Chiang in the struggle against Japan and declaring:

> In these dark days of crisis in China there must be a considerable number of intelligent Chinese young men who are puzzling their brains on how their country might be able to stop Japan. All Chinese are, of course, worrying about the danger threatening their homeland, but there must be many who are doing more than worrying, who are studying and thinking about things that ought to be done to meet the crisis.[5]

Powell's call to resist was loud and clear, but he was regularly intimidated. His car was stolen and he even had a hand-grenade thrown at him one day after lunch (it was faulty and didn't explode) as he left the American Club where he was living. He was shot at twice and reduced to working on the *Review* at night for his own safety with the door, recently steel-plated, guarded by tough Mauser-toting Shandong bodyguards. Ralph Shaw, who stayed on at the *North-China*, described entering Powell's office as "... like entering a citadel".[6]

The Japanese also intimidated Randall Gould who had a bomb that did explode planted on the steps of his building. The *China Press* came in for a lot of attention from the Japanese and the situation became even more hazardous as the pro-Japanese *Shanghai Times* had offices in the same building which were a target of Chiang's secret police chief Dai Li and the Nationalist underground movement.

The situation in Shanghai worsened as the Japanese encroachment across China proceeded. Powell's *China Review*, AP, the *China Press* and several other newspaper offices were all on the same street known as "Newspaper Row" and they came in for almost daily attacks. Milton Chase's AP offices were bombed twice and he was blown down the stairs and left with severe concussion on one occasion. Six gunmen raided the *China Press*'s printing works. When a security guard tried to stop them entering, the police became involved and a full-scale gun battle broke out on the street which left two dead, including a local American bar owner Tug Wilson, and several more people wounded. Despite these threats the *Press* kept on putting out daily editions. In September 1939, Alex Buchman received a "Black Hand" note — a death threat from the Japanese — and realising his time was up, he left for California and then went to Coyoacn to see Trotsky in exile with a letter of introduction from Harold Isaacs. Malcolm Rosholt and others, including Wu Kia-tang, decided to stay on in Shanghai. In 1940 Wu became managing editor and re-employed Rosholt as night editor but the pressures on journalists were mounting. Rosholt went to work with his old night-time colleague K. S. Chang who told him that he had not had a day off since Black Saturday almost three years previously.

Shortly afterwards, in July 1940, Sammy Chang, editor-in-chief of the *Shanghai Evening Post*'s Chinese-language edition, and a neighbour of the long-time journalist C. H. Lowe, was killed with four shots in the back by an unknown assassin while having *tiffin* in a German-run tea shop. A hired killer from the pro-Japanese puppet government was blamed but was never caught. J. B. Powell and his remaining staff at the *Review* set about organising funerals and memorial ceremonies for the dead Chinese journalists.

Carroll Alcott, with an estimated radio audience of 500,000 listeners, despite continuing attempts by the Japanese to jam the signal, was forced to live in the

YMCA, and send his wife and daughter back to America. After the Japanese ordered him "expelled" from Shanghai, he had to carry a Colt .45, travel around town wearing a flak jacket for protection over his somewhat bulky frame and be accompanied everywhere by his White Russian driver, loyal bodyguard Jan Egeberg (a Danish member of the SMP) and Chang, a Chinese detective. He had annoyed them in numerous ways ranging from constantly referring to the Japanese New Order as the "New Odour" to running a series of witty and politically incorrect sketches featuring two Japanese named Mr. Suzuki and Mr. Watanabe, who were symbols of Japanese militarism and arrogance. Mr. Suzuki was based on the actual Japanese agent who had dedicated himself to Alcott's destruction. Several assassination attempts were made on Alcott and his car was forced off the road a number of times. The Japanese eventually caught up with him and beat him viciously after dragging him out of a rickshaw near XHMA's studios, but he finally managed to escape their boots and fists and fled through an alley. After that, he travelled around in a Packard with bullet-proof glass. While he had his trusty Colt .45 for protection, his bodyguard Egeberg traded up to a tommy gun and his Chinese bodyguard got the most powerful automatic pistol he could find. Alcott eventually left Shanghai for America in September 1941 still in one piece, thus defeating Mr. Suzuki.

Things went from bad to worse to deadly. James Cox of Reuters was murdered at the Japanese police headquarters, with the Japanese claiming that he had admitted to being a British spy. The *New York Times*'s correspondent Hallett Abend was burgled repeatedly and then badly beaten at gun-point by Japanese thugs in his 16th floor Broadway Mansions apartment. He reluctantly returned to the US in 1941 amid grave concerns for his life should the Japanese return to finish the job as they had with Cox.

Then, on 15 July 1941, Wang Jingwei's Japanese-controlled puppet government issued a blacklist of their "Most Wanted Foreigners" still in Shanghai who were to be expelled. Journalists featured prominently, including Powell, Alcott, Gould, Hal Mills of AP, Vic Keen, J. A. E. Sanders-Bates, who published a group of anti-Japanese Chinese-language newspapers, and the newspaper proprietor and insurance magnate C. V. Starr.

Gould had continued publishing the *Shanghai Evening Post* despite mounting pressure from the Japanese. However, after the list was published, he quit and made it to New York in 1941. While it lasted in Shanghai, the paper's most popular columnist had been the aging H. G. W. Woodhead (now an OBE) of *Tientsin Times* fame, the best-known British newspaperman in China. Woodhead was by now a commanding figure in the press corps and nearly a 40-year China veteran. As well as his acerbic columns for Gould, he self-funded and edited a monthly magazine called *Oriental Affairs* and edited the annual

China Year Book. During the fighting in Shanghai in 1937, Woodhead published a day-by-day account of the events which was a sort of prototype blog that was hand-printed, distributed and widely read. His offices became a focal point for newly arrived correspondents looking to understand the background to the situation, though this wasn't always very peaceful as Woodhead's office was next to Emily Hahn's and the old veterans faithful black King Charles Spaniel Puppety regularly fought with Hahn's furiously masturbating gibbon Mr. Mills, creating mayhem until Hahn decamped for Hong Kong.

There were some foreign journalists who did not automatically take the Chinese side. Lord Killanin had left Shanghai, where he had been the British right-wing *Daily Mail*'s special correspondent on the "Sino-Japanese Hostilities" and went to Kobe where he told the Japanese news agency Domei that he regretted "… the anti-Japanese stand taken by 'some people and organisations' in Great Britain, 'especially the Labour Party'" and ascribed this anti-Japanese sentiment to "vigorous Chinese propaganda". Killanin, born Michael Morris and an Irish peer, did indeed represent the view of some of the British community and some among the establishment in England. Apologist reporters like Killanin were to look at best foolish and at worst tragically wrong as events in Nanjing were to take the horror of the Japanese attack to an altogether higher level.

Killanin and a few journalists took an overt pro-Japanese stance out of political belief but others went over to the Axis side for less ideological reasons. Royal Navy gunner John Kenneth Gracie agreed to be a broadcaster on the pro-Axis radio station XGRS which was based in Shanghai during the war and run by the Nazis. He used the on-air name Sergeant Allan McIntosh. Gracie had developed a deep loathing of upper- class Shanghailanders and the pompous British Residents' Association in particular and saw working for the Germans simply as a form of revenge for their perceived slights against him. Robert Lamb was another Western journalist who worked for XGRS during the war, as was Herbert Moy, a young Chinese-American who was the Nazi station's main newsreader. When the war in Europe ended with the Nazi surrender, Moy committed suicide by jumping out of the studio window. The Japanese made use of certain individuals too. For instance, Don Chisholm, a generally disliked American who claimed to be British and who had founded *The Shopping News* in Shanghai in 1932, worked for them apparently without being forced and became known as "Shanghai's Lord Haw-Haw". His *Shopping News* was aimed at women and featured mostly fashion news surrounded by adverts. The main selling point of the magazine was its regular gossip and rumour pieces about local Shanghailanders. Most believed that Chisholm ran a blackmail sting, threatening to reveal prominent Shanghailanders' infidelities if they didn't pay up. When the Japanese reopened the old XHMA radio station, Chisholm became the announcer in an attempt to replicate Alcott's former popularity but his pro-Axis stance was generally ignored and he lacked charm. Chisholm was arrested at the end of the war but was eventually released on the orders of the US Justice Department in 1946. It seems he knew where enough Shanghailander social skeletons were hidden to make sure he never had to face a jury without embarrassing some important people.

Witnessing the Rape of Nanking

As if the fighting to date had not been terrible enough with the slaughter in Shanghai, worse was to come as the Japanese army swarmed into Nanjing and, after defeating the Chinese army, went on a horrific and genocidal rampage through the city for six weeks in what swiftly became known as the "Rape of Nanking". Some journalists had been in Nanjing prior to the Japanese occupation of the city and they mostly congregated in the city's rather down-at-heel International Club. Indeed, shortly before the Japanese swept into the city, many had travelled there to hear the views of Dr. T. T. Li, the Ministry of Foreign Affair's director of publicity and intelligence at a sociable gathering in the club.

Hallett Abend felt he could not leave Shanghai to travel to Nanjing as he had lost his long-time assistant Douglas Robinson. He persuaded the *New York Times* to send Elbert Clifton Daniel instead. Daniel didn't last long and returned to the US, which was a smart career move as, after being posted to Russia and Paris, he ended his career as chief of the *Times*'s Washington bureau and then the paper's managing editor, jobs made easier presumably by the fact that he had married Margaret Truman, the daughter of President Harry S. Truman. Into the breach stepped the reliable and smart Till Durdin, who resigned from the *China Press* to take up the *New York Times* post. Durdin was plunged in at the deep end and started out for the *Times* by reporting the Nanjing atrocities.

Other foreign correspondents who covered the horrific events included Lesley Smith of Reuters and Arthur Menken, a Paramount newsreel cameraman, along with the *Chicago Daily News*'s Arch Steele and UPI's Earl Leaf. All of them despatched strong articles about the tragedy at Nanjing. "Wholesale looting, the violation of women, the murder of civilians, the eviction of Chinese from their homes, mass executions of war prisoners and the impressing of able-bodied men turned Nanking into a city of terror", wrote Durdin in the *New York Times* on 17 December 1937, two days after he managed to escape the massacre aboard the *USS Oahu*, a Yangtze cruiser that evacuated foreign nationals from the city.[7] Steele headlined his last piece from Nanjing simply as "Four Days of Hell" in the *Chicago Daily News* which hit home with his audience as he was considered a balanced and well-informed reporter by many of his readers and his contemporaries in the press corps. Another correspondent, AP's C. Yates McDaniel — a "mishkid" born in Suzhou who was to go on to become famous for covering the fall of Singapore before dramatically escaping the city — noted: "My last remembrance of Nanking: Dead Chinese, dead Chinese, dead Chinese".[8]

Harold John "H. J." Timperley, a Shanghai-based Australian China Hand, swiftly edited a book with Alexander Buchman that was one of the first accounts of the Rape of Nanking, with eyewitness testimonies of both victims and the foreigners that worked in the International Safety Zone.[9] "Tim" Timperley had arrived in China in 1928 and set up a small agency which translated and interpreted articles from the Chinese press while working for the *Manchester Guardian*. He was also the local representative of the Institute of Pacific Relations, a body that held meetings around China that were popular with journalists. Indeed the elegant and aristocratic-looking Timperley was a very popular member of the press corps. He was described by Ilona Ralf Sues as "… like a marquis from the court of Louis XV"[10] and was known as a caring man who in his spare time organised medical aid for hundreds of apprentices who worked without pay in industrial sweatshops in Shanghai. Nanjing was a busy beat for Timperley. Somehow he found time in between air raids to marry a young American woman who was working in Nanjing, as well as reporting. His *Manchester Guardian* articles, filed from Shanghai after being smuggled out of the besieged city of Nanjing by his new wife, created a furore and a diplomatic storm in England despite the attentions of the Japanese censors. In an attempt to discredit him, Japanese historians have accused him of being in the pay of Chinese Intelligence. However, according to the *Guardian*'s archives, his articles from Nanjing were initially prompted by members of the ad-hoc International Committee for the Nanking Safety Zone.[11] He was also to annoy the British authorities in China when he accused British diplomats in Nanjing of negligence for having gone on their summer holidays despite the growing crisis. Undeterred, Timperley was to address the question of Japanese atrocities again in *Japan: A World Problem* (1942). In 1997 the fuller testimonies that Timperley had worked from were reportedly discovered under a bed in the city of Hefei in Anhui province. For his part, Timperley left journalism in 1939 to become an adviser to the Chinese Ministry of Information, though he continued to be consulted regularly by the long-serving editor of the *Guardian*, W. P. Crozier.

The Japanese immediately and consistently denied that any massacre had taken place. Strenuous denials flowed from most of the 120 Japanese correspondents and photographers who travelled with the Japanese army from the *Asahi Shimbun*, the *Osaka Mainichi*, *Yomiuri Shimbun*, *Kokumin Shimbun*,

Tokyo Nichi Nichi Shimbum and the *Shanghai Nichinichi Shimbum* (which issued a daily Chinese-language edition and combined had a circulation of 6,000 copies in Shanghai) as well as Domei which all resolutely supported Tokyo's invasion of China. However, a number of Japanese soldiers did immortalise their roles in the carnage by photographing their atrocities, providing incontrovertible proof.[12] Many soldiers returned to Shanghai after the massacre and put their rolls of film in to be developed as macabre souvenirs and shocked Chinese technicians gave copies of the prints to foreign journalists which allowed images of the events to get out to the wider world. It was also the case that their own people suppressed the truth of the horrific events, with Tokyo's censors heavily cutting their press corp's articles. Tokyo and the local military officials quickly imposed a gag order, under the Japanese law Governing the Dissemination of False Rumours and the Publishing Supervision, which affected several writers. Ishikawa Tatsuzo's book *Ikiteiru heitai* (*Living Soldiers*) was scheduled to appear in instalments in the monthly leading opinion magazine *Chuo Koron*, but it was banned after the first instalment appeared in March 1938 under the false rumours law and deemed an anti-war statement. Ishikawa, who spent time in both Shanghai and Nanjing in 1937–38, depicted the indiscriminate slaughter of Chinese soldiers and non-combatants, Japanese looting and mass rape but it was all suppressed. However, in general the denial of any massacre stuck. Along with many others, the following all denied witnessing any massacre in Nanjing when they first returned home: Sato Shinju, a photographer with the *Tokyo Nichinichi Shimbum*; Asai Tatsuzo, a photographer and newsreel cameraman with Domei's Motion Picture Department; Taguchi Toshisuke, war correspondent with the *Hochi Shimbum*; Imai Masatake, special correspondent with the *Tokyo Asahi*; and Koike Shuyo, a reporter with the *Miyako Shimbum*. They realised how total the news blackout had been back in Japan and how vicious the recriminations were against those who told the truth about what they had seen.

With the passing of time, some admissions slowly surfaced. Asai Tatsuzo later recalled witnessing mass executions, while Imai Masatake, who wrote patriotic "soul-stirring" articles in the late 1930s, admitted in the 1950s that he had witnessed a mass execution of between 400 and 500 Chinese near the *Tokyo Asahi*'s Nanjing office and had seen dead bodies piled up at the city's wharves. Others only talked much, much later: Adachi Kazuo and Moriyama Yoshio, both reporters with the *Tokyo Asahi*, finally recalled, in 1975, a mass murder near the paper's office: "Plain-clothes soldiers were shot to death one after another, right in front of their wives and children, who were weeping and screaming".[13] Others also wrote later. For example, Suzuki Jiro of the *Tokyo Nichinichi Shimbum* wrote of witnessing executions and later Matsumoto Shigeharu,

Domei's Shanghai bureau chief, interviewed Japanese journalists who admitted seeing charred and burned bodies littering the streets of the city.

Even decades later, the clamp-down and suppression of the events in Nanjing was still enforced. *Tokyo Nichi Nichi Shimbum* correspondent Goto Kosaku denied the massacre throughout the 1960s; Hara Shiro, *Yomiuri Shimbum*'s Shanghai correspondent who was still alive in the 1980s, vehemently denied he had seen any brutalities; and, despite his book, later Ishikawa once again denied witnessing any massacres. Hashimoto Tomisaburo, a colourful figure who headed the *Asahi Shimbun*'s Shanghai bureau, claimed never to have heard a thing about a massacre and neither, so he claimed, did the dapper and urbane English-speaking Moriyama Takashi of the *Asahi Shimbun*, though another of the paper's Nanjing reporters, Imai Seigo, admitted witnessing the massacre and later wrote about it. Clearly even long after the actual events, the Japanese censors were determined not to face the facts about Nanjing. Never was an event so dreadful and the suppression of the facts so overt by a group of journalists as the Japanese press corps' almost total denial of the Rape of Nanking.

Fighting continued to rage around Nanjing. In early December two Japanese newspapermen were killed — Yoshio Amano, a cameraman with the *Tokyo Asahi* and Keniro Ashizawa, a reporter for a Japanese wire service, both of whom were shot dead by Chinese forces. One other event of the time that garnered massive press coverage and left the Japanese in a bad light was the evacuation of Americans and other neutrals from Nanjing in December 1937 aboard the *USS Panay*. Many of the press corps headed to the city to cover the exodus. The *Panay* and three nearby Standard Oil vessels were attacked by Japanese fighter planes which strafed and bombed the American gunboat, wounding both seaman aboard and people ashore.

Several journalists had sought refuge aboard the *Panay*, disastrously as it transpired. Colin McDonald, Far East correspondent for the London *Times*, was in one of the boats that left the *Panay* to take the wounded sailors ashore. He tore up handkerchiefs and rags to stuff in the bullet holes in the boat and then started to bail rapidly with the only thing available, a battered helmet. Weldon James, UPI's Nanjing bureau chief, put down his notebook to help the wounded and was later awarded the Navy Expeditionary Medal. James Marshall, Far East correspondent for *Collier's*, was seriously injured during the Japanese strafing, receiving shrapnel wounds in the neck, shoulder, stomach and chest. Despite his injuries, Marshall managed to walk 20 miles before being picked up by Japanese soldiers and flown to Shanghai.

Eventually the beleaguered aboard the *Panay* were got ashore. Once on land, Sandro Sandri of *La Stampa*, an Italian journalist known as "the Floyd Gibbons of Italy", lay mortally wounded with stomach wounds on the banks of the river, hidden among the 10-foot-high reeds. Luigi Barzini Junior, the son of the correspondent Luigi Barzini Senior who had covered the Boxer Rebellion in 1900, comforted him with an occasional cigarette before Sandri died from his wounds.

Universal's Norman Alley and George Krainukov, as well as Movietone's Eric Mayell, captured the Japanese attack on the *Panay*. Their footage was rushed by destroyer to Manila, then by clipper to America's west coast, where it was met by a chartered airplane to New York and finally was taken by armoured car to a processing lab in Brooklyn, all at a cost of US$25,000. Along with the newsreels, American audiences learnt of the *Panay*'s fate from the photographs of the *New York Times*'s Norman Soong, a Hawaiian-born Chinese-American who snapped the attack. Alley, Mayell and Soong's images would prove the attacking Japanese planes had been low enough, on more than one approach, to identify the *Panay* clearly as an American ship. Soong's photos were accompanied by Hallett Abend's exclusive story that the machine-gunning was done on the personal command of the reactionary secret society member Colonel Kingoro Hashimoto who was later sentenced to life imprisonment by the International Military Tribunal for the Far East for his deadly actions in China.

Between Black Saturday in August and the attack on the *Panay* in early December 1937, more foreign journalists had been killed in China than since the *Canton Press* issued its first edition in 1827 over 100 years before.

Peiping and Tientsin: Every Vestige of Independence Gone

By the end of 1937 Beijing had ceased to have an independent press (known as the "Nanking press" for its allegiance to the Chinese capital) or foreign press as the Japanese took control of the city which was briefly called Peiping, or capital of peace, at the time. The attempt to shut down all publications not openly sympathetic to Tokyo's cause was total as the city lacked the protection of a foreign concession. The major Chinese newspapers were all suppressed and only those under Japanese control and/or ownership were left publishing. For some time the city had been run by the Hopei-Chahar Political Council [14] but the Japanese disbanded it. This doomed the *Peiping News*, an English-language newspaper the council had established. The paper had described itself as neutral before the Marco Polo bridge (*Lukouchiao*) incident in July 1937, when Japanese soldiers provoked a firefight with Chinese forces, but afterwards it fell in loyally behind the Nanjing government. As they occupied the city, the Japanese swiftly arrested Dr. Wilson Wei, the paper's editor, accused him (falsely) of being a communist and detained him for several weeks.

The British-owned *Peiping Chronicle*, which had been started in the early 1930s as the *Peking Chronicle*, lasted slightly longer than the *News* but, after repeated and serious threats to his life, the editor Sheldon Ridge eventually closed the paper. The *Chronicle* was not the best newspaper ever produced in China by any stretch of the imagination but many foreigners found it amusing and read it avidly. To save costs most of the paper's journalists were Chinese with less than fluent English and Chinese typesetters who knew no English at all laid up the paper. When two skaters fell through the ice on a lake, the *Chronicle* reported: "They eyed ice angrily for some time before leaving in disgruntle" and a famous headline declared "PRINCESS ELIZABETH TO BECOME MOTHER OF HER OWN CHILD". Ridge had been brought in to make improvements but he couldn't do much with the limited resources, though he was highly knowledgeable about both China and Mongolia and had previously been a managing editor with the Far Eastern Times Syndicate. The *Chronicle* later reappeared as an overtly pro-Japanese paper. A further casualty was Edgar Snow's *Democracy* that was shut down and killed before it had really had a chance to establish itself.

Tianjin fared little better than Beijing, despite having a degree of protection in the foreign concessions. The Chinese papers were swiftly shut after the Japanese bombed the city in July 1937. With the Japanese occupation of the city on 30 July, the English- language afternoon paper, the *Tientsin Evening Post*, which had only been launched in early 1937, was forced to close. The long-established *Peking and Tientsin Times* survived a bit longer under the shelter of the British Concession. Woodhead's replacement editor, the monocle-wearing Wilfred Victor "W. V." Pennell, had formerly worked on Woodhead's monthly *Oriental Affairs* as the paper's Tianjin correspondent. As well as trying to keep the *Times* going, Pennell kept filing for Woodhead in Shanghai on what he saw as the "unprecedented lawlessness and anarchy" in northern China.

At the same time, an American, Dr. Charles James Fox, the president of Tianjin's American Chamber of Commerce who had been in China for several decades, was publishing the *North China Star* in Tianjin. The *Star* lasted longer than the other foreign papers as it was perceived to be sympathetic to the Japanese and perhaps even secretly funded by them, though J. B. Powell in his *Review* claimed that these charges could be "emphatically denied" and it did indeed seem unlikely, given that an early board member and editorial staffer at the *Star* had been the ubiquitous KMT-insider Holly Tong.[15] By December 1937 a *China Weekly Review* editorial declared that every vestige of independence in Beijing and Tianjin's press was gone.

Last Ditchers and Iconoclasts

The worsening situation, of course, attracted a new crop of journalists chasing the China story. The reporters on the Japanese black-list were now highly limited in what they could do, but at the same time new ones, often unaccredited freelancers, arrived who were not on the list and could move around with more freedom compared to their more closely watched colleagues. Among these were a number who congregated in the temporary Nationalist retreat of Hankou in 1938. They became known as the "Last Ditchers" and based themselves in the former British Concession. For a brief time Hankou became the centre of life for the foreign press corps in China. Many old China Hands based themselves there, but so too did many new arrivals chasing the next war, in this case the next Madrid now that Franco's forces had secured their victory and the Spanish Civil War was waning. The Last Ditchers reported, wrote, socialised, drank, quarrelled and, quite often, slept with each other. They included a number of fascinating characters worthy of a mention.

A leading Last Ditcher was the London-born socialist Winifred "Freda" Utley. She had been a member of the Communist Party of Great Britain and had also been close to the Fabians and George Bernard Shaw. She had become entranced with the USSR and moved to Moscow where she married a Soviet citizen. Her husband got himself caught up in Stalin's purges and was sent to a Siberian gulag, and he died without ever making contact with her again. She left Moscow, surprisingly not totally disillusioned with Stalin's Russia, and went to America where she freelanced for *Reader's Digest*.

In her memoirs, *Odyssey of a Liberal*, Utley, who had been to Shanghai briefly 10 years previously carrying messages for the Comintern, was as keen to report the political situation in China when she arrived in 1938 as she was to report that she was incredibly beautiful and highly desirable. She did, however, admit that the lack of available white women in the war zones of China, combined with the testosterone-fuelled reporting environment, probably contributed to her self-proclaimed popularity among her male colleagues. She soon formed an attachment based on gender and politics with the *Manchester Guardian*'s correspondent Agnes Smedley and Anna Louise Strong, basically the only other unattached white women around the journalist community in Hankou (though most men admitted to being afraid of them!), along with Ilona Ralf Sues who was now working for Holly Tong's government Propaganda Ministry. Smedley, Strong and Sues shared rooms at Bishop Logan H. Roots's house. This unlikely partnering of the Stalinist Smedley, the intensely revolutionary Strong, the liberal Sues and the good bishop made more sense when it is remembered that Roots, the American Bishop of Hankou, was widely known as the "Pink Bishop" due to his alleged sympathy for the Communists: it was rumoured he had once sheltered Zhou En-lai and his wife in the 1920s. In truth, he did admire their social improvement efforts but was also rather keen on the KMT's New Life Movement too. This strangely thrown together household got arguably even stranger with regular evening soirees featuring Roots's wife Francis playing the piano while, to pass the time, Smedley taught the Pink Bishop and the visiting Bishop Huntington of Anqing to sing such revolutionary classics as *The Man on the Flying Trapeze*. According to Sues, who was the press-ganged audience for many of these recitals, Smedley couldn't resist finishing the evening with an anticlerical rendition of *You'll Get Pie in the Sky, When You Die* which the bishops politely applauded but declined to join in. Roots, clearly a very liberal chap, even allowed Smedley and Strong to address him as "Comrade Bishop" and invite Communist Eighth Route Army commander Peng Dehuai over for tea.

Despite the strength of the various characters at Bishop Roots's house, they seem to have generally kept the peace. Strong was at least used to religious folk as she was the daughter of a Nebraskan missionary and pastor of the Congregational Church. She had been awarded a Ph.D. by Chicago University where she had championed the cause of child welfare. She then moved into journalism, working for the *New York Evening Post*, and covered the 1916 Everett Massacre when the Industrial Workers of the World (the "Wobblies") clashed with vigilantes in support of striking lumber workers. She then vocally opposed the First World War and openly supported the Bolshevik Revolution. After some pieces in various papers dealing with organised labour in the US, in 1921 she became the Moscow correspondent of the International News Service, supporting the fledgling USSR. During the 1920s and 1930s she travelled throughout China, Asia and Russia and then went to see the Spanish Civil War. Throughout her life Strong may at times have described herself primarily as a journalist but she was really always a political activist whether in her journalism, books or the causes she championed. Much of her writing was published in highly partisan publications, but as she was often groundbreaking this didn't always rule her out as a serious commentator.

Strong's fellow-lodger, Agnes Smedley, was from Osgood, Missouri. She had rebelled against her drunkard father and seen her mother die of malnourishment. She had been a leftist since her student days when she had invited the likes of anarchist Emma Goldman, muckraking writer Upton Sinclair and the five times socialist candidate for president, Eugene Debs, to speak. She became a member of the American Socialist Party, which earned her expulsion from San Diego College. She had then gone to New York and managed to annoy the authorities by simultaneously stirring up agitation against British rule in India and promoting birth control. She dabbled in journalism, writing for the *New York Call* and the *Birth Control Review*. In 1919 she founded the Friends of Freedom for India movement and, though approached, decided not to join the American Communist Party. She moved to Berlin, then Russia, covering Weimar society for *The Nation* and the *New Masses* and finally to China in 1928 where she wrote for a variety of newspapers including the *Manchester Guardian* and Powell's *Review* while completing her novel, *Daughter of Earth* (1929). The book received good reviews on the left: *The Nation* described it as "America's first feminist-proletarian novel".

Smedley's ultra-radical politicisation had begun in 1930 when she started a relationship, physical and intellectual, with Richard Sorge, the German journalist and Soviet super-spy, working under cover in Shanghai for the *Frankfurter Zeitung*. He held court in the bar of the Cathay Hotel, a Shanghai press corps watering-hole, picking up useful titbits as he looked to recruit. Smedley had written reports on the Japanese occupation of Manchuria for the *Frankfurter Zeitung* that had been praised in Germany. This led her to have direct contact with the Communist Party and its forces; she was probably an agent of the Comintern already anyway. She kept a wide range of friends and associates but steered clear of most journalists except Edgar Snow, Frank Glass, Harold Isaacs and Powell. She thought Powell was a man of integrity, despite their different politics, and he did publish her work occasionally. One British journalist described her as "... tall, rather grim and Eton cropped, about forty, an ardent communist of the Chinese not the Russian variety".[16] She certainly did cause a stir soon after arriving in China. Those easily titillated found her vocal espousal of "free love" something of a turn-on and she does seem to have had many lovers; and the exasperated Bishop Roots eventually evicted her for being "immoral". What titillated many in the press corps who met her caused consternation among the women and wives of the Long March members when she visited them in their Yenan caves.

The rather vain Utley, the somewhat butch and severe-looking Smedley and the determined and imposing Strong were to spend much of 1938 in Hankou as the nucleus of the Last Ditchers, who drank in the evenings on the roof of the *China Press* building, in the gardens of the Navy "Y", in the Terminus Hotel or at Rosie's Dine, Dance and Romance Restaurant, a small Russian-run bar where the favoured tipple was the United Front cocktail. Having recently spent time in both the USSR and the USA, Utley preferred the company of the American journalists in town to the Brits. She believed Americans to be more genuinely liberal in their outlook while Brits were, according to Utley at least, almost wholly pro-Japanese and obsessed with the European situation and the Nazi threat to England rather than any threats to China. Utley stuck close to

Smedley and Edgar Snow, who was also in Hankou still writing for the British *Daily Herald*. For much of the time Smedley was seething as all her notes and photographs taken during a visit to the Eighth Route Army had been lost in the post either due to the growing chaos across China or, as she believed, because "plenty of people" in Hankou didn't want them to be found again. It turned out to be chaos rather than censorship or malice and her papers eventually arrived in New York to be published in 1938 as *China Fights Back*.

The Last Ditchers were a cosmopolitan bunch. As well as Utley, Smedley, Strong and Snow, they included Walter Bosshard, the pioneering photojournalist now working for New York's Black Star agency. The Swiss citizen was constantly troubled with stomach problems but was a good photographer and earned some money on the side stringing for a variety of Swiss papers. There was also Eppie Epstein who had moved from the *Tientsin Times* to Hankou to work for UPI, though he was still barely 20; Luigi Barzini who had just witnessed the attack on the *Panay* and Sandro Sandri dying in his arms; and Lily Abels of the *Neue Zürcher Zeitung* who was a well-known author in her native Switzerland. The most senior correspondent in Hankou, and the group's doyen, was UPI's Francis McCracken (or "Mac") Fisher, a journalist who had been around China since the late 1920s and was based in an office in Hankou's Lutheran Mission run by the eponymous Bishop Roots. The mission became an informal gathering centre and a clearing-house for news, with the radio kept on all day.

Fisher, who had started out with UPI in Beijing, was a workaholic and, though disruptive to his daily schedule, he preferred the other correspondents to come to him as he rarely left his typewriter and wires ticker to socialise anywhere else. He worked closely with his colleague, the dashing, slightly aristocratic, rugby-playing Englishman George Hogg who had been just 23 when he arrived in Shanghai for a two-day visit in 1937 as part of a round-the-world trip before starting a banking career in London. Brought up in a pacifist family, it's not clear when he actually became interested in China, though while at Oxford he was one of many young undergraduates who came under the spell of the well-known warden at Wadham College, Maurice Bowra, who had been born in China, the son of a Chinese Imperial Maritime Customs official. In Shanghai, Hogg had stayed with Frank and Aimée Millican of Shanghai's Christian Literature Society and the Christian Broadcasting Station. They and his staunchly pacifist family in England introduced him to the *Manchester Guardian* which he started freelancing for and through that paper he met its Hankou stringer Smedley who in turn got him rooms with Bishop Roots. This was a good thing in that Hogg, himself brought up in a liberal and somewhat radical Christian family, found much common ground with Roots; but it was often a bad thing as proximity to Smedley meant endless lectures on the virtues of communism and repeated attempts at luring him away from Christ as well as into the bedroom.

Hogg decided he preferred China and journalism to banking and high finance, and was hired by AP as a stringer but was expelled from China by the Japanese. He promptly made his way back to Beijing via Korea and started working for UPI and ended up being present at the Rape of Nanjing, entering the city secretly to avoid the Japanese censors. In Hankou the demands for more copy meant that both Fisher and Hogg often ended up sleeping in their office along with UPI's Chinese correspondent George Wang. The UPI-Lutheran Mission also became a virtual hostel for visiting journalists as the events in Hankou reached their climax. Utley described Mac Fisher as a "bamboo American", meaning that he had been in China so long he couldn't envisage living anywhere else and was fluent in Chinese. He did indeed love China and later worked for the OWI in Chongqing but was eventually forced to leave the country in 1945.

Another major Hankow Last Ditcher well known to many in the old China press corps was Haldore Hanson, who was a star correspondent in the 1930s, despite remaining freelance and not being made a full-time correspondent by AP until 1937. He arrived in 1934 from his native Minnesota barely into his twenties and was famous for repeatedly riding his bicycle up to one frontline or another and being arrested by one side or the other — first either the Japanese or Chinese and then later, during the civil war, either the Nationalists or the Communists.

The Hankou contingent also included a number of German journalists who were assumed by most to be Nazi spies. On the other hand, the political affiliations of Vladimir Rogov were unquestionable: he represented TASS and wrote for *Pravda*. Still, Rogov was popular. Born a Russian peasant, he left his village at 22 completely illiterate and, by 30, was fluent in English, German, French and Chinese, amazing the Chinese press corps with his ability to read the Chinese classics. He had been in Manchuria first and then moved to Hankou. Despite political differences, most of the foreign press corps liked him, not least for his tradition of dispensing gossip, *zakuska* (Russian-style hors d'oeuvres) and chilled vodka to anyone who dropped by for a chat at his house, which was actually in the *China Press* building that also housed Reuters on the ground floor and TASS on the third. Rogov knew more than most in Hankou as he had reports coming in from the 10 TASS correspondents reporting from different fronts where they were "embedded" with the Communists. Ralf Sues maintained that the KMT officials in Hankou were always keen to see Rogov's telegrams as he had a better impression of the development of the war than they did.

Hankou also saw perhaps one of the best times for relations between the KMT and the foreign press. Bill Donald, now called "the evil spirit of China" by the Japanese, and Madame Chiang's man Holly Tong, assisted by Sues and the tall, blond Australian journalist Buzz Farmer, held daily press briefings that were always well attended due to the fact that even if real news was scant the corps was guaranteed tea and cookies. Tong wasn't altogether to blame. He could only reveal to the corps what had been revealed to him by the Chiangs, Donald and the military, which typically wasn't much, and usually left him apologising profusely: "My dear friends: Unfortunately I have no news for you, but we will have a friendly cup of tea together and some Chinese sweets — we call them *dien-hsin*, which means 'touch heart'. I hope they will touch your heart and you will forgive me …".[17] This approach was not likely to cut much ice with tougher hacks like Mac Fisher or those already hostile to the KMT such as Smedley. In any case, Tong wasn't a total walkover and placed Sues in charge of press censorship where she had the unenviable task of monitoring all cables sent from Hankou, which did little to endear her to the Last Ditchers.

Like most of the press corps in Hankou, Utley wanted to get to the frontlines and did manage it with the help of people such as Jimmy Wei and Eddie Tseng of the Central News Agency. At the front, away from the by now claustrophobic and incestuous milieu of Hankou, Utley mixed with a new crowd. Those that had made it to the forward lines were slightly more experienced than many of the keen amateurs back in Hankou. They included Till Durdin, Arch Steele, Lesley Smith of Reuters and UPI's Jack Belden, "a ferocious woman hater" according to Utley but considered one of the great China correspondents by Owen Lattimore despite suffering severe mood swings and being a functioning alcoholic. They constituted a sub-clique of the Last Ditchers that became known, largely by themselves it must be admitted, as the "Iconoclasts", believing only what they saw with their own eyes. Utley was one of the only women correspondents to reach the front around Nanchang in Jiangxi province due to her connections with the Chinese Red Cross and the Chinese Army Medical Corps. As more of an author rather than a practising journalist, she had trouble with her copy. Bob Murphy, a 19-year-old UPI correspondent from Kansas City, helpfully coached her on "cablese".

Utley praised Till Durdin for his knowledge of Chinese politics and the infighting that marked the Nationalist-Communist alliance. Durdin was still working for the *New York Times* and was by now firmly a bamboo American but he never became overly pro-communist. In Hankou he thrashed Jack Belden at chess and annoyed everyone with his dreadful violin playing late into the night. However, his years on the *China Press* and other Shanghai publications had given him "top-flight correspondent" status in Hankou among the newcomers.

Freda Utley was charmed by him writing: "Scholarly, sensitive and reserved, with a slight physique but great endurance and singular charm, Till Durdin was an "egghead," physically as well as metaphorically. Although only in his early thirties, his thinning red hair had already receded far back over both sides of his wide forehead".[18]

Indeed many of the Hankou contingent were among the best foreign correspondents in China. The wonderfully named Archibald Trojan Steele ticked all the boxes in Hankou — a top-flight correspondent, Last Ditcher and Iconoclast who was a very good friend of Walter Bosshard. At the time Steele was working for the *Chicago Daily News* and the *New York Herald Tribune*, having taken over the job from Frank Smothers. Utley described him as "tall and lanky with a thin, angular face, high bony forehead, prominent nose, tight lipped mouth and a western drawl".[19] Altogether, given his looks and Californian background, she saw him as being reminiscent of the "strong, silent hero of a western movie". However, despite his demeanour, Steele was a deep-thinking journalist who had developed a strong compassion for China and the Chinese since his arrival in 1932. When Utley returned to the front in late 1938, Arch Steele accompanied her, at one point dragging her from their army truck to take shelter in a roadside ditch as the Japanese strafed their convoy. Utley was partially deaf and so the noise of falling bombs affected her less than her colleagues who could clearly hear the bombers approaching. She claimed that this physical handicap saved her a lot of unnecessary worry during the war and also, later, allowed her to get a good night's sleep when covering Vietnam in the late 1960s as she never heard the Viet Cong mortar attacks. The two raced around on a borrowed motorcycle to cover the shifting frontline and found themselves climbing steep hillsides along with the Chinese army and a TASS correspondent who was living permanently with the troops. Steele's reports would earn him the sobriquet of the "Dean of the China Correspondents".

Durdin and Steele were almost unique in that, according to Utley, neither ever claimed to be an expert on China or the Far East and, unlike just about every other Last Ditcher and Iconoclast in Hankou in 1938 (including Utley), they never wrote a book about the period: "Whereas other correspondents with far less knowledge rushed home to write books about China, neither Durdin nor Steele ever wrote one".[20]

Eventually, as the Japanese advance continued, Hankou ceased to be the official capital and Chongqing was declared the site for the final stand. The Last Ditchers and Iconoclasts started to drift apart in late 1938. Smedley went to work for the Chinese Red Cross with the Communist Fourth Route Army but continued to send the odd despatch to the *Manchester Guardian* when she had time. Utley returned to America on a lecture tour and became a celebrity along the way after the Japanese refused to let her land in Yokohama. Belden left Hankou, recruiting George Hogg to take his place at UPI before leaving, visited the New Fourth Army for the *Shanghai Evening Post and Mercury* in 1939 and then went on to follow the Burma campaign. Yet others, including Till and Peggy Durdin (the daughter of American missionaries in China), relocated to Chongqing to continue following the war in China and form the nucleus of the Chongqing press corps for the duration.

However, for a period in 1938, Hankou had been the place to be — and one of the most heavily bombed places to be too as there were nightly air raids — and most of the left-leaning journalists, writers and assorted sojourners looking for a war had gathered there. Ilona Ralf Sues remembered the somewhat dangerous and always chaotic time favourably. Evenings were spent on the roof of the *China Press* building watching Japanese air raids with the Central News Agency's Francis Yao; and the congregating press corps would occasionally be joined by local celebrities such as Claire Lee Chennault of the Flying Tigers, diplomats and senior Nationalist officials watching the dog fights between Chennault's raffish band of mercenary pilots and the Japanese. Despite the deteriorating situation, editors back home didn't always seem to understand how serious the war was in and around Hankou. Sues was once faced with an agitated Eppie Epstein who had been ordered by his bosses at UPI to double-check the colours of Madame Chiang's polka dot sweater. Nobody knew the answer. Epstein's editors cabled again yet more urgently and Sues declared: "Hell, Eppie, cable them it's yellow with brown dots. Who cares?"[21]

It was the end of an era. Some journalists left China; others stayed on to cover the war from Chongqing and form an arguably even tighter-knit clique at the top of the Yangtze; and some famous sojourners popped in for a quick look.

Amateur War Correspondents — Auden and Isherwood

Writers kept on visiting as China's increasingly desperate situation attracted the curious, many of whom had already "done" Spain. In Shanghai the city's legendary status as the "Whore of the Orient" or the "Paris of the East", depending on your point of view, had grown in the 1930s and took on an even more decadent and daring tinge after Black Saturday. Few celebrity writers came with as much fanfare and reputation or as much attention lavished upon them as the two celebrated British writers Christopher Isherwood and Wystan Hugh "W. H." Auden who arrived in China as "amateur war correspondents" in February 1938. Though leftist intellectuals, it was not necessarily clear that

Auden and Isherwood would sympathise with China's plight any more than some other foreign leftists had. Many in the peace movement were still refusing to take sides, blaming war in general and as a concept rather than any particular nation's policy.

Their English publishers Faber and Faber had encouraged Auden and Isherwood to undertake an Asian tour in which China was to be just one stop among many. They were commissioned to produce a book of their experiences. However, war loomed and they only made it to Singapore, Macau, Hong Kong and China. They eventually delivered their jointly-authored mix of reportage and poetry *Journey to a War* in 1939. Isherwood was responsible for most of the prose narrative and Auden the sonnets that accompanied the text. Their first proper stops after London were Hong Kong and Macau. In Hong Kong, after meeting senior officials, Sir Victor Sassoon and the governor, Auden wrote:

> Here in the East the bankers have erected
> A worthy temple to the comic muse. [22]
>
> And in Macau ...
>
> A weed from Catholic Europe, it took root ...
> And grew on China imperceptibly ...
> Churches beside the brothels testify ...
> That faith can pardon natural behaviour. [23]

Obviously the two poets quickly got the measure of Hong Kong and Macau, as they had done with Singapore during a brief stopover, where they noted that, like Hong Kong, Singapore suffered from bankers' bad taste in terms of architecture. However, this was a simple challenge for two men who were used to the pomposity of the British Empire as well as Catholic Europe, after visiting Spain. China was to be more of a challenge and they wisely decided to head for the hinterland first, before Shanghai, probably guessing correctly that Shanghai would appeal to their baser desires a little too much and probably lead to the abandoning of the rest of the trip if they visited it first. They headed to Guangzhou and were dubbed Au Dung and Y. Hsiao Wu, and then moved on to Wuhan despite Japanese bombing of the rail line. They felt safe as they were in the first class carriage, the only one painted with camouflage! From Wuhan they took a Yangtze steamer to Hankou where they met Holly Tong as well as Bishop Roots and his lodger Agnes Smedley — the "Moscow-Heaven Axis" as they dubbed the unlikely pair. Smedley was depressed at the news of the German *anschluss* with Austria and didn't take too warmly to the two poets, considering them a little bourgeois for her austere tastes but they decided they liked her, "with her close-cropped grey hair, masculine jaw, deeply lined cheeks and bulging, luminous eyes".[24]

They also visited the Chinese opera with Francis Yao and took tea with Madame Chiang who wondered if poets ate cake or stuck to just spiritual food? They all ate cake. They also drank with the foreign press corps and the Last Ditchers and met old friends including Robert Capa, "the 23-year-old stocky and swarthy" Hungarian photographer for *Life* Auden had met in Spain covering the civil war. Capa was waiting for permission to join the Eighth Route Army to make a film about them. He was a star among the Hankou mob due to his instantly iconic photographs from the Spanish Civil War. His work in China would become less well known but was widely seen at the time. Capa was to go on to photograph D-Day and visit the USSR with his friend John Steinbeck and become a founder of the Magnum photo agency before heading to Vietnam to capture the collapse of French Indo-China. Sadly, he stepped on a landmine and was killed. He was perhaps best immortalised as the gritty classic war photographer in the Alfred Hitchcock movie *Rear Window* where Jimmy Stewart based his grizzly old war-snapper character on Capa.

They travelled on, by now flea-bitten and constipated, and eventually did visit the frontlines, somewhere near Suzhou, but it was a very quiet and uninteresting part of the front and so they moved on again northwards to Xian. Back in Hankou, they had socialised with Peter Fleming, who was in town for the *Times*, this time as the paper's war correspondent rather than its special travel correspondent as before, and with his infamously uncomplaining movie star wife Celia Johnson. The pair had travelled up the Burma Road into China, a not necessarily easy route though Johnson proved a particularly hardy traveller for a glamorous star of stage and screen while Fleming claimed he was so fit from walking most of the way (a slight exaggeration as they did most of the trip by bus) that he could crack nuts between his buttocks. The notoriously clumsy Fleming was routinely short on small talk but amused the writers "… with his drawl, his tan, his sleek, perfectly brushed hair, and lean good looks, a subtly comic figure — the conscious living parody of the pukka sahib. He is altogether too good to be true — and he knows it".[25]

The pair hung around Hankou, where they visited the local film studios and interviewed the gangster Big Eared Du, who was introduced to them as a leading philanthropist and member of the Shanghai Red Cross Committee. Then they went on to Nanchang near the front again and met Fleming once more. The two "amateur war correspondents" now felt decidedly amateurish in their padded coats and galoshes next to the über-correspondent Fleming: "… in his khaki shirt and shorts, complete with golf stockings, strong suède shoes, waterproof wristwatch and Leica camera, he might have stepped straight from a London tailor's window, advertising Gent's Tropical Exploration Kit".[26] Together the three got back close to the front again and interviewed Chinese peasant guerrillas, one of whom told them how he had bashed in a Japanese soldier's head with a stone and then drowned him. "Oh, jolly good!" was Fleming's only comment which proved that he still held his unassailable position as the William Boot of the China press corps.

Though they were all posh Englishmen and Oxbridge-educated, the contrast between Fleming and the two writers could not have been greater. Things nearly came to a head on a tough march through a 4,000 foot high pass near the front where Auden and Isherwood found themselves huffing, puffing and trailing "The Fleming Legend" and passing the time by reciting invented passages from an imaginary travel book they invented to be called "With Fleming to the Front". Fleming studiously ignored the two: after his 1935 trek across China with Ella Maillart, a woman, he was now patrolling the wartime frontline with two effeminate and slightly camp men. This was not the image Fleming wished to cultivate for the readers of the *Times* who thrilled at his manly and decidedly hetero exploits of derring-do. For their part, Auden and Isherwood thoroughly enjoyed their time with the Squire of Nettlebed, which included not a little teasing of the great correspondent. Auden commented after they finally left Fleming to head back to Nanchang, "Well, we've been on a journey with Fleming in China, and now we're real travellers for ever and ever. We need never go farther than Brighton again".[27] However, rather than heading for the English south coast, they finally went to Shanghai and provided probably the best or worst, depending on your tastes, description of the city at the time:

> The tired or lustful businessman will find here everything to gratify his desires. You can buy an electric razor, or a French dinner, or a well-cut suit. You can dance at the Tower Restaurant on the roof of the Cathay Hotel, and gossip with Freddy Kaufmann, its charming manager, about the European aristocracy, or pre-Hitler Berlin. You can attend race meetings, baseball games, football matches. You can see the latest American films. If you want girls or boys, you can have them, at all prices, in the bathhouses and the brothels. If you want opium you can smoke it in the best company, served on a tray, like afternoon tea. Good wine is difficult in this climate, but there is whisky and gin to float a fleet of battleships. The jeweller and the antique dealer await your orders, and their charges will make you imagine yourself back on Fifth Avenue or in Bond Street. Finally, if you ever repent, there are churches and chapels of all denominations.[28]

The two *bon vivants*, with cigarettes permanently hanging between their fingers, enjoyed Shanghai's decadence and frivolity. They had drinks at the

Shanghai Club's Long Bar, which disappointingly proved to be far shorter than they had been led to believe. They also had discussions with Rewi Alley on factory conditions and luncheons with the British ambassador, Sir Archibald Clarke-Kerr, and his charmingly beautiful blonde Chilean wife Tita, who was shortly to ditch him. In between frequent visits to the male brothels and bathhouses of Shanghai, with British Intelligence in tow to keep an eye on them, they found time to broadcast back to England for the BBC on conditions in China, and then they left. However, despite their sometimes flippant and disdaining tone, Auden and Isherwood did comprehend China's precarious situation in 1938, though it is not always apparent in their book. *Journey to a War* ends with a sonnet sequence entitled *In Time of War*:

> But ideas can be true although men die,
> And we can watch a thousand faces
> Made active by one lie:
>
> And maps can really point to places
> Where life is evil now:
> Nanking; Dachau.[29]

News for the Displaced — Jews, Russians and Internees

As the global situation deteriorated, still more refugee Jews came to Shanghai and gave the Jewish press a new lease of life. The oldest Jewish newspapers, *Israel's Messenger* (bi-weekly and strongly pro-Zionist) and *Die Gelbe Post* (daily and in German) were still running and they were joined by the weekly *Jewish Voice* (formerly known as the *Jüdisches Nachrichtenblatt*, and originally the long winded *Gemeindeblatt für die Jüdisches Kultus-Gemeinde*) which was launched in 1939 and lasted until 1946 and the *Shanghai Jewish Chronicle*, a weekly issued from May 1939 to October 1945. In addition, *Undzer Lebn* (*Our Life*) began publication in Russian and Yiddish in May 1941 and also put out an English supplement between 1942 and 1945. Others kept on coming, such as the *Chaverim News*, the voice of Reform Judaism in China, which was also launched in 1941, and later still the *Bundeszeitung der Brith Noah Zioni*, the first issue of which appeared in 1943.

The Jewish press, as well as those other papers that took an anti-fascist stance and managed to remain in business, naturally fought out the issues of the day with the pro-fascist press, much of which was supported by Nazi or Japanese interests in Shanghai. German propaganda included the *China Daily Tribune*'s German supplement and *The Shanghai Herald*'s German-language supplement. The Russian fascist newspaper *Nash Put* had been closed by the Japanese in Harbin but was still operating in Shanghai. Its editor M. M. Spassovsky, who wrote under the name M. Grott, wrote an article entitled "Can't We Dispense With The Jews" which led to a fight with P. A. Savintzev, the editor of *Novoe vremia* (*New Times*). Spassovsky had taken issue with Jewish doctors working at the Shanghai Russian Emigrants Hospital. Savintzev's reply, that doctors were hard to come by in Shanghai at the time, was hardly a strident defence of the Jewish doctors. Savintzev's *Novoe vremia*, a Japanese-sponsored White Russian publication, argued that this was an issue for the Japanese authorities while making sure everyone knew the paper had no fondness for Jews. At the same time, both the Nazis and the Japanese set up radio stations to broadcast Axis propaganda across China in their own languages and, in the case of Domei, in English and Chinese too. Also, the German Resident Association (*Deutsche Gemeinde*) had a radio station in Shanghai that broadcast war propaganda to Germans in China with a show called *Shanghai Calling*, the content of which was determined by a committee formed from delegates of the German consulate general. The Soviets weren't to be left out, however, and had two newspapers, *The Russian World* and *New World*, that supported the USSR, and by extension for much of the time the Nazi-Soviet Pact. Perhaps the best read to emerge from the Russian émigré community in China was *Na Rodinu* (*To Motherland*), a newspaper funded and published during the war by the well-known and very popular Oleg Lundstrem Jazz Band. All profits from their concerts and their paper were donated to the Red Army Foundation.

For those neither stateless, non-aligned or from the Axis countries, life took a decided turn for the worse. The Japanese forced the *North-China Daily News* to cease publishing: in truth reporting had become increasingly difficult and most people read the paper largely in the hope of seeing the announcement "US AND EUROPEAN MAIL DUE TODAY" for some news from home. They also started to seize radios from foreigners. Left with little news but the long-standing pro-Japanese *Shanghai Times*, which carried verbatim the proclamations of the Japanese authorities, many Shanghailanders didn't believe that the attack on Pearl Harbour could possibly have been so devastating while later in the internment camps they were even less believing of the rumours of massive bombs falling on Nagasaki and Hiroshima. However, arguably, people could read between the lines of the *Shanghai Times* Tokyo-determined news agenda. Some believed that they could tell which Pacific islands the Japanese had lost as those previously reported as being in Japanese hands then became islands being bombed and so must have been lost to the American advance.

Arrest and internment was the fate of many after Pearl Harbour in December 1941. The unluckiest were those deemed to be most influential and likely to organise resistance and subversion; and those able to speak fluent Chinese were sent to the notorious Haiphong Road Camp, an all-male camp whose inmates included the major Shanghailander business tycoons, SMC officials and others of note. The best-known press corps inmate was J. B. Powell who had annoyed the Japanese so much for so long with his *Review* and radio broadcasts. Haiphong Road was to be feared as it meant torture and regular trips to the infamous Bridge House Jail for questioning. Arthur de Carle Sowerby was arrested and survived three very unpleasant months in Bridge House, as did Hal Mills, the New Orleans-born editor of the Chinese language *Hwa Mei Wan Pao* who had earlier been the target of an unsuccessful Japanese hand-grenade attack. Also, George Bruce, the vice-president of the *Shanghai Evening Post and Mercury* was taken for questioning at Bridge House where he was tortured, and when he was taken back to the Pootung Internment Camp he promptly dropped dead of a heart attack.

Bridge House was a fearful place for the remaining press corps. Howard Roda and Alfred Pattison, two Americans, had been operating a clandestine radio station in Shanghai broadcasting anti-Japanese stories, and both ended up in Bridge House and were tortured. Powell was arrested and then tortured in a 12-by-18-foot lice-ridden cell with six-inch bars that he had to share with consumptives, lepers and syphilitics. Powell was effectively starved by only being given rotten food and forced to sit, head bowed, for as long as eight hours at a stretch facing Tokyo — a torture known as the "New Order Kneeling Posture". The Japanese worked hard to keep the existence of Bridge House a secret from the outside world. However, M. C. Ford, correspondent for the *Chicago Daily News* and International News Service, managed to get a story on the American newsmen held in "Japanese death cages" into *Collier's*.

With the entry of America into the war, the International Settlement's days were numbered, internment or Bridge House loomed and the exodus of journalists from Shanghai turned into a scramble. The former *North-China Daily News* editor O. M. Green worked tirelessly in London to help British citizens and journalists get out of Shanghai as the official representative of the British Residents' Association to Parliament. In 1942, the Italian liner *TSS Conte Verde* and the Japanese ship *Asama Maru* carried American citizens 6,000 miles on a 24-day voyage from Shanghai and Hong Kong to the neutral port of Lourenço Marques in Portuguese East Africa for exchange and repatriation.[30] The *Conte Verde,* a rusty, battered old freighter, carried 636 Americans aboard, including 26 journalists from Shanghai. It was a harsh voyage on which the wife of the American consul at Yantai died and was buried at sea. Around the same time, the Swedish ship *MS Gripsholm*, which had been chartered by the US government as an exchange and repatriation ship under the protection of the Red

Cross, ferried yet more Americans home via Lourenço Marques. The Japanese had become worried that Powell would die in custody, causing problems for them, and so allowed him out on the *Gripsholm* accompanied by another refugee Shanghailander, the wealthy and socially connected Dr. William Gardiner. However, after his treatment at Bridge House Powell's weight had dropped from his normal 160 pounds to just 64. He developed beriberi which caused his feet to swell up and turn black from infection and he had to have all 10 toes amputated. Despite escaping Bridge House and being accompanied by a doctor, it was too late; Powell's feet continued to rot and he eventually had both feet amputated during the voyage. He was to die several years later at just 56 years of age but not before going to Tokyo to testify at the Japanese War Crimes trials.

The *Gripsholm,* termed a "mercy ship", was even more crowded than the *Conte Verde* with 1,510 passengers, including 15 American newspapermen. Conditions on the *Gripsholm* were considered even worse too. Some of the passengers were mentally deranged after captivity, and decades later one Swedish crew member wrote that he could still not forget their terrified screams. Upon arrival at Lourenço Marques, the journalists immediately starting filing stories back to their papers with many, including *Time*, running stories about the horrors the well-known Powell had suffered in Bridge House at the hands of his Japanese torturers.

Internment camps, the so-called "Civilian Assembly Centres", around the country were to become home for other members of the foreign press corps. Daphne Mosley of the *Peiping Chronicle* was interned in Weihsien in northern China, as were the Italian journalist Maria Prodan, the naturalised British journalist Anna Alexandrovna Ore and Willett Dorland, a journalist and writer specialising in medicine. Some seem to have coped with camp life. For example, the *North-China Daily News*'s editor, Ralph Thomas "R. T." Peyton-Griffith, was interned in Shanghai's Lunghwa Camp where he was a popular figure, managing to produce a series of fine watercolours while imprisoned; and newspaper proprietor Eric Cumine proved to be the best baseball pitcher in Pootung Camp.

For many more, however, life in the internment camps was brutal. Mike Fox, a talented but cynical and outspoken Reuters reporter, was interned in Weihsien Camp, a forced home to many Allied nationals who had been based in Beijing, Tianjin and the northern China treaty ports. Fox had a big ego and was highly strung but he had been carving out what looked to be a stellar career before internment. The son of a high-caste Indian woman and a British *taipan*, he and his brother had been socially ostracised by stuffy British society in India due to their mixed-race background and consequently the family had moved to China. Fox's journalistic success had ended the snobbish blackballing and he was well regarded by many for his barb-tongued critiques of China. However, camp life at Weihsien, where he worked as a hospital orderly, depressed him terribly and he eventually attempted suicide by ingesting a mix of morphine and aspirin. It didn't work and he survived but was living proof that seemingly innocuous terms such as "Civilian Assembly Centre" could not mask the horrors of internment camp life.

The *North China*'s Ralph Shaw was interned in Shanghai's Kiangwan Camp and made it through the war, only to be liberated and then nearly die from dysenteric fever contracted at Kiangwan. Also, Arthur de Carle Sowerby, having survived the brutality of Bridge House, was sent to an internment camp barely able to walk as his feet had been so badly beaten.

Internally produced camp newspapers were largely morale-lifting exercises which tried to raise people's spirits and get them involved in camp life by volunteering for duties in the growing programmes of sports, education classes and, of course, wherever there were Brits, endless amateur dramatics. Giving people something to do with their time was essential for survival and to relieve tension and boredom. The hand-written *Camp Chit Chat* featured camp news, gossip and cartoons and was published in Shanghai's Yangtzepoo camp with the slogan "Long live our iron rations, and God save the man with parcels". It helped lighten the dark times, claiming to be "registered in Kamp-Chat-Ka as first class matter". Shanghai's Pootung Camp was well served with newspapers too. Noel Jacobs produced the *Noon Bulletin* while Robert Davis of the *North-China*, along with George Laycock and Alex Hoorin of Havas, put out a camp paper called simply *The Q*, in honour of the activity that took up most of their time. Another interned journalist, Carl Mydans, produced his own paper, the *Assembly Times*, in Shanghai's Chapei Camp. All were roughly typed up and circulated by hand throughout the camps and did much to raise spirits and get people through the seemingly never-ending horror of it all.

Internment also affected many journalists who weren't actually interned themselves. Former *China Press* managing editor Woo Kyatang's American-born wife and son were interned in Shanghai, dividing the family and creating a strain on their marriage that ultimately contributed to its breakdown shortly after the war.

Hong Kong fell on Christmas Day 1941. Immediately the press was suppressed and replaced by the Japanese-sponsored *Hongkong News* which was produced by English-speaking Japanese staff in the *South China Morning Post*'s seized offices. Though pro-Japanese, internees would scour the paper trying to read between the lines to decipher what was really happening outside and which way the war was going. Those interned in Hong Kong's Stanley Camp also produced their own internal newspapers and A. J. Savitsky, a member of the

Hong Kong Volunteer Police Reserve, was the unofficial camp cartoonist. Journalists were well represented in Stanley. George Wood Giffen, the editor of the *Post*'s sister paper, the *Hong Kong Telegram*, shared a cramped room with four *Post* journalists: Benjamin Wylie, John Luke, Richard Cloake and Vincent Jarrett. The interned hacks obviously became close. Ben Wylie was a long-serving managing editor at the *Post* while Dick Cloake, originally from Toowoomba in Queensland, was a former editor of the paper. Uncomfortable as Stanley was, some *Post* journalists suffered a worse fate. For example, reporter Reg Goldman joined the Hong Kong Volunteers and died defending the colony against the Japanese invasion and Australian Norman Stockton, a former *Hongkong Telegraph* editor, was killed while working as a war correspondent for the *Sydney Sun*, accompanying a doomed RAF bombing raid over Germany.

Norman Allman ended up in Stanley briefly. The big, blonde and straight-talking Virginian was from farming stock but had become a lawyer, was a gifted linguist and had a passion for horse racing. He had been posted as a student interpreter to the American legation in Beijing in 1916 and went on to serve at various US consulates in China. Allman was a very well-known figure in Shanghai before the war as a member of the SVC, the honorary consul for Mexico, a law lecturer at Suzhou University and a member of the SMC too. He became involved in journalism and was the editor of the *Shen Bao* from 1937 to 1941. With such a high profile, he was forced to leave, arriving in Hong Kong just in time for the colony's surrender and got himself imprisoned in Stanley. However, internment didn't slow him down much as he was out in six months and became chief of the Far East Section of the Secret Intelligence Branch of the US Office of Strategic Services (OSS).

Others also managed to get themselves interned and then released. Gwen Dew was an intrepid reporter and noted photographer for the *Detroit News* and *Popular Photography* who roamed around Asia, touring Japan and Singapore in the 1930s. She then travelled to China where she was granted a rare interview with Madame Chiang in 1936, the first she had granted to anyone for three years. Later Dew was hired as a special correspondent for UPI and headed back to Asia in 1941, getting caught in Hong Kong as the colony fell. She managed to film the battles and the eventual surrender of Hong Kong for the *South China Morning Post*. She was eventually sent to Stanley where she kept notes about the occupation and conditions at the camp, hiding them in the collection of dolls she had amassed while travelling which she had somehow been allowed to take into Stanley with her. She eventually made it back to America on the *Gripsholm* and immediately returned to work, writing a series of popular eyewitness articles for the *Detroit News* and *Reader's Digest* entitled "I Was a Prisoner of the Japs".

The Gung Ho Kids

Another group gathered outside Shanghai in 1940 to avoid internment. Calling themselves the "Gung Ho Kids", they comprised Edgar and Helen Snow, Rewi Alley (who had given the world the term "gung ho" from the Chinese name for his Chinese Industrial Cooperative Movement) and Evans Carlson, among others. Helen Snow, whose friends loved her but was considered hard to get along with and shrill by many not so close, coined the name and also chose a location for them all to go for some rest and recuperation in the Philippines resort of Baguio where the Snows rented a cottage for a month. The Snows were well known for their journalism and books and Rewi Alley was a perennial figure on the left who organised the Gung Ho movement which aimed at rebuilding Free China's industrial base through a network of small, easily movable factories. Evans Carlson, however, is less well known as a journalist. That was because primarily he wasn't one but he did become associated with the group of pro-communist supporters among the foreign press while technically a military man.

Evans Fordyce Carlson had come to Shanghai in 1927 with the US Fourth Marines as a battalion operations officer planning the defence of the International Settlement. He became the regimental intelligence officer, despite having no real training in the field. He then went to Beijing in 1933 where he became the editor of the *Legation Guard News* and used the army paper to try to foster better relations and understanding between the marines stationed in Beijing and the local Chinese, primarily by trying to help the soldiers understand their posting better. Carlson then started writing more lengthy and learned papers on China and the Asian political situation that were published in the *Naval Institute Proceedings* and the *Marines Corps Gazette*. Later, while still in the army, he started submitting anonymous book reviews and editorials to Powell's *Review*. However, he was becoming increasingly disillusioned with military life and eventually resigned from the marines in 1939, voluntarily forfeiting his pension.

While in Shanghai, Carlson had become close to both the Snows and Powell. However, as time moved on, he was to come to admire Snow ever more while growing disappointed with Powell who, in Carlson's view, retained the outlook that he was still living in his more radical days of 1926–27. Carlson considered J. B. to be a man of fine character and a fighter, but when Powell dismissed most of his views following Carlson's visit to the Eighth Route Army, the two became distant. Carlson marched over 2,000 miles with the Red Army and wrote about his experiences in his 1940 book *Twin Stars of China*. As his politics moved further to the left, his relationship with Snow flourished and he continued to be a regular visitor to the offices of the *Review* where Snow was an editor working for Powell. Snow remembered Carlson: "In the late 1920s a tall open faced, long jawed intelligence officer in the Fourth Regiment, US Marines, dropped in once a week to exchange information with me at the *Review*".[31] Snow hired Carlson to write editorials and in return Carlson strenuously defended Snow against the mounting accusations from Army Counter Intelligence, which maintained extensive files on Snow, Powell and other senior figures at the *Review*. Carlson also used his military position to bombard President Roosevelt with letters arguing a pro-communist position during the war which, to be fair, FDR had requested he send, with many letters going between Carlson wherever he was and FDR's loyal secretary Marguerite "Missy" LeHand.

A sort of phoney war existed for some time. Papers kept coming out, people still went to work and organisations like the Shanghai Short Story Club and the Royal Asiatic Society went on meeting until internment kicked in. For a time though, before Pearl Harbour, newsreels and moving pictures became increasingly important. The *History Today* newsreel team was filming on the frontline in China as it had done previously in Spain. Where the cameras went, so did the print journalists. Carlson, for instance, popped up alongside a *History Today* crew snapping away beside them in 1940 as the Chinese army scored a victory over the Japanese at Taierchwang, near Suzhou. Carlson had followed the New Fourth Army, the counterpoint of the Eighth Route Army in the north, along with Rewi Alley who was touring the country inspecting his industrial co-operatives. Carlson recorded his images of his time on the march and the battles of the New Fourth in the *China Defence League Newsletter*, which was being published in (the about to fall) Hong Kong. Carlson remained highly sceptical of Washington's developing China policy. He died in 1947 at just 51 of complications brought on by stress and overwork and was buried with full military honours in Arlington Cemetery. Agnes Smedley spoke at his memorial service, which was arranged by the Committee for a Democratic Far Eastern Policy, of which Carlson had once been chairman.

By the end of 1941 most of the press corps had been forced to leave China, and others had been interned, tortured or killed. As the Japanese advance continued, many of the remaining press corps and a host of visiting writers and journalists congregated in the besieged wartime capital of Chongqing at the top of the Yangtze to witness the final showdown between China and Japan.

10
In Air Raid Shelters and Caves — Covering the War

"Chungking, China's wartime capital, is marked on no man's map ... Men great and small, noble and corrupt, brave and cowardly, convened there for a brief moment; they are all gone home now."

Teddy White and Annalee Jacoby, *Thunder Out of China* (1946)

"Where I want to be, boy, is where it is all blowing up."

Martha Gellhorn

The Chungking Contingent — The Press Corps at War

In October 1938 the government retreated to Chongqing which is geographically closer to India than Shanghai and where the population swelled to a million. The government and the refugees were followed by a horde of foreign correspondents pouring in for either brief visits or the duration. War correspondents were to become stars on their newspapers, widely read and by-lined but not always writing exactly what they saw. Notions of censorship both in China and at home still applied while patriotism and political expediency to support the Allies was actively encouraged and ordered by editors. For many arriving with friendly intentions to report on an allies' struggle, Chongqing was a shock. For example, Till Durdin wrote a letter to Evans Carlson from the beleaguered and humid city in June 1939, describing the situation as he saw it:

> Coming to Chungking was a distinct letdown. The sentiment here is flabby. Everybody is money-grubbing. Even Hollington Tong's boys are going in for restaurants, brick factories, transport companies, etc. I think there's

distinctly a danger that the Central Government people will get so busy with "reconstruction" that they will forget to do much about the fight which goes on, but dimly felt here, on fronts a thousand miles away.[1]

At the time, both men were becoming increasingly political and increasingly veering away from Chiang towards the left. Others who were based in the city or just visiting chose to remain faithful to Chiang, or at least to paper over the cracks in the name of preserving the Nationalist-Communist alliance against the Japanese. Veteran Shanghailander Carl Crow came to Chongqing for the pro-Chiang *Liberty* magazine, having sailed from New York to Southampton, taken the flying boat to Rangoon and then traversed the far-from-completed Burma Road to get to the city. He endured the constant bombing raids of the summer of 1939, when Chongqing was the most heavily bombed city on earth, a situation that somewhat contradicts Durdin's idea of a fight being "dimly felt" and remote.

Almost all the foreign correspondents reporting from China during the war came to see the conflict between the Nationalists and the Communists as a struggle between the forces of reaction and the forces of progress, even if they couldn't always report this to the folks back home. The Americans had particular reasons to be shocked by the apparent venality and corruption of the Chiang government as from 1941, after the US senate had approved the Lend-Lease programme, Washington was the Nationalists' largest source of weapons, equipment and money. That much was stolen, while perhaps yet more was held back in reserve to fight the Communists rather than the Japanese, naturally angered many and shaped their personal views, whatever glowing prose they had to file for their papers at home. It wasn't a small sum either: though it's difficult to calculate just how much the Nationalists received through Lend-Lease, it was in the region of several hundred million dollars.

To many, a victory by what they perceived to be the progressive, democratic forces of the Communists was not only desirable but inevitable, even though the majority were what came to be known as "softliners" and were not paid-up members of the Communist Party. According to the historians Stephen MacKinnon and Oris Friesen, except for the Philippines-born Frederick Marquardt who had started out on the *Manila Free Press*, all the Chongqing press corps were liberal to left in persuasion and tended to group together and feed off each others liberalism and gossip: "They met frequently and avidly clipped each other's work. During the Chungking period they even mostly lived together in the notoriously run-down KMT-run Press Hostel. Through such interaction, consensus was reached about legitimacy of sources. Together they decided what was news and what should be reported and how".[2] The Press Hostel was soon damaged by Japanese bombing which helped to foster a decidedly blitz spirit among the press corps as they suffered the privations of Chongqing and wartime China, while also finding time for games of tennis and long drinks parties with the assorted foreigners of the city — missionaries, diplomats, aid workers, spies and various driftwood drawn to such places.

John Hersey was the link that sent more than one journalist to Chongqing during the war. A Tianjin "mishkid", he had studied at Hotchkiss and then Yale where he dabbled in poetry, got interested in journalism writing for the *Yale Daily News* and then headed to Cambridge where he was the novelist and playwright Sinclair Lewis's personal secretary. He left Cambridge to work for *Time* in the autumn of 1937 and two years later was transferred to the magazine's Chongqing bureau as one of its foreign correspondents. Like all *Time* correspondents in China, Hersey was answerable to Whittaker Chambers, then *Time*'s foreign news editor and a former member of the American Communist Party before leaving and becoming obsessively anti-communist. He was later to play a major role in the Alger Hiss case and the rise of McCarthyism, and the persecution of many former members of the old China press corps. While in Chongqing, Hersey also contributed to the *New Yorker*, winning a Pulitzer Prize in 1945. Hersey had the ear of *Time*'s proprietor Luce (they both were "mishkids") and was responsible for the arrival in Chongqing of the journalist who was to become perhaps America's best-known wartime correspondent in China — T. H. White.

Theodore H. White, though small and unprepossessing physically, loomed large over the Chongqing press corps despite not yet being 25 when he arrived. He quickly became a doyen of the wartime press corps. Raised in an impoverished Jewish family in Boston, he consistently maintained that China was a mystery to him, despite being fluent in Mandarin and having a degree in Chinese history from Harvard. After college he had freelanced for the *Boston Globe* and the *Manchester Guardian*. Like many before him he had arrived in Shanghai to meet J. B. Powell who referred him to Holly Tong who gave him a job with the Chinese Ministry of Information crafting press releases to distribute to the press corps. Later he would be teased mercilessly for this by the old China press corps who went to Chongqing and remembered the young man who worked for Holly Tong. Arch Steele, who competed with White for the crown of doyen, held his past against him; others like Till and Peggy Durdin didn't and liked him immensely. Eventually Hersey hired him to cover East Asia for *Time*, and he eventually became chief of its China bureau and a close friend of Luce, though they argued constantly. In 1946 he was to resign in a dispute with Luce, claiming that Whittaker Chambers had introduced a "monotone of paranoia" to the publication's China coverage. Hersey, though offered a managing editorship, was also to quit; like White, he objected to Chambers's doctoring of his copy. White's 1946 China memoir, *Thunder Out of China*, which was written with fellow *Time* correspondent Annalee Jacoby, was considered one of the best, but White was not always the easiest person to get along with. He later declared: "When a reporter sits down at the typewriter, he's nobody's friend".[3]

Teddy White and Annalee Jacoby produced the most widely read scathing indictment of American China policy in the Second World War and Luce's overt and misguided flattery of Chiang, which obviously did little to endear them to the Generalissimo- infatuated Luce who pulled out the stops to try to suppress the book. However, *Thunder Out of China* made waves in America, selling over a half million copies at its first printing. Starting from the brief moment of patriotic glory after the Nationalist retreat to Chongqing, the book then covered the period when disillusionment and corruption set in and a "credibility vacuum" was created that allowed the Communists to gain ground. There was little doubt that White got his hands dirty in China, angering the Nationalist censors and press minders when he visited famine-stricken Hunan with Harrison Forman. Chongqing's *Chung Kung Pao* newspaper, arguably the most independent Chinese newspaper at the time, reported the famine in February 1943 and was suppressed for three days for its trouble. White also marched with the Sixty Second Army when it attempted to break the Japanese siege ring at Hengyang in Hunan. White, with Reuters correspondent Graham Barrow, wriggled through the mud with the troops, many of whom were hastily conscripted peasants who fully expected to lose the battle as they were armed with little more than First World War vintage rifles. White, though impressed by the bravery of the rank and file, was not impressed by the senior command: "All that flesh and blood could do the Chinese soldiers were doing. They were walking up hills and dying in the sun, but they had no support, no guns, no directions. They were doomed".[4] After these experiences White felt he had no choice but to break ranks, annoy his employer and accuse the American government of slavishly propping up Chiang, preferring stability to an argument. He was not to be alone in consciously defecting from the official line.

While Hersey brought White to Chongqing, it was Shelley Smith of *Life* magazine who introduced him to his collaborator and co-author Annalee Jacoby which reflects the instantly tight-knit nature of the Chongqing press corps. Smith had arrived to cover the bombing of Chongqing in 1939. She was married to the photographer Carl Mydans and Luce sent both of them to cover the Japanese bombardment of China. Their Chongqing home was a "single cubicle with a mud floor and thatched roof". In Chongqing they had a circle of old Stanford University friends, including the independently wealthy China scholar Melville Jacoby and Smith's old classmate Annalee Whitmore, who had been the managing editor of the *Stanford Daily,* the campus newspaper. Melville Jacoby was delighted to be in China as he found he could escape his privileged wealthy background and also the anti-Semitism he had suffered in California when growing up, where, despite being good enough to get into Stanford, as a Jew he was unable to join any of the elite fraternities.

Mydans had previously worked on the *Boston Globe* and *Boston Herald* before marrying Shelley and becoming one half of *Life*'s first husband and wife overseas photojournalism team who, reputedly, carried with them just "a jackknife, a poncho, a canteen, a cup, a spoon and a helmet". Mydans, known as "Stump" due to his short, stocky build, was considered good company. He had come from a highly cultured Boston family and was also a gifted photographer, and had been a colleague and contemporary of the likes of Margaret Bourke-White and Dorothea Lange. Shelley was also from cultured stock, the daughter of a university professor, and after graduating she had worked in New York for the *Literary Digest* before joining *Life* in 1936. In New York she met Carl who was working on the *American Banker* and they married in 1938 before setting out for China.

The dark and pretty Annalee Whitmore had come to China at just 28 via a rather unconventional route even by the standards of the time. She had spent three years in Hollywood with MGM as a successful screenwriter, with her credits including contributing to Mickey Rooney's *Andy Hardy Meets Debutante* and the Clark Gable and Lana Turner vehicle *Honky Tonk*. However, she desperately wanted to go to China. She knew Shelley Mydans who knew Melville Jacoby at *Time*, who was then still close to Luce. Smith got Jacoby to get Whitmore a job with the United China Relief Fund in Chongqing in 1940, which placed her in close proximity to Madame Chiang. As the bombing got worse, the Mydanses and Melville Jacoby decamped to Manila. Melville pleaded with Annalee to marry him. She resisted at first, agreeing with Emily Hahn that he was "arrogant", but eventually relented and moved to Manila to be with him. This was a terrible case of bad timing as Pearl Harbour happened and all four of them were put in the POW camp at Santo Tomas University. They eventually escaped to Australia on a small ship where, shortly after arriving, Melville was killed in an air crash after the couple had been married for barely a year. The Mydanses went to Shanghai where they were held in an internment camp for another year before being repatriated on the *Gripsholm* and finally arrived home in 1943. They were soon back in Asia and Mydans's career was made in 1945 with his classic shot of General MacArthur wading ashore on his promised return to Luzon in the Philippines.

Annalee, however, managed to get back to Chongqing in the autumn of 1944 with *Time* — after demanding "… an 18-hour-a-day job — right in the middle of the war if possible". She was the only full-time woman correspondent in Chongqing and started working with Teddy White. She claimed to have no problem adapting to the Spartan conditions in Chongqing having had a rough upbringing and she always delighted in telling people that she had been born on the kitchen table of her family's home in Price, Utah.

For a while White and Annalee Jacoby had the best jobs in Chongqing. The Luce budget was lavish, and as Luce's man White was feted by the diplomatic core and the government and, arguably, the most important people in Chongqing: the Soong family. However, especially after the pro-Chiang Luce actually visited China during the war and White had to escort him around, their relationship started to deteriorate seriously and the mogul refused to believe their stories of the corruption that suffused the Chiang court. Annalee claimed that Chambers in New York fabricated a large part of her features on Chiang arguing that her interview with the Generalissimo was published "... with questions I did not ask and answers Chiang did not give".[5] Certainly, White was under no illusion about Luce and his pro-Chiang line by now. In Chongqing White commandeered a shack and declared it the *Time* bureau complete with a sign on the front door that read:

ANY RESEMBLANCE TO WHAT IS WRITTEN HERE AND WHAT IS PRINTED IN *TIME* MAGAZINE, IS PURELY COINCIDENTAL.[6]

The veteran *New York Times* journalist Harrison Salisbury, who had come to China as a foreign correspondent after being inspired by Vincent Sheean's memoirs, summed up the "Luce problem": "Just as the puritan image of the communists stemming out of *Red Star Over China* influenced many, so the image of the Nationalists given by Luce, and his journals, *Time* and *Life*, influenced many Americans as well".[7] This was nothing new: Luce had made the Chiangs "Man and Wife of the Year" and stuck them on his cover in 1937; and Madame Chiang was to adorn the cover several more times during the war due to Luce's obvious infatuation with her.

The "line" was fixed for *Time-Life* reporters but others also found Chongqing very strange surroundings, full of competing agendas. Brooks Atkinson had been the drama critic for the *New York Times* since 1925 and would be again after the war until 1960, even having a Broadway theatre named after him. However, with the shortage of human resources in wartime, he found himself despatched to China as an "accidental Orientalist". He'd got his start on local papers including *The Springfield Daily News* and *The Boston Evening Transcript*. Then the *New York Times* snapped him up to edit its book review section before appointing him chief drama critic. In 1941 Atkinson moved from championing the work of Eugene O'Neill to being dumped in China until 1945 where the *Times* was also using Eppie Epstein as a stringer after he had moved on from Hankou following the retreating government. Atkinson found that the change of scene — from the Great White Way to the Middle Kingdom — was not as bad as he had initially dreaded and he developed a taste for the life of a foreign correspondent. After the war he moved to Moscow and won a Pulitzer Prize in 1947 for his writing on life in the Soviet capital.

Others found Chongqing just another stop on the Asia beat. Harold Isaacs came back to China chastened, distinctly less political and a totally new character, reporting for *Newsweek*. Long-time Japan Hand Ernest O. Hauser reported for the *Saturday Evening Post* from Chongqing and went on to cover China till the end of the conflict for various publications including *Harper's* and the *New Yorker*, to which he submitted a series of pieces from deep inside Free China. By the time he was posted to Chongqing, he had already been bouncing round the region for a dozen years and before the war was most often to be found between assignments nursing a scotch and soda in Tokyo's Imperial Hotel. Hauser, primarily a Japan Hand, was prolific in turning out multiple books on everything from Shanghai's development to Italian culture, along with a few novels for good measure. Other old Asia Hands offered some distractions in Chongqing too where, despite being a wartime capital, major boredom was a factor. UPI's Robert "Pepper" Martin came pre-prepared for the rather austere atmosphere of the city with his Nanjing mistress and they both enlivened evenings at the rather rickety Press Hostel as their energetic love-making shook the building. When Pepper Martin was busy, his assistant Karl Eskelund covered for him and attracted a lot of attention himself as he was a handsome Dane whose father had been the king of Siam's dentist while Karl went on to write a series of best-selling books on his many later postings around the world.

Aside from the rampant inflation (Teddy White had to spend a sack containing 1,300 Chinese dollars, or US$2.50 in treating a contact to three glasses of milk that were two-thirds water and one-third milk), one of the biggest problems in Chongqing for correspondents was dealing with the egos and personalities of the main characters in China's wartime drama. As if the Generalissimo and Madame Chiang weren't enough, there were also General "Vinegar Joe" Stilwell and Claire Lee Chennault of the Flying Tigers, who were schmoozing correspondents to promote themselves in China and back home to their bosses (in Vinegar Joe's case) and the public (in Chennault's case). Stilwell certainly had his fans, including Teddy White and Jack Belden, and also had his favourites who were rewarded with greater access, such as *Internews*'s veteran correspondent John Goette whom Stilwell had known in Beijing. Indeed all these writers let Stilwell increasingly turn them against Chiang as Vinegar

Joe fell out with the "Peanut", as Chiang was dubbed by Stilwell on account of his rather small head. Chennault was looking for a good public image and the syndicated newspaper columnist Joseph Alsop, whose column "The Capital Parade" appeared in 300 US papers, helped him out, even basing himself inside Chennault's Kunming HQ and ruthlessly promoting Claire's attractive Chinese wife Anna. The Chongqing press corps had to perform a balancing act with, on the one hand, the Chiangs, the Nationalist's press-control machine and sympathetic media moguls like Luce and, on the other, a whole range of alternate voices from the Communists to Stilwell. Added to this, the corps then had to deal with the visits of the big names who came to see the war.

The Bell Tolls for China — Hemingway and Gellhorn

Chongqing was a magnet to some superstars and celebrities who, but for the war, would never have ventured there. Undoubtedly the biggest literary icon to arrive in Chongqing was Ernest Hemingway who came with his correspondent wife, the chain-smoking 32-year-old Martha Gellhorn. Later in the 1970s, aged nearly 70, she decided to write about the journeys she had taken in her long reporting career in her memoir *Travels with Myself and Another*. By far the funniest section of what is a very wry read was the story of her trip to the Far East with her "UC" — Unwilling Companion — a fitting nickname for the reluctant Hemingway. The American literary Titan and Gellhorn were only recently married and their trip to Asia was basically their typically untypical honeymoon and also marked the start of the end of their brief tempestuous marriage. The excited Gellhorn and the largely disinterested Hemingway quarrelled, fought, made up and laughed their way around the continent for three months during the war.

Their trip came about after Gellhorn was asked by *Collier's* magazine, a weekly with a circulation of about three million, to go to China, Hong Kong, Singapore, the Dutch East Indies and Burma to cover the Chinese front, the state of British forces in the Far East and the scale of the Japanese threat, and to take a trip up the Burma Road, Chongqing's vital supply line. This was a popular route for intrepid journalists at the time; as well as Carl Crow, Ian Morrison (G. E. Morrison's son) traversed the infamous road while the intrepid woman journalist Alice L. B. Moats had also driven the entire length of the road as far as Chongqing for *Collier's* already. Gellhorn had never been to Asia, but she wanted desperately to cover the war. She was an ardent supporter of American aid for China and was also keen to remain financially independent and not just sink into being Hemingway's wife, chief groupie and camp-follower as she could so easily have done. Hemingway for his part was decidedly cool about the idea of traipsing around China, despite the fact that his favourite uncle had been a medical missionary in Shaanxi and had been awarded a medal by Sun Yat-sen. However, he eventually relented under Gellhorn's insistence and was himself commissioned by the New York tabloid *PM* — a short-lived, advertising-free magazine founded by the crusading liberal Ralph Ingersoll — to report on the war in Asia with an accent on how the newly passed Lend-Lease Act was helping the Allies to win.

Though he had previously professed a desire to emulate Jack London and roam around the Far East, Hemingway was tempted to stay at home, or at least in Havana, and enjoy life a little with his recently cashed cheque for the then phenomenal sum of US$100,000 for the movie rights to *For Whom the Bell Tolls*. He was suddenly wealthy and respected and didn't really need to rough it around Asia. Hemingway, 41 at the time of the trip, moaned incessantly from the start and suffered from his usual high-highs and low-lows, being what would now probably be diagnosed as bipolar. Their voyage was dismal: onboard service was non-existent under austere wartime conditions and they were pitched about in rough seas for most of the trip. A seasick Hemingway struggled ashore in Honolulu where, to his annoyance, he was smothered in garlands and mobbed by the locals, which led the combative novelist to declare to Gellhorn: "The next son of a bitch who touches me I am going to cool him". The trip had not started well.

The pair reached Hong Kong where life improved dramatically. Gellhorn recalled Somerset Maugham-type visions of colonial life in the Orient and Hemingway, whose arrival had been anticipated eagerly in the pages of the *South China Morning Post*, was happy to find a ready circle of hangers-on to praise his books and pour his drinks in his base at the Hong Kong Hotel's bar. They were able to enjoy the last, and distinctly hedonistic, days of Hong Kong before the Japanese invasion. Gellhorn filed some colourful pieces, hiring the well-known photographers Norman Soong and Newsreel Wong to shoot the accompanying pictures. However, duty beckoned and in March 1941 she flew to Chongqing, at night and at high altitude to avoid the Japanese planes. Hemingway decided to stay in Hong Kong, enjoying his new circle of admirers and hunting for pheasant. He was busy: Emily Hahn, who met Hemingway in Hong Kong claimed he introduced the concept of the Bloody Mary to the colony. Gellhorn departed with her notebook to take "the pulse of the nation", while Hemingway predictably looked for yet more wildlife to kill, occasionally in the company of Morris "Two Gun" Cohen, Sun Yat-sen's old Cockney bodyguard who was in semi-retirement in Hong Kong.

Gellhorn's flight was rocky, with plenty of turbulence. When the plane's air-speed dial froze, the pilot had to open the window to estimate the speed, knowing that if it fell below 63 miles per hour the plane would fall out of the sky. They made it to Kunming where Gellhorn reported from the Chinese end of the Burma Road and then headed back to Hong Kong where Hemingway was risking life and limb for *PM's* readers by drinking, boxing and playing with firecrackers in their hotel room. She decided that Hemingway was just fine on his own and set off to explore Hong Kong and its crowds, brothels, dance halls, floods of Chinese refugees and squatters.

Eventually Hemingway could put off the trip to Chongqing no longer. Gellhorn, an obsessive on matters related to hygiene, stocked up on Keating's Flea and Lice Powder and off they went. Hemingway was required to give rousing speeches to the troops at the frontline, a task he found not to his liking. However, as had been seen in the Spanish Civil War, Hemingway was a double-sided character, simultaneously deeply engaged in the cause while remaining the detached and cynical writer. Moving around on ponies did little to improve his mood as the great author's feet grazed the ground when he was sitting on the back of the small but stout Mongolian steeds. When his pony got tired, Hemingway claims to have literally picked it up and carried it for a while, to Gellhorn's great embarrassment. The inns they stayed in were full of bedbugs and broken plumbing which further exacerbated the mood of the great man. By this time Gellhorn too was starting to seriously tire of the vicissitudes of travel in war-torn China.

They eventually made it to Chongqing where Hemingway showed his compassionate side. Gellhorn noticed that the skin between her fingers was rotting and oozing puss, a condition known by the press corps as "China rot". She had to apply a horrible smelling cream and wear gloves, which was not an easy process; and to compound her misery she contracted dysentery too. Hemingway's response to his wife's plight was: "Honest to God, M. You brought this on yourself. I told you not to wash". Gellhorn, the hygiene obsessive, was distraught and later recalled: "In 50 years of travel, China stands out in particular loo-going horror". [8] Hemingway, who was perfectly happy to go without a bath for a while, didn't find much in Chongqing to like and Gellhorn was angry that the local *Chungking Central Daily News* pointed out that she was a bottle-blonde after the Hong Kong papers had praised her as a beauty — "For Whom the Belle Falls", as the *Post's* "Birds Eye View" gossip column had put it. The pair were lucky as the Japanese didn't bomb the city during their stay. They were shocked to meet Chiang Kai-shek without his dentures, which apparently was deemed a great honour, and Madame Chiang, who was dubbed by Hemingway "The Empress of China", a sobriquet that dogged her to her death and featured in several of her obituaries. They also met Zhou En-lai but neither American writer had any idea who this founding member of the Communist Party was or what to ask him, though apparently both were charmed by him (as were so many in the war-time press corps) and wrote to friends about how nice he seemed. At a point when she just wanted to escape the dirt, grime and skin infections of Chongqing, Gellhorn, who interviewed Zhou in French, wrote:

> If he had said take my hand and I will lead you to the pleasure dome of Xanadu, I would have made sure that Xanadu wasn't in China, asked for a minute to pick up my toothbrush and been ready to leave.[9]

The couple left Chongqing for Rangoon where they parted and Hemingway returned to Hong Kong and his twin passions of hunting and drinking and perhaps, in a story he told repeatedly for years, enjoying an encounter with three Chinese prostitutes (at once). Hemingway enjoyed cocktails with Emily Hahn's boyfriend Charles Boxer who said Hahn was suffering from stomach ulcers and couldn't join the party, though she was of course secretly pregnant with Boxer's child. Gellhorn found Rangoon "hotter than the inside of a steam boiler", while Hemingway wrote to her that he was lost without her, proving that he was more romantic on the page than in person. Eventually both made it back to America. At home they walked into an argument with the editor of *Collier's* who accused Hemingway of scooping Gellhorn with his *PM* articles. Hemingway, annoyed at the accusation, declared: "The only reason I went along was to look after Martha on a son of a bitching dangerous assignment in a shit filled country".[10] China and Hemingway had not really hit it off. The argument fizzled out, with the editor opting not to get into any more serious debates about "shit filled countries" with the angry Hemingway. Gellhorn's articles attracted a lot of attention, though she later admitted that she had been struck with wartime patriotism, glossed over the truth and didn't reveal the corruption she had seen in the Generalissimo's Chongqing. Hemingway too refrained from mentioning corruption to support the wartime Nationalist-Communist alliance. The superstars of Chongqing were as susceptible to the charms of Zhou En-lai, the cause of the Generalissimo and the dazzling nature of Madame Chiang as any new cub reporter.

What wasn't known at the time was that Hemingway's reporting was a secondary function of his trip. His primary task was to spy for US treasury secretary Henry Morgenthau. Perhaps it seems a little strange that the request for information came from the treasury rather than the president or the War Office but the shy, professorial and uncharismatic Morgenthau was, in his own quiet way, trying to mount a resistance to fascism while America was still technically neutral. Morgenthau, who was not always easy to please, was said to be delighted and impressed by Hemingway's briefings; and all would have gone well, except that all the correspondence passed through the hands of Morgenthau's right-hand man, Harry Dexter White, who was later revealed to be a Soviet spy. Both Morgenthau (and by extension Roosevelt) and Stalin had all seen Hemingway's briefings. It was also the beginning of the end of the Hemingway-Gellhorn marriage. When together on the trip they rowed and fought; and when they were apart they pined for each other. But the relationship was too combustible and later, in London during the later stages of the war, the marriage collapsed completely. All in all, the entire Hemingway-Gellhorn sojourn in China had been a mixed experience: both later professed their admiration and love for China and conversely their depression and hatred of the place. Hemingway perhaps summed up their journey best as an "unshakeable hangover".[11]

The Guardians — The Press Corps' Minders

Celebrity correspondents like Hemingway got star treatment from the Nationalists but as the Chongqing press corps became more questioning of the Nationalists' handling of the war and then especially as they demanded access to the front, and particularly the Communist-held sections of it, relations soured distinctly.

Traditionally relations between the Nationalists and the press corps had been fractious at best; indeed there was a long history of the government frustrating journalists, banning publications and generally making life difficult. The old Qing dynasty *Tsungli Yamen* had used the tactics of delaying permits and travel documents to frustrate journalists and was hardly the sort of organisation that held regular press briefings; and the Nationalists largely, though often less subtly, carried on this tradition. Journalists in the 1920s and 30s had regularly been refused permission to travel to remoter areas of the country, particularly the west, while the *North-China* had suffered from periodic censorship in the 1920s and, so some argued, altered its political line to be more pro-nationalist as an act of appeasement.

Some publications had been favoured by the Nationalists. The *China Press*, for example, had had several well-connected KMT activists on its board since it was launched in 1911 and it was also widely known that Chiang had been buying up large quantities of Powell's *Review* throughout the 1930s for posting abroad at government expense, believing it to be the most effective form of pro-Chinese propaganda overseas. However, in general the KMT was becoming more wary as it, increasingly correctly, perceived that the foreign press corps was either starting to criticise it for corruption and ineptitude if not outright cheerleading for the Communists which many journalists (and not just those politically committed to the left) increasingly saw as more progressive.

In the immediate aftermath of Black Saturday and the Rape of Nanking, the relationship changed slightly from distrust to qualified acceptance, in large part driven by Madame Chiang's conviction that the Generalissimo needed the foreign press on his side to engender support and secure funding and supplies from overseas to maintain the fight against the Japanese which they had already realised would be long, drawn out and possibly to the death. The media-savvy Madame Chiang's view was partly one of understanding that support for China among the wider American public could be won through the press and also, in typical Soong family style, a belief in keeping your friends close and your enemy's closer. Also, over the years, a good number of foreign journalists had worked directly for the government in an advisory capacity, and who could be better in anticipating and knowing best how to frustrate journalists than their colleagues? Tom Millard, Charles Webb (who helped pen Dr Sun's appeal for worldwide recognition in 1911), Holly Tong (who had written for the *China Press* and the *China Review* and other papers as well as being editor of the *Peking Daily News*) and, of course, Bill Donald had all been journalists who switched over to become government aides while others like Tim Timperley and Ilona Ralf Sues worked for the KMT Ministry of Information during the war.

In late 1937 the Generalissimo, largely at his wife's insistence, started to hold more briefings and receptions for the foreign press in the temporary capital, Nanjing. These receptions attracted all the major foreign correspondents, particularly those based relatively nearby in Shanghai. At one such event, John Morris, a roving UPI manager based mostly in Shanghai, spent time huddled with Madame Chiang to decipher the Generalissimo's long-term strategy. He found that she could articulate the Generalissimo's intentions and plans better in her fluent, lightly accented English which had been perfected during her student days at Wellesley College than the Generalissimo himself. These briefings were attended religiously by Red Knickerbocker for the International News Service; Till Durdin for the *New York Times*; Clifton Daniel, the *New York Times*'s Nanjing stringer; Powell; Vic Keen for the *New York Herald Tribune*; and Thomas Chao, Reuters's Nanjing correspondent. Chiang would speak through an interpreter with Madame doing the back channel briefings to favoured correspondents while Donald ensured the press had the story "right". These briefings were considered positive in the long-term. However, immediately after the bombing of Shanghai in 1937, the short, dapper and smooth KMT chief of press at the *Waichiaopu* (Foreign Office) Dr T. T. Li started treating the foreign press corps with extreme caution.

A problem for the Nationalists was duplication of responsibilities: T. T. Li controlled the Chinese Press Agency while the weary-looking and worn-out Cheng Kung-po controlled the Propaganda Ministry, otherwise known as the Fifth Department. In addition, Chiang Kang-li was running the KMT Publicity Office and the gaunt and always serious General Yang ran the Military Intelligence Bureau, which was also known as the Enemy Propaganda Bureau. All four organisations and all four men claimed to be the ultimate sanction for where and what foreign journalists could do and where they could go after Black Saturday. In reality, journalists found themselves faced with indecision as they were passed from Li to Cheng, to Chiang and finally to General Yang who sent them back to the indefatigable T. T. Li who apparently refused to ever use the word "defeat". Isherwood described him as: "... the most optimistic of Walt Disney's Three Little Pigs".[12] Li would tell journalists he couldn't release potentially sensitive information; Cheng would claim the same; Chiang would say everything was a Party secret and General Yang would claim everything was militarily sensitive and barred foreign journalists from even visiting his HQ — yet all four claimed to be autonomous and omnipotent and have priority in releasing information. To confuse things further, Bill Donald distrusted all of them, thought Cheng a spy for Wang Jingwei (the Chinese Pètain) and enlisted the help of Madame Chiang to assist in circumventing the bureaucratic foursome when necessary.

Donald had also established his own control mechanism with trusted old friends outside Nanjing handling press and propaganda. He had Tim Timperley installed in Shanghai distributing all foreign publicity directly to the press corps there. However, usually, by the time the press had done the rounds of the four possible sources, the deadline for cables had passed and arguably the Nationalists' press control operation had worked as nobody got to file a story, either positive or negative. Ultimately things improved a bit when Sues, then working for Cheng Kung-po, suggested a more rational organisation and got it to Donald's attention. He enlisted Madame Chiang's support and she gave her approval to reorganise things. Sues's system involved articles going from her in Nanjing direct to Timperley in Shanghai and circumventing Cheng completely. Donald's plan all along was to kick out Cheng and his gang eventually and install Holly Tong as boss of a proper (i.e. Madame Chiang/Donald-controlled) publicity machine, which is indeed what happened. But the intrigue did not stop there. Later, when Sues was planning to leave China, Tong asked her to open a Chinese News Centre in Europe for him without Donald's knowledge. The tall, skinny and bespectacled Earl Leaf was offered the same deal in New York, though neither went behind Donald's back and both went on to spend time with Mao at Yenan, much to Tong's annoyance.

In Chongqing itself the foreign press had two major organisations to deal with: Holly Tong's Ministry of Information — Madame Chiang hated the word "propaganda" and insisted on either "information" or "publicity" — and the US government's American Military Attaché's Office which was keen to see that the right message about the Generalissimo, the progress of the war in China, Vinegar Joe's (and later General Wedemeyer's) role and the Nationalist-Communist alliance got out.

For the government side, Tong was also the head of the International Department of the Board of Information which engaged in various propaganda activities and, along with the National Military Council, provided journalists, visitors and embassy officials with a regular weekly press conference. The Board of Information published bulletins, special handouts, state documents, speeches by the Generalissimo, a monthly magazine in English and *China at War*; and it was overseeing local newspapers including the *Chungking Reporter* and *Chungking National Herald*, the latter of which was printed on rice paper due to wartime paper shortages. Most important, Tong controlled access to the Generalissimo and Madame Chiang. Donald's original idea of using Sues in Nanjing and Timperley in Shanghai to circumvent the four overbearing press-handling organisations had worked and Tong was in control. Cheng was sent away with a $50,000 bonus and did, as Donald had predicted, eventually join Wang Jingwei's pro-Japanese puppet government.

The new problem for the foreign press corps was that, though the four previous smaller blockages had been removed, they were now faced with one very large and experienced obstacle — Tong, who at first declared himself avowedly independent but soon collapsed under the sledgehammer of the Chiang/Donald political spin machine. In reality, the Chiang propaganda engine of the Generalissimo, Madame and Donald was now firmly in control. Sues had little doubt that it was Donald who held the immediate power. Tong may have been a likeable "soft spoken, well-groomed gentleman, with a swaying apologetic gait" but the contrast between Donald and Holly Tong was like "the lion and the little white rabbit" respectively.[13] Meanwhile the top Communist in town at the time, Zhou En-lai, looked after his own press relations.

The Americans too were active in behind-the-scenes control. Their military attaché's office had a large staff, though not all of them were experienced press handlers. John Hlavacek was posted to the Chongqing attaché's office following Pearl Harbour when the stakes increased dramatically for America overnight. Originally from La Grange, Illinois, Hlavacek had come to China in 1939 and spent a couple of years teaching English in Japanese-occupied Shanxi, followed by a stint driving Red Cross trucks to deliver medical supplies to mission hospitals, before he was sent to Chongqing where he stayed until 1944. Meanwhile the OSS became active in China after Pearl Harbour and established the Morale Operation (MO) in Chongqing and Kunming. MO's function was to engage in "black propaganda", i.e. to make up rumours and other disinformation to confuse and impact on Japanese morale in China. Parts of this involved making sure as many foreign correspondents as possible were "on message". To do its work most effectively, MO hired a number of journalists. Raymond Cromley, the long-time Tokyo correspondent for the *Wall Street Journal*, who had been considered a spy and imprisoned by the Japanese when war broke out, was an employee, as were journalist Elizabeth McDonald and the cartoonist William Smith. They engaged in various activities which included parodying the Japanese war effort and satirising the foolishness of the famed Japanese *bushido* ethic. And, of course, the OWI had its own hired journalists, such as John Caldwell who was in reality a spy posing as a journalist (indeed in his spying career he adopted both of the most obvious "covers" used by spies (journalist and keen bird watcher!) and Christopher Rand who had left Yale to work at the *San Francisco Chronicle* and then became a China correspondent for the OWI in 1943. After the war Rand stayed on as China correspondent for the *New York Herald Tribune*, following the Chinese Civil war and the 1949 revolution.

The British press had its own problems in Chongqing and elsewhere in China and launched "Operation Remorse" in 1944. Remorse was run from the British Embassy in Chongqing by the Special Operations Executive (SOE) and was designed to prepare the ground for the reassertion of British pre-war trade and influence across Asia as well as ensure the smooth recovery of Hong Kong. British journalists were encouraged to support the aims and objectives of Remorse as keenly as the Americans sought support from their people for the activities of MO.

Of course, as is always the case in the murky world of spooks and spies, turf wars and rivalries soon appeared. The OSS complained that its work was hampered by rivalries with the Sino-American Cooperative Organization, known by everyone as SACO, a group jointly run by the US Navy and the Chinese Secret Service under the shadowy and much-feared KMT secret police chief Dai Li. The navy and Dai rarely found themselves in agreement about objectives and the acceptable methods employed to achieve them. Also, all the time the Chongqing press corps did its utmost to get round them all and find out what was really happening and that meant heading to Yenan to see Mao and his comrades.

Day Trips to Yenan and "Group Think"

The biggest problem for all the groups seeking to control reporters in China was, of course, those journalists, a group growing in number after 1941, who were becoming pro-communist, or at least wanted to know what was going on with the other half of the anti-Japanese alliance. This group, which could be found in Chongqing, Hankou and Shanghai and dotted around elsewhere after 1937, included relative "hardliners" such as Epstein, Smedley, Strong and Gunther Stein as well as Edgar and Helen Snow among others, many of whom were to end up offering life-long support to Mao.

Behind the "hardliners" were those not directly aligned with the Communists, the "softliners", who were increasingly anti-Chiang after their experiences and observations in Chongqing. They included Till and Peggy Durdin, Harrison Forman, Brooks Atkinson and Maurice Vota, all of whom wanted to visit the Eighth Route Army. Eventually Jack Belden, George Hogg and James Bertram did; and obviously Snow, Smedley (who got completely infested with lice while there) and the various TASS correspondents who all disliked the KMT, an elite group of hardliners, were received in Mao's own roomy cave. Smedley was the common point for many as, with her excellent connections to the Communists, she could organise trips for those she liked or was courting (romantically, politically or both). Anna Louise Strong was another who went and would brook no opposition to her visiting the Eighth Route Army, with the Central News Agency's Francis Yao as interpreter. On her trip, Strong got a lot of information, especially from the likes of Generals Zhu De and Peng Dehuai, as well as a bad cold that did nothing to soften her legendary temper which had already led to a non-stop argument with Yao throughout the trip who came to hate her and her demands. Yao had also been under immense pressure from the fascistic KMT Blue Shirts who threatened him and his family if he didn't collaborate with them. He avoided their attentions by escaping their control, becoming a battlefield reporter and earning a reputation as a daredevil correspondent.

The Nationalists and the American government had always been interested in anyone who visited Yenan, with the Nationalists regularly threatening to withdraw accreditation from anyone who went there. Russian-born American citizen Philip Jaffe was one intriguing figure that turned up in Yenan to some consternation and bemusement from Allied and Nationalist censors. Jaffe, a businessman who had made a fortune in the greeting cards business, had a special interest in the Chinese Communists and had been close to the American Communist Party. He was also a co-founder of the magazine *Amerasia* that succeeded the communist-leaning *China Today*.[14] *Amerasia* was popular in American left-wing circles and Jaffe worked closely with the American Friends of the Chinese People organisation. He had first visited Mao in 1937 which prompted his investigation by the FBI which tracked him remorselessly throughout the war and afterwards.

Trips to the front, particularly the Communist-controlled front, grew and caused headaches. OSS, MO, SACO, SOE, Dai Li and Holly Tong's organisation were all thrown into a fit of pique and open anger when in June 1944 a large delegation of foreign correspondents visited Yenan, but there was little they could do and they were forced to sanction trips by first four American correspondents and then by star names such as Teddy White and Brooks Atkinson. Much to Tong's further consternation, some liked it and went over to the Communist side. Gunther Stein of the *Christian Science Monitor* ended up staying for five months; Arch Steele said that after the corruption and graft of Chongqing, Yenan "...was like going from hell to heaven"; and Teddy White saw only "agrarian liberals" rather than hardline communists. Many of the softliners were unfathomable to Tong and his team. For instance, the former university professor Maurice Votaw had been an adviser to Tong's Ministry of Information in 1939. Tong was particularly perturbed to see him apparently embracing the other side and was probably right to be worried. Later Teddy White was to lay the blame for the general favouring of the Communists over the KMT squarely at the door of the government and Tong's organisation: "Nonpartisan opinion, both Chinese and foreign, usually favored the Communists in their great debates with the Kuomintang. The reason for this was simple. The Central Government until 1944 forbade any journalist or observer to travel in Communist territory; it insisted that its own version of the Communist problem be fully accepted".[15] Naturally this attitude was like a red rag to the bulls of the press corps.

The "mishkid" (and a former neighbour of Pearl Buck in Nanjing) James Thompson who would later become professor emeritus of journalism, history, and international relations at Boston University, wrote: "Mao's capital at Yenan became for many frustrated Chungking correspondents 'the Camelot of China'". The truth was that since the publication of Snow's *Red Star Over China* a certain aura had hung over Yenan. Trips to the Communist zone were becoming the fashionable thing to do, not only for the growing number of socialist-leaning journalists but for others too. Much earlier, Edgar Snow and Evans Carlson had both visited the Communist bases and interviewed their leaders; and by now others, mostly unaccredited freelancers who were often under the censor's radar, were wandering round the battlefields and among the Communist and Nationalist troops at will, avoiding both the KMT and other would-be censors who were heading there too. It was becoming a circus.

The accredited journalists themselves, of whatever political persuasion, in Chongqing felt it was professionally required of them to break out of the straightjackets their minders sought to place them in, and ordering trips to Yenan was one way to assert their independence. Subsequently they went further and formed their own Foreign Correspondents' Club (FCC) as a lobby group and with a 24-room clubhouse. Eventually it seemed that just about every correspondent was taking a trip to Yenan. Even the Reverend Patrick O'Connor, working as a war correspondent for the Catholic News Service, visited and celebrated Mass for the handful of interested Americans in the Communist base caves.

All in all, the combination of the hardliners, a growing number of softliners and those "embedded" in Yenan — as well as a foreign press at home which was increasingly disenchanted with Chiang — meant that, despite the soft-soap sell of Holly Tong and his team, the KMT's attempt to control foreign reporting in China during the war had largely failed and had actually been significantly counter-productive.

Indeed, it had been a major factor in generating the amazing level of sympathy for the Communists by Western, and particularly American, correspondents, though this was perhaps understandable given the overt corruption of the Nationalists in Chongqing. The chorus of sympathy had even come from those whose employers were extremely pro-Chiang and anti-communist, including Teddy White and Richard Lauterbach at *Time-Life* as well as the correspondents for *Harper's*, *The Atlantic*, the *New Republic* and the *Nation*. Sometimes it was not just the correspondents on the ground who leant to the left but also their editors back home. The *New York Herald Tribune*'s foreign editor Joseph Barnes was left-leaning, as was Maxwell Stewart at the *Nation*.

However, despite a healthy dislike of Nationalist censorship, why did this obsession of so many foreign correspondents with the Communists grow? Ignoring the overtly communist reporters, what attracted the likes of White, Jacoby and so many others who were not paid-up Party members? It seems it was the specific circumstances they found themselves in and reporting from. Till Durdin, another candidate for the title of "dean" of the American press corps in China, told Freda Utley his theory in 1946 when she pondered why so many seemed so enthralled with Mao and the Communist Party:

> "You must understand" he said "how easy it was to believe in the communists. It was so utterly hopeless in Free China! The graft, misery, the lack of will to fight anymore. Even I felt that it could not be worse, and must be better in communist China. You Freda", he impressed on me, "missed the depressing hopeless years in China following the fall of Hankou. You have got to get the feel of them in order to understand why so many Americans fell for the communists". [16]

The political links that had been formed earlier in places like Hankou in 1938 and then Chongqing during the war seemed to continue afterwards and were later to add victims and fuel to Joe McCarthy's fire at home. Utley noted that in the 1940s the book review pages of the *New York Times* and the *New York Herald Tribune Sunday* edition were a "closed shop" containing only those with pro-communist sympathies formed in China in the late 1930s and during the war:

> If one looks through their back numbers, one finds that it was rare that any book on China was not given to one of a small group of reviewers. Week after week, and year after year, most books on China, and on the Far East, were reviewed by Owen Lattimore, John K. Fairbank, Edgar Snow, Nathaniel Peffer, Theodore White, Annalee Jacoby, Richard Lauterbach, and others with the same point of view.[17]

Annalee Jacoby appears to have been a major force in continuing the political and ideological arguments of the late 1930s and the war in China through to the newspapers of peacetime America. She caused a stir with her damning review of the book *Way of a Fighter* by Claire Lee Chennault and then raised the hackles of many old China Hands of varied political stripes by criticising J. B. Powell's autobiography *My Twenty-Five Years in China*. The recently deceased Powell was bizarrely described by Jacoby as a "reactionary". At the same time it seemed that members of this group were allowed to review their own books: Snow favourably reviewed Lattimore and Harrison Forman's books; Lattimore praised Israel Epstein's *Unfinished Revolution in China*; and the communist-sympathising Columbia University Professor Nathaniel Peffer, who had lived in China previously for 25 years and worked as the Beijing correspondent for the *China Press*, favourably reviewed Gunther Stein's equally sympathetic *The Challenge of Red China*. Clearly ideological decisions and stances decided late at night on the roof of the *China Press* building in Hankou or in the social gatherings of the wartime press corps in Chongqing's Press Hostel were to have long-lasting repercussions when the reporters arrived home in peacetime. By the 1950s when Jack Belden and others were publishing their memoirs, which in Belden's case extolled the virtues of the Communist armies in the war, McCarthyism was in full swing and reviews were squashed.

The End of the Old China ... and a Great 'What If?' of History

As the Second World War ended and civil war resumed, the uneasy truce between Chiang and Mao collapsed. Henry Lieberman, in China reporting for the *New York Times*, arrived in 1945 and stayed till 1949. He continued the general preoccupation with the advanced nature of the Communists and the degeneration of the Nationalists and fell, like many before him, completely under Zhou En-lai's spell. He later concluded that he had been duped, and he was far from being the only one. It had happened to the veteran Carl Crow on his 1939 trip and to Teddy White, Gellhorn and Hemingway among many, many others. Jonathan Mirsky, in his essay *Getting the Story in China*, claims that Zhou "... charmed foreign reporters, even though they were occasionally shocked by his lies".[18]

MO was still active and still employing Raymond Cromley in January 1945. Cromley travelled to Yenan and developed a rapport with Mao good enough to become the courier by which Mao sent a remarkable cable to President Roosevelt seeking a path towards Sino-American cooperation. According to Cromley, Mao genuinely wanted to meet FDR and go to Washington with Zhou to talk about Sino-American trade, US investment in China, and the resumption of American sales in China and Chinese sales in America. What might have been a major breakthrough in Sino-American relations that could have changed the entire shape of the relationship between Beijing and Washington after 1949 came to nought after the US ambassador to China, the vehemently anti-communist Patrick J. Hurley, intercepted and seized the telegram and made sure it never reached FDR. When Cromley got word out later about Hurley's actions, he started decades of speculation about one of the great "what ifs?" in history.

11
Interregnum —
End of a War, Start of a Revolution

"'You must understand' he said 'how easy it was to believe in the communists. It was so utterly hopeless in Free China!'"

Tillman Durdin to Freda Utley

"But if you think China is going to give you all the answers you are as innocent as — as an American newspaperman."

Emily Hahn, *China To Me* (1944)

The Last of the Old Boys

As the war against Japan ended, renewed civil war erupted between the Nationalists and Communists. For those who had been active in the press corps before the war, the writing was clearly on the wall, though they didn't always immediately see it and tried to restart life as before. In 1948 Norman Allman returned to Shanghai to be the editor and publisher of the *China Press*, but eventually could find no accommodation with the new regime, and so gave up and left China. Randall Gould tried to relaunch the *Shanghai Post and Mercury* and attempted to reach some sort of deal, first with the collapsing Nationalists, and then the triumphant Communists. As the end neared, the Nationalists' censors blanked out so many of his stories that the paper ran with massive white gaps throughout. Gould infuriated the censors by refusing to replace the excised text so that readers would understand his problems. Prior to the fall of Shanghai to the Communists, the paper's readership had swiftly declined anyway as inflation made the price of the paper a staggering 750,000 yuan — just 25 US cents, but the amount required a large and rather inconvenient paper bag in which to carry the bills. The Communists infiltrated agents, posing as reporters, into his press room and they insisted he print pro-communist stories and eventually forced Gould to give up and leave China. He returned to America, worked on various newspapers and wrote several books about China, but committed suicide in 1979.

Harry Morriss, son of the legendary Mohawk Morriss and whose family had done so much to define Shanghai's foreign-language press, watched the liberation of Shanghai from his office on the Bund and decided to relaunch the *North-China Daily News*. R. T. Peyton-Griffin, known to many simply as "Peyt", was to be the paper's last editor. A long-time member of the *North-China*'s staff, and assistant editor through most of the 1930s, Peyt, a stickler for grammar, had always insisted on maintaining the hyphen in the title and had helped promote the paper's star writers; and he also wrote a regular column of witty comments under the by-line "Ip" (in parentheses). In 1937 he had started providing opinionated weekly cables to the Australian Broadcasting Corporation that annoyed the Japanese intensely. After the fall of Shanghai he had been interned and then after the war he resumed his career as the paper's editor but, as the Communists occupied the city in May 1949, he was summoned to appear before the Foreign Affairs Department of the Shanghai Military Control Commission to explain himself. In September the Communists banned distribution of news by foreign news agencies, thus rendering the paper effectively pointless. Unable to publish any real news, Peyt ran a story about a minor squabble between an Englishwoman and a Japanese consul that had happened 28 years previously, a series of articles on the philosopher Lao Tzu and another on Hittite hieroglyphics. In a front-page box, Peyt, slightly tongue-in-cheek as normal, announced: "This journal is petitioning the appropriate authorities for permission to cease publication". The paper lasted a surprisingly long time after the Communists took over the city, indeed right up until the morning it announced that North Korea had invaded South Korea — a political interpretation of events that went too far for the new government. Harry Morriss remained in Shanghai and eventually died there; and Peyt did not survive long after the closure of the paper, dying in 1950, with his remains being interred in Shanghai's Holy Trinity Cathedral.

Others had left earlier. For example, Bill Donald, who had arrived in China in 1903, finally called it quits on advising the Chiangs and told an AP reporter that he was sailing to Tahiti in his yacht to write his memoirs. Rumour had it that Donald had confronted Madame Chiang about the rampant corruption surrounding the Chiang clan and she had curtly informed him that his remit did not extend to family matters. Fed-up, he retreated in disgust, typed a letter of resignation expressing his fears and concerns, promptly ripped it up and sailed off into the sunset. Donald died in 1946 without ever releasing his full memoirs.

However, he did confide in the former *China Press* journalist, Earle Selle, then working in Hawaii, who wrote his rather hagiographical biography. Despite falling out with the Chiangs, Donald's legacy remained. He was buried with a state funeral in Shanghai's International Cemetery and shortly afterwards the US weekly *New Republic* described him as "one of the most influential men in modern history".

Arthur de Carle Sowerby kept on publishing books, remained active in the North China Branch of the Royal Asiatic Society and was the honorary director of the Shanghai Museum even after the Japanese had shut down his *China Journal*. Sowerby, who had lived in China for over 40 years, had been interned and all his personal property confiscated. He left China in 1949 to settle in America with his third wife, Alice. She was British but Arthur had been born in China and, despite having served in the First World War, became a stateless citizen for a time, expelled from the US and forced to roam to Manila, Hong Kong, Buenos Aires and Cape Town before being officially admitted back into America.

Some of the old press corps found other callings. For instance, former Hankou "Last Ditcher" George Hogg left journalism, though he still occasionally sent in mood pieces to the *New Statesman*. Following an introduction, courtesy of Agnes Smedley, he worked as a teacher in one of Rewi Alley's training schools in Shaanxi — the so-called Bailie Schools named after Alley's friend Joseph Bailie, an Irish-American missionary. As the Japanese advanced in 1944, Alley and Hogg moved the school 700 miles further inland to Shandan on the old Silk Road in Gansu close to the Mongolian border. Alley appointed Hogg as headmaster where he introduced the motto "Create and Analyse", imposed English public-school rules and taught most of the classes himself. Hogg unfortunately stubbed his toe and died of tetanus a year later. Still, he had clearly taught his boys well. When he was suffering from lockjaw, they attempted to keep him alive by knocking his teeth out one by one to feed him soup through a straw. According to the British geologist and holder of the Royal Geographic Society Founder's Medal, Professor Brian Harland, who was prospecting nearby and met Hogg a few days before his death, his pupils sang the school song to him as he died and then the carpentry class stayed up all night to make him a wooden coffin. A statue of Hogg remains outside the school in Shandan and his tomb on campus has been maintained by his surviving "old boys".

Some, of course, didn't have too many choices even though the war was over. Shanghai's displaced Jewish community was still largely in a condition of stateless limbo. Ossie Lewin, who had founded the *Shanghai Jewish Chronicle* in 1939 remained active, launching *Tagar* in 1946, a pro-Zionist bi-weekly in English and Russian that mixed strident editorials with a highly modernist look. The stateless White Russians had nowhere much to go either until the refugee agencies could deal with them. As they left China, the number of Russian publications dropped though some, such as the Shanghai-based *Kitaisko-Russkaia Gazeta* and the pre-USSR Russian paper *Novosti Dnia* (*News of the Day*), continued up until the revolution, serving the remaining few Russians. Polish speakers still had *Echo Szanghajskie* but their numbers soon dropped too. Pro-communist publications lasted a little longer: the Russian language *Novaia Zhizn* (*New Life*), a Shanghai version of the old pro-Bolshevik newspaper from Petrograd in 1917, survived into the 1950s.

Others were getting out as quickly as possible as chaos reigned and passports became available. The cartoonist Sapajou was one of hundreds of White Russians who decamped with the help of the UN for the Philippines. He had been forced to work for a pro-Nazi paper during the war to make ends meet and this meant he was largely ostracised by his old employers at the *North-China* after the war. He was offered a job in America with the Hearst organisation but sadly died in the chaos of a pestilential UN relocation camp for Russians in the Philippines. Sapajou's rival cartoonist Schiff fared better. Though he was also forced to leave Shanghai, he departed for Buenos Aires in 1947 where he continued to work as an artist and cartoonist until his death in 1968.

A few tried to get back into China but, having annoyed the Nationalists during the war, they were punished and not readmitted. Most notably, Edgar Snow was denied entry as the *Saturday Evening Post*'s China correspondent, as was Harold Isaacs, who tried to come back to report for *Newsweek*. Vincent Sheean, the *New York Times*'s Brooks Atkinson and the *Chicago Daily News*'s Leland Stowe were all barred too for their anti-Chiang articles during the war. Worried members of the press corps who feared being expelled asked a Chongqing official what they had to do to stay acceptable. He replied blandly and not very helpfully: "Use common sense".

Yet another to be punished was the well-liked Darrell Berrigan who had worked for UPI before the war and now wanted to return as Far East correspondent of the *New York Post*. His crime appeared to be that he had been very friendly with Snow. Berrigan had been a popular figure in the press corps and was one of the founders of the Shanghai FCC before leaving in 1939 to establish UPI's Bangkok bureau. However, the Japanese military followed him and he was forced to leave Thailand, moving on to report from Burma and India. Unable to report from China, he moved back to Bangkok to become the editor of the *Bangkok World* and the doyen of the city's foreign press corps. Berrigan was murdered with a single bullet through the back of the head in 1965 in a sensational unsolved case that may have been linked to the journalist's political connections or openly gay lifestyle. An arrest was made but a clear-cut answer to why Berrigan was murdered was never forthcoming.

Others got back in by hook or by crook. In December 1946 Jack Belden landed illegally near Tianjin after bribing a customs official to let him ashore in return for US$200 and a gold wristwatch. He travelled to Beijing where students had stopped protesting against the Japanese and were demanding "GI go home! We are free now. Down with American imperialism". Belden saw that the demonstrations of 1936 and 1946 had one thing in common, namely that they were both staged in defiance of the Generalissimo's orders. He considered travelling to Yenan but decided "… that cave village had become a kind of tourist centre with every foreign correspondent in China hopping over to have a quick look at Mao Tze-tung and Chu The (*Zhu De*), leaders of the Communist party and army, and I had no desire to get mixed up in that circus …".[1] However, Belden had made an ideological turn between his earlier and later sojourns in China. Before returning, he had thought Snow's flattering portrait of the Eighth Route Army in *Red Star Over China* overly idealised. Also, he felt that the likes of Smedley and Evans Carlson had been suckered by the Communists into supporting them without really understanding their ultimate aims and motivations: he thought at the time that the pair enjoyed the romance of the rebellion without appreciating the imminent totalitarianism. Visiting the front in the 1930s, Belden maintained, in a somewhat Hemingwayesque style, that men fought to acquire the respect of their own comrades rather than fighting for an ideology or out of simple patriotism. He doesn't seem to have considered two of the oldest reasons for joining an army in China, official, rebel or warlord: the desire to avoid hunger and press-ganging. However, during the civil war, Belden began to openly and vociferously support the Communists and became close to any number of openly-declared foreign communist sympathisers in China, even to the extent that some, such as Utley, found his conversion overly dramatic and his new-found respect for the likes of Smedley slightly odd.

After returning, he produced *China Shakes the World* (1949), a popular but pro-communist book of the war period and the Eighth Route Army which just made Freda Utley detest him even more, while others praised him. However, he never made any decent money out of the book as, by the time it came out, America had changed, the war was receding, "Red China" was rising and McCarthyism was getting into its stride.

In Hong Kong the Americans had wanted Britain to surrender the colony. FDR suggested an international free port similar to Trieste, an idea London was loath to entertain. The British colonial secretary Franklin Gimson contacted London the moment he was released from Stanley Camp, accepted the post of lieutenant governor and swiftly reasserted British rule. Roosevelt's plan died a quiet death. The Japanese puppet press in the colony was instantly redundant as the English-language occupation newspaper, the *Hongkong News*, had been produced from the seized offices of the *Post* on Wyndham Street. On 30 August 1945 the *Post*'s pre-war editor, the Australian-Chinese Henry Ching was joined by former general manager Ben Wylie and journalist George Giffen (both recently freed from Stanley) to confront the stunned and disbelieving Japanese journalists, reclaim their offices and publish the first post-war edition of the *Post* as the British fleet steamed into the harbour. It was a single free sheet on 31 October with the headline "EXTRA — FLEET ENTERING". For a while a joint edition of the *Post* and the *Hong Kong Telegraph* was published. It wasn't easy as they had to beg, steal or borrow newsprint and ask all the other businesses in Wyndham Street to switch off their lights and fans so that the *Post* had enough electricity to run the presses. Eventually, after the fleet anchored, Ching arranged for a hook-up to a British submarine's generator, with the presses being powered by a line strung up from Wyndham Street down to the harbour.

The *Post* had hired British-born Giffen in 1933 after he had worked on a number of English regional newspapers but he found life in depression-era Britain depressing and headed to Hong Kong. Life there was certainly different from his last job at the *Derbyshire Times*. He described his life as a general reporter in 1930s in the colony as "… a lot of waiting, drinking, rickshaw riding and boredom", a life he seems to have heartily approved of. When Hong Kong fell to the Japanese, he was working as the editor of the *Post*'s sister paper, the *Hong Kong Telegraph*. He was shipped off to Stanley for the duration while his wife was repatriated to Canada. Giffen, Wylie and Ching had kept in touch, though the former two journalists were interned while Ching maintained a clandestine existence, sporadically being arrested by the Japanese and then repeatedly talking his way out of their clutches. Ching had been appointed editor of the *Post* in 1922 following the retirement of the Scotsman Thomas Petrie who had edited the paper since 1911. Ching had been a risky appointment: he was just 31 and, though born in Queensland, he was ethnically Chinese (though speaking only passing Cantonese). Many European reporters argued that this meant he would never be "one of us", but Wylie, the paper's general manager, and others supported his appointment. Those concerned need not have worried as Ching was to be a fierce defender of the *Post's* editorial independence, even to the point of facing down advertisers who objected to his editorials and boycotted the paper intermittently. Ching stood firm and despite the advertisers' anger, increased the paper's circulation among both the European and Eurasian communities and generally elevated the *Post*'s reputation. Throughout his tenure as editor, up till he retired in 1958, he wrote the *Bird's Eye View* column which was full of witty comments about local and international affairs.

Hong Kong swiftly got back into the swing of things as a British crown colony and put the war behind it. The newspapers played their part. The reinstalled colonial government told the newspapers to leave alone stories of collaboration by Hong Kong residents with the Japanese during the occupation for the sake of the recovery effort and the resumption of trade without scapegoats and reprisals. By and large, the papers and their editors complied with the request, despite evidence that some of the major business families and groups had openly fraternised and traded with the enemy in both Hong Kong and Macau throughout the war.

Peace and a certain normality returned in Hong Kong but on the Mainland a new war was raging for control of China.

Covering the Liberation

With the end of the war in the Pacific and the liberation of Shanghai, a new crop of journalists arrived. Their journey was ultimately to be a different one from those who covered China in the first half of the century. Jack Belden spelled out the situation in 1946 when it looked as if Chiang would retain the upper hand:

> Under his (*Chiang's*) command, he now had an army of four million men, thirty nine divisions of which had been American trained and equipped; he had the largest air force any Asiatic mainland power had ever possessed and he held captive or made innocuous nearly every warlord or politician who had ever opposed him. The only possible challenge to his power was a band of Communist guerrillas whom eight years before had been penned up in the barren loess and cave country of the north-west and all but liquidated.[2]

Those journalists who got to meet Chiang at this point all agreed that he was determined to smash the Communists. The Far Eastern manager for UPI, Miles Vaughn (known as "Peg" to the press corps), who was mostly based in Tokyo and seen as the dean of the American press corps in Japan, got an interview with the Generalissimo who told him, in no uncertain terms, that no deals were to be done and he would fight the Communists to the bitter end. It was set to be a vicious showdown with no quarter given or taken. Men like Roy Rowan, who turned up in Shanghai in July 1946, were to follow the Nationalists as their fortunes reversed and crumbled while also seeking out the Communists to tell their story as they slowly took control of the country. Rowan came to China initially to work as an aid worker with the UN Relief and Rehabilitation Administration (UNRRA), a job that allowed him to roam the Chinese countryside in a jeep. However, he had long craved the life of a foreign correspondent to satisfy his "innate desire for adventure" and find "exciting stories to write about as a freelance journalist".[3]

Rowan resigned from the UNRRA in Shanghai, disgusted by the corruption he had seen, and went for a drink at the Palace Hotel bar. Standing next to him was the well-connected Bill Gray, the Shanghai bureau chief for *Time-Life*, who had been posted to China by Luce after Teddy White had finally quit in disgust. They got talking and drank a lot of vodka, and Gray asked Rowan to write a "situationer" on the civil war with "plenty of color, and make sure the facts are straight".[4] A month later, Rowan was the China and Southeast Asia correspondent for *Life* and went on to spend time with Mao and Zhou. He became best known for his coverage of the 1948 Siege of Mukden (Shenyang), a major victory for the Communists that the Nationalists denied to the world's press for as long as possible. The defeat was as good as the writing on the wall for many people. Most foreigners were evacuated from Beijing and the foreign press in the city was finished as the *Peiping Chronicle*'s circulation shrank from 8,000 to a few hundred overnight. With the city surrounded by the Communists, the *Chronicle* reluctantly shut up shop.

Rowan was a close friend and colleague of the American photographer Jack Birns, "a burly, high spirited Californian" who was known as a "rookie" freelance who "could shoot news".[5] He was just 28 when he arrived in December 1947 with three ten-year-old German Rolleiflex cameras and he stayed until 1949, leaving a compelling portfolio of pictures of the upheaval of the postwar period — refugees and beggars, dead children in coffins, street executions, defeated and bedraggled Nationalist soldiers, the last days of Shanghai's notorious Blood Alley bar street and violent demonstrations, all of which were photographed for *Life* magazine in Shanghai, Beijing and northeast China.

Travelling around the country following the civil war, Rowan and Birns took some fairly hairy plane rides seated next to fellow passengers that included monks, orphans, cows, exhausted pilots and millions of dollars of Nationalist funds. The two spent a rather nervous time in Shenyang as the city fell to the Communists and had to make a frantic last-minute escape from a bombarded airstrip with some *gung-ho* ex-Flying Tigers fighter pilots. Rowan and Birns got the scoop largely due to the fact that they were the only reporters who made it into Shenyang while the Nationalists were refusing to report the defeat. When they got back to Shanghai and told their story to the crowded FCC bar, they met disbelieving stares. The Nationalists' refusal to talk about the stunning defeat left the two journalists with a problem. Rowan could cable his scoop back in time for the week's edition, but Birns' photographs would take longer as they could only travel by air. To solve the conundrum, the two men booked passage for the film on a 40-hour flight to America and persuaded *Life* to hold the presses for 12 hours and set up an ad-hoc darkroom at San Francisco airport. A charter pilot agreed to fly the wet negatives to a fog-bound Chicago, but he couldn't land and so diverted to Cleveland, where *Life*'s photo editor arrived from New York to collect them. He then selected the photos by using the window of his taxi as a light box and delivered them to the printer just in time for the issue.

Due to their employment by Luce, Birns and Rowan also got access to Chiang in his last days as leader just after Manchuria fell to the Communists at the million-man Battle of Xuzhou (named the Battle of Huai-Hai by the Communists) in December 1948, the Nationalists' "Gettysburg". It was the biggest land battle since the Second World War, with Chiang losing 550,000 men while the Communists captured 300,000 in just 65 days. Birns and Rowan recalled that the "Gimo" was understandably testy and querulous. Both also made it back to witness the fall of Shanghai in May 1949 and watched wide-eyed farm boys roam the former International Settlement marvelling at flush toilets and elevators while the defeated Nationalist soldiers retreated to the red-light district, threw their rifles into the Huang Pu River and swapped their uniforms for civilian clothing.

Birns's pictures captured effectively the everyday horror of the civil war and the effects on ordinary people of the internecine fighting and destruction wrought by the retreating Nationalists as well as the advancing Communists. This meant he ran afoul of Chiang's old supporter Luce. His pictures remained largely unpublished and in the *Time-Life* archive for 50 years, despite his having earned the Correspondent of the Year award from the Overseas Press Club of America for his work.

Rowan and Birns were actually part of a triumvirate of *Time-Life* reporters covering the civil war. After Rowan had been despatched out to the field, Robert Doyle had been hired to cover the *Time-Life* bureau in Shanghai. A graduate in Far Eastern history at Columbia and Chinese at Yale, Bob Doyle had covered the battle for Suzhou and then the fall of Shanghai with Rowan. He opted to stay in Shanghai after the Communists took over of the city, and was put under house arrest and kept incommunicado for three months. Tragically, while Rowan and Birns went on to have long and illustrious careers, Doyle left China to cover the Dutch colonial exodus from Asia and the creation of Indonesia where he was dragged from his car and murdered by bandits in Central Java.

The *Time-Life* men followed the Nationalists on orders from Luce but others shadowed them from the other side of the lines with the Communists. Seymour Topping, another graduate of the Missouri University School of Journalism (after Columbia University's Graduate School of Journalism had rejected him) had just left the army where he had served as an infantry officer in the Philippines and described himself as "very green" when he arrived in China. He first went to northern China for the International News Service for the princely sum of $50 a month and in 1948 joined AP in Nanjing where he was the first correspondent to report the fall of the city to Communist forces in 1949 and described Chiang as a "beaten man". After the Communist occupation of Nanjing, Topping continued to report from the city for six months.

Another soldier-turned-correspondent was John Roderick who had originally joined AP in 1937 where he worked in the Maine and Washington bureaus before being drafted in 1941. The army taught him Japanese and he was recruited by the OSS who sent him to Kunming and Chongqing and allowed him to roam around the remoter parts of western China during the war. Afterwards he decided he wanted to stay but get closer to the action and rejoined AP who posted him straight back to Chongqing. The wartime capital was winding down and the Nationalist-Communist alliance was in tatters, but Roderick still got to meet Zhou En-lai at the city's Press Hostel. Zhou spoke eloquently of the immediate post-war situation while stabbing at his teeth with an ivory toothpick. The AP man was impressed: Zhou's legendary urbaneness and charm were still working on foreigners. Roderick also visited Yenan, spending seven months there between 1945 and 1947, including having two Christmas lunches with Mao in which he was able to feast on pheasant in a decorated dining hall complete with a Christmas tree. Later, after Mao had left Yenan, Roderick was to meet him again. He had dinner with Mao and listened to his complaints about the Communists being encircled by the Nationalists. Roderick was surprised at the lavish banquet laid on for him but Mao simply replied that "… although we are Communists, we are also Chinese and we like good food", adding for the record: "Of course, we don't eat like this every day". Mao was also worried that supplies had broken down and the movement of goods across China was too slow, and he accentuated the post-war recovery. Roderick was not a little surprised when Mao asked: "Would Sears Roebuck or Montgomery Ward be interested in coming to China?" [6] Roderick was to move on to cover events from Nanjing, Beijing and Hong Kong. It was to be a long time before American mail order companies started deliveries to China again.

Others popped in for shorter periods of time to look at the progress of the civil war. Peter Fleming returned briefly for the *Times* but couldn't get to the frontlines and ended up spending his trip once again shooting game with the Keswick family. Keith Murdoch had spent some time in China as a war correspondent in the 1930s, leaving his young son Rupert in Australia. By the 1940s he was a powerful newspaper proprietor in Australia and despatched Rohan Rivett to China for the *Melbourne Evening Herald* to cover the civil war. Rivett had been a POW on the infamous Burma-Thailand Railway and his despatches from China, though liberal in tone, impressed the virulently anti-communist Murdoch who promoted him to be the *Herald*'s London correspondent. Many journalists found the ever-shifting front and fortunes of the two sides confusing and never really managed to get a handle on what was going on, when and where during the civil war. Keyes Beech of the *Chicago Daily News*, who was to go on to some fame in reporting the Korean War, freely admitted he could never quite work out where the front was.

Another brief sojourner during the civil war was Ian Morrison who had been born in Beijing, the eldest son of Morrison of Peking, a fact of life that perhaps meant he was destined to be a journalist in the Far East. After an education at Winchester and then Trinity College, Cambridge, he became a professor of English at Sapporo's Hokkaido Imperial University, where he remained until 1937. He then spent two years as private secretary to Sir Robert Craigie, the British ambassador in Tokyo, before working for the British and Chinese Corporation in Shanghai until October 1941, followed by a short stint as deputy director of the Far Eastern bureau of the Ministry of Information in Singapore. He then followed almost directly in his father's footsteps by becoming a war correspondent for the *Times* in Southeast Asia, having previously contributed to the paper on a freelance basis. He spent six months travelling in China in 1948 reporting the progress of the civil war, before going on to cover the Korean War in 1950 where he was killed in a bomb blast. Though not as intimately connected to China as his father, Morrison is perhaps best known to fiction readers from the book *A Many Splendoured Thing* by Chinese-Belgian author Han Suyin that recalled her love affair with Morrison while she was working as a medical doctor in Hong Kong. In 1955, the book was made into a phenomenally popular movie that won three Oscars — *Love is a Many Splendoured Thing* — with William Holden (as Morrison, and called Mark Elliot and an American in the film) and Jennifer Jones (somewhat incongruously cast as Han). The film's promotional tagline was the immortal: "She was Han Suyin, the fascinating Eurasian. He was Mark Elliot, American correspondent ... In each other's arms ... they found a love that defied 5,000 years of tradition!"

As the situation deteriorated and it became increasingly obvious that Chiang and the Nationalists were finished, it was clear that it was just a matter of time before the Communists mopped up the remaining cities of China. Things looked like escalating if the Nationalists held out much longer. The *Chicago Daily News*'s George Weller reported a scoop that excited political interest in Washington when he wrote that there was a secret agreement reached in January 1946 between the Soviet High Command and the Chinese Communists pledging 5,000 Russian soldiers to help fight the Nationalists and obligating the Chinese

Communists to subordinate their army to the Russian command. If such a pact existed, it was never ultimately implemented.

The collapse of the Nationalists came thick and fast. Seymour Topping became part of the running lottery among the travelling pack of reporters for the chance to file their stories first as one Nationalist stronghold after another crumbled. When Nanjing fell, he flipped a coin with Bill Kwan of AFP. Kwan won, and wired his editors in Paris, "Reds Take Nanking". Topping, with no reason to rush for an exclusive, filed about 300 words. However, Kwan's French editors were more cautious and opted to wait for more details and Topping subsequently got his first world exclusive as Kwan's Paris editors dithered.

After chasing the story for so long, few in the press corps actually managed to witness the final handover of power. Chang Kuo-sin had been born on Hainan Island but his family had emigrated in search of a better life to Kuching in Borneo when he was a small child. When war broke out in China, Chang had rushed to offer his services to the mother country. He ended up enrolling in Kunming's National Southwest Associated University, the hastily thrown together wartime amalgamation of Peking, Tsinghua and Nankai universities. When he graduated in 1945, he joined the Central News Agency in Chongqing as a reporter, but Holly Tong quickly despatched him to Nanjing, by then once again the capital of Nationalist China. A year later he landed a job with UPI to cover the bitter, failing peace talks between the Nationalists and Communists, and also to report on the Communists' mounting victories over the crumbling Nationalists on the battlefield. Chang and UPI were the first to report the conclusions of the six agreements between the Nationalists and the Communists under General Marshall's mediation in 1946, the Generalissimo's decision to step down in December 1948, and the fall of Nanjing in April 1949.

Chang's biggest problem was getting his notes and writing out of Nanjing and past the Communist authorities and their censors. His imaginative solution was to buy a Chinese dinner set for 12 people comprising porcelain bowls, dishes and spoons, all packed in a big camphor chest. He wrapped the entire dinner set, using his notes as wrapping paper. The suspicious Communist guards examined the chest, but only saw an innocent dinner set wrapped up in used paper. They let Chang and his chest pass unmolested and he got the story out. He reached Hong Kong, wrote up his notes and published one of the first exposés of life under the new communist system —*Eight Months Behind the Bamboo Curtain* (1952).

Some found reporting on the Communist advance a dangerous and potentially lethal occupation. Melbourne-born Graham Jenkins of Reuters and George Vine, the assistant editor of the *North-China* (who later also worked for Reuters) found themselves rather alarmingly condemned to death. Jenkins, based in Nanjing, had written about the Red Army crossing the Yangtze and the imminent fall of Chiang's forces in April 1949. Vine, in Shanghai, ran the story in the *North-China* along with a map that Vine cobbled together. The Nationalists weren't happy with either man: Jenkins was quickly arrested by the KMT secret police and Vine was picked up later the same day at his apartment in Shanghai. Both refused to name their sources and were accused of rumour-mongering and sentenced to execution. Vine called the British consulate, but the staff who came were turned away at gunpoint. In the end the president of the Shanghai FCC, Clyde Farnsworth, a former UPI man and *New York Herald Tribune* correspondent, approached the Generalissimo and the two, along with the secret police, launched into 36 hours of negotiations. The men were freed, minus a few teeth after repeated scraps with their guards, while newspapers around the world erroneously flashed the news that Jenkins had been executed by a firing squad.

Shortly after his release from prison, Vine watched Shanghai's Bund fall to Communist forces from his Broadway Mansions apartment just across Suzhou Creek. He then attended his own farewell party at the FCC, housed in the same building along with the offices and apartments of 50 foreign correspondents. Even for those who weren't based in Broadway Mansions, the FCC was a regular stop. Fred Hampson, the well-liked AP correspondent in Shanghai, had his offices in Frenchtown, but both he and his wife Margaret visited the FCC often. During the fall of Shanghai, fighting broke out along the Suzhou Creek all around the FCC's building. Margaret, who had stopped in for a gossip, ended up phoning in the details from Broadway Mansions to her husband Fred who was sitting in his Frenchtown office a couple of miles away from the action.

Vine's "Farewell to Shanghai" party — farewell to Vine and, as was now obvious, to the old Shanghai too — was to be the last held at the Club's Shanghai HQ. Parties could be wild at the FCC as, after the American military personnel and offices on the lower floors moved out, the press corps had the building to itself. But now the Communist Fifth Column was seen as too much of a threat to journalists. After the Chinese capital had moved from Chongqing to Nanjing, the FCC had followed with UPI's Walter Logan as president and a new clubhouse in a large, terraced Tudor-style mansion, along with three jeeps from the US Army motor pool at a cost of only US$150 each. At Vine's party the FCC's assets, including the Club's furniture and the three jeeps, were sold for the then handy sum of US$10,000. *Time* and *Life* magazines bought one each and AP got the third. Vine then took the cheque to Hong Kong to help start up the Hong Kong FCC.

Clyde Farnsworth, the saviour of Vine and Jenkins, moved to Hong Kong to run the FCC where it thrived after a somewhat rocky start. Deprived of premises in the overcrowded colony when they arrived in 1949, the club held meetings in a variety of places including the old Dairy Farm Restaurant on the mezzanine floor of Windsor House. The restaurant became the major hangout for journalists in Hong Kong for some years despite being very cramped, but in 1949 the FCC had only 11 full members. Eventually a more permanent home was found in a small house on the residential Kotewall Road, which they were allowed to occupy if they promised to "keep the noise down". One nice touch about the early FCC in Hong Kong was that it managed to help many of its former Chinese staff across the border from Shanghai and settle them with jobs in the Hong Kong club. Had they remained in Communist Shanghai they would certainly have been considered immediately suspect as spies and collaborators. It must have felt like old times on the Kotewall Road as most of the early members of the Hong Kong FCC were former members of the Shanghai club (Rowan, for instance, had moved the *Time-Life* China bureau into the bridal suite at the posh Peninsula Hotel in Kowloon) and the first president was Farnsworth and the second was a former Reuters man in Shanghai, Monty Parrott.

The chaos of the civil war also attracted a few chancers to China. The foreign press corps was not sorry to see the back of the obese and flamboyant Reynolds Packard (or his equally obese Chinese girlfriend dubbed the "Manchu Monster"). He was eventually fired by an exasperated UPI which had been fooled by him repeatedly after promoting his by-line heavily for a time. To say that Packard was loose with the truth was an understatement: he had falsely claimed that the Russians had led an evacuation of Manchuli, and also claimed to have discovered a human-headed spider in the Chinese countryside and a Soviet atomic bomb plant near Lake Baikal. Eventually, it was deemed necessary for Walter Rundle, UPI's China bureau chief based in Shanghai to travel to Beijing to fire him personally as they'd tried before but he'd ignored the telegrams. UPI was not pleased when Packard announced his belief that "If you've got a good story, the important thing is to get it out fast. You can worry about details later. And if you have to send a correction, that will probably make another good story".[7]

The Generalissimo Departs

While all this was occurring Chiang was, of course, fleeing to Taiwan to establish the Republic of China. After the Battle of Xuzhou, the Generalissimo had realised that his military position was hopeless but he was not prepared to surrender. Instead he expressed a Chinese New Year's wish for a peaceful settlement and said that he would not stand in the way if one could be arranged.

On 19 January 1949, the Executive Yuan (parliament) proposed a cease-fire and peace negotiations with Mao; and two days later Chiang announced his retirement from the presidency. The Communist military machine rolled on unabated and Shanghai fell to the Communists on 27 May.

The inevitable happened. The Generalissimo gave up the ghost and decamped to Taiwan, which China had only managed to regain from the Japanese in 1945 as part of the post-war settlement favouring the Allies. He left with a bunch of loyalists, some treasure, a substantial amount of art and a load of gold from the Central Bank of China. (Roy Rowan witnessed the late-night loading of the gold while taking a stroll from the *Time-Life* offices in the *North-China* building on the Bund, but it was only later that he realised what he had actually seen.) And this was to be followed by hundreds of thousands of supporters and the establishment of the Republic of China on Taiwan, with further riches and cultural treasures having been sent on ahead.

Before the flow of refugees was cut off, nearly two million Chinese crossed to join Chiang in Taiwan. Reporting from Taiwan was not easy. The veteran Rodney Gilbert did get an interview with Chiang in Taiwan in 1950 where he wrote that he believed that Chiang was capable of building a strong nation from his island retreat, which certainly wasn't a majority opinion of the Generalissimo's chances at the time. [8] The KMT was highly suspicious of journalists on the island, a suspicion verging on paranoia that went back to 28 February 1947 when a massacre had occurred which the KMT would rather not be made public. News about the massacre was due in part to several key foreigners, notably George H. Kerr, who was working at the US consulate in Taipei at the time. A protest over a woman selling cigarettes led to riots that were put down by KMT troops sent from the Mainland. The numbers vary but it seems that between 18,000 and 28,000 people were killed. The press was discouraged from reporting it and the incident was rarely mentioned in Taiwan until the 1990s. Kerr leaked out information and then more details in his 1965 book *Formosa Betrayed*. As well as Kerr, Henry Lieberman and Till Durdin reported the massacre for the *New York Times*, and Peggy Durdin wrote two powerful essays in *The Nation* which raised awareness.

After Chiang fled to Taiwan, the press corps was not encouraged to follow. The dwindling number of foreign correspondents on the Mainland, including Clyde Farnsworth and Randall Gould, attempted to comprehend Chiang's strategy of retreat. Some did highlight the antagonisms between the new arrivals from the Mainland and the indigenous Taiwanese population. For example, an editorial in the *London Daily News* speculated, rather glibly, that the arrival of Chiang and his cohorts was so disruptive to the economy and society of the island that the native Taiwanese may be the only Asians keen to see the return of the

Japanese. Also, Till Durdin noted that the poor conduct of the KMT refugees was destroying the fabric of Taiwanese life since robbery and rape shot up as the desperate soldiers arrived to find little in the way of financial support, available women or gainful employment to occupy them.

However, the major story was really back on the Mainland where the surviving press corps found itself thrust into revolutionary China. Walter Sullivan arrived on the eve of the revolution as the travelling correspondent for the *New York Times*. Sullivan had been the paper's science editor, having accompanied four research expeditions to Antarctica, before following the veteran Hallett Abend on the China beat. He travelled as far west as Xinjiang and remained for another year on the periphery of China, primarily in Korea and Hong Kong. In Shanghai, Sullivan reported Mao's official appointment as chairman of the Communist Party's Central Committee before going on to cover the outbreak of the Korean War.

Problems for Those Who "Lost China"

Mao's ferocious politically-motivated attacks on writers, journalists and scholars in China were still to come, but in America scapegoating was already underway even before the revolution had been consolidated in China. The later McCarthyism period was to be brutal but the recriminations and accusations had started in 1945 even before the official end of the war as the "China Lobby" looked for scapegoats and many members of the old China press corps were to become embroiled in the vicious "who lost China?" argument.

The ball started rolling with the prominent case of official displeasure in America with Philip Jaffe, of *Amerasia* fame, who had visited Mao in Yenan in 1937. Jaffe was already under suspicion for his long-time friendship with American Communist Party general secretary Earl Browder, his visits to Mao, Zhou and other Chinese Communist leaders in the 1930s as well as the political tone of *Amerasia* (which had a circulation of only about 2,000 copies). He had been labelled a "Super Fellow Traveller" and it also didn't help that Jaffe was Russian-born. The FBI arrested him in June 1945. Also arrested were his co-editor Kate Mitchell, herself another US Communist Party sympathiser, and Andrew Roth who in the 1930s had been Jaffe's assistant and who, despite a secret government report labelling him a fellow traveller, had still somehow ended up working in the Office of Naval Intelligence. After wiretapping *Amerasia*'s New York offices and tailing Jaffe and his staff, the FBI and the OSS claimed that Emmanuel Sigurd "Jimmy" Larsen, a State Department expert on Far East affairs, and Roth had both passed sensitive documents to Jaffe who had then passed them on to Mark Gayn, a freelancer who had started with J. B. Powell in Shanghai and was now working for *Collier's* and the *Saturday Evening Post*. The *Amerasia* case was not one of pure and simple espionage: nothing was passed to the Soviets and it seemed that Jaffe only used the documents to argue for support for the communist movement in Asia. Consequently, Jaffe, Roth and Larsen were charged with stealing, receiving or concealing government documents rather than treachery. In these pre-McCarthy days before the TV cameras and headlines highlighted the witch hunts, a deal was done and Jaffe was let off with a warning against his "excess of journalistic zeal" and a US$2,500 fine, which he paid on the spot. Larsen was fined US$500 which Jaffe, who was independently wealthy, also paid while all charges against Roth were dropped.

Soon, however, to comment too closely on China could be hazardous. The China lobby tried to get those reporters with pasts that had not been supportive of Chiang fired. *Newsweek* was urged to fire Harold Isaacs but refused. However, the China lobby's pressure was nothing compared to the infamous senator from Wisconsin, Joseph McCarthy, who accused Owen Lattimore of being a "Red" and a spy in 1950 and thereby started a horrific ball of persecution rolling. Lattimore was to be the first of the old China press corps to have the finger pointed at him, but he was certainly not the last. Veteran correspondent Haldore Hanson of AP was accused of having "pro-Communist proclivities" and of being on "a mission to communize the world" in 1950. McCarthy offered no proof and Hanson, backed up by the State Department, simply replied "I am a loyal American".[9]

Initially thwarted, McCarthy swiftly resurrected the earlier *Amerasia* case that he felt had been insufficiently pursued and prosecuted. Through the links between Jaffe and the government officials Larsen and Roth, he used the case as part of his hounding of foreign service officers and journalists in the early 1950s. But, by then, many things had changed: *Amerasia* had folded; Jaffe was passing his time dabbling with a planned history of Asia; Mitchell was collecting material for a planned book on the Far East; Roth had joined the staff of the leftist *Nation* and was living in Holland; Gayn was freelancing in central Europe; and Larsen was running a shoestring agency called the Far East Information Bureau in Washington.

Those with unorthodox political views who had returned to the US were immediately suspect. After receiving his "Black Hand" death threat in Shanghai and then visiting Trotsky in Mexico, Alexander Buchman had returned to America. To McCarthy, Buchman's sins were legion — a dedicated communist in China, a bodyguard to Trotsky and a union organiser in California, not to mention his having associated with the black left-wing poet and homosexual

Langston Hughes in Tokyo and having married Debbie Bloomfield, a Shanghailander whose mother was Japanese and father a Jewish Englishman. (They had waited till returning to the US to marry but California's laws against bi-racial marriages had meant they had to drive to Gallup, New Mexico, in 1941 to tie the knot.) In the late 1940s the FBI began an investigation of Buchman while he was working for North American Aviation (later Rockwell International). He lost his security clearance, was suspended from work and was accused of being a communist. Buchman fought back, angered that being called "communist" intimated he was supportive of the USSR, which as a Trotskyist he obviously wasn't. After a lengthy hearing in 1951, Buchman was cleared and returned to work, though the names of his old friends at the China press corps, such as Frank Glass and Harold Isaacs, came up frequently during the hearing.

Having a famous father didn't help either. J. B. Powell's son, John W., had returned to Shanghai after the war and his father's death to open a news bureau for the OWI and take back control of the *China Weekly Review*. Powell's life was intricately linked to China; he had been born in a rickshaw rushing his mother to hospital in Shanghai. He divided his childhood between Hannibal, Missouri, and the International Settlement. Then, following in his father's footsteps, he attended the Missouri University School of Journalism before heading back to Shanghai to visit his family and getting caught up in the war. Only 26 years old, he decided to restart the *Review*. When he went to the old offices on Avenue Edward VII just days after the Hiroshima and Nagasaki bomb blasts, he found the place completely looted, including the loss of the *Review*'s 4,300-volume library of English-language books on the Far East, the majority of which J. B. had probably actually read. He officially re-launched the *Review* in October 1945 declaring he would "... aim at the same high standards of journalism and to follow the same basic principles of truth and accuracy as those established by its founders".[10] Powell published the magazine until June 1953, first as a weekly and then, when revenues slumped, as a monthly.

John W. was to the left of his father politically and was later to be hauled before the House Un-American Activities Committee (HUAC) accused of pro-communism in his *Review* articles. What followed was a five-year legal fight by Powell, his wife Sylvia, a San Francisco writer who had been on the *Review*'s editorial staff, and their friend Julian Schuman. In 1956 all three were charged with treason and sedition following articles they published during the Korean War in which they accused the US of using aircraft to attack North Korea with biological weapons. The Powells said they were simply reporting what they were told by Chinese officials returning from the frontlines (which they were). However, the *Review* had also been full of articles arguing against European colonialism in Asia and urging America not to isolate China — nothing overly radical but dangerous in the hey-day of McCarthy — while Henry Luce called Powell "an outright apologist for communism".[11]

Eventually the treason charges were dismissed in July 1959, and in 1961 attorney general Bobby Kennedy also dropped the sedition charges after a public campaign in their defence led by the "Queen of the Muckrakers" Jessica Mitford and other celebrities. However, the Powells had broadly supported the revolution and had been marginalised by many influential and former colleagues in America when they had returned from China in 1953. Powell was reduced to working as a salesman after being blacklisted from working in the media. The largely ostracised couple eventually became property restorers and ran an antiques shop in San Francisco. For his part, Schuman returned to China later as a consultant on the English-language *China Daily*.

The End of the Old China Press Corps

Standing on the rostrum at Tiananmen Square on 1 October 1949, Mao had officially founded the People's Republic of China, declaring that "The Chinese people have stood up!" Not one foreign correspondent was there to witness the historic event. Once the Communists had secured total victory, access to Mao and the senior leadership became virtually impossible for those not confirmed and trusted supporters. Some journalists were allowed to stay as it suited Mao's purposes. In return for remaining, many would allow themselves to be used for propaganda purposes and see no evil, hear no evil and, most importantly, speak no evil. By the spring of 1950 all foreigners were required to register with the police and submit to an interview asking them, among other things, whether they owned a radio, a camera, any weapons such as guns or swords and what they thought of Marxism.

By the late 1950s China was becoming an unknown and mysterious place once again as the divisions of the Cold War separated foreigner from Chinese almost totally. By the late 1950s only Reuters, AP and AFP were officially left to represent the independent Western media in China and they could not easily leave Beijing to report from the countryside or send a single line out of the country without the approval of the government. David Lancashire, a Canadian hired by AP in 1956, was one of the very few able to send back reports from Mao's increasingly authoritarian and reclusive state. Lancashire spent six weeks travelling over 5,000 miles across China and wrote a lengthy series of stories on life behind the "Bamboo Curtain", as it was now known. He got the job after the State Department refused AP permission to send a US citizen as a correspondent. In reality, Washington didn't want anyone to be reporting from

China and even threatened AP with serious sanctions, which led to outrage from journalists. AP's board of directors also objected to this blatant interference and despatched Lancashire in defiance of the State Department (which had secretly opened diplomatic channels of communication with the Chinese in Warsaw in the mid-1950s), arguing that Americans had a right to learn through their own news organisations rather than just their government about conditions in China. Lancashire appeared quite impressed by what he had seen reporting back that:

> Red China today is an immense machine with 600 million moving parts, running at top speed. Its 600 million individuals are sacrificing individually at Communist behest in an all-consuming drive to change a backward, poverty ridden nation into a modern state.[12]

But perhaps the greatest survivor of them all, and the last of the real old China press corps, was the monocle-wearing arch-cynic Jacques Marcuse, a Belgian journalist who was still representing AFP in the Chinese capital in the 1960s after originally arriving in Shanghai in the 1930s to work for *Le Monde* and Havas, and having been a member of the Chunking Contingent during the war. Marcuse never became a fellow-traveller; though he was not slow to comment on those who did, describing Rewi Alley as "eminently useable rather than eminently useful".[13]

K. S. Rana, a young Indian diplomat posted to Beijing in 1963 recalled that Marcuse had a standing arrangement with the bar at Beijing Airport which kept his own personal bottle of fiery *Maotai* white spirit. Friends were apparently welcome to dip into it as they awaited the inevitably frequently delayed flights: all one had to do was to call for Mr. Marcuse's bottle. When Marcuse left and the Cultural Revolution began, the end had come. The last of the old China press corps went home, not to return until China was on the brink of becoming a very different country … but that's another story.

Notes

Introduction — Through the Looking Glass

1. Millie Bennett (1993) *On Her Own: Journalistic Adventures from San Francisco to the Chinese Revolution, 1917–1927*, Armonk, NY: M. E. Sharpe, p. 229.
2. Peter Fleming (1933) *One's Company: A Journey to China in 1933*, London: Penguin, p. 14.
3. Anonymous, "Work of the foreign newspaper correspondent in China", *China Weekly Review*, 10 October 1928.
4. Hallet Abend (1943) *My Life in China 1926–1941*, New York: Harcourt, Brace & Co., p. 96.
5. Earl H. Leaf, "The bookworm turns," *China Weekly Review*, 1 May 1937.

Chapter 1   God, Mammon and Flag

1. *Canton Register*, vol. 1, no. 1, 8 November 1827.
2. ———, vol 1, no. 1, 8 November 1827
3. Rosmarie Lamas (2006) *Everything in Style: Harriet Low's Macau*, Hong Kong: Hong Kong University Press, p. 97.
4. Joseph Conrad (1902) *Heart of Darkness*, Edinburgh: Blackwood and Sons.
5. Maurice Collis (1946) *Foreign Mud*, London: Faber and Faber, p. 108.
6. ———, p. 108.
7. *Chinese Repository*, issue 1, May 1832.
8. ———, 3 April 1835, pp. 559–70.
9. Which Downing later compiled into a book *The Fan-Qui in China in 1836–7* (1838). A *fan-qui* is a foreign devil, a phrase many of the British sailors revelled in.
10. Canton Gunpowder, a mixture of rum and tobacco, was also seen as a good cure for sailors who had been flogged, as was common in the Royal Navy. This accounted for the rum and the lash; when the sodomy, which was infamously the third element of naval tradition, occurred is not clear.
11. Rowlandson's pictures of drunk and carousing British sailors were not Guangzhou-specific but, as British sailors tended to act pretty much the same everywhere in the world when they got on shore, readers got the point.
12. Basil Lubbock (1933) *The Opium Clippers*, Glasgow: Brown, Son & Ferguson.
13. An impressive triple rise to wealth chronicled in his autobiography (1857) *An American Merchant in Europe, Asia, and Australia*, New York: Sampson Low.

14 Jack Gray (1990) *Rebellions and Revolutions*, Oxford: Oxford University Press, p. 27.
15 Maurice Collis, *Foreign Mud*, p. 111.
16 ——, p. 189.
17 *India Gazette*, 1840.
18 The early 1800s were a time of political turmoil in Portugal. The 1807 invasion by Napoleon's armies forced the Portuguese court into exile in Brazil. In 1820 the regency was overthrown and a conflict erupted between Constitutionalists and Monarchists that did not end until 1834.
19 *Friend of China*, 17 March 1842.
20 H. J. Lethbridge, "Hong Kong Cadets, 1862–1941", http://sunzi1.lib.hku.hk/hkjo/view/44/4401180.pdf
21 The parallel is obvious but would not have been made at the time as Kipling's classic short story of two British ex-soldiers who set off from British India in search of adventure and end up as kings of Kafiristan was only published in 1888, the same year as de Mayréna arrived in Hong Kong.
22 J. S. Thomson (1909) *The Chinese*, Indianapolis: Bobbs-Merrill Company.
23 *Friend of China*, 2 April 1856. William Caine got the last laugh returning as the fifth governor of Hong Kong (1859–65).
24 ——, 23 September 1848.
25 Edward Said (1978) *Orientalism*, London: Penguin, p. 36.

Chapter 2   Civil and Other Wars — Rebels, Mercenaries and More Dope

1 Issachar Jacox Roberts, *Chinese and General Missionary Gleaner*, 6 October 1852.
2 Now People's Square and previously the racecourse and public recreation ground which shows how small Shanghai was at the time.
3 *North China Herald*, 4 August 1860.
4 His sister, Helen, was an opium addict and had had to be restrained by the Lunacy Commission before dying of her addiction.
5 Niall Ferguson (2004) *Empire*, London: Penguin, p. 166.
6 Karl Marx, "The case of the Lorcha Arrow", *New York Daily Tribune*, 23 January 1857.
7 Daniele Varé (1936) *The Last of the Empresses*, London: John Murray, p. 38.
8 The first formal treaty signed between the US and China. It served as an American counterpart to the 1842 Anglo-Chinese Treaty of Nanjing.
9 See Regine Thiriez (1998) *Barbarian Lens*, London: Routledge.
10 *North China Herald*, 3 August 1850.
11 Which technically it is, as the fourth-most senior of the British Orders of Chivalry.
12 Prescott Clarke and Frank King (1965) *A Research Guide to China Coast Newspapers*, Cambridge, MA: East Asian Research Center; Caleb Carr (1992) *The Devil Soldier*, New York: Random House, p. 95.

13 Charles George Gordon, "Military strength of China and its development", *China Mail*, 25 August 1880.

Chapter 3 Boxers and Treaty Porters — Headlines Change History

1   Peter Fleming (1959) *The Siege at Peking*, New York: Harper & Brothers, p. 137.
2   Now renamed Wanfujing.
3   George Ernest Morrison (1895) *An Australian in China*, London: H. Cox.
4   *Kipling Journal*, no. 45, March 1938.
5   Hugh Trevor-Roper (1977) *Hermit of Peking*, New York: Knopf, p. 42.
6   James M. MacPherson, "The canny Scot who advises China's president", *New York Times*, 11 August 1912.
7   Daniele Varé (1936) *The Last of the Empresses*, London: John Murray, p. 180.
8   *Novoe vremia*, 8 June 1900.
9   *Grazhdanin*, 13 June 1900.
10 This didn't ultimately help Amfiteatrov much: in 1902 he was exiled for writing a satirical article lampooning the imperial family.
11 Jay Denby (1910) *Letters of a Shanghai Griffin*, Shanghai: China Printing Company, p. 69.
12 Fleming, *The Siege at Peking*, p. 20.
13 *Hongkong Telegraph*, 5 August 1903.
14 *South China Morning Post*, 6 November 1903.
15 Tse Tsan-tai (1924) *Secret History of the Chinese Revolution*, Hong Kong: South China Morning Post.
16 *Hongkong Telegraph*, 1 September 1906.

Chapter 4 The Vultures Descend

1   Maurice Baring (1905) *With the Russians in Manchuria*, London: Methuen, p. 124.
2   Charles Russell, "The men behind the dreadnoughts", *New York Herald*, 3 March 1906.
3   Ilona Ralph Sues (1944) *Shark's Fin and Millet*, New York: Garden City Publishing, p. 63.

Chapter 5 Writing in a Republic — Printing What They Damn Well Liked

1   *Chinese Public Opinion*, vol.1, no. 1, 1908.
2   John Benjamin Powell (1945) *My Twenty-Five Years in China*, New York: Macmillan, p. 7.
3   ——, p. 8.

4 Extraterritoriality is the system that put foreigners beyond the reach of Chinese justice and subject to penalties only from their own courts and judges in China's treaty ports. The system greatly annoyed the Chinese, and massively benefited the foreigners though many felt it unhelpful to better relations.
5 Simon Winchester (1985) *Outposts*, London: Penguin, p. 125.
6 Stella Dong (2001) *Shanghai*, New York: Perennial, p. 176.
7 Peter Rand (1995) *China Hands*, New York: Simon and Schuster, p. 24.
8 *Peking and Tientsin Times*, No. 1, 10 March, 1894.
9 ———, No. 1, 10 March, 1894.
10 "British gift", *Time*, 14 September 1936; *China Weekly Review*, 17 July 1937, p. 226.
11 Brian Power (2005) *The Ford of Heaven*, Oxford: Signal Books, p. 177.
12 J. W. Sanger, (1921) *Advertising Methods in Japan, China, and the Philippines* Washington DC, p. 65.

Chapter 6   The Roaring Twenties — Substituting Action for Talk

1 Rodney Gilbert, "Downfall of Tsao the Mighty: Minister literally bites the dust", *North China Herald*, 10 May 1919, pp. 348–9.
2 Rodney Gilbert (1926) *What's Wrong with China*, London: John Murray. The historian Robert Bickers makes the apposite comment that Gilbert's title never bothered to feature a question mark.
3 Carl Crow, "The most interesting character I ever knew", Crow archive, folder 107A, Western Historical Manuscript Collection, University of Missouri.
4 ———, "The most interesting character I ever knew".
5 Actually a true story and somewhat of a necessary skill for any horse in the dramatically steep geography of Chongqing.
6 G. F. Shecklen, "Modern China will communicate by radio", *China Weekly Review*, 10 October 1928, p. 58.
7 Arthur Ransome (1927) *The Chinese Puzzle*, London: Unwin Brothers.
8 ———, *The Chinese Puzzle*.
9 Nicholas Clifford, "A revolution is not a tea party: The 'Shanghai mind(s) reconsidered", *The Pacific Historical Review*, vol. 59, no. 4 (November 1990), pp. 501–26.
10 Hallett Abend (1943) *My Life in China 1926–1941*, New York: Harcourt, Brace & Co., p. 9.
11 Baruch Hirson and Arthur Knodel (2007) *Reporting the Chinese Revolution: The Letters of Rayna Prohme*, London: Pluto Press, p. 48.
12 Vincent Sheean (1934) *Personal History*, New York: Houghton Mifflin, p. 273.
13 Abend, *My Life in China*, p. 19.
14 Bertram Lenox Putnam Weale (1917) *The Fight for the Republic in China*, New York: Dodd, Mead & Co., p. 89.

Chapter 7   The Decadent Thirties — Celebrities, Gangsters and the Ladies of the Press

1. To be fair to Fleming, these sorts of comparisons were common among English (and other) writers. Jules Verne had compared Hong Kong to a town in Kent or Surrey in the 1870s; Auden and Isherwood described the countryside around Guangzhou in 1938 as reminiscent of the Severn Valley; and the famous sinologist Joseph Needham compared Fuzhou to Clapham and, perhaps most bizarrely, wartime Chongqing to Torquay!
2. Peter Fleming (1936) *News From Tartary*, London: Jonathan Cape, p. 54.
3. Fleming was possibly in Waugh's mind when he wrote *Scoop*, published in 1938 after Fleming's *One's Company* and *News From Tartary*.
4. Edna Lee Booker (1940) *News is My Job*, New York: Macmillan, p. 7. Dinty Doyle went on to become a well-known radio personality in America in the 1930s.
5. Emily Hahn (1944) *China To Me*, New York: Doubleday, Doran & Co., p. 113.
6. Ilona Ralf Sues (1944) *Shark's Fins and Millet*, New York: Garden City Publishing, p. 95.
7. Sues, *Shark's Fins and Millet*, p. 56.
8. Carroll Alcott (1943) *My War With Japan*, New York: Henry Holt & Co., pp. 68–9.
9. Ralph Shaw (1973) *Sin City*, London: Everest Books, p. 88.
10. Sapajou and R. T. Peyton-Griffin (2007) *Shanghai's Schemozzle*, Hong Kong: China Economic Review Publishing.

Chapter 8   The Dirty Thirties — Left Wing, Right Wing, Imperialists and Spies

1. Ilona Ralf Sues (1944) *Shark's Fins and Millet*, New York: Garden City Publishing, p. 106.
2. Harold Isaacs (1932) *Five Years of Kuomintang Reaction*, Shanghai: China Forum.
3. Published as (1938) *The Tragedy of the Chinese Revolution*, London: Secker and Warburg.
4. US Department of State, Document 893.91, 5 June 1919.
5. *The Weekly Review*, vol. XXII, no. 8, 21 October 1922.
6. Brian Power (2005) *The Ford of Heaven*, Oxford: Signal Books, p. 177.
7. Consultation with Edward Hunter, Tuesday, March 13 1958, US House of Representatives, Committee on Un-American Activities, Washington DC.
8. Hallett Abend (1943) *My Life in China 1926–1941*, New York: Harcourt, Brace & Co., p. 163.
9. Randall Gould (1946) *China in the Sun*, Garden City: Doubleday, p. 148.
10. Arthur de Carle Sowerby, "While Rome burns", *China Journal*, vol. XVI, April 1932.
11. According to Utley in her book *The China Story* (1951), the passage critical of the Soviets appeared in the 1938 Random House edition. The passage was omitted from

the editions published in 1939 (Garden City Publishing Company) and in 1944 by the Modern Library (then owned by Random House).
12   "Interview with the British journalist James Bertram, 25 October 1937", Mao Tse-tung (1967) *Selected Works of Mao Tse-tung*, Beijing: Foreign Languages Press.
13   Irene Kuhn (1938) *Assigned to Adventure*, Philadelphia: J. B. Lippincott & Co., p. 43.
14   Carroll Alcott (1943) *My War With Japan*, New York: Henry Holt & Co., p. 112.
15   ———, p. 112.
16   Sues, *Shark's Fins and Millet*, pp. 309–10.

Chapter 9   Too Hot — China Fights for Its Life

1   John Keay (1997) *Last Post*, London: John Murray, p. 156.
2   The Japanese sort of apologised for this by establishing the Robert Guillain Prize for excellence in journalism on issues pertaining to Japanese–European relations in the 1980s.
3   *China Weekly Review*, 20 November 1937, p. 282.
4   "Jap's enemy no. 1", *Time*, 7 September 1942.
5   *China Weekly Review*, vol. 81, no. 12, 21 August 1937.
6   Ralph Shaw (1973) *Sin City*, London: Everest Books, p. 102.
7   Tillman Durdin, "All captives slain," *New York Times*, 18 December 1937.
8   C. Yates McDaniel, "Nanking horror described in diary of war reporter," *Chicago Daily Tribune*, 18 December 1937.
9   *Japanese Terror in China* (1938) also called *What War Means* in the British edition published by the famous left-wing publisher Victor Gollancz.
10   Ilona Ralf Sues (1944) *Shark's Fins and Millet,* New York: Garden City Publishing, p. 183.
11   John Gittings, "Japanese rewrite Guardian history", *The Guardian*, 4 October 2002.
12   At least to the rest of the world — there are plenty of people in Japan who still dispute the Massacre ever occurred — see Iris Chang (1997) *The Rape of Nanking*, London: Penguin.
13   Katsuichi Honda (1999) *The Nanjing Massacre*: *A Japanese Journalist Confronts Japan's National Shame*, Armonk, NY: East Gate Books, p. 239.
14   Established in December 1935 in Beijing under Chinese General Song Zheyuan.
15   *China Weekly Review*, 4 December 1937, p. 3.
16   George Hogg, quoted in James MacManus (2007) *Ocean Devil*, London: Harper Perennial, p. 60.
17   Sues, *Shark's Fins and Millet,* p. 178.
18   Freda Utley (1951) *The China Story*, Chicago: Henry Regnery Company, p. 192.
19   ———, p. 192.
20   ———, p. 144.
21   Sues, *Shark's Fins and Millet*, p. 177.
22   Christopher Isherwood and Wystan Hugh Auden, *Hong Kong*, a poem contained within (1939) *Journey to a War*, London: Faber & Faber.

23   Selected lines from Auden's *Macao*, contained within *Journey to a War*.
24   Isherwood and Auden, *Journey to a War*, p. 52.
25   ——, p. 209.
26   ——, p. 207.
27   ——, p. 232.
28   ——, p. 237.
29   *In Time of War*, sonnet XVI, *Journey to a War*.
30   Lourenço Marques is now Maputo in Mozambique.
31   Edgar Snow (1958) *Journey to the Beginning,* London: Victor Gollancz.

Chapter 10 In Air Raid Shelters and Caves — Covering the War

1   Letter 13, Evans F. Carlson to Marguerite LeHand, Evans F. Carlson on China at War 1937–41.
2   Oris Friesen and Stephen MacKinnon (1987) *Reporting China,* Berkeley: University of California Press.
3   *Newsweek*, 23 October 1972.
4   Theodore H. White and Annalee Jacoby (1946) *Thunder Out of China*, New York: William Sloane Associates, p. 188.
5   Jacoby quoted in Walter Sullivan, "The crucial 1940s", *The Nieman Foundation for Journalism at Harvard University*, double issue: vol. 53, no. 4, Winter 1999/vol. 54, no. 1 Spring 2000.
6   Roy Rowan (2004) *Chasing the Dragon*, CT: Lyon Press, p. 177.
7   Jonathan Mirsky, "Getting the story in China: American reporters since 1972", *Harvard Asia Quarterly*, vol. VI, no.1, Winter 2002.
8   Peter Moreira, (2006) *Hemingway on the China Front*, Dulles, VA: Potomac Books, p. 113.
9   Moreira, *Hemingway on the China Front*, p. 129.
10 ——, p. 113.
11 ——, p. 179.
12 Christoper Isherwood and Wystan Hugh Auden (1939) *Journey to a War*, London: Faber & Faber, p. 68.
13 Ilona Ralf Sues (1944) *Shark's Fins and Millet*, New York: Garden City Publishing, p. 151.
14 An American-based publication and not to be confused with the later English language *China Today* magazine issued by the Chinese government in the 1950s as overseas propaganda.
15 White and Jacoby, *Thunder Out of China*, p. 213.
16 Freda Utley (1951) *The China Story*, Chicago: Henry Regnery Company, p. 143.
17 ——, p. 144.
18 Jonathan Mirsky, "Getting the story in China: American reporters since 1972", *Harvard Asia Quarterly*, vol. VI, no.1, Winter 2002.

Chapter 11 Interregnum — End of a War, Start of a Revolution

1. Jack Belden (1949) *China Shakes the World*, London: Pelican, p. 19.
2. Roy Rowan (2004) *Chasing the Dragon*, CA: Lyon Press, p. 86.
3. ———, p. 86.
4. ———, p. 94.
5. Excerpt from a speech by John Roderick to the Hong Kong Foreign Correspondents' Club, *The Correspondent*, April–May 2002.
6. "China incident", *Time*, 21 April 1947.
7. Belden, *China Shakes the World*, p. 36.
8. Rodney Gilbert, "Dangerous thoughts: Feathers from the right wing", *The Nation*, vol. 170, issue 24, 17 June 1950.
9. Bruce Lambert, "Haldore Hanson, 80, Chronicler of China and victim of McCarthy", *New York Times*, 5 October 1992.
10. John Maxwell Hamilton, "The Missouri news monopoly and American altruism in China: Thomas F. F. Millard, J. B. Powell, and Edgar Snow", *The Pacific Historical Review*, vol. 55, no. 1, February 1986.
11. Robert Speer, "Dirty secrets", *San Francisco Bay Guardian*, 27 June 2006.
12. David Lancashire, "China's goal to equal the industrial power of the United States", *AP*, 15 December, 1956.
13. Jacques Marcuse (1967) *The Peking Papers: Leaves From the Notebook of a China Correspondent*, London: Arthur Barker.

Bibliography

Old China Press Corps Books

Abend, H. E. (1930) *Tortured China*, New York: Ives Washburn.
—— (1943) *My Life in China, 1926–1941*, New York: Harcourt, Brace & Co.
Alcott, C. (1943) *My War With Japan*, New York: Henry Holt & Co.
Auden W. H. and Isherwood, C. (1938) *Journey to a War*, London: Faber & Faber.
Balfour, F. H. (1887) *Leaves from my Chinese Scrap Book*, London: Trubner.
Belden, J. (1943) *Retreat with Stillwell*, New York: Alfred A. Knopf.
—— (1949) *China Shakes The World*, New York: Harper Bros.
Bennett, M. (1993) *On Her Own: Journalistic Adventures from San Francisco to the Chinese Revolution, 1917–1927*, Armonk, New York: M. E. Sharpe.
Bertram, J. M. (1937) *Crisis in China*, London: Macmillan.
—— (1939) *Unconquered: Journal of a Year's Adventures Among the Fighting Peasants of North China*, New York: John Day.
Birns, J. (2003) Assignment Shanghai, Berkeley: University of California Press.
Bland, J. O. P. (1921) *China, Japan and Korea*, London: Heinemann.
Bland, J. O. P. and Backhouse, E. (1910) *China Under the Empress Dowager*, London: Heineman.
Booker, E. L. (1940) *News is My Job*, New York: Macmillan.
Bosshard, W. (1938) *Kuhles Grasland Mongolei*, Berlin: Deutscher Verlag.
Carlson, E. (1940) *Twin Stars of China*, New York: Dodd, Mead & Company.
Chen, P. (1979) *China Called Me: My Life Inside the Chinese Revolution*, Boston: Little, Brown & Co.
Chesterton, A. E. (1933) *Young China and New Japan*, Philadelphia: J. B. Lippincott.
Clark, G. (1932) *Economic Rivalries in China*, New Haven: Yale University Press.
—— (1935) *The Great Wall Crumbles*, New York: Macmillan.
—— (1936) *A Place in the Sun*, New York: Macmillan.
Close, U. (Josef Washington Hall) (1924) *In the Land of the Laughing Buddha: The Adventures of an American Barbarian in China*, New York: G. P. Putnam's & Sons.
—— (1927) *The Revolt of Asia: The End of the White Man's World-Dominance*, New York: G. P. Putnam's & Sons.
Cooke, G. W. (1861) *China and Lower Bengal*, London: Routledge, Warne, and Routledge.
Creelman, J. (1901) *On the Great Highway*, New York: Lothrop.
Crow, C. (1913) *The Travelers' Handbook for China*, Shanghai: Hwa-Mei Book Concern.
—— (1937) *Four Hundred Million Customers*, New York: Harper & Brothers.

_____ (1937) *I Speak for the Chinese*, New York: Harper & Brothers.
_____ (1938) *The Chinese Are Like That*, New York: Harper & Brothers.
_____ (1940) *Foreign Devils in the Flowery Kingdom*, New York: Harper & Brothers.
_____ (1940) *Master Kung: The Story of Confucius*, New York: Harper & Brothers.
_____ (1942) *Japan's Dream of World Empire: The Tanaka Memorial*, New York: Harper & Brothers.
_____ (1944) *China Takes Her Place*, New York: Harper & Brothers.
Denby, J. (1910) *Letters of a Shanghai Griffin*, Shanghai: Kelly and Walsh.
Dew, G. (1943) *Prisoner of the Japs*, New York: A. A. Knopf.
Dingle, E. (1911) *Across China on Foot*, Edwin Dingle, Bristol: J. W. Arrowsmith.
_____ (1912) *China's Revolution, 1911–1912*, London: T. F. Unwin.
Dorn, F. (1970) The Forbidden City: The Biography of a Palace, New York: Charles Scribner's & Sons.
_____ (1974) *The Sino-Japanese War, 1937-41*, New York: Macmillan.
Downing, T. (1838) *The Fan-Qui in China in 1836–7*, London: Henry Colburn.
Durdin, P. (1959) *Mao's China*, New York: Foreign Policy Association.
Epstein, I. (1939) *The People's War*, London: Gollancz.
_____ (1947) *The Unfinished Revolution*, Boston, Little, Brown & Co.
Eskelund, K. (1946) *My Chinese Wife*, New York: Garden City Publishing Co.
_____ (1961) *The Red Mandarins*, New York: Taplinger.
Etherton, P. T. and Hessell Tiltman, H. (1932) *Manchuria: The Cockpit Of Asia*, London: Jarrolds.
Farmer, R. (1945) *Shanghai Harvest*, London: Museum Press.
Fleming, P. (1933) *One's Company: A Journey to China in 1933*, London: Penguin.
_____ (1936) *News From Tartary*, London: Jonathan Cape.
_____ (1959) *The Siege at Peking*, London: Rupert Hart-Davis.
Forman, H. (1945) *Report From Red China*, New York: Henry Holt.
_____ (1948) *Changing China*, New York: Crown Publishers.
Gayn, M. J. (1944) *Journey From the East: An Autobiography*, New York: Alfred A. Knopf.
Gellhorn, M. (1979) *Travels with Myself and Another*, New York: Dodd, Mead.
Gilbert, R. (1926) *What's Wrong with China,* London: John Murray.
_____ (1929) The Unequal Treaties: China and the Foreigner, London: John Murray.
Gilman, L. (1954) *The Dragon's Mouth*, New York: William Sloane Associates.
Gould, R. (1946) *China in the Sun*, Garden City: Doubleday.
Green, O. M. (1945) *The Story of China's Revolution*, London: Hutchinson.
Gunther, J. (1939) *Inside Asia*, New York: Harper & Brothers.
Hahn, E. (1941) *The Soong Sisters*, New York: Garden City Publishing.
_____ (1944) *China to Me*, New York: Doubleday, Doran & Co.
_____ (1963) *China Only Yesterday, 1850–1950: A Century of Change*, Garden City: Doubleday.
_____ (2000) *No Hurry to Get Home*, Emeryville, California: Seal Press.
Hanson, H. (1939) *Humane Endeavor: The Story Of The China War*, New York: Farrar & Rinehart.
Hauser, E. O. (1940) *Shanghai: City for Sale*, New York: Harcourt, Brace & Co.

Hersey, J. (1985) *The Call*, New York: Alfred A. Knopf.
Hogg, G. (1944) *I See a New China*, New York: Boston, Little, Brown & Co.
Hyde, R. (1939) *Dragon Rampant*, London: Hurst & Blackett.
Isaacs, H. R. (1932) *Five Years of Kuomintang Reaction*, Shanghai: China Forum.
_____ (1938) *The Tragedy of the Chinese Revolution*, London: Secker and Warburg.
_____ (1985) *Re-Encounters in China*, Armonk, New York: M. E. Sharpe.
Kuhn, I. (1938) *Assigned to Adventure*, Philadelphia: J. B. Lippincott & Co.
Lattimore, O. (1943) *America and Asia: Problems of Today's War and the Peace of Tomorrow*, California: Claremount Colleges.
_____ (1990) *China Memoirs: Chiang Kai-Shek and the War Against Japan*, Tokyo: University of Tokyo Press.
Lowe, C. H. (1984) *Facing Adversities With a Smile*, San Francisco: Chinese Materials Center Publications.
McCormick, E. (1923) *The Unexpurgated Diary of a Shanghai Baby*, Shanghai: Chinese American Publishing Co.
McCormick, F. (1913) *The Flowery Republic*, London: John Murray.
MacLellan, J. W. (1889) *The Story of Shanghai: From the Opening of the Port to Foreign Trade*, Shanghai: *North China Herald*.
Maillart, E. (1940) *Forbidden Journey: From Peking to Kashmir*, London: Heinemann.
Marcuse, J. (1968) *The Peking Papers: Leaves from the Notebook of a China Correspondent*, London: Arthur Barker.
Medhurst, W. H. (1872) *The Foreigner in Far Cathay*, London: E. Stanford.
Mennie, D. and Putnam Weale, B. L. (1922), *The Pageant of Peking, Shanghai*, Peking: A. S. Watson & Co.
Millard, T. F. (1919) *Democracy and the Eastern Question*, New York: The Century Company.
_____ (1931) *The End of Exterritoriality in China*, Shanghai: The ABC Press.
Misselwitz, H. F. (1941) *The Dragon Stirs: An Intimate Sketch-book of China's Kuomintang Revolution, 1927–29*, New York: Harbinger House.
Montalto de Jesus, C. A. (1909) *Historic Shanghai*, Shanghai: *Shanghai Mercury*.
Moorad, G. (1949) *Lost Peace in China*, New York: Dutton.
Morrison, G. E. (1895) *An Australian In China*, London: H. Cox.
Morrison, I. (1943) *The War Against Japan*, London: Faber and Faber.
Mossman, S. (1867) *China. A Brief Account of the Country, Its Inhabitants, and Their Institutions*, London: Society for Promoting Christian Knowledge.
Mydans, C. (1959) *More Than Meets the Eye*, New York: Harper.
Nichols, F. (1902) *Through Hidden Shensi*, New York: Charles Scribner's & Sons.
Pennell, W.V. (1974) *A Lifetime With the Chinese*, Hong Kong: South China Morning Post Publications.
Peyton-Griffin, R. T. and Sapajou (1938) *Shanghai's Schemozzle*, Shanghai: *North-China Daily News*.
Powell, J. B. (1945) *My Twenty Five Years in China*, New York: Macmillan.
Putnam-Weale, B. L. (1907) *Indiscreet Letters From Peking*, New York: Dodd, Mead & Co.
_____ (1917) *The Fight for the Republic in China*, New York: Dodd, Mead & Co.

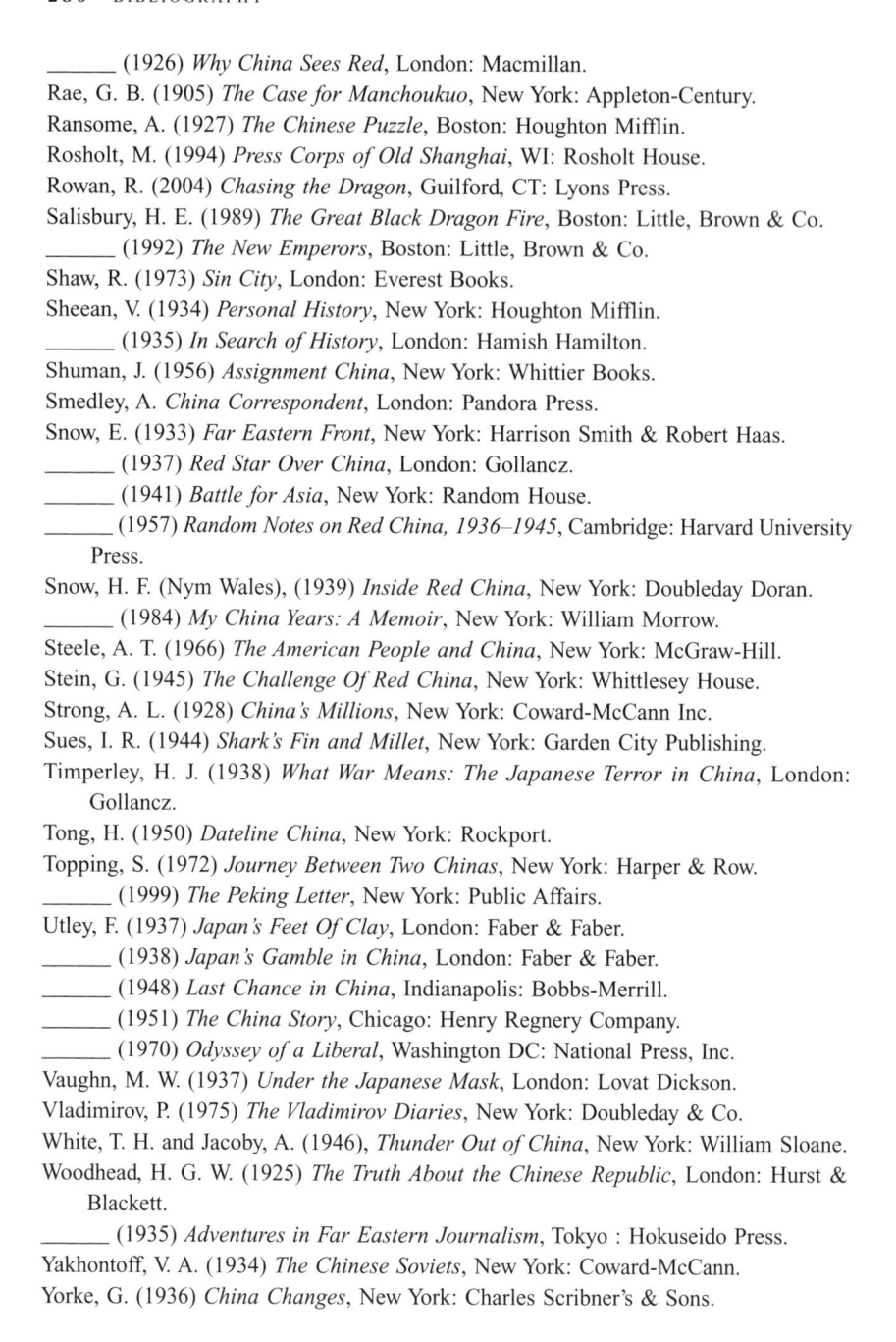

_____ (1926) *Why China Sees Red*, London: Macmillan.
Rae, G. B. (1905) *The Case for Manchoukuo*, New York: Appleton-Century.
Ransome, A. (1927) *The Chinese Puzzle*, Boston: Houghton Mifflin.
Rosholt, M. (1994) *Press Corps of Old Shanghai*, WI: Rosholt House.
Rowan, R. (2004) *Chasing the Dragon*, Guilford, CT: Lyons Press.
Salisbury, H. E. (1989) *The Great Black Dragon Fire*, Boston: Little, Brown & Co.
_____ (1992) *The New Emperors*, Boston: Little, Brown & Co.
Shaw, R. (1973) *Sin City*, London: Everest Books.
Sheean, V. (1934) *Personal History*, New York: Houghton Mifflin.
_____ (1935) *In Search of History*, London: Hamish Hamilton.
Shuman, J. (1956) *Assignment China*, New York: Whittier Books.
Smedley, A. *China Correspondent*, London: Pandora Press.
Snow, E. (1933) *Far Eastern Front*, New York: Harrison Smith & Robert Haas.
_____ (1937) *Red Star Over China*, London: Gollancz.
_____ (1941) *Battle for Asia*, New York: Random House.
_____ (1957) *Random Notes on Red China, 1936–1945*, Cambridge: Harvard University Press.
Snow, H. F. (Nym Wales), (1939) *Inside Red China*, New York: Doubleday Doran.
_____ (1984) *My China Years: A Memoir*, New York: William Morrow.
Steele, A. T. (1966) *The American People and China*, New York: McGraw-Hill.
Stein, G. (1945) *The Challenge Of Red China*, New York: Whittlesey House.
Strong, A. L. (1928) *China's Millions*, New York: Coward-McCann Inc.
Sues, I. R. (1944) *Shark's Fin and Millet*, New York: Garden City Publishing.
Timperley, H. J. (1938) *What War Means: The Japanese Terror in China*, London: Gollancz.
Tong, H. (1950) *Dateline China*, New York: Rockport.
Topping, S. (1972) *Journey Between Two Chinas*, New York: Harper & Row.
_____ (1999) *The Peking Letter*, New York: Public Affairs.
Utley, F. (1937) *Japan's Feet Of Clay*, London: Faber & Faber.
_____ (1938) *Japan's Gamble in China*, London: Faber & Faber.
_____ (1948) *Last Chance in China*, Indianapolis: Bobbs-Merrill.
_____ (1951) *The China Story*, Chicago: Henry Regnery Company.
_____ (1970) *Odyssey of a Liberal*, Washington DC: National Press, Inc.
Vaughn, M. W. (1937) *Under the Japanese Mask*, London: Lovat Dickson.
Vladimirov, P. (1975) *The Vladimirov Diaries*, New York: Doubleday & Co.
White, T. H. and Jacoby, A. (1946), *Thunder Out of China*, New York: William Sloane.
Woodhead, H. G. W. (1925) *The Truth About the Chinese Republic*, London: Hurst & Blackett.
_____ (1935) *Adventures in Far Eastern Journalism*, Tokyo : Hokuseido Press.
Yakhontoff, V. A. (1934) *The Chinese Soviets*, New York: Coward-McCann.
Yorke, G. (1936) *China Changes*, New York: Charles Scribner's & Sons.

Others

Bard, S. (2003) *Voices from the Past: Hong Kong 1842–1918*, Hong Kong: Hong Kong University Press.
Bernard, T. S. (1996) *Season of High Adventure: Edgar Snow in China*, Berkeley: University of California Press.
Brady, A. M. (2002) *Friend of China: The Myth of Rewi Alley*, London: RoutledgeCurzon.
Clarke, P. and King, F. H. H. (1965) *A Research Guide to China-Coast Newspapers, 1822–1911*, Cambridge: Harvard East Asian Research Center.
Clifford, N. J. (2001) *A Truthful Impression of the Country: British and American Travel Writing in China, 1880-1949*, Detroit: University of Michigan Press.
Cuthbertson, K. (1999) *Nobody Said Not to Go: The Life, Loves, and Adventures of Emily Hahn*, New York: Faber & Faber.
Farnsworth, R. M. (1996) *From Vagabond to Journalist: Edgar Snow in Asia, 1928–41*, St Louis: University of Missouri Press.
French, P. (2006) *Carl Crow — A Tough Old China Hand: The Life, Times, and Adventures of an American in Shanghai*, Hong Kong: University of Hong Kong Press.
Hamilton, J. M. (1988) *Edgar Snow: A Biography*, Bloomington, IN: Indiana University Press.
Hart-Davis, D. (1974) *Peter Fleming: A Biography*, London: Jonathan Cape.
Hirson, B. (2004) *Frank Glass: the Restless Revolutionary*, London: Porcupine Press.
Kerr, D. and Kuehn, J. (2007) *A Century of Travels in China: Critical Essays on Travel Writing from the 1840s to the 1940s*, Hong Kong: Hong Kong University Press.
Klehr, H. and Radosh, R. (1996) *The Amerasia Spy Case: Prelude to McCarthyism*, Chapel Hill, NC: University of North Carolina Press.
Lazich, M. (2000) *E. C. Bridgman (1801–1861), America's First Missionary to China*, Lewiston, NY: Edwin Mellen Press.
Lo Hui-min. (1976) *The Correspondence of G. E. Morrison* (2 vols), Cambridge: Cambridge Univesity Press.
Hirson, B. and Knodel, A. J. (2007) *Reporting the Chinese Revolution — The Letters of Rayna Prohme*, London: Pluto Press.
Long, K. A. (2007) *Helen Foster Snow: An American Woman in Revolutionary China*, Colorado: University Press of Colorado.
Lu, S. (2004) *They Were in Nanjing: The Nanjing Massacre Witnessed by American and British Nationals*, Hong Kong: Hong Kong University Press.
MacKinnon, J. R. and MacKinnon, S. R. (1988) *Agnes Smedley: The Life and Times of an American Radical*, Berkeley: University of California Press.
MacManus, J. (2008) *Ocean Devil: the Life and Legend of George Hogg*, London: Harper Perennial.
Moreira, P. (2006) *Hemingway on the China Front*, Dulles, VA: Potomac Books.
Price, R. (2005) *The Lives of Agnes Smedley*, Oxford: Oxford University Press.
Rand, D. (1995) *China Hands*, New York: Simon & Schuster.
Rawlinson, J. (1990) *The Recorder and China's Revolution: A Topical Biography of Frank Joseph Rawlinson, 1871-1937*, Notre Dame, IN: Cross Cultural Publications.

Selle, E. A. (1948) *Donald of China*, New York: Harper & Brothers.
Strong, T. B. and Keyssar, H. (1983) *Right in Her Soul: The Life of Anna Louise Strong*, New York: Random House.
Thompson, P. A. and Macklin, R. (2004) *The Man Who Died Twice: The Life and Adventures of Morrison of Peking*, London: Allen & Unwin.
Trevor-Roper, H. (1976) *Hermit of Peking: The Hidden Life of Sir Edmund Backhouse*, New York: Knopf.
Winchester, S. (2008) *Bomb, Book and Compass: Joseph Needham and the Great Secrets of China*, London: Viking.

Appendix

Chinese Provinces

Then	*Now*	*Then*	*Now*
Anhwei	Anhui	Kiangsu	Jiangsu
Chekiang	Zhejiang	Kirin	Jilin
Fengtiang	Liaoning	Kwangsi	Guangxi
Formosa	Taiwan	Kwangtung	Guangdong
Fukien	Fujian	Shansi	Shanxi
Honan	Henan	Shantung	Shandong
Hopei	Hebei	Shanshi	Shanxi
Hupei	Hubei	Shensi	Shaanxi
Kansu	Gansu	Sinkiang	Xinjiang
Kiangsi	Jiangxi	Szechuen	Sichuan

Chinese Cities and Towns

Then	*Now*	*Then*	*Now*
Amoy	Xiamen	Ningpo	Ningbo
Anking	Hefei	Pakhoi	Beihai
Canton	Guangzhou	Peitaiho	Beidaihe
Chefoo	Yantai	Peking (Peiping)	Beijing
Chengchow	Zhengzhou	Port Arthur	Lushan
Chengtu	Chengdu	Port Edward	Weihaiwei
Chinkiang	Zhenjiang	Saianfu	Xiangyang
Chungking	Chongqing	Shasi	Jinsha
Dairen	Manchuli	Sian (Sianfu)	Xian
Foochow	Fuzhou	Soochow (Hsuchow)	Suzhou
Hangchow	Hangzhou	Swatow	Shantou
Hankow	Hankou	Tientsin	Tianjin
Kalgan	Zhangjiakou	Tsinan	Jinan
Kiukiang	Jiujiang	Tsingtao	Qingdao
Mukden	Shenyang	Yunnanfu	Kunming
Nanking	Nanjing	Wenchow	Wenzhou
Newchwang	Yingkou	Wusih	Wuxi

Index

* = Brackets indicate country of publication

Abels, Lily, 211
Abelha da China (Macau), 34
Abend, Hallett, arrival in China, 126; in Guangzhou, 130; appointed *New York Times,* 138–139; targeted by government, 139–140; employed by *Peking Leader*, 167; employed by *Shanghai Times,* 170; in Manchuria, 174; on Chiang Kai-shek kidnapping, 181; assistants, 195–196; 197; clashes with Japanese, 197, 200; in Nanjing, 202; on *USS Panay* incident, 206
Ackerman, Fred, 103
Adachi Kazuo, 204
Adamson, Sydney, 71
Addis, Charles Stewart, 111
Agence France-Press (AFP), 196, 260, 267, 268
Alcott, Carroll, 129; arrival in Shanghai, 155; the star of XHMA, 188–189; targeted by Japanese, 199–200
Alexander, William, 48
Alley, Norman, 191, 206
Alley, Rewi, 182, 197, 219, 225–226, 251, 268
Allman, Norman, 224, 249
Alsop, Joseph, 234
Altes und Neues aus Asiens drei Kaiserreichen (China), 83
Amerasia (USA), 243–244, 264–265
American Banker (USA), 231
American Board of Commissioners for Foreign Missions, 24

American Church Mission, 137
American Episcopal Church Mission, 53
American Socialist Party, 209
Amfiteatrov, Aleksandr, 80
Anderson, Roy, 120, 122–123
Anglo-Chinese College, 26
Anti-Opium Information Bureau, 150, 152
Arnold, Julean, 103
Artemieff, Colonel, 92
Asai Tatsuzo, 204
Asahi Shimbun (Japan), 203, 205
Ashmead-Bartlett, Ellis, 91
Asia (USA), 82, 138
Assembly Times (China), 223
Associated Press (AP), 66, 114, 126, 138, 174, 199, 200, 203, 212, 250, 258, 261, 265, 267–268
Atkinson, Brooks, 232–233, 243, 244, 252
The Atlantic (USA), 147, 245
Auden, Wystan Hugh "WH", 215–219
A Aurora Macaense (Macau), 34
Australian Broadcasting Corporation (ABC), 250
Aw Boon Haw, 159

Babb, Glenn, 174
Babylon of Babylon (China), 123
Backhouse, Sir Edmund, 75; partnership with JOP Bland, 77–78; working with GE Morrison, 78
Bailie, Joseph, 251
Bain, George Murray, 35–36
Balfour, Frederick, 54, 57, 59

Baltimore Sun (USA), 133–134
Bangkok World (Thailand), 252
Barbosa, Major Paulino da Silva, 33–34
Baring, Maurice, 91
Barnes, Joseph, 245
Barrow, Graham, 230
Barzini, Luigi (Jr.), 206, 211
Barzini, Luigi (Sr.), 79
Bass, Gertrude, 89
Bass, John Foster, 89
Bass, Robert, 89
Beato & Co., 48, 49
Beato, Antoine, 48
Beato, Felice (Felix), 45, 48–50
Beech, Keyes, 259
Belden, Jack, 213, 233, 243, 246, 253, 255
Bell, Moberley, 70, 72–74
Benckendorff, Count Alexander, 91
Bennett, Milly, 131
Bennett, Roy, 127
Berlin am Morgan (Germany), 176
Berliner Illustrierte Zeitung (Germany), 175
Berliner Tageblatt (Germany), 176, 180–181
Berrigan, Darrell, 252
Bertram, James, 182, 243
Billingham, Anthony, 196
Bingham, Senator Hiram, 138
Biograph Company, 190
Birns, Jack, 256–257
Birth Control Review (USA), 210
Black, John Reddie, 59–60
Black Star Agency, 211
Blakeney, Louise, 148
Bland, John Otway Percy "JOP", early career, 75–76; relationship with GE Morrison, 76–77; partnership with Edmund Backhouse, 77–78; arguments with Morrison, 78–79; *Verse and Worse*, 88; chairman of the SMC, 115; 139
Bloomfield, Debbie, 266
Boletim Official do Governo de Macau (Macau), 34

Booker, Edna Lee, 147–148, 177
Boone Review (China), 137
Borghese, Prince Scipione, 79
Borodin, Mikhail, 129–130, 132
Bosshard, Walter, 175, 191, 211, 214
Boston Evening Transcript (USA), 232
Boston Globe (USA), 229, 231
Boston Herald (USA), 231
Bowker, John, 53
Bowlby, Thomas, 45–47
Bowra, Maurice, 211
Bowring, Sir John, 43–44, 54
Boxer, Carolla, 154–155
Boxer, Charles, 154–155, 182, 237
Boxer, Ursula, 154
Bredon, Boyd, 76
Bridgman, Elijah Coleman, 22, 23–25, 30, 41
Bridgman, James Granger, 24–25
Brigade–Zeitung (China), 83
British North Borneo Company, 55
British Residents' Association (Shanghai), 201, 221
British Topical Film Company, 191
Brooklyn Eagle (USA), 65
Browder, Earl, 264
Bruce, Frederick, 51
Bruce, George, 221
Bruce, Lord James (see Elgin, Lord)
Buchman, Alexander, 156, 199, 203, 265–266
Buck, Pearl S, 78
Buckle, George Earl, 73
Bundeszeitung der Brith Noah Zioni (China), 219
de Bunsen, Maurice, 74
Burgevine, Henry, 56, 62
Burleigh, Bennet, 91
Burlingame, Anson, 50–51
Burton, Wilbur, 131, 157–158
Butler, Lady Elizabeth, 47

The Calcutta Englishman (India), 56
Caldwell, John, 242

Call of Ukraine (see *Ukrains'ky I Holos Dalekomu Skhodi*)
Camp Chit Chat (China), 223
Canton Chronicle (China), 85
Canton Courier (China), 16–22
Canton Daily News (China), 85
Canton Gazette (China), 131
Canton Mission Press, 24, 25
Canton Press (China), 16–22, 30, 31–32, 37, 206
Canton Miscellany (China), 19
Canton Register (China), 16–22, 30, 31–33, 37
Canton Times (China), 114
Capa, Robert, 217
Capra, Frank, 192
Carlson, Evans, 225–226, 244
Carol Broadcasting Station, 186
Carol Corporation, 186
Catholic News Service, 245
Celestial Empire (China), 57, 59
Central China Post (China), 114
Central News Agency (China), 145, 150, 212, 215, 243, 260
Central News Agency (UK), 86
Chaicheck, Max, 170, 199
Chambers, Whittaker, 229–230, 232
Champly, OH, 176
Chancellor, Christopher, 126, 177
Chang, Kuo-sin "KS", 159, 199, 260
Chang, Samuel, 158, 199
Chao, Thomas, 239
Charles Urban Trading Company, 94
Chase, Milton (see Chaicheck, Max)
Chater, Paul, 84
Chaverim News (China), 219
Chefoo Daily News (China), 101
Chen Duxiu, 169
Chen, Eugene, 130–131, 135–137
Chen Jiongming, 124
Cheng, Hawthorne, 159–160
Cheng Kung-po, 240
Chennault, Claire Lee, 215, 233–234, 246
Chesterton, Ada, 143

Chiang Kai-shek, interview with Peter Fleming, 144; clash with Bill Donald over opium, 151; and Emily Hahn, 152–153; kidnapping of, 181–183; interview with Hemingway and Gellhorn, 236; interviews in Taiwan, 263–264
Chiang Kai-shek, Madame, introduction to Bill Donald and experiences together, 95–96; interview with Peter Fleming, 144; tea with Auden and Isherwood, 217; interview with Gwen Dew, 224; Henry Luce's infatuation with, 232; interview with Hemingway and Gellhorn, 236; attitude to foreign press, 239; argument with Bill Donald and split, 250
Chiang Kang-li, 240
Chicago Daily News (USA), 129, 132, 172, 176, 178, 202, 214, 221, 252, 259
Chicago Tribune (USA), 135, 140, 174
China Association, 57
China and Far East Finance and Commerce (China), 96
China at War (China), 241
China Christian Advocate (China), 114–115
China Christian Conference Bulletin (China), 115
China Courier (China), 131
China Critic (China), 138, 141
China Daily (China), 85, 267
China Daily Tribune (China), 219–220
China Defence League Newsletter (Hong Kong), 226
China-Dienst (China), 185
China Forum (China), 168–169
China Imperial Maritime Customs Service, 56, 76, 82, 88, 128, 211
China Inland Mission (CIM), 40
China Journal of Science and Arts (China), 116–118, 149, 162, 167, 251
China Mail (Hong Kong), 29, 34, 35–36, 62, 63, 84, 94, 100

China Mission of the Methodist Episcopal Church for South Shanghai, 114
China Monthly Magazine (Malacca), 23
China Press (China), establishment of, 102–103; design and aims, 106; "girl reporters", 147–149; freelancers and editors, 155–161; in Manchuria, 173; on First Shanghai War, 176; Gareth Jones on assignment for, 180–181; bought by Edward Ezra, 184; radio station, 186–187; bombed, 199; in Hankou, 210, 212; edited and published by Norman Allman, 249
China Review (UK), 57
China Weekly Review (China), establishment of, 103; "women's interest" page, 148; 159; freelancers, 168; employed Edgar Snow, 178; "War Edition", 198–199; Agnes Smedley employed, 210; employs Evans Carlson, 225; reestablishment of after the Second World War, 266
China Today (USA), 243
China Who's Who (China), 171
Chinese and General Missionary Gleaner (UK), 40
Chinese Drama Research Society, 141
Chinese Evangelization Society, 40
Chinese Industrial Cooperative Movement (INDUSCO), 225–226
Chinese Public Opinion (China), 100, 112
Chinese Recorder and Missionary Journal (China), 114, 120, 127, 196
Chinese Repository (China), 19, 23–28, 30, 31–32, 37, 41
Chinese Students Monthly (USA), 137
Chinese Times (China), 111
Chinese Union, 27
Ching, Henry, 254
Chinnery, George, 21
Chirol, Valentine, 73–74, 79
Chisholm, Don, 201–202
Christian Broadcasting Station, 187, 211
Christian Herald (USA), 100
Christian Literature Society of Shanghai, 187, 211
Christian Science Monitor (USA), 177, 244
Chung Kung Pao (China), 230
Chungking Central Daily News (China), 236
Chungking National Herald (China), 241
Chungking Reporter (China), 241
Chuo Koron (Japan), 204
Church and State (USA), 65
Ci Xi, Empress Dowager, 51, 75, 77
Civil and Military Gazette (India), 139
Clark, Grover, 167–168
Clark, JD, 59–60
Clarke, Prescott, 61
Clarke-Kerr, Sir Archibald, 219
Cloake, Richard, 224
Close, Upton (see Hall, Joseph)
Cohen, Morris 'Two Gun', 135, 235
Colledge, Dr Thomas, 30–31
Collier's (USA), on Russo-Japanese War, 89–90; on *USS Panay* incident, 205; on imprisonment of Americans in Shanghai by Japanese, 221; employed Martha Gellhorn, 234–238; McCarthyism, 265
Collis, Maurice, 22, 31, 32
Columbia-Missouri Herald (USA), 105
Columbia University Journalism School
Committee for a Democratic Far Eastern Policy, 226
The Commonwealth (China), 59
Communist League of China, 134
Communist Party of Great Britain (CPGB), 208
Communist Party of the United States of America (CPUSA), 210, 229, 264
Compton, Charles Spencer, 51, 55–56
Cooke, George Wingrove, 45
Cordier, Henri, 70
Corriere d'America (USA), 79
Corriere della Sera (Italy), 79
Cosmopolitan (USA), 65

Courier d'Haiphong (Vietnam), 35
Le Courrier de Changhai, (China) 60
Cox, James, 177, 200
Crane, George (see Krainukov, George)
Creelman, James, 65, 72
Cromley, Raymond, 242, 247
Crow, Carl, hired by *China Press,* 103; establishes UPI in China, 104; early career, 105; as director of Chinese newspapers, 127; office romance, 149; night shift on the *China Press,* 155; sensitive stories, 159–160; Carl Crow Inc., 161; report for the State Department, 171; on Jiangxi Soviet, 178; on Chiang Kai-shek kidnapping, 181; on Black Saturday, 195–196; leaves Shanghai, 198; in Chongqing, 228; Burma Road, 234
Crozier, WP, 203
Cumine, Eric, 124, 223
Cunningham, Arthur, 65, 84–85
Cushing, Caleb, 24
The Cycle (China), 53

Dai Li, 242, 244
Dailey, Charles, 135, 140
Daily Advertiser (Hong Kong), 34
Daily Express (UK), 137, 197
Daily Herald (UK), 197, 211
Daily Mail (UK), 68–71, 147, 201
Daily News (UK), 134–135
Dal'nevostochnoe Vremia (China), 186
Daily Telegraph (UK), 79, 82, 91, 197
Daily Worker (USA), 170
Daniel, Elbert Clifton, 202, 239
Das Volk (Germany), 44
Davis, Robert, 223
Deen, Victor, 176
Ha Dagel (China), 186
Delane, John, 46
Democracy (China), 169, 207
Denby, Jay, 80–81
Dent and Company, 18, 53
Dent, Lancelot, 18

Denver Post (USA), 188
Derbyshire Times (UK), 254
Destrées, 169
Detroit News (USA), 224
Deutsch-Asiatische Warte (China), 83
Deutsche China Post (China), 183
Deutsch-Mandschurische Nachrichten (China), 183
Deutsch-Chinesische Nachrichten (China), 183
Deutsches Nachrichtenburo (DNB), 180, 183
Deutscher Nachrichtendienst fr Ostasien (China), 83
Deutscher Ostasien-Bote (China), 183
Deutsche Shanghai Zeitung (China), 183–184
Deutsche Zeitung fr China (China), 109
Dew, Gwen, 224
Die Reform (Germany), 44
Diemer, Christine, 177
Dingle, Edwin, 96–97, 107
Disraeli, Benjamin, 29
Dockray, ST, 125
Domei News Agency, 201, 204, 205, 220; Motion Picture Department, 204
Donald, William Henry, career and early life, 94–96; 1911 revolution, 108; editor of *Far Eastern Review,* 120–121, 171; on opium, 151; in Hankou, 213; control of foreign journalists, 239–241; departure from China and death, 250–251
Dorland, Willett 222
Downing, Dr Twogood, 26
Doyle, J Edward, 147–148
Doyle, Robert, 257
Du, Yue-Sheng, 151–152, 166, 187, 217
Dublin University Magazine (Ireland), 36
Duncan, Chesney, 36, 85
Dundee Advertiser (UK), 103
Duranty, Walter, 180
Durdin, Peggy, 215, 229, 243, 263

Durdin, Tillman, 156, 158, 183; in Nanjing, 202; in Hankou, 213; relocation to Chongqing, 215; in Chongqing, 227, 229, 239, 243, 245; in Taiwan, 263–264

East Asia Central Conference of the Methodist Episcopal Church, 114
East-West Monthly Examiner (China), 24, 27–28
Eastern Sketch (China), 81
Echo Szanghajskie (China), 186, 252
L'Echo de Chine (China), 61, 101
L'Echo de Shanghai (China), 61
L'Echo de Tientsin (China), 101
Eckardt, Theo, 185
Egeberg, Jan, 200
Ekins HR, 177, 197
Elgin, Lord, 43, 45–47
Elliot, Captain Charles, 32
Elliston, HB, 121
Engels, Frederick, 44–45
Epstein, Israel, employed at the *Peking and Tientsin Times,* 113; employed at the *China Press,* 169–170; in Hankou, 211, 215; in Chongqing, 233; visiting Yenan, 243; books reviewed, 246
Eskelund, Karl, 233
Etherton, Colonel PT, 173
Evening Express (China), 53
Evening Telegram (USA), 65
Evreiskoe slovo (China), 140
Ezra, Edward, 115, 184

Fairbank, John K, 246
Far East (Japan), 49, 60
Far Eastern Economic Review (China), 96
Far Eastern Review (Philippines/China), 171
Far Eastern Times syndicate, 82, 207
Farmer, Buzz, 213
Farnsworth, Clyde, 261–262, 263
Feng Yuxiang, 167
Ferguson, Dr John Calvin, 117, 127

Der ferne Osten (China), 83
Le Figaro (France), 93
Fink, Carl, 83
Fisher, Francis McCracken, 211–212
Fisher, William, 157
Fleisher, Benjamin, 106
Fleming, Ian, 144
Fleming, Peter, on the Boxer rebellion, 69, 82; *One's Company,* 144–145; travels with Ella Maillart, 145–147; with Auden and Isherwood, 217–218; return to China in 1946, 258
Floyd, William Pryor, 50
Ford, MC, 221
Foreign Correspondents' Club (Chongqing), 245, 261
Foreign Correspondents' Club (Hong Kong), 261–262
Foreign Correspondents' Club (Nanjing), 245, 261
Foreign Correspondents' Club (Shanghai), 196, 252, 256, 261
Foreign Correspondents' Club (Tokyo), 173
Forman, Harrison, 191–192, 197, 230, 243, 246
Fort-Worth Star Telegram (USA), 103
Forum (China)
Fox, Dr Charles James, 207
Fox, Mike, 177, 223–224
Fox Movietone, 190, 191, 206
Francis, JJ, 36
Frank, Ladislaus, 185
Frankfurter Zeitung (Germany), 176, 184, 210
Fraser, David, 125–126
Fraser-Smith, Robert, 34–36
Free Press (USA), 44
Freemasons, 57
Friend of China (Hong Kong), 34, 36, 53

Gannes, Harry, 170
Gardiner, Dr. William, 222
Gayn, Mark, 265

Gazeta de Macao (Macau), 34
Die Gelbe Post (China), 184–185, 219
Gellhorn, Martha, 234–238
Gemeindeblatt für die Jüdisches Kultus-Gemeinde (see *Jewish Voice*)
German Resident Association (*Deutsche Gemeinde*), 220
Gibbons, Floyd, 174, 193
Gibson, Charles Dana, 90
Giffen, George, 224, 254
Gilbert, Rodney, 120–121, 124, 139, 263
Giles, HA, 57
Gillis, Fay, 175
Gilman, La Selle, 157
Gimson, Franklin, 253
Givens, Patrick, 169
Gladstone, William, 43
Glass, Frank, 134, 156, 169
Goette, John, 233
Goldman, Reg, 224
Gordon, Charles George, 62
Goto Kosaku, 205
Gould, Randall, 157, 167, 177, 196, 197, 199, 200, 249–250, 263
Gracie, John Kenneth, 201
The Graphic (UK), 45, 47, 71
Gray, Bill, 256
Gray, Willis, 59
Grazhdanin (Russia), 80
Green, OM, 54, 106–107, 139, 221
Griscom, Lloyd, 90
Griffith, Miriam, 149
Gros, Baron, 45
Guangzhou Revolutionary Government's Propaganda Department, 131
Guillain, Robert, 196
Von Gundlach, Herr, 83
Gundry, RS, 54, 56–57
Gunther, John, 129
Gützlaff, Karl, 22, 27–28, 30

Haden, GW, 54, 57
Hahn, Emily, 149; arrival in China and background, 152–155; offices 201; on Melville Jacoby, 231; on Ernest Hemingway, 235, 237
Hale, Lyman, 115
Hall, Joseph, 121, 148
Hamburg Frendemblatt (Germany), 176
Hamilton, Angus, 86
Hammond, Jim, 156, 183
Hampson, Fred, 261
Hampson, Margaret, 261
Han Suyin, 259
Hankow Daily News (China), 83, 109
Hankow Herald (China), 114,137, 138, 174
Hankow Short Wave Radio Station, 189
Hanson, Haldore, 212, 265
Hara Shiro, 205
Harding Davis, Richard, 89–91
Harkness, Ruth, 159
Harkson, US, 187–188
Harland, Brian, 251
Harmsworth, Alfred, 68–69
Harper's Weekly (USA), 93, 233, 245
Harris, Morris, 177
Hart, Elizabeth, 159
Hart, Sir Robert, 56, 76, 88
Hashimoto Tomisaburo, 205
Hauser, Ernest O, 233
Havas, 131, 156, 169, 223, 268
Hawaiian Shell News (USA), 117
Haward, Edwin, 76, 139
Hawks-Pott, Dr FL, 103
Hayter, HWG, 81
Healey, Mike, 188
Hearst Group, 89, 138, 174, 190, 252
Hearst International News Service, 147, 174, 180, 193, 198, 209, 221, 258; Hearst International Newsreel, 190–191
Heiburg, Hans, 176
Heis, Paul, 190
Hemingway, Ernest, 234–238
Hergé, 169
Hersey, John, 229–230
Hessell Tiltman, H, 173

History Today, 226
Hlavacek, John, 241
Hochi Shimbun (Japan), 204
Hogg, George, 211, 215, 243, 251
Holmes, Earnest, 97
Holmes, WM, 176
Hollssen, Henry, 151
Hong Xiuquan, 39, 51
Hong Kong Mercury and Shipping Gazette (Hong Kong), 34
Hong Kong Standard (Hong Kong), 159
Hong Kong Telegram (Hong Kong), 224
Hongkong Daily Press (Hong Kong), 34, 42, 65, 84
Hongkong Government Gazette (Hong Kong), 34
Hongkong News (Hong Kong), 223, 253–254
Hongkong Telegraph (Hong Kong), 34–36, 64, 68, 84, 86, 87, 109, 115, 224, 254
Hongkong Times (Hong Kong), 34
Honolulu Advertiser (USA), 157
Honolulu Star-Bulletin (USA), 138
Hoorin, Alex, 223
Horiguchi, Robert, 197
Horton, Jack, 188
Hotung, Robert, 115
House Un-American Activities Committee (HUAC), 266–267
Hsiao, TT, 150, 215, 217, 243
Hsien Feng, Emperor, 46, 51
Hsueh Huan, 52
Huang Hua, 179
Huldermann, Paul, 184
Hull, Peggy, 177
Hunter, Edward, 138, 174
Hunter, William, 28, 30
Hurley, Patrick J, 247
Hwa Mei Wan Pao (China), 221
Hyde, Robin, 182–183

Illustrated American (USA), 65
Illustrated London News (UK), 31, 46, 47–48

L'Illustration (France), 176
Imai Masatake, 204
Imai Seigo, 205
Imperial Gazette (China), 27
India Gazette (India), 32
Ingersoll, Ralph, 235
Institute of Mentalphysics, 97
Institute of Pacific Relations, 166, 203
International Famine Relief Commission, 121
International Psychoanalytical Press, 184
Internews, 233
Isaacs, Harold, 106; 156, 168, 169, 199, 233, 252, 265
Isherwood, Christopher, 215–219, 240
Ishikawa Tatsuzo, 204, 205
Israel's Messenger (China), 184, 219
Itier, Jules, 48

Jacobs, Noel, 223
Jacoby, Annalee, 230–232, 245, 246
Jacoby, Melville, 230–231
Jaffe, Philip, 243–244, 264–265
James, Lionel, 89
James, Weldon, 205
Jamieson, Dr RA, 53, 54, 56
Jansen, William, 191
Japan Advertiser (Japan), 106, 137, 138, 158
Japan Gazette (Japan), 32, 60
Japan Herald (Japan), 60
Japan Times (Japan), 167
Jardine Matheson, 16, 22, 27, 111, 145
Jardine, William, 16, 21, 24, 27–28, 29–30, 33, 36
Jarrett, Vincent, 224
Jenkins, Graham, 260–261
Jewish Voice (China), 219
Johnson, Celia, 144, 146–147, 217
Jones, C Treasure, 53
Jones, Gareth, 180–181
La Journal (France), 176
Journal de Pekin (China), 139
Journal de Shanghai (China), 101, 176

Jüdisches Nachrichtenblatt (see *Jewish Voice*)

Kang Tung-yi, 127
Kansas City Star (USA), 103
Kanzo, Uchiyama, 141
Keating, Arthur Saunders, 18
Keen, Victor, 158, 200, 239
Keniro Ashizawa, 205
Kerr, George H, 263
Kettner, P, 183
von Ketteler, Baron, 68
Kiautschou Post (China), 83
Killanin, Lord, 201
King, Frank, 61
Kingoro Hashimoto, Colonel, 206
Kipling Journal (UK), 76, 139
Kipling, Rudyard, 35, 100
Kirton, Captain Walter, 99–100
Kitaisko-Russkaia Gazeta (China), 252
Knickerbocker, Hubert Renfro, 157, 174, 197, 198, 239
Kobe Electrical Equipment Company, 186
Koike Shuyo, 204
Kokumin Shimbun (Japan), 203
Koo, Wellington, 167
Krainukov, George, 191 206
KRC Radio, 186–187
Kroker, Bruno, 117
Kruzenshtern, Iustina, 148
Kuh, Frederic, 174
Kuhn, Irene Corbally, 148, 187
Kwan, Bill, 260

Lacks, George, 191
Laging Una (USA), 134
Lamb, Robert, 201
Lancashire, David, 267–268
Landor, Henry Savage, 71
Lang, Hugh, 53, 59
Larsen, Emmanuel Sigurd, 264–265
Larson, Frans August, 125–126
Lattimore, Owen, employed at the *Peking and Tientsin Times*, 113; employed by *Pacific Affairs*, 166–167; on Jack Belden, 213; as a reviewer, 246; persecuted by McCarthy, 265
Laurens, Marguerite 177
Laurens, Rene, 176–177
Lauterbach, Richard, 245, 246
Laycock, George, 223
Leaf, Earl, 181, 202
Lee, CH, 136–137,167
Legation Guard News (China), 225
Lehrbas, Lloyd, 126–127
Lethbridge, HJ, 34
Lewin, Ossie, 185, 251
Lewis, Herbert, 157
Li, Dr TT, 202, 239–240
Li Fang, Colonel, 150
Li Hongzhang, 52, 190
Li Yuanhong, 107
Lieberman, Henry, 246–247, 263
Life (USA), 192, 217, 230–231, 256–257, 261
Lillico, Stuart, 117
Lin, Alfred, 150
Lin Tse-Hsu, 32
Literary Digest (USA), 231
Literary Society for the Promotion of Benevolence, 84
Little, RW, 54, 57–58, 88
Loch, HB, 46
Logan, Walter, 261
London, Jack, 89, 93, 235
London Daily News (UK), 44, 173, 263
London Missionary Society (LMS), 23, 25
London Morning Post (UK), 91
London News Chronicle (UK), 181
Londres, Albert, 176
Look (USA), 192
Loureiro, Pedro, 59
Los Angeles Herald (USA), 147
Los Angeles Sentinel (USA), 134
Los Angeles Times (USA), 156
Low, Harriet, 17, 18
Lowe, CH, 137–138, 199

Luce, Henry, 190, 229–230, 232, 256–257, 267
Lucey, Acheson, 188
Luke, John, 224
Lunt, Carroll, 171
Lyall, LA, 128

McCarthy, Senator Joseph, 137, 246, 265–267
McCormick, Elsie, 148
McCormick, Frederick, 89
McDaniel, C Yates, 203
MacDonald, Sir Claude, 81
McDonald, Colin, 205
McDonald, Elizabeth, 242
Macgowan, Daniel Jerome, 42
McGrady, Patrick, 157
Maclellan, JW, 54
Mackrill Smith, J, 55
Maillart, Ella, 145–147
Manchester Guardian (UK), 86, 128, 134–135, 180, 203, 208, 210, 211, 214–215, 229
Manchuria Daily News (China), 171
Manila Bulletin (Philippines), 127, 177, 188
Manila Free Press (Philippines), 228
Mao Zedong, 152; Jiangxi Soviet and interview with Edgar Snow, 178–179; 182; visited by journalists in Yenan, 243, 253, 256, 258; appointment as chairman of the Communist Party, 264; declares formation of PRC, 267
March of Time (USA), 191
Marconi Wireless Telegraph Company, 125
Marcuse, Jacques, 268
Marjoribanks, Charles, 17
Marines Corps Gazette (USA), 225
Marquardt, Frederick, 228
Marshall, James, 205
Martin, Robert, 233
Marx, Karl, 43–45
Matheson, Alexander, 16

Matheson, James, 16, 21, 29, 33, 36
Le Matin (France), 176
Matsumoto Shigeharu, 204–205
Mayell, Eric, 191, 206
de Mayréna, David, 35
Meadows, Thomas, 41, 50
Medhurst, Walter, 41, 50, 54–55
Medical Missionary Society in China, 24
Melbourne Evening Herald (Australia), 258–259
Menken, Arthur, 202
Mennie, Donald, 126
Meshcherskii, Prince Vladimir, 80
Meyer, Alfred, 188
Michie, Alexander, 111
Miles, Basil 133
Millard, Thomas, early career and background, 102–103; establishment of *China Press*, 103–104; coverage of 1911 revolution, 107–108; "girl reporters", 148
Millard's Review (China) 102
Miller, Milton, 48, 50
Millican, Aimée, 152, 187, 211
Millican, Dr Frank, 187, 211
Millington Ltd, 187
Millionton Radio Station, 187
Mills, Hal, 200, 221
Mills, James, 158, 197
Milne, William, 23
Mingxing Film Company, 190
Misselwtiz, Frank, 132, 138
Mitchell, Kate, 264–265
Mitchell, Mildred, 131
Mitford, Jessica, 267
Mitteilungs-und Verordnungsblatt der Landesgruppe China der NSDAP (China), 184
Miyako Shimbun (Japan), 204
Moats, Alice LB, 234
Mody, Hormusjee, 84
Le Monde (France), 196, 268
Montague-Bell, Henry Thurburn, 54, 112
Montalto de Jesus, CA, 60

Moorad, George, 156–157
Moore, Frederick, 138
Moresthe, George, 176
Morgenthau, Henry, 237–238
Moriyama Yoshio, 204
Morris, John, 239
Morris, Michael (see Killanin, Lord)
Morrison Education Society, 24
Morrison, Dr GE, 70; early career, 72–73; falsely declared dead, 74; Boxer rebellion and Siege of the Legation, 74–75; relations with Backhouse and Bland, 75–79; arguments with Bland, 78–79; on Sir Claude MacDonald, 82; as adviser to Yuan Shih-kai, 79, 108–109
Morrison, Ian, 234, 259
Morrison, Robert, 18, 22, 23, 25–28, 30
Morriss, Gordon, 124
Morriss, Hailey, 124
Morriss, Harry, 124, 166, 250
Morriss, Henry, 63–64
Mosley, Daphne, 222
Mossman, Samuel, 54, 56
Moy, Herbert, 201
Mueller, Dr Herbert, 180, 183
Münchner Illustrierte Presse (Germany), 175
Murdoch, Keith, 258–259
Murphy, Bob, 213
Mydans, Carl, 223, 230–231
Mydans, Shelley, 231

Na Rodinu (China), 220
Nash Put (China), 186, 220
The Nation (USA), 210, 245, 263
National Broadcasting Corporation (NBC), 192
National Geographic (USA), 121
National Manufacturers Association (USA), 137
National Review (China), 99–100
Naval Institute Proceedings (USA), 225
Navarra, Bruno, 83

Needham, Joseph, 116
New Masses (USA), 210
Neue Welt (Australia), 185
Neue Zürcher Zeitung (Switzerland), 211
New Republic (USA), 88, 245, 251
New Series of the Far East (China), 60
New Statesman (UK), 251
New World (China), 220
New York Call (USA), 210
New York Daily News (USA), 177
New York Daily Tribune (USA), 44
New York Evening Post (USA), 209
New York Evening Sun (USA), 86, 90
New York Herald (USA), 65, 92, 102, 107
New York Herald Tribune (USA), 58, 158, 174–175, 176, 188, 214, 239, 242, 245, 246, 261
New York Post (USA), 137, 252
New York Times (USA), 49; on Boxer Rebellion, 66; on Russo-Japanese War, 89; 132; in Manchuria, 175; on Ukrainian famine, 180; 192; on Nanjing Massacre, 202; on *USS Panay* incident, 206; in Hankou, 213; in Chongqing, 232–233, 239; book review pages, 246; on Chinese civil war, 247, 264; correspondents banned, 252; on Taiwan, 263
New York Times Magazine (USA), 137
New York World (USA), 65
New Yorker (USA), 148, 152–153, 229, 233
News of the World (UK), 124
Newsreel Wong, 190, 191, 192–193, 235
Newsweek (USA), 233, 252, 265
Nichi-Nichi (Japan), 197
Nichols, Francis, 100
Nielson, Gordious, 115
Nishinshinjishi (Japan), 60
Noble, Dr Joseph, 115
Noon Bulletin (China), 223
North American Newspaper Alliance, 132
North China Commerce (China), 113

North-China Daily News (China), founding of, 54–56; on Boxer rebellion, 68; on 1911 revolution, 108; headquarters building, 123; censored, 139, 220; woman's page, 148–149; Emily Hahn freelancing, 152; cartoonists, 161; notorious typos, 166; radio station XCDN, 189; internment, 222–223; relaunched after the Second World War and subsequent forced closure, 250
North China Herald (China) 21; on the Taiping Rebellion, 40–42, 50; on the Ward Corps, 51–52, 62; establishment of, 52, 54–55; *North China Herald and Market Report,* 53; early editors, 54–58; early influence, 61; on Russo-Japanese War, 88; 134, 196
North China Star (China) 113–114, 207
Northern Star (UK), 43
Northcliffe, Lord (see Harmsworth, Alfred)
Le Nouvelliste de Shanghai (China), 60–61
Novaia Zhizn (China), 252
Novi Krai (China), 92
Novoe vremia (Russia), 80, 220
Novosti Dnia (China), 252

O'Connor, Reverend Patrick, 245
Observer (UK), 134
Ochs, Adolph, 140
Office of Strategic Services (OSS), 224
Office of War Information (OWI), 170, 212, 242, 266
Ohara, Koson, 94
Oliver, Frank, 177
Ore, Anna Alexandrovna, 222
Oriental Affairs (China), 113, 200, 207
Osaka Mainichi (Japan), 203
Osborn, EG, 186
Osborn Radio Station (XRO), 186
Ostasiatischer Beobachter (China), 184
Ostasiatischer Lloyd (China), 82–83, 109, 184

Overseas Press Club of America, 257
Oxford Group of Shanghai, 187
Ozaki, Yei Theodora, 89

Pacific Affairs (USA), 166
Packard, Reynolds, 262
Pall Mall Gazette (UK), 47, 86
Palmerston, Lord, 31, 43
Paramount Newsreel, 191, 202
Paris Herald (France), 65
Paris Soir (France), 148, 177
Parker, Dr Peter, 24
Parkes, Sir Harry, 28, 33, 43, 45–47
Parrott, Monty, 262
Pattison, Alfred, 221
Pavlov, Alexander, 93–94
Payne Whitney, Dorothy, 88
Peel, Sir Robert, 29
Peffer, Nathaniel, 246
Peiping Chronicle (China), 137, 207, 222, 256
Peiping News (China), 206–207
Peking and Tientsin Times (China), 68; coverage of the First World War, 111; establishment of, 111–112; censored, 139; cartoonists, 162; on Japanese in Tianjin, 172; shut by the Japanese, 207
Peking Daily News (China), 100, 112
Peking Gazette (China), 27, 52, 82, 109, 136
Peking Leader (China), 82, 130, 137, 138, 167–168, 174
Peking People's Tribune (China), 130–132, 136
Peking Post (China), 109–110
Peking Standard (China), 168
Pekinger Deutsche Zeitung (China), 83
Peng Dehuai, 209, 243
Pennell, Wilfred Victor, 207
The People's Paper (USA), 44
von Perckhammer, Heinz, 126
Le Petit Parisien (France), 145, 176
Petrie, Thomas, 254
Peyton-Griffin, Ralph Thomas, 161, 223, 250

Philadelphia Inquirer (USA), 90
Philadelphia Ledger (USA), 137
Philadelphia Press (USA), 90
Philadelphia Record (USA), 90
Pickwood, Edwin, 63
Pickwood, Janet, 63
Pickwood, Una, 63–64
Pitt, William (the Younger), 30
PM (USA), 235–238
Ponting, Herbert, 93
Poole, Francis Gordon, 71
Popular Photography (USA), 224
O Portuguez na China (Macau), 34
Pottinger, Sir Henry, 33
Powell, John Benjamin, 102; takes over editorship of *Millard's Review,* 103; early career, 105; member of Shanghai Good Roads Committee, 115; argument with Arthur de Carle Sowerby, 117; employment of radicals, 168; dislike of the *Far Eastern Review,* 171; accused of being a communist, 174; on Jiangxi Soviet, 178; starts radio station, 189; opposition to Japan, 198–199, 200; imprisoned by Japanese, 221; deported, 222; and Evans Carlson, 225–226, 227; and Teddy White, 229; accused of being "reactionary", 246; son's persecution, 266–267
Powell, John W, 266–267
Powell, Margaret, 148
Powell, Sylvia, 266–267
Powers, Mildred, 149
Pratt, FL, 160
Pratt, John, 160
Pravda (USSR), 212
Press Wireless Radio, 189
O Procurador dos Macaistas (Macau), 34
Prodan, Maria, 222
Progres (China), 61
Prohme, Rayna, 130–133, 167
Prohme, William, 130–133
Prokudin-Gorskii, Sergei Mikhailovich, 93

Pruitt, Ida, 169
Pu Yi, 171–172
Punch (UK), 62, 81
Putnam Weale, BL, 81–82, 126, 136, 168

The Q (China), 223
De Quincey, Thomas, 16

Radio Corporation of China, 186
Rana, KS, 268
Rand, Christopher, 242
Ransome, Arthur, on the Shanghai mind, 128–129; reporting activities, 134–135
Raphaelson, Sampson, 130
Ravenshaw, Charles, 17
Rawlinson, Frank, 120, 196
RCA-Victor China, 188
Rea, George Bronson, 171
Reader's Digest (USA), 208, 224
Reid, Dr Gilbert, 109–110
Reinsch, Dr Paul, 110, 120
Reuters, on Russo-Japanese War, 88; establishment in China, 104; Beijing Bureau, 125–126; Shanghai Bureau, 126; 143; Guangzhou Bureau, 150; Tokyo Bureau, 177; radio station in Shanghai, 187; reporter murdered, 200; on Nanjing, 202; in Hankou, 213; in Chongqing, 230, 239; on civil war, 260–261; post-1949, 267
Reyher, Rebecca, 130
Ricalton, James, 88–89, 93
Ridge, Sheldon, 207
Rivett, Rohan, 258–259
Rivington, C, 59
Roberts, George, 94
Roberts, Issachar Jacox, 40, 51
Roberts, JP, 59
Robertson, Douglas, 195–196, 202
Robertson, James, 48–49
Robinson, Viola, 168
Roda, Howard, 221
Roderick, John, 258
Rogov, Vladimir, 212

Roots, Bishop Logan, 208–209, 211–212, 216
Roots, Francis, 209
Rosenthal, Joseph, 94
Rosholt, Malcolm, 149, 156, 158, 159–160, 173, 176, 183, 192, 196, 197, 199
Rossiia (Russia), 80
Rosta (see Soviet Russian Telegraph Agency)
Roth, Andrew, 264–265
Roube-Jansky, Alexandra, 148
Rowan, Roy, 255–257, 262, 263
Rowlandson, Thomas, 26
Roy, NM, 129
Royal Asiatic Society, 117, 226, 251
Royal Commission on Opium in Shanghai, 53
Rubezh (China), 140
de Ruffe, D'Auxion, 176
Ruker, Joe, 191
Rundle, Walter, 262
Ruskoe Slovo (Russia), 92
Russell and Company, 17, 28
Russell, Charles, 92–93
Russell, William, 46
Russian Daily News (China), 140
Russian Daily News (USSR), 136
Russian World (China), 220

St. John's Dial (China), 134
St. John's University, 103, 159
St Louis Post-Dispatch (USA), 137
Salisbury, Harrison, 232
San Antonio Express (USA), 156
San Francisco Call Bulletin (USA), 147
San Francisco Chronicle (USA), 242
San Francisco Examiner (USA), 130
Sanders-Bates, JAE, 176, 200
Sanderson, Sir Thomas, 74
Sandri, Sandro, 205–206
Sanger, JW, 102
Sapajou (see Sapojnikoff, Georgii Avksentievich)
Sapojnikoff, Georgii Avksentievich, early life and career, 160; cartoon style, 161; 176
Sassoon, Sir Victor 126, 152–153, 216, 252
Sato Shinju, 204
Saturday Evening Post (USA), 121, 233, 252, 265
Savintzev, PA, 220
Savitsky, AJ, 223–224
Schiff, Friedrich, 162–163, 252
Schonberg, John, 71
Schuman, Julian, 266–267
Scribner's (USA), 90
Scott, CP, 135
Scott, EO, 159
Secker, Fritz, 83, 183
Selle, Earle, 156, 157, 251
Semantza, Nevada, 149
Shanghai Budget and Weekly Courier (China), 59
Shanghai Courier (China), 59
Shanghai Courier and China Gazette (China), 59
Shanghai Daily Times (China), 53
Shanghai Echo (China), 185
Shanghai Evening Courier (China), 53
Shanghai Evening Gazette (China), 59
Shanghai Gazette (China), 115, 136, 137
Shanghai Herald (China), 219–220
Shanghai Jewish Chronicle (China), 185, 219, 251
Shanghai Mercury and Evening Post (China), 59, 60, 103, 113, 124, 134, 138, 157, 177, 186, 188, 199, 200, 215, 221, 249–250
Shanghai Newsletter (China), 49, 59
Shanghai Newsletter For California and the United States (China), 59
Shanghai Nichinichi Shimbun (China), 203
Shanghai Opium Suppression Bureau, 151–152
Shanghai Polish Union, 186

Shanghai Recorder (China), 53
Shanghai Short Story Club, 134, 226
Shanghai Times (China), 59, 115, 134, 155, 170–171, 191, 220
Shanghai Zaria (China), 101, 140
Shankhaiskaia Zaria (China), 148
Shaw, Bruno, 114
Shaw, Ralph, 161, 166–167, 199, 223
Shearman, Henry, 52, 54, 63
Sheean, Vincent, arrival and early career, 131–132; in Moscow, 133; influence on Harrison Salisbury, 232; banned from China, 252
Shelepina, Evgenia Petrovna 135
Shen Bao (China), 186, 224
Shiwubao (China), 83
Shopping News (China), 201
Shun Pao (China), 126–127
Siegelberg, Dr Mark, 185
Simons, Grace, 131,134, 157
Simplicissimus (Germany), 109
Simon-Eberhard, Max, 184
Simpson, Bertram Lenox (see Putnam Weale, BL)
Sin Wan Pao (China), 127
Sioux City Tribune (USA), 188
Siren, Osvald, 126
Skinner, Lieutenant, 31
Slovo (China), 101, 140
Smedley, Agnes, 106, 176; in Hankou, 208–211, 216–217; at the front, 214; in Yenan, 243
Smith, Lesley, 202, 213
Smith, Shelley, 230
Smith, William, 242
Smothers, Frank, 178, 214
Snow, Edgar, 103, 169; covering the Jiangxi Soviet, 178; *Red Star Over China,* 179; kidnapping of Chiang Kai-shek, 182; on Black Saturday, 197; publishes *Democracy*, 207; in Hankou, 211; "Gung Ho Kid", 225–226; in Yenan, 243–244; as a book reviewer, 246; denied entry to China, 252

Snow, Helen Foster, 169, 178, 179, 182, 225, 243
Social Shanghai (China), 101
Society for the Diffusion of Useful Knowledge, 24
Society for the Restoration of China, 84, 85
Society for the Suppression of the Opium Trade, 36
Sokolsky, George, 122, 136–137, 139
Sokolovskii, SF, 80
Solitario na China (Macau), 34
Soong, Charlie, 95
Soong Ching-ling (Madame Sun), 133
Soong, Mei-ling (see Madame Chiang Kai-shek)
Soong, Norman, 206, 235
Soong, TV, 132
Soré (see Sokolovskii, SF)
Sorge, Richard, 180–181, 210
Soualle Jean-Baptiste, 55
South China Morning Post (Hong Kong), establishment of, 83–84; early years, 85–86; merger with *HongKong Telegraph,* 115; during Japanese occupation of Hong Kong, 223–224; welcome for Martha Gellhorn, 235, 236; reestablishment after the Second World War, 254–255
Soviet Russian Telegraph Agency 129–130, 212, 243
Sowerby, Alice Muriel Cowans, 251
Sowerby, Arthur de Carle, as editor of the *China Journal,* 116–118, 176; imprisoned by Japanese, 221, 223; departs China, 251
Spassovsky, MM, 220
Spectator (UK), 70, 144
Sprague, Marshall, 113–114
Springfield Daily News (USA), 232
La Stampa (Italy), 205–206
Stanford Daily (USA), 231
von Starnburger, Ungtaren, 176
Starr, Cornelius Vanderbilt, 175, 200

Steele, Archibald T, 177, 202, 212, 214, 229, 244
Stefani News Agency, 184
Stein, Gunther, 180–181, 243, 244, 246
Stephens, Philip Pembroke, 197
Sterling Clark, Robert, 116
von Sternberg, Josef, 122
Stewart, Maxwell, 245
Stilwell, Joseph W, 182, 233–234, 241
Stockton, Norman, 224
Stoessel, General Anatoly, 92
Storfer, Albert Joseph, 184–185
Story, Douglas, 85
Stowe, Leland, 252
Straight, Willard Dickerman, 88
Strong, Anna Louise, 133; in Hankou 208–211; in Yenan 243
Sues, Ilona Ralph, on Donald of China, 96, 151; arrival in China and early career, 149–150; on opium and Du Yue-sheng, 151–152; on Shanghai, 166; on Chiang Kai-shek's kidnapping, 181; as a radio announcer, 189–190; on Tim Timperley, 203; in Hankou, 208, 212, 215; on controlling foreign journalists, 240–241
Sullivan, Walter, 264
Sun Fo, 137
Sun Yat-sen, relationship with the *South China Morning Post*, 84–85; interview with Edna Lee Booker, 148; on radio, 186
Sunday Herald (USA), 65
Supreme Court and Consular Gazette (China), 53–54
Sutterlee, FW, 69–70
Sutton, Christian, 176
Sutton, Frank "One Armed", 126
Suzuki Jiro, 204
Sweetland, Reginald, 176
Sydney Daily Telegraph (Australia), 94
Sydney Sun (Australia), 224

Tagar (China), 251

Tageblatt fr Nordchina (China), 83
Taguchi Toshisuke, 192, 204
Taylor, A Cecil, 114
Taylor, Bayard 58–59
TASS (see Soviet Russian Telegraph Agency)
Temple, Henry (see Palmerston, Lord)
Le Temps (France), 176
Thackrey, Theodore Olin, 175
Thomson, John, 49–50
Thompson, James, 244
Thorbecke, Ellen, 190
Thorbecke, Dr Willem, 190
Thorne, John, 59
Tien Hsia (China), 182
Tientsin Evening Post (China), 207
Time (USA), 198, 229–230, 231, 261
Time-Life (USA), 157, 190, 232, 245, 256, 257, 262
Times (UK), 86; on Opium Wars, 44, 45; on the Elgin Mission, 45–47; on the Taiping, 51; on Boxer rebellion, 69–70; appointment of GE Morrison, 72–75; on Russo-Japanese War, 87, 89; death of Basil Miles, 133; Peter Fleming as Special Correspondent, 143–146, 217–218, 258; Gareth Jones on assignment for, 180; kidnapping of Chiang Kai-shek, 182; on *USS Panay* incident, 205; Ian Morrison as correspondent, 259
Timperley, Harold J, 203, 240–241
Tokyo Asahi (Japan), 204, 205
Tokyo Nichi Nichi Shimbun (Japan), 203
Tong, Au Huna, 149
Tong, Hollington, 160, 207, 208, 212, 216, 229, 240–241, 244, 245, 260
Topping, Seymour, 257–258, 260
Train, George Francis, 28
Transocean News Service, 183, 185
Trans-Pacific News Service, 114
Die Tribüne (China), 183
Tse Tsan-tai, 84–85
Tseng, Eddie, 213
Tseng Yang-fu, Mayor, 150

Tsingtao Times (China), 114
Tsingtauer Neueste Nachrichten (China), 83
Twombley, Howard, 59

Ukrainian National Committee in East Asia, 186
Ukrains'ky I Holos Dalekomu Skhodi (China), 186
Ullstein Publishing Company, 184
Underwood, Bert, 93
Underwood, Elmer, 93
Undzer Lebn (China), 219
United China Relief Fund, 231
United Nations Relief and Rehabilitation Administration (UNRRA), 255
United Press (UPI), 104, 131, 167, 170, 174, 177, 181–182, 196–197, 202, 205, 211, 212, 215, 224, 233, 239, 252, 255, 260, 261, 262
Universal Newsreel, 191, 206
Ustein Syndicate, 191
Utley, Freda, on Edgar Snow, 179; in Hankou, 208–211; on Mac Fisher, 212; on Jack Belden, 213; on Tillman Durdin, 213–214, 245; at the front, 214–215; on the foreign press corps, 246

Vanity Fair (UK), 82
Varé, Daniele, 47, 78
Vaughn, Miles, 131, 255
Varges, Ariel, 190–191
La Vérité (France), 169
Vine, George, 260–261
Vogel, Dr V, 176
Voice of America (USA), 148
Voila (France), 126
Votaw, Maurice, 133, 243, 244
Des Voeux, Sir William, 35

Wales, Nym (see Snow, Helen Foster)
Wall Street Journal (USA), 242
Waln, Nora, 147

Walter, Wilhelm, 190
Wang, Betty, 149
Wang Jingwei, 240–241
Wang, George, 212
Wanstall, Mary, 28
The War (China), 109, 185
Ward, Frederick Townsend, 41, 51–52, 62
Ward, Sir Leslie, 82
Warner, Gertrude (see Bass, Gertrude)
Wau Wau (China), 109
Wei, Jimmy, 213
Wei, Dr Wilson, 207
Weller, George, 259–260
Wells, Linton, 175
Die Welt des Ostens (China), 83
Western Mail (UK), 180
White, Harry Dexter, 238
White, Theodore, 229–230, 232, 233, 244, 245, 246, 256
Whitehead, Theodore, 73
Whiting, Fred, 71
von Wiegand, Karl, 174, 176
Williams, AD, 196
Williams, Samuel Wells, 24–25
Wilson, Tug, 199
Wong Hai-Sheng (see Newsreel Wong)
Woo Kyatang, 159, 223
Wood, Richard, 103, 107, 110
Wood, William, 17
Woodhead, HGW, early career, 112–114; and the Institute of Pacific Relations, 166–167; on the Japanese in Tianjin, 172–174; *Shanghai Evening Post* columnist, 200–201; edits *Oriental Affairs*, 200
The World (USA), 65
Wright, Paul Randall, 172–173
Wu Hsu, 52
Wu Peifu, 121, 148, 171–172
Wu Ting-fang, 102–103, 107, 148
Wu Youru, 45
Wylie, Benjamin, 224, 254

XCDN Radio, 189

XGOW Radio (see Hankow Short Wave Radio Station)
XGRS Radio, 189, 201
XMHA Radio, 134, 187–188, 200
XQHB Radio, 189
Xu Qian, 137

Yakhontoff, Victor, 170
Yale Daily News (USA), 229
Yancey, Marguerite, 148–149
Yang, General, 240
Yang Tilin, 149
Yao, Francis (see Hsiao, TT)
Ye Mingchen, 45
Yomiuri Shimbun (Japan), 203, 205
Yorke, Gerald, 143
Yoshio Amano, 205

Young, Clarence Kuangson, 160–161
Young, Jack, 149
Young, Quentin (see Yang Tilin)
Young, Su-Lin, 149
Yuan Shih-kai, 79, 108–109, 116
Yuen-cham (YC) Tong, 99

Zarya (Russia), 170
Zau Sinmay, 152–154
Zeng Guofan, 52
Zhang Leping, 163
Zhang Xueliang, 95, 181–183
Zhang Zongchang, 168
Zhang Zuolin, 130–131, 148, 168
Zhou En-lai, 152, 179, 209, 236–237, 241, 247, 256, 258
Zhu De, 178, 243, 253